THE HOUSE THAT ZEE BUILT

Praise

The book reveals to readers the story of how an entertainment-starved India made Zee a success despite the many hurdles that are faced by a pioneering venture, especially at a time when India was at the cusp of emerging from socialist policies and was opening up its economy.

Dr Dahiya interviewed me at length and I have complete faith in her capabilities to tell our story, and through her able research, do due justice to it. Through first-hand accounts of all that buzzed behind the curtains as we sowed the first seeds of Zee, to captivating accounts of how we went on to chart magnificent successes, the book brings to life our past, dwells on the present and looks to the future.

From when my forefathers traded in grains, to the trust they placed in me as a young man with dreams in my eyes, to what eventually resulted in the largesse of the Essel Group and Zee today, the narrative is balanced between tangible figures and abstract motivations which compound the axis upon which Zee rotates.

I hope the book serves well the students of media, mass communication and management. I am sure that the readers will have a great experience as they thumb through the pages of this honest chronicle and read about our journey.

4.2.2021

Dr Subhash Chandra
Chairman Emeritus, Zee

THE HOUSE THAT ZEE BUILT

SURBHI DAHIYA

RUPA

Published by
Rupa Publications India Pvt. Ltd 2021
7/16, Ansari Road, Daryaganj
New Delhi 110002

Sales Centres:
Allahabad Bengaluru Chennai
Hyderabad Jaipur Kathmandu
Kolkata Mumbai

ISBN: 978-93-90918-68-3

First impression 2021

10 9 8 7 6 5 4 3 2 1

Printed by Parksons Graphics Pvt. Ltd Mumbai

In loving memory of my father

Sh. Rajinder Bhalla
16.12.1949–04.05.2021

CONTENTS

FOREWORD

The twenty-first century has witnessed the rise of global media and technology companies around the world. Media companies produce the content we access for entertainment and information, while technology companies distribute the content across multiple platforms and devices. Many of these companies are well-known brands: Disney, Viacom/CBS, AT&T, Comcast, Alphabet (Google), Apple, Microsoft and Netflix to name just a few.

One characteristic these companies have in common is their location in the Western Hemisphere. These companies are also known for their mogul-like leaders—individuals who are so well-known they are synonymous with the companies they lead (or have led): Rupert Murdoch, Robert Iger, Steve Jobs and Tim Cook, Brian Roberts, Reed Hastings and Bob Bakish are names we read and hear about connected with the global media business. These companies are so large that they tend to define for us what constitutes a media giant.

There are media conglomerates outside of the Western Hemisphere; the problem is these companies are not so well known outside of their domestic boundaries, and scholars in the 'West' may not have knowledge of these entities. Such is the case with India. One of the world's two largest nations, India, is a country with a rich and diverse culture. When scholars in the West think of Indian media, they may think of 'Bollywood' or perhaps STAR TV which was formerly part of the Fox empire ruled by Rupert Murdoch. Or they might be familiar with Doordashan, the country's well-established public service broadcaster.

The House That Zee *Built* tells the story of Zee Entertainment Enterprises Ltd and Zee Media, and its founder Subhash Chandra, from its formation to the present day. Zee Entertainment and Zee Media has its roots in the Essel Group, a private holding company founded in India in 1926 by Jagannath Goenka, the grandfather of Subhash Chandra.

In 1992, Chandra took leadership of the company and expanded its operations and scope into the media and communication industries with the establishment of Zee TV. As the book details, Dr Chandra is a fascinating individual. He is a combination of an entrepreneur, a business executive, a visionary and, clearly, one of India's media 'moguls.'

This book is authored by Dr Surbhi Dahiya, a professor at the Indian Institute of Mass Communication and a well-known scholar in her country and field. Dr Dahiya is an exceptional scholar; she examines Zee and its founder from many different perspectives, using a very objective and structured approach.

This volume fits within the realm of other books broadly recognized as part of media management and economics. However, what is unique is that this book details both the managerial and economic aspects of ZEE, something rarely found in the literature of this field. Further, Dr Dahiya uses a 'mixed-methods' approach in her exhaustive research on the company and its founder. Methods employed range from historical analysis to the discussion of various aspects of ZEE's development to in-depth interviews, including that of Dr Subhash Chandra. All of this is very rare in a scholarly work on a media company. The level and breadth of analysis are quite remarkable.

The author employs both a SWOT (Strengths, Weaknesses, Opportunities and Threats) and PESTLE (Political, Economic, Social, Technology, Legal and Environmental) analysis to further 'drill down' and provide a comprehensive examination of the company. This analysis will be appreciated by scholars and students who want to know more about Zee and serve as a heuristic source of information on other Indian companies.

Dr Dahiya takes the reader on a journey to understand the development of Zee over its first three decades of operation. She presents a discussion of the business models used by the company throughout its subsidiaries. She details the company's innovative rational strategy, built on recognizing different purposes, demographics and nationalities of India. One thing the reader will appreciate about the book is the omission of any ideological or political slant. Professor Dahiya writes as a seasoned journalist, giving us the facts and not opinions.

One of the more interesting parts of the book is the overarching discussion of the 2006 breakup of Zee into four different entities: Zee Entertainment Enterprises, Zee News, Wire & Wireless India Ltd and ASC Enterprises Ltd. The breakup was driven by the concomitant changes across the communication industries driven by technological, social, economic, globalization and political forces. The discussions presented help us to understand the strategy behind the decision-making and how this important decision positioned the company for the 21st century.

Media and communication companies operate in a continually evolving and changing marketplace. The book captures the driving forces that led to changes in Zee from its initial role as a terrestrial broadcaster to its current position as a multiplatform media conglomerate. To that end, Dr Dahiya details how the company became the first over-the-top (OTT) provider in India, as consumers began the adoption of streaming media channels over multiple devices.

The House That ZEE Built is a welcome addition to the scholarly literature on media companies and media management. The book also has utility as a text in courses in communication, media and business schools alike. Further, it will be surely be cited as a reference work for many years, by researchers interested in the history and development of Zee Entertainment and Zee Media.

7.6.2020

Dr Alan B. Albarran,
Professor Emeritus,
University of North Texas, USA

PREFACE

The House That Zee Built offers an in-depth narration on the conglomerate whose name resounds in every Indian household—Zee. It is an analytical chronicle of the first satellite channel of India, Zee Telefilms Ltd (ZTL). It tracks the development of the conglomerate through various ages. It extensively takes on observations of the media giant, right from the humble days of its inception in the post-liberalisation era, to its transformation into many powerful business empires in three decades, up until its current enviable stature as a media conglomerate. Without any ideological or political slant, the book aims to deconstruct the journey of Zee fact by fact, and present a holistic understanding of the manner in which the company has managed to scale skyscraping heights.

The narration begins with a holistic insight into the earliest germinations of the Zee identity, when it hadn't taken on the shape of a brand yet. The reader is pulled back into the pre-genesis era in a remote corner of north India, on the homeground of media baron Subhash Chandra. The story begins in a small Haryana village, where Chandra's forefathers entered into the business of foodgrains. When Chandra came of age, he took over, and took the foodgrain family business to dizzying heights, diversifying further into the business of packaging and lamination. During these upward developments, the company assumed the identity of Essel Group, the precursor to ZTL.

Chandra's gaze shifted to the media and entertainment (M&E) industry soon after, and the narration continues onward from Essel, into the workings of Chandra's thoughts and innovations as he began to shape a new brand. At a time when India was a distant participant of the Gulf War, Chandra dared to kickstart his venture into the media world with the brainchild he named Zee.

Hereafter, the book follows a detailed account of the phenomenal growth Zee achieved in every sphere it stepped into. The narrative analyses the company's progress through the business decisions it made and advances year-by-year, chronicling the successes and failures inherent in each. Through an analysis of the company's annual reports, interviews with the founder, MD, CEO, and messages from the chairman and CEO, the book tries to gauge how all these torchbearers have constantly been the forces behind the company's dynamic and adaptive missions, values and visions all through these years. This aspect of the narrative places importance on the way in which Zee has achieved superior audience targeting techniques and brand identity, all while keeping its mind open to the changing markets of the changing world.

Keen notice has been taken of the company's efforts to maximize its regionalization projects through all its channels of communication. With a specialized focus on every aspect of its audience, no matter how varied, Zee managed to gather clout in the market. It branched out each of its broadcast ventures into the regional sector, with focused programmes for different demographics, cultures and even nationalities. One witnesses the robust rigour of Zee to fearlessly travel overseas into international markets, giving imminence to the diaspora public, as well as global audiences.

Detailed also are the motivations that pushed Zee to diversify into a varied genre of product offerings, ranging from Zee News, Zee Cinema to Zee Music, understanding how these new ventures simultaneously shaped public imagination and the media industry. Given its pioneering nature, Zee's launch of the first cable service became a decision that rocked the market and changed the meaning of M&E forever.

At the dawn of a new millennium, Zee made boundless growth. It created a household name for itself in the homeland, as well as the subcontinent, through its pay bouquet of channels. The author maps how, early in the game, Zee realized the importance of partnerships and joint ventures with other players in the game, a move that yielded fruitful results for the company. Regional expansion and penetration also became an important brand identity for Zee during this phase of its timeline, as it sought to cater to a vast mix of audiences and take everyone along on its journey together. The book also makes note of Zee's entry into the film business, a decision that was a precursor to the company's subsequent film connections.

In the run-up to its infamous demerger, the Essel giant had expanded its multifaceted interests in fields like education, direct-to-home (DTH) services and infrastructure, understanding how this contributed to the company's vast business and high output value. This was also contributed to by the company's global reach into the Americas, Europe, MENAP (Middle East, North Africa, Afghanistan and Pakistan) and APAC (Asia-Pacific) regions, exceeding numbers over the previous years. Several branch-outs of Zee's news offering were also launched during this phase, including a print segment, which gives the reader an insight into the company's forecasting of its upcoming demerger of product offerings into four laterals.

The big break in the book comes with the 2006 demerger of ZTL, which caused a divide into four differentiated segments: ZEEL, Zee News Ltd (ZNL), Wire and Wireless India Ltd, and ASC Enterprises Ltd. The book chiefly approaches the former two undertakings, dedicating two complete chapters to the developments pursued by each of those companies after the demerger. Though separate, it seamlessly streamlines the successes claimed by both ZEEL and ZNL (now Zee Media Corporation Ltd), appreciating in great detail, the channels launched by both companies every year, and the elevated manner of their holistic visions, adjusted to the world around them.

A full chapter is dedicated to the developments pursued by ZNL post the 2006 demerger, with a recapitulation of all events and achievements up until the latest period, mapping the journey from ZNL to Zee Media Corporation Ltd (ZMCL). It looks at how ZNL braved the global economic slowdown, and emerged afresh against the tides with renewed stamina to serve its audiences. The narrative pursues the company's dedication to bring news across platforms, cutting across regions and mediums, which has worked towards creating a loyal customer base for its various product offerings. ZNL has made many innovations in the field of news and television, especially as far as technology is concerned, that contribute to its status as a patriarch in the business industry. The section also focuses on how the company diversified into segments like print, and looks into whether or not that has proved fruitful for it.

The chapter that follows offers a detailed insight into ZEEL's developments post the demerger. The lows and highs of Zee on the waves of dynamic market conditions and audience feedback makes for an exciting read, seeing as how during this phase, the Zee brand managed to hold sway over people's imagination and entertainment preferences. With élan, the company entered the sports market, kids' entertainment, live events, theatre and radio segment, quickly grabbing the top spot in each segment.

The narrative also keenly observes the masterful technique with which ZEEL dipped its fingers into all the regional markets, across north, south, east and west India, and even abroad. The company attained many milestones during this phase of its life, each of which is given prominence in the chapter. It also deals with the technological leaps the company has been taking, that have placed it on the path to a seamless transition to the digital age.

Since the book is bare in facts and lacks any biased prejudices, it makes mention of instances of conflict objectively, which facilitates readers' understanding of the company's aspirations. While it looks at the excellence some channels achieved, it also flips the coin to point out channels that shut shop mid-career. With insight from key faces and news anchors of the Zee bouquet, courtesy personal interviews with the author, several of the company's internal functions find a detailed outline in the book. These inputs attempt to factor in the latest developments in the company, right from its downward spiral of shares to Chandra's step-down from his post as company chairman.

The book also offers factual insight into Zee's business functions, the visionary leadership that guides it, an overview of strategies that the company has employed to extend its reach in the domestic and international markets and how these practices have contributed towards creating a brand identity and the way in which the business model has anchored Zee's ship all these years.

With the changing times, the phenomenon of convergence is responsible for opening up new ventures and product ideas in an organization. Companies from different media sectors have been joining hands, giving rise to cross-media ownership. This has been giving birth to new business models in the media industry. The business model of an organization thus forms a crucial part of the analysis, as it is mandated to undergo constant change while adapting in response to the ever-changing external and internal environment. The author analyses how the group has responded to the ever-changing political, economic, social, technological, legal and environmental (PESTLE) conditions while maintaining its business streak, given the organization's SWOT. Only through an analysis of the organizations, is the author able to study the diversification in its business and reasons for strengthening its operations.

Against this backdrop, the book will look at the changing media management perspectives, revenue generation model and the business models of this Indian media giant. The book focuses on the changing practices of the group from one decade to another, as it gradually orients and re-orients its strategic positioning to the pulse of the media market and the opportunities under various regulatory regimes. It is replete with a meticulous analysis of the business dynamics and models upon which the foundation of Zee has been laid, the ripples that it has created in the media world and how it is constantly being modified to suit the tastes of the modernizing market.

Changes in leadership, organizational structuring and re-structuring and division of management roles steer conglomerates towards their targets and visions and signify their ability to maintain their competitive spirit through trials and tribulations. Thus, the book in its concluding chapters, outlines the company's leadership structure, business overview, brand strategies and business model, while simultaneously offering an analysis into how these propositions can be duly aligned and re-aligned. This segment is especially important to understand the management processes of the company, with enough space for the leisurely reader, the student, the professor and other interested parties, to review their own thoughts and come to objective conclusions about the future of Zee, in addition to the author's views and analysis.

As the book traces the journey, rise and management practices of a major media house in India, the author has attempted to cover both the journalistic and managerial aspects of this media hub, and has attempted to analyse the birth, primary products, product development and diversification along with the organizational structure, hierarchical charts, changing ownership of the papers and respective groups, editorial policies, HR policies, technological upgradation, market expansion, geographical spread and regional penetration, competitive strategy, edge over rivals and many more aspects.

By duly recapping all the significant events mentioned in each chapter in a clean nutshell, the narrative culminates with transformative scopes as well as the company's outlook going forward. Simply put, this holistic compendium offers multiple perspectives on how this media organization has grown from strength to strength, towards the goals that had been envisioned for it.

1

ON A ZEE ADVENTURE: ZOOMING BACK TO HUMBLE BEGINNINGS (1890-1991 AND 1992-1994)

Prelude—The Life and Times of Zee Then and Now

Sowing the First Seed of Success: The Essel Group Is Founded

A Man and A Dream: The Story of Subhash Chandra

Multi-Billion Dollar Business Conglomerate: Media and Non Media Sectors

New Business Paradigms: The Genesis of Empire Holdings

Environmental Scanning: A War and A New Economy

Zee Telefilms Dawns on Indian Entertainment

Visions During War: Chandra Dreams Big

Next in Line, News

Managing the Company, Marwari Style

New Stratagems for a New Decade

In a Nutshell

Fig. 1.1: Chapter Insights

'In this journey, every moment has had excitement and anxiety. In all these years, there have been no dull days. Hardships have been a constant game. Whatever seems like a hardship today, doesn't tomorrow. When you look back, you just wonder at what had seemed like a hardship earlier. You understand you handled it well.[1]

The word impossible is still not there in my dictionary. Once I am convinced, I develop a strong sense of conviction and the courage to follow through on my commitment. I seek thrill in the new ideas that I explore—the joy of a challenge, the excitement of conquest over a challenge. I am not scared of jumping into situations that would scare others. I do not fear anything.

We should continue to strive for something better. We should keep trying to create a more challenging goal for ourselves. That's how I drive myself all the time.[2] *Good things don't come easy. We have had our share of trials and tribulations throughout, which made the journey exhilarating. Starting with the longwinded process of leasing a transponder for the launch of our first channel, to constantly contending with peers with immense financial resources, there has seldom been a day without a challenge. However, each impediment made us even more determined to succeed.'*[3]

—Dr Subhash Chandra, Chairman, Essel Group

PRELUDE—THE LIFE AND TIMES OF ZEE: THEN AND NOW

ZTL had its roots in the vision of a small-time mofussil town entrepreneur, Subhash Chandra, who dared to dream so big that he created not just an organization, but an institution, which revolutionized entertainment business in India. At a time when the business of entertainment was defined by the distribution system, requiring the customer to reach out to the place of entertainment, he reversed the direction of this flow by taking entertainment to the living rooms of the customers. In this, he was facilitated by the advent of the then new communication technology of satellite/cable television. Chandra was quick enough to seize the opportunity offered by this new technology and to develop a new business model, with few competitors. In anticipating the technological change and scripting the birth of a media goliath, Chandra's name will be remembered in the annals of entertainment business as a master strategist and as a visionary leader, who began with a dream in one hand, and an iron will in the other. In Chandra's visionary leadership of ZTL lie the seeds of its market-focused strategic management. From the days of its inception to its present-day growth as a multinational institution, Zee has come a long way on the strong back of its dynamic founder. It is his sensitivity towards the customers and their needs on which Zee was built, and which even today, it strives to achieve.

ZTL, as it began and progressed, operated in four main areas of business, namely, content and broadcasting[4] (consisting of developing, producing and procuring television programming and film content and delivering via satellites, thereby earning revenues by way of advertisement, subscription revenues and syndication); access (consisting of multi-system operators [MSO] operations, distribution of satellite channels and Internet over cable); education business (consisting of distance learning programmes and ground learning centres); film production and distribution (consisting of production, acquisition and distribution of films, animation films and programmes).

However, ZTL did not remain ZTL forever. As the years advanced, so did the company's identity. It underwent multiple facelifts, shuttling between many interests and undertakings. The education business became a separate entity, while access was also demerged.[5] Needless to say, content creation and broadcasting remained its prime focus and that of subsequent media ventures that the market endowed it with. Today, Essel Group is present in the media domain through two companies—ZEEL and Zee Media Corporation Ltd (ZMCL). It also brings out the Daily News and Analysis (DNA).

ZEEL has a presence in over 190 countries with 3000+ brands consumed by more than 750 million users. The five business verticals of Zee cater to the diversified content demand of India's population, making Zee the go-to source for viewers not just in India, but also across the globe. Broadcast, digital, international, movies and music and live events are the five different realms ZEEL encompasses.

Today, it has considerable clout in the market. On the domestic front, ZEEL has 47 channels and broadcasts in 11 native languages. It has over 620 million weekly viewers. It includes a bouquet of Hindi general entertainment channels, regional channels, Hindi movie cluster and niche channels. Internationally, ZEEL serves not only the South Asian diaspora with channels and programming in Indian languages but the wider international audience in their native languages as well. ZEEL serves 190 countries (including broadcast in eight foreign languages and 120+ channels in the Americas, Europe, Africa, MENA, APAC regions, etc.) On the digital front, on-demand and live content is delivered to the new-age consumer across connected devices. On the domestic front, Zee 5 has 150+ exclusive originals, 4,500+ movie titles, in 12 Indian languages, 125,000+ hours of on-demand content, 11.2 million+ daily active users, 100 million+ downloads and 100+ live channels.

On the international front, it is a front runner in the South Asian over-the-top (OTT) platforms in Bangladesh and the Middle East. It has the largest presence among South Asian OTT platforms, with 60+ live channels in 190+ countries (12 Indian and six international languages). It has 25+ global partnerships across key countries.

ZMCL has over 345 million viewers consuming multilingual news from 14 channels in eight states today. The many threads of the network come together to constitute an ever-blooming bouquet. As is apparent, with ZEEL and ZMCL leading the group, the company's media visions have not corroded over decades, and with every new vision statement they appear to be promising their continuance even in the near future.

The Zee Entertainment belief lies in the phrase 'Extraordinary Together'. The company believes in the power of 'We', reflected through their focus on 'We are stronger together' i.e. 'Sum>Parts'. It is in the industry to take everyone along with it, and for everyone to lift each other up in life. It claims, 'Everything that we create, not only has to be better than what was, but it has to be extraordinary, everyday. Because we inspire to go beyond; it's not a goal, it's a standard. It's not for any particular individual. It's for everyone.' Zee's ambitious and audacious nature is reflective in the mission statement that defines it today. The company aims 'to become the world's leading global content company from the emerging markets. As a corporation, we will be driven by content leadership based on innovation and creativity. Our focus will be on growth while delivering exceptional value to our customers, viewers and stakeholders.'[6] The corporation believes in the mantra of 'customer first', to anticipate, understand and meet needs of internal and external customers, ensuring high levels of service delivery. It goes for 'big, hairy, audacious goals', transcending the fear of failure, criticism and ambiguity, in an effort to set and achieve bigger targets. There is a focus on the ability to 'solve big problems', and identify and resolve problems which have a high impact on business, by providing innovative solutions and ensuring implementation with creative execution. The company believes in 'being frugal', focusing on need-based resource utilization and to do more with less, while simultaneously working on continuous improvement and on-time delivery. Principles like 'respect, humility and integrity' aim to honour each individual's unique talents, life choices and work styles, and to be fair, humble, honest, transparent and ethical in conduct. 'Speed and agility' are of essence and the company continues to deliver on responsibilities while anticipating and responding to the evolving environment. The company encourages an entrepreneurial spirit, wherein the team and individual employee take full accountability of results, claiming ownership of decisions and actions and ensuring timely delivery of the commitment made with high quality results.

Essel Group, the parent company of Zee, which has grown into a multi-billion dollar business conglomerate, is known across the world for achieving great endeavours and has become a brand synonymous with success. It has an impressive track record of value creation over nine decades, in all businesses across media, entertainment, real estate, infrastructure, education, finance, precious metals and technology sectors. With worldwide operations and a workforce of over 40,000 employees, Essel Group is growing in strength day by day and strives to bring the latest innovations and the best value offerings to all consumers.

This chapter is significant with regard to the growth of Essel Group and ZTL as it traces the roots of the phenomenal and paradigmatic growth of the group and ZTL to the unique personality of its founder and his traditional business. No study of ZTL can be ever complete without an analysis of the personality of its founder. The growth of ZTL derives almost exclusively from the visionary leadership of one man—Subhash Chandra.

TIMELINE 1

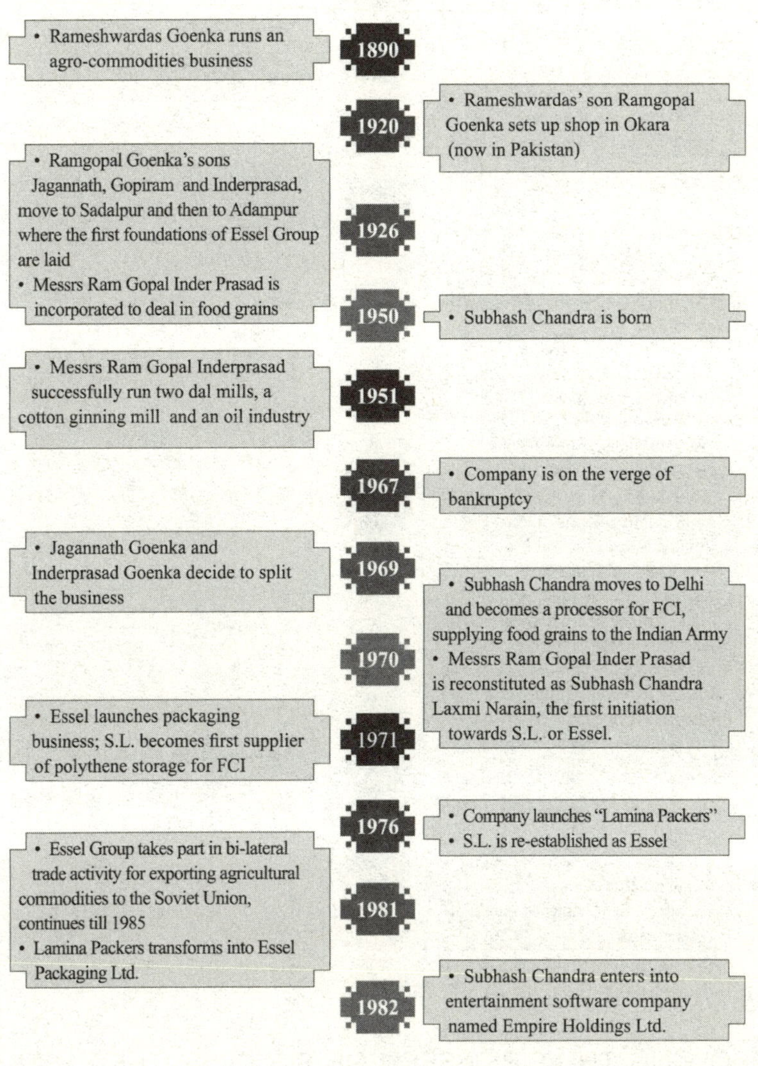

• Rameshwardas Goenka runs an agro-commodities business
1890
1920
• Rameshwardas' son Ramgopal Goenka sets up shop in Okara (now in Pakistan)
• Ramgopal Goenka's sons Jagannath, Gopiram and Inderprasad, move to Sadalpur and then to Adampur where the first foundations of Essel Group are laid
• Messrs Ram Gopal Inder Prasad is incorporated to deal in food grains
1926
1950
• Subhash Chandra is born
• Messrs Ram Gopal Inderprasad successfully run two dal mills, a cotton ginning mill and an oil industry
1951
1967
• Company is on the verge of bankruptcy
• Jagannath Goenka and Inderprasad Goenka decide to split the business
1969
• Subhash Chandra moves to Delhi and becomes a processor for FCI, supplying food grains to the Indian Army
• Messrs Ram Gopal Inder Prasad is reconstituted as Subhash Chandra Laxmi Narain, the first initiation towards S.L. or Essel.
1970
• Essel launches packaging business; S.L. becomes first supplier of polythene storage for FCI
1971
1976
• Company launches "Lamina Packers"
• S.L. is re-established as Essel
• Essel Group takes part in bi-lateral trade activity for exporting agricultural commodities to the Soviet Union, continues till 1985
• Lamina Packers transforms into Essel Packaging Ltd.
1981
1982
• Subhash Chandra enters into entertainment software company named Empire Holdings Ltd.

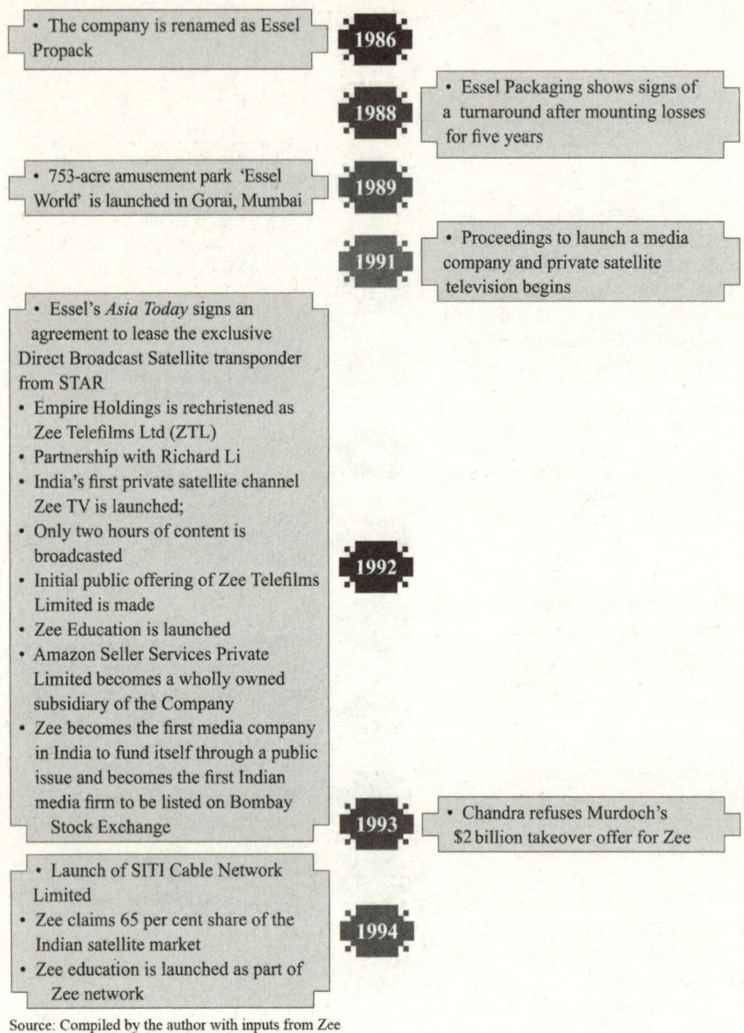

Source: Compiled by the author with inputs from Zee

SOWING THE FIRST SEED OF SUCCESS: THE ESSEL GROUP IS FOUNDED

A proper study of the genesis and growth of Zee can only be carried out by going back to where it all began and reaching far into the early beginnings of the Essel Group. The story can be traced back almost nine and a half decades, with a rich heritage in arenas that were far from the media establishment set up by the Essel Group.

Subhash Chandra's ancestors made humble beginnings by dealing in foodgrains, in Adampur, Haryana; an initiative that came to form the foundation of the Essel Group. Sharing an anecdote on the genesis of the name Essel, Subhash Chandra, in a personal interview with the author narrated, 'My grandfather and his younger brother had separated. Our original firm in 1926 was Ram Gopal Inderprasad. Ram Gopal was my great grandfather and Inderprasad was one of my three grandfathers. So, the firm, Ram Gopal Inderprasad, was handed over to my grandfather. This firm was reconstructed as Subhash Chandra Laxmi Narain (after my name and my brother's). I used to deal in foodgrains and so when it was time to get the gate pass and receipts, people would see the company trucks and say, "S.L. ki gaadi hai" (it is S.L's vehicle). SL was derived from the S in Subhash and L in Laxmi. In 1970, I changed this distinguished acronym into "Essel"'.

The legacy of the group traces its origins back to 1890, when Rameshwardas Goenka, the great-great grandfather of Subhash Chandra, used to run an agro commodities business under the banner of Jagannath Rameshwardas. Jagannath, in the name, referred to his partner.

Ramgopal Goenka, son of Rameshwardas Goenka, bought a plot of property in Okara, Punjab (now in Pakistan) in 1920. Ramgopal birthed three children—Jagannath, Gopiram and Inder Prasad. Subsequently, they set up shops on this plot they had purchased, under a new establishment called Inder Prasad Harchand Rai (Harchand Rai was a family friend). The setup, however, came to be known to the customers and surrounding public as 'Okara dukaan' (Okara shop). Since business at Okara dukaan was slow, Ramgopal Goenka's son Jagannath Goenka began surveying for better opportunities.

In 1926, Subhash Chandra's forefathers migrated to Haryana. From scratch, they raised a humble grain empire there. A market was set up and came to be known as Mandi Adampur (which was then situated in undivided Punjab and in present times is located in Haryana), for which the residents of Hisar were greatly thankful. In 1930, Nand Kishore Goenka, Subhash Chandra's father, was born in Sadalpur village, a place near Mandi Adampur. In 1941, the family shifted base to Hisar itself. In 1948, Jagannath Goenka moved to Delhi and procured a plot at Mothiakhan, where, he set up a pulse factory that rolled out polished pulses. But upon suffering heavy losses in this business, the machinery was moved back to Hisar. A new unit of the business started functions in Hisar and provided polished gram to the Southern regions of India and to Gujarat. This actually turned out to be a profit-making venture.[7]

A MAN AND A DREAM: THE STORY OF SUBHASH CHANDRA

Subhash Chandra was born on 30 November 1950 to Nand Kishore Goenka and Tara Devi in Adampur, Haryana. He was the oldest of seven siblings—Laxmi Narain Goel, Jawahar Goel, Ashok Goel, Kusum, Urmila and Mohini. From an early age, he showed an aptitude and acumen for business. He attended the local village school, which had classes only up till primary school. From the fifth grade onwards, he attended CAV School in Hisar, where he was put under the care and guidance of Jagannath Goenka, his grandfather. Jagannath Goenka's company was involved in purchasing grain and retailing them for a flat commission, money-lending and warehousing. When Chandra returned from school each day, his grandfather would sit him down and teach him to write letters to several clients. This was among the principal teachings he received from his grandfather.

His grandfather, Chandra claims, was one of the most influential people he ever came across and from whom he gained indispensable wisdom about life, values and the family business. Everything he learnt, he learnt from what he metaphorically called the 'Jagannath Goenka University'. His grandfather taught him the three most important lessons that would come handy in life: first, to be fearless; second, to not go back on commitment under any circumstances; third, to not abandon the route of truth. Perhaps the most impactful lesson he learnt was about commitment, since even to this day, Chandra is known in the industry to seal his deals with a simple handshake which is as good as an official paper agreement.

Jagannath Goenka taught Chandra his earliest lessons in the field of business, one of the most important of which was to understand the techniques of analysing people. He gave the young boy lessons in observing people closely and comprehending their motives and purposes through their behaviour. These sessions have held him in good stead even today.

Ever since he was a child, Chandra remained awestruck with what he called his grandfather's 'native wisdom'. During vacations, Chandra went around the village markets with his grandfather, gathering information about people. This taught him to develop strong senses that picked up the tiniest of details. Even today, Chandra is said to be much the same in business. He is known to listen to what people say and doesn't deem it below him to take advice from his employees.

By the time Subhash Chandra was a young boy of eight, he was leading a content life in a large family. Since the grain business was a family-run operation, Chandra too was assigned roles. In his memoir, *The Z Factor*, Chandra recalls an anecdote from the time: 'As the business grew in Hisar, I was given major responsibilities by Dadaji at a relatively young age. I was 12 or 13 years old when I was asked to accompany trucks that carried our goods for sale to Delhi and other destinations… Ludhiana, Hoshiarpur and Pathankot. For a small-town boy, travelling to a big city like Delhi was a delight.'[8]

This boy with rapture in his eyes soon grew up, and in 1965, at the age of 15, moved to the neighbouring city of Sirsa to attend college at Punjab Polytechnic Institute. By 1966, the firm M/s Ramgopal Indraprasad was running one dal mill and two cotton-ginning factories, and things were going smoothly.

Unfortunately, he was not able to finish his education there. The youthful college chap soon received a letter from his grandfather in Hisar asking him to return home because he couldn't afford his grandson's expenses any longer. Reeling from the shock, Chandra rushed back to try and make sense of what had happened in the time that he had been away. He came home to discover a business in shambles and his grandfather in despair. Some bad business decisions had set the family grain business back, and having incurred heavy losses, everything had come to a standstill, almost on the precipice of bankruptcy. Working capital was gone and the earning wasn't more than 3–4 lakhs. In 1967, the young lad was overcome by a new wave of motivation to get his family back on its feet again and to pay off all the debt. Charged with motivation to do something for his family, the seventeen-year-old dropout, with a mere ₹11 in his pocket, took over the reins from his grandfather and moved to Delhi to further expand his patrimonial foodgrain business. Thus, began Chandra's entrepreneurial career as a dal trader in Hisar. He also revived some of their other old mills that had been lying dysfunctional. Navigating a bankrupt business was not an easy task for a 17-year-old boy.

On the bus ride from Hisar to Delhi, Chandra struck up a conversation with a man called Aman Singh, who was an assistant manager for the Food Corporation of India (FCI). FCI was the main buyer of grain in India during those days. Yet, the armed forces used to purchase grain from the Ministry of Food and Agriculture.[9] The Army was a major client of grains, pulses and dry fruit. But FCI was incapable of meeting the tall criterions set by the Army. Sharp witted as he was, Chandra offered a very innovative technical solution of processing foodgrains from his end for the Indian Army, which could then be passed on by FCI to the Army. Chandra suggested that his business could upgrade the product by polishing pulses and cleaning barley. The FCI approved his proposal and Chandra's family was back in business due to his efforts to find a way to add significant value to the product without any substantial investment. Chandra also persuaded the FCI to supply him with whole dal that could be split and delivered to the Army.

Though Chandra was supplying foodgrains from Delhi, he did not possess enough money at the time. He had only about ₹50,000 in his pocket from his dal mill profit savings. It was a huge risk for him to be functioning like this, since if ever he was not able to raise capital, he would stand to lose the factories, bids, and most of all, his stature.

Therefore, he entered a partnership with C. Lal, B.D. Hansaria and B.R. Chopra in a 50:50 deal. It was decided that the others would invest the money, while Chandra would manage the business. Forever a 'street smart' man who thought on his feet, Chandra's business acumen was being honed with each turn of events in his self-established grain kingdom.

It had only been a year in Delhi for Chandra when, one day, after the completion of a few contracts, he found out from the accountant that the business had 'made a small loss instead of profits.' Chandra suspected some miscalculation by the accountant, but failed to convince his partners about the same. He felt that his partner had cheated him of a few lakhs' worth of profit. Chandra was left feeling helpless.

When he visited his family next, they all agreed that he was not ready yet to venture out and work in the big bad world all alone. Since everybody was skeptical about the long-term success of this entire arrangement, Chandra wrapped up his functions in Delhi, packed his bags and returned home to Hisar. A slight disillusionment was setting in, and Chandra 'could not stomach the thought of doing the same work' for the rest of his life.

In 1976, he made a foray into the world of packaging under the name 'Lamina Packers' and manufactured laminated tubes for FCI to store surplus agricultural harvests. His solution of storing foodgrains in the open, under polythene sheets saw a positive response from FCI. Chandra stepped foot into this business by obtaining polythene sheets and then cutting and welding them into tents. But the buck didn't stop here. Chandra recounts, 'Along with Lamina Packers, we considered other businesses too. We started work in the fiberglass moulding business.'[10] The grain business even went international during this time, as the company began exporting rice to the USSR through FCI. Rama Associates, an establishment set up by Chandra in 1976, had won a profitable deal which required the export of rice to the Soviet Union. On 21 May 1981, an agreement was signed, approving the export of 30,000 tonnes of rice to Russia under the bilateral trade agreement, at a cost of ₹5,500 per tonne.

This venture too was not without its share of glitches. Moments before the agreement was signed, the deal was on the verge of slipping through his hands as a result of a communication gap between the Russian delegation and the company. Chandra, who was in Belgium at the time, cut his visit short and rushed back to Delhi in order to salvage the settlement. Fortunately, he subsequently also won an additional contract for the export of soya bean. In 17 months, the company had exported grains worth a billion.

Lamina Packers transformed in 1981, with the nomenclature of Essel Packaging Ltd, denoting the company's primary packaging business. It was set up in Mumbai, and manufactured laminated tubes for packaging pharmaceutical tablets and other groupings of paper, plastic and aluminum files of international standards on basic indigenous machinery.

Soon, he also set up a manufacturing plant which supplied empty capsules to the pharmaceutical industry, and bought a company that manufactured hand tools. As 1982 approached, the turnover of the business was in excess of ₹1 billion, far from the bankrupt company whose reins he had taken over in 1973. By 1986, the company was in full swing, and was renamed Essel Propack.

At the time, toothpaste was mainly packed in aluminum tubes in India. In the West, aluminum tubes had been replaced by multi-layered lamination ones, which had earlier dominated the medicine, cosmetics and toothpaste businesses. Chandra imported a new technology that made laminated tubes. Unfazed by the counsel of well-wishers that this product would not find a space in the Indian market, Chandra proceeded with his endeavour as he believed these new tubes would replace metal tubes as toothpaste containers. But as predicted, this Western innovation unfortunately arrived ahead of its time in India, and Chandra fought long and hard for five years, to survive the low utilization and swelling losses. Nevertheless, he stood his ground, confident that this was a product that would succeed one day. Around the late 1988–89, his 50 million tube capacity packaging businesses started to show signs of a turnaround. It was a new dawn for India that saw the launch of gel toothpastes, which exclusively required a non-aluminum format filling, courtesy Essel Packaging.[11]

Chandra wrote in his 2016 autobiography, *The Z Factor: My Journey as the Wrong Man at the Right Time*, 'After years of struggle, our commitment to laminated tubes had paid off well. Essel Packaging became so successful… Now we are the biggest tube makers in the world—manufacturing about eight billion tubes in the world. One third of humanity uses our tubes while brushing their teeth.'[12]

From then on, there was no looking back for Chandra. What began as a business in foodgrain, that were even exported globally, he began extending into newer avenues like fiberglass moulding, packaging, laminated tubes, storage and pharmaceutical lamination, all stamped with the legacy of his forefathers under the name Essel.

With this company name, Chandra even ventured into adventure and entertainment. Subhash Chandra used his business acumen and the surplus of funds generated from his real estate businesses to establish Essel World in 1989 in Mumbai. Chandra recounts an interesting anecdote in his autobiography, which many may not know: 'Though the name sounds as if it was the natural extension of the group's name, this was not so. We had started a public competition to name the place. Out of the thousands of entries we received, we picked the name ESSEL (Educational Sports and Science Exhibition Land).'[13] Essel World was inaugurated as a 753-acre popular amusement park in Mumbai, and became another gemstone in the legacy of the Essel Group. There was, at the time, opposition from powerful state politicians and protests from environmentalists, but Chandra's PR agency suggested the idea to dedicate the amusement park to honour Jawaharlal Nehru's love for children on his birth anniversary.[14]

This was also a time of deep spiritual peace in Chandra's life. He discovered the art of Vipassana practices, an event that transformed him into a different person altogether. He was also made the chairman of Global Vipassana Foundation, a public trust. As a tribute to the practice that had brought him immense faith and confidence, Chandra donated a piece of land within Essel World to the organization.

The most satisfactory notes of success however wafted in with the setting up of Chandra's media empire upon the foundations of bringing entertainment to the drawing room of every household in the country. What began as a humble foray into the media industry, called Empire Holdings, quickly tumbled, phase after phase, into success. Along the way, Chandra broke many barriers inherent to the Indian communication industry. From paving the way for the first private satellite broadcaster to the first privately broadcasted channel, he is a pioneer in many ways. The name of his new broadcast media undertaking, Zee, was enough to elicit sentiments of awe for Chandra and his mammoth efforts to transform the M&E industry in India.

The media baron also dipped his fingers into politics. In 2016, Chandra was elected to the Upper House of the Indian parliament as a Bharatiya Janata Party candidate for the state of Haryana in the Rajya Sabha elections. In November 2019, Chandra stepped down from his position as chairman of Zee. He is now chairman emeritus at ZEE.

MULTI-BILLION DOLLAR BUSINESS CONGLOMERATE: MEDIA AND NON-MEDIA SECTORS

'Faith in innovative and organized growth' has been the mantra behind Essel group's whopping achievements. Close to a century later, Essel Group now stands as a multi-billion dollar business conglomerate. The establishment now spans across both media and non-media sectors. Its chief businesses can be classified into segments, namely media, technology, education, entertainment, infrastructure, health and lifestyle, precious metals and finance services. Media consists of TV broadcasting and includes ZEEL, ZMCL, DNA and India.com. Technology and TV distribution includes Dish TV India Ltd and Siti Networks Ltd. It also includes a company named Cyquator Technologies; diversification over the years has also brought some non-media ventures under the Essel umbrella. Education includes Zee Learn and Liberium; entertainment sector includes companies liker Pan India Network Ltd, Pan India Paryatan Ltd (Essel World, Water Kingdom), E-City Bioscope Entertainment Ltd and E City Digital Cinemas Pvt. Ltd; infrastructure, includes Essel Infraprojects Ltd (EIL), Smart Utilities and E-City Real Estates Pvt. Ltd; health, lifestyle and wellness includes Living Foodz; precious metals includes the company Zee Gold and Shirpur Gold Refinery Ltd (SGRL); and finance services consist of Essel Finance.[15]

The Essel empire stands neatly allocated to each of Subhash Chandra's brothers with independent charge, who own majority stakes in the company. Laxmi Narain Goel owns and manages real estate, film and gas distribution, Jawahar Goel has the media distribution and DTH businesses, while Ashok Goel looked after the Essel Propack (now a Blackstone-owned company) and amusement park businesses. While the group presents a union through Subhash Chandra's iconic image, the businesses are run independently. Chandra has however mentioned, 'The finances of each brother's businesses are also separate, but we help each other if someone requires any support.'[16]

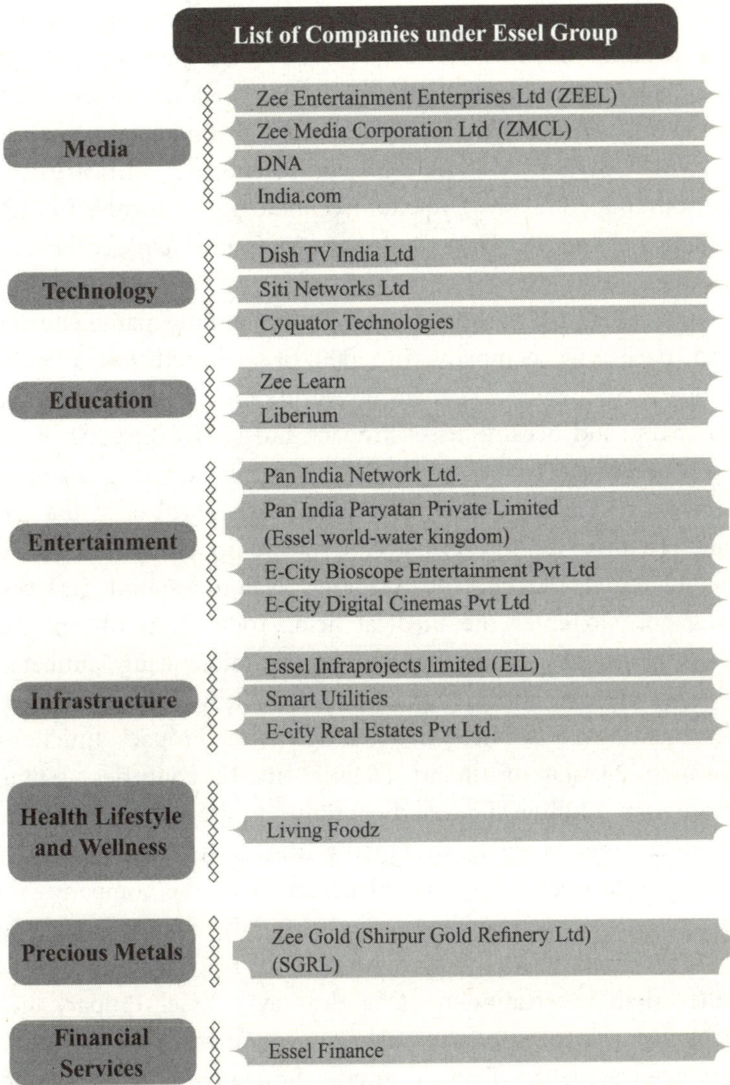

Source: Compiled by the author with inputs from ZEE

Fig. 1.2: List of Companies under Essel Group

The Essel Group's technological operations are carried out via three main outlets, namely Dish TV, Siti Network Ltd and Cyquator Technologies. Dish TV is Asia Pacific's largest DTH company, while Siti Networks Ltd is one of India's largest Multi System Operator (MSO). An end-to-end, IT infrastructure outsourcing company, Cyquator Technologies, is involved in the business of Internet Data Center and high-end managed hosting services.

Essel Propack was the company's longstanding manufacturing and packaging company. In 2000, it acquired Switzerland's Propack AG, which was then the world's fourth largest lamitube company, and became Essel Propack Ltd (EPL). In 2002, it set up a greenfield facility in Danville, Virginia, US to provide its services to P&G. In 2004, it acquired Arista Tubes of the UK and renamed it Essel Propack, UK, and in 2006, it acquired manufacturers Tacpro Inc, US and Avalon Medical Services, Singapore to enter the medical field. Today it is one of the leading specialty packaging company manufacturing laminated and seamless or extruded plastic tubes. With over 2,500 people representing 25 different nationalities, Essel Propack functions through 24 state-of-the-art facilities in 12 countries, selling more than 5 billion tubes and continues to grow every year. The product range is extensive, ranging from beauty and cosmetics to home care, oral care and pharma.[17] Now the company is a Blackstone-owned company.

For Essel's vision going forward, with respect to businesses other than entertainment, Chandra says, 'Essel Propack has become a global specialty packaging company; that objective has been achieved. I would advise the team that they should now widen their horizon and come out from the specialty packaging, expand into other areas of packaging, or they have to exit their business. For our infrastructure business, we are working to become the most admired [business] in the country.

For education, we recommend both models of education to be continued in parallel—one to provide free education in the public sector, and second to also allow private educational institutions to start taking profits, which currently is not allowed. If that is done, then I think we have a vision for Zee Learn to become an admired education company. The future is to create your own IPR (intellectual property rights) in every business.'[18]

Education is another spectrum on the Essel Group scale of success, with Zee Learn Ltd and Liberium. Zee Learn is growing with a chain of K–12 schools and pre-schools in its portfolio. Liberium offers an array of services around training, temporary staffing, lateral hiring and other allied human resource business process outsourcing services.

Outdoor as well as digital entertainment has also been a venture that Essel has excelled in with Pan India Network Ltd, Pan India Paryatan Pvt. Ltd, E-City Bioscope Entertainment Pvt. Ltd and E-City Digital Cinemas Pvt. Ltd Pan India Network Ltd is in the business of providing infrastructure, data communication, marketing support and service to facilitate a secure online lottery network. Playwin is the lottery and gaming brand of Pan India Network Ltd, part of the Essel (Subhash Chandra) Group. Pan India Paryatan Pvt. Ltd is the holding company of EsselWorld Leisure Pvt. Ltd and Water Kingdom, the largest amusement parks in India, and a subsidiary of Essel (Ashok Goel) Group. E-City Bioscope Entertainment Pvt. Ltd (ECBEPL) was formed to establish a chain of commercial complexes, housing complexes, construction businesses and multiplex cinema-cum-family activity centers (FACs) across non-metro towns all over India and is a part of the Essel (Jawahar Lal Goel) Group. E-City Digital Cinemas Pvt. Ltd, a part of Essel (Laxmi Narain Goel) Group was established in April 2004, and revolutionized the Indian movie business by implementing modern digital technology at the various independent cinema houses in the industry.

Under infrastructure, the group has three main subdivisions: Essel Infraprojects Ltd, Smart Utilities and E-City Real Estates Pvt. Ltd. Having diversified interests in infrastructure projects, Essel Infraprojects Ltd is a successful venture by Essel (Subhash Chandra) Group with three SBUs and six business verticals comprising of an order book value $3.5 billion and a national footprint in more than 14 states and across 52 cities. Smart Utilities, an integrated utilities brand—a consumer-centric integrated utility services brand delivering smart value and efficiency is another successful venture of Essel (Subhash Chandra) Group. A part of Essel (Laxmi Narain Goel) Group, E-City Real Estates Pvt. Ltd is the force behind the successful lifestyle brand Fun Republic, which currently operates three lifestyle malls in Mumbai, Lucknow and Coimbatore. The company aims to operate successful retail formats that align the interests of operators, retailers and consumers providing an ideal size and brand mix.

Health, lifestyle and wellness is another product brand for the group, offered mainly through Living Foodz and Veria Living. The premium food and lifestyle channel Living Foodz specializes in exploring the evolving social status of food; moving out of the confines of the conventional kitchen into a world of entertainment and adventure with food. Living Entertainment Enterprises Private Ltd is a part of Essel (Subhash Chandra) Group. Veria Living is one of the leading media brands devoted to showcasing healthy lifestyle and wellness programming and related content across multiple media platforms in the United States and beyond.

The precious metals department is shouldered solely by the Shirpur Gold Refinery Ltd (SGRL), a part of Essel (Subhash Chandra) Group, which is one of the leading players in the precious metals market in India. With ultra-modern refining and minting processes and professionally driven management coupled with experienced manpower, the company produces gold and silver bars and coins that meet international standards in quality.

The company's financial services are showcased through Essel Finance. The umbrella brand for the financial businesses, it is a private sector financial services company offering a range of services and products across corporate finance and retail sectors. Headquartered in Mumbai, the company has a vast network spread in almost all major cities in India. This well-diversified financial services firm offers a range of financial products and services such as private equity and SME business loans through its non-banking financial company (NBFC), housing finance, distribution of mutual funds and insurance, forex money-changing and remittance and investment banking.

However, expansion has not just been limited within India. Essel Group's boundaries expand even into the Middle East, Africa and other parts of the world. Essel Group Middle East (EGME) operates subsidiary businesses in the natural resources sectors. Its natural resources portfolio includes oil, gas, potash and iron ore assets. EGME pursues growth through the acquisition of underdeveloped assets at competitive valuations. Its flagship assets are located across Africa and the Middle East, in sectors and locations with significant growth potential and a competitive cost environment. Their assets are strategically located close to existing infrastructure links to enable quick monetization and transport to end customers. They invest where they can see project returns in the mid-teens levels, using a locally adjusted cost of capital assessment. At EGME, the company contributes to the development of the areas and communities where they work. They are very active in supporting local community initiatives through oil and gas investments in Africa. Pan Asia Infrastructure FZ-LLC (free zone limited liability company) has been incorporated under Dubai Technology and Media Free Zone. It is located in the midst of Dubai Media City (DMC), Dubai, United Arab Emirates. Pan Asia Infrastructure provides Real Estate Research, Management and Development services across the UAE.

On the milestone success of 90 years, a press release quoting Subhash Chandra said, 'This journey of 90 years has been filled with remarkable successes as well as challenges and obstacles. It has been a journey of creating history, venturing into unknown territories, only to emerge as leaders, capitalizing on our pioneering vision and sheer entrepreneurial spirit. Today, Essel Group is a multi-billion dollar diversified business conglomerate, enriching billions of lives across the world. As we look to the future, I am confident that we will carry forward the legacy of the Group with complete passion, dedication and above all, the spirit of #YoungAt90!'[19]

The event was attended by many dignitaries, including the prime minister and the president. Prime Minister Narendra Modi described Essel as an 'epitome of Indian culture where family values run supreme'. He recalled, 'This journey is more of a journey of economic development. I have been associated with the family for long. Nand Kishore ji used to invite me for meals at their house,' referring to Subhash Chandra's father. President Pranab Mukherjee also said, 'I would like to appreciate the adjective "young" at 90. You should continue to look at new dimensions of the job in which you are engaged in. You had a modest beginning. But over 90 years we have witnessed how things have changed.'[20] Chandra also announced that he had pledged a ₹5,000 crore fund for India's development, and inaugurated an entity called Development Support Centre (DSC) Foundation for capacity building towards start-ups that would create jobs.

PRE GENESIS: EMPIRE HOLDINGS AND NEW BUSINESS PARADIGMS

The Essel story never really ends, since it still stands as the backbone to the Zee story that begins here. Subhash Chandra's entry into the media world began in no ordinary manner. Like the plot of an exciting film, this particular story too is riddled with its unique share of ups and downs, many unexpected twists, and an ultimate breakthrough.

Chandra had made long leaps in the fields of packaging, trading and amusement. Wishing to make further forays into the industry, he decided to go for media production. India at the time had been witnessing a boom in the trend of video parlours. Chandra, in the beginning, toyed with the concept of outfitting a fleet of video vans that were enabled to tour the countryside, wherein people could be charged to watch the videos. He was also prepared with calculations about the revenue he would be capable of earning through advertisements. To this end, he set up Empire Holdings Ltd, an entertainment software company.

The company was incorporated on 25 November 1982 and it obtained the Certificate of Commencement of Business on 5 January 1983 as Empire Holdings Ltd in the state of Maharashtra. Chandra's Essel Group of companies, comprising Sanjay Badgamia, Vasant Parekh and Ashok Kothari, promoted it. The main objective of the company was the business of entertainment software. This company is the one whose name was ultimately changed to Zee Telefilms Ltd.

Empire Holdings produced Hindi films, serials, game shows and children's programmes among other media products of various kinds. The company also commissioned serials, game shows, etc. through directors and producers on contract basis, purchased rights of Hindi films, serials and other programmes from the producers for a predetermined period. Simultaneously, the company co-promoted Essel Packaging Ltd, the partnership company of the Essel group in 1982.

Signatories to the Memorandum of Association subscribed for 70 equity shares. 2,47,930 equity shares of ₹10 each were then issued at par, of which 97,930 shares were reserved for allotment to the directors and their relatives, among others. The remaining 1,50,000 shares were issued to the public on 25 February 1986. Besides these, another 4,96,000 shares were offered on rights basis in the proportion 2:1.

ENVIRONMENTAL SCANNING: A WAR AND A NEW ECONOMY

To understand the launch of Zee, it becomes important to scrutinize the environmental conditions that surrounded it at the time. This environmental scanning is led first and foremost by the fact that Doordarshan, with a logo and signature tune that has high recall value even today, was the only public television broadcaster in India in 1990 by law. No other television system was permitted to broadcast from Indian soil.

This situation was turned on its head by the momentous Gulf War, which began with Iraq's invasion of neighbouring Kuwait in 1990. Many Indian families had relatives working in the Gulf States and they were desperate for news from the region. In January 1991, warfare began between Iraq and America and other allied military forces. People would huddle around television sets in the lobbies of Taj and other five-star hotels that subscribed to international television news networks like CNN. Punit Goenka also confirmed, 'During the Gulf War that created the penetration of cable television in this country, CNN was the most watched channel.'[21]

In 1991, the Narasimha Rao government launched a series of economic and social reforms. Under the new policies, the government allowed private and foreign broadcasters to engage in limited operations in India. It increased the inflow of private and foreign investments into the country's economy. This created the second spark in the early '90s with the broadcast of satellite TV by foreign programmers like CNN, followed by Star TV and a little later by domestic channels such as Zee TV and NDTV into Indian homes. As a consequence, 1991 onwards, India began to get wealthier.

ZEE TELEFILMS DAWNS ON INDIAN ENTERTAINMENT

Subhash Chandra, during this time, was generating immense positive business with Essel Group. But even though he was riding high on the wave of success, Chandra's ambitions and desires were not fully satiated. His drive was not motivated solely by profit or expansion. It was based primarily upon offering something more to his country's people. Sensing great margins for this in the M&E industry, Chandra sought to diversify his business from rice trading and packaging to the M&E business. This was an important step, as it put him on the high road of future growth in an ever-growing M&E industry. The decision to go into packaging had been nothing more than a horizontal integration of the business of rice trading with that of its safe transportation and preservation, but the decision to venture into M&E was a paradigmatic business policy shift. Chandra had the vision and the guts to take such a policy decision and to make it work.

VISIONS DURING WAR: CHANDRA DREAMS BIG

Chandra outgrew the traditional model of entertainment business by deciding to take entertainment right into the homes of his customers. This was a revolutionary idea in practical terms too. Owing to the country's tropical climate, one can't expect clients to travel in the sweltering heat of the summer sun to the point of sale of entertainment service. Taking advantage of the advent of the satellite technology, a seed germinated in Chandra's visionary mind. But Chandra, being a man with a simple background, wasn't familiar with the nitty-gritties of technology. He writes in his book, 'When we started Zee, we did not know what satellite meant. The chief engineer of the state-run Doordarshan gave me a simple and effective description of a satellite. He said it's a bit like a big mirror in the sky. Whenever a signal or a beam of light is sent up, it reflects it back within a certain area. That's the footprint or reach of that satellite.'[22]

Prakash Pednekar, area manager, Hathway Cable and Datacom, Bangalore, which was a key competitor to the Zee Network, commented, 'Subhash Chandra has grown remarkably fast. Clever visionary that he is, he has found answers in technology. He has captured the Indian market with a host of services.'[23] Chandra foresaw the importance of satellite technology, along with Shashi Kumar, a journalist who ran the Press Trust of India's television production arm, and was the first to realize that money could be made out of it.

The idea of Zee can be attributed in part to the Gulf War, when Chandra had watched CNN in the office of Ashok Kurien, an advertising executive who was marketing Essel World. Kurien, recalls Chandra asking him whether launching a private television channel like CNN was possible in India. Kurien had replied that Chandra could make it happen and that he would help him.

In December 1991, there were incipient developments of this venture into mass media. At a time, when the business of entertainment was defined in terms of the distribution system, which required the customer to reach out to the place of entertainment, Chandra sought to reverse the direction of this flow. The idea behind it was, as Chandra said, 'Some people do not want to travel three hours for entertainment, so let us take entertainment to them.'[24]

Punit Goenka, discussing the Zee mantra for popularity with the author, reiterated this, 'I think the biggest reason for our success at Zee is that we understood the idea that people were not willing to travel long distances for entertainment. People wanted entertainment at their beck and call, and television was the medium that would lead to that. When we launched Essel World, I remember our consultant came up with the projection that 1 million visitors would come to Essel World in the first year. Less than half showed up. That's when we realized that if we bring entertainment to people's homes, our brainchild would be far more successful.'[25]

Chandra was thus shown the way to STAR (Satellite Television Asian Region) Ltd. His point of contact was David Manion, a middle-level executive at Star TV, whom he approached with a request to 'lease a transponder on AsiaSat1'. Nalin Mehta, in his book *India on Television*, quotes Subhash Chandra who said that when he first approached STAR to hire one of the 24 transponders on AsiaSat, he was not taken seriously by anyone. Then in a 2016 interview with Gurbir Singh, Chandra explained, 'STAR had transponders on the AsiaSat satellite and it was a monopoly. On the other hand, STAR had not launched in India and wanted access in our markets. With hindsight, I can say it may have been better if Zee had gone with a Russian satellite that was also available. I was in favour of that, but our investors had a problem. They wanted us on AsiaSat.'[26] Thereafter, Chandra and Kurien together produced a show reel for trial. Manion enjoyed the production and suggested that the two friends pursue a joint venture. Kurien and Chandra entered into a 50:50 joint partnership, with the transponder lease cost decided at $1.2 million per year.

Chandra faced several challenges in the business of packaging

M&E, the biggest being the lack of institutional mechanism and structures for promoting a media business primarily in television. At that time, the restrictions on private broadcasting space was another problem, and it took Chandra and his team some time to understand the legal bindings upon making use of a foreign satellite to stream into India. Launching a private satellite channel was not going to be an easy task, and this endeavour locked horns with roadblocks at every stage of development. When Chandra proposed the subject to the then secretary for Information and Broadcasting, the official became livid. 'You will introduce consumerism and destroy the country. Your proposal can fructify only over my dead body,' the secretary boomed.[27]

Punit Goenka, opines that his father, Dr Chandra, was truly the visionary who had the courage and the bare resolve to see his idea through. He stated, 'I used to hear people saying, "Subhash, you've lost your mind! You will lose everything with this idea. This is not something that the Indian government or any investors would really see through." But I think he had the conviction that India was ready to see what the world had to offer.'

REVERSING THE BUSINESS MODEL

In December 1991, Chandra and Kurien flew to Hong Kong for a meeting fixed with the businessman Richard Li, who was to supply the transponder. Nothing went as planned. Li refused the offer with a view that this business opportunity would not yield much profit in India. Chandra recalls, 'Nobody thought it was a viable proposition. I didn't know anything, maybe that's why I had faith in it. The fear of failure wasn't there in me, since there was no knowledge about anything.'[28] But he persisted.

After some discussion, Li agreed, but not without inflating the cost to $5 million a year. Chandra, helpless yet motivated, gave in to the offer. He figured that if the channel was going to work, it was going to do so even at $5 million.' Unfortunately, Li was still unconvinced about the profit returns and didn't sign the deal.

Subsequently, an unsure Li was invited over by Chandra to visit the campus of his Essel Packaging worth $345.5 million. Among the biggest flexi-packaging companies across the globe, Essel Packaging was enough to convince Li that a partnership with Chandra would prove to be fruitful. The confirmation letter was signed on 21 May 1992, and India witnessed the launch of his channel in October of the same year.[29] Zee TV, India's first Hindi satellite channel, was launched with a vision to create a platform that would converge media and communications and help viewers find a mirror that is relevant to the changing times.

It was launched as a Hindi general entertainment channel (GEC). Zee TV's content library delivered a variety of choices for the Indian middle class ranging from non-fiction formats that celebrated the talent of India's common man to fiction shows which delivered strong messages and drove positive change in society while entertaining the viewers. Zee TV's content resonated with its core ethos. It aimed to inspire viewers to take charge of their destinies giving wings to their dreams and aspirations.

But new troubles awaited. Chandra says, 'One was the initial lack of capital to run such a business. We started it, and then realized that we'll need lots of money. It was challenging to raise funding in the initial period. Banks were not ready to lend; even SBI refused, which was an imperial bank and had been our bank since 1926. I met almost a hundred venture capitalists abroad—Singapore and Hong Kong, mainly, and some even in London. Eventually people trusted us and invested. We raised about $12.5 million from the venture capitalists, and from our end, we contributed almost ₹10 cr.'[30] He raised the kickstarting resources from British businessman, Sir James Goldsmith, and from Indians living overseas.

The branding of the channel was paramount. Chandra recounts, 'After raising the money, I started work on branding the channel. The name of the production company that made the programmes would be the same as that of the channel. In the end, we went with Zee as the brand name for the TV channel. We changed the name of an existing group company in India to Zee Telefilms Ltd.'[31]

Punit Goenka stated, 'I was just a young boy in 1992 when we launched Zee. A large part of the liberalization period that followed post the launch of Zee was also on account of how we showed India what was happening around the world, outside the country, by using the television medium to reach masses. I give some credit of liberalization to my father. He was instrumental in making that happen at the pace at which it happened in the early 90s.'

As such, the giant ZTL was incepted. Asia Today Ltd became the corporation that launched Zee TV. Chandra approached producers and directors, like B.R. Chopra and Subhash Ghai, in search of support from these bigwigs during his maiden venture. In this first instance, Chandra acquired the rights to almost 3,000 movies for broadcasting on his channel.

The channel gained momentum soon enough. Chandra wrote, 'We started getting letters from viewers complimenting us and sharing feedback on the shows.' Hooking onto the love, Chandra used this as proof to invite advertisers and media buyers into the fold of his business. There was even talk of Zee venturing into the satellite communication space which had started to emerge under the aegis of Motorola and ICO, but Chandra then decided to dedicate his focus to the media industry only.[32]

The initial period of ZTL's growth is significant for a number of developments, which include the identification of the company as a new business paradigm of M&E industry, apart from the various strategic initiatives taken to make the new paradigm successful.

Several environmental factors such as the need for ever-growing information in the wake of the Gulf War, the economic reforms of the government, and the need for entertainment, created a conducive cocoon from which Zee emerged like an illustrious butterfly. Thus, right at the onset, exemplary leadership and efficient use of technology became the pillars of foundation of the Zee group. Chandra's vision behind this new business paradigm was of paramount importance, when there were many who were shirking from investing in Asia.

NEXT IN LINE, NEWS

Chandra went on to develop Zee as India's most popular satellite television network, and positioned it as a global brand in the US, UK and South Africa. In 1993, Amazon Seller Services Private Ltd (ASSPL) became a wholly owned subsidiary of the company. During the year, the company entered into an agreement with the Mauritius Broadcasting Corporation for the supply of programme software to Zee TV. During the same year, Chandra visited Marché International des Programmes de Communication (MIPCOM), a global trade exhibition in France, and bought some Latin American soaps. These shows were then aired on Zee TV with Hindi dubbing. At MIPCOM, Chandra was struck with an idea: 'Why not have a weekly news round-up on Zee?'[33]

As had been the case with private satellite broadcasting when Zee had first launched, the company was met with hurdles once again. They did not allow domestic private networks to air news; DD was still the only channel with that power. The old adage—where there is a will, there is a way—isn't without reason. A way was found around this problem.

The idea of satellite television networks broadcasting in India had programming uplinked to satellite transponders from Hong

Kong, Singapore, Moscow, or other sites outside India. Until late 1998, each private network in India sent videos by courier to one of these sites, and its programming was then uplinked for satellite transmission to India. This helped the news channels to circumvent the Indian government's prohibition on broadcasting news from Indian soil. Those practices are long gone now. Seen in this perspective, it was a revolutionary change in the history of Indian broadcasting. The show that was uplinked for Chandra's venture was on Zee TV, branded as Zee News. Thus, was born the 'first private daily news bulletin of India' in 1994.

Despite the success Zee achieved, Punit Goenka maintained, 'Even today, Zee carries the brand of one individual—Dr Chandra. The vision is his; my team and I are just implementers of his vision and that's where we complement each other. I don't try and bring my vision into the picture. But now, I think, having been in the business for 12 years in Zee, I can read what he wants before he can tell me what his next target for me is going to be. So, while I would've already started the journey with the team, it still comes from him that this is what the goals are. So, I think that's what works best for us as a family, as a chairman and CEO relationship or a chairholder and MD relationship.'[34] Punit Goenka even showed two papers to the author which he received from his father, mentioning goals set for him.

An employee of Zee, in conversation with the author, remarked, 'Chandra is perhaps the first Indian who has successfully harnessed media in all its forms to pass on the fruits of entertainment, education and information to millions of viewers'.

MANAGING THE COMPANY, MARWARI STYLE

The Zee family ethos reflected in Chandra's keen management style, that even to this day is an exhibit of the affection with which the company was started. Elaborating on his system,

Chandra writes in his autobiography: 'I started a system and process of meeting all the important executives in the group. Once a year, I interview and discuss with them their issues with the company, or with their boss… One has to keep one's eyes and ears open. And the feet should be on the ground.'[35]

In an interview at Wharton U-Penn, Subhash Chandra revealed that the key to a successful business in the broadcast and entertainment industry was to look at every programme as a viewer, not as a chairman. The most important thing, according to him, was to be responsive to the viewers.[36] In an interview with the author, he maintains, 'This is not rocket science. I even tell my sons, as long as you listen to your viewers and don't behave as if you are the only one who knows what entertains or brings out emotions in people, it'll be okay. Steven Spielberg for TIME said, if anyone who makes films says they know what will work and what won't, they are telling a lie. Different content works for different audiences.'[37]

While some perceived Chandra's business style as being a traditional Marwari one, he was the first in the television industry to introduce employee stock options. In 1993, Zee TV became the first media company in India to fund itself through a public issue, and became the first Indian media firm to be listed on the Bombay Stock Exchange. The value of Zee's stock rose by a whopping 15,000 per cent in seven years after the company went public in 1993, making it the fastest-rising Indian stock of all time. In the words of a Zee employee, 'It is one of the most spectacular, sustained, stock price increases that the Indian equity markets had experienced over the decade.'

In August 1993, the company issued 89,28,000 rights equity shares of ₹10 each at a premium of ₹20 per share in proportion 12:1. Another 90,00,000 shares were offered at a premium of ₹20 per share through a prospectus as follows: 9,00,000 shares and 27,00,000 shares reserved for allotment to FIIs and NRIs (repatriation basis) respectively. Only 21,90,300 shares taken up by NRIs. Of the balance, 10,000 shares were reserved for allotment on preferential basis to employees (only 4,100 shares taken up). The remaining 45,90,000 shares along with 5,15,600 shares not taken up were issued to the public (of these 4,98,000 shares taken up by FIIs and 17,600 by the public). Four lakh Redeemable Cumulative Non-Convertible Pref. shares were issued during the year.

Nalin Mehta notes in *India on Television* that private television came to India as a foreign entity. Therefore, Indian producers in the early years largely followed Western formats, which served as a benchmark for them. He adds that television has been Indianized because news channels put global practices of television through an Indian lens, remarrying them with reconstituted elements of what are seen as Indian practices to create new hybrid genres of programming. Mehta also opines that as the competition intensified, economic pressures turned news producers into mediators of what they understood to be an Indian identity. They tapped into Indian oral traditions and traditional patterns of social communication that historians and sociologists have long documented and channelized them into television.[38]

Chandra elaborates on the intent behind the content being presented to viewers during the initial days of Zee: 'Zee gave many firsts to the viewers. Though seemingly these issues were a reflection of the reality in society, some of them were taboo. Issues such as extramarital relations and single motherhood were brought by Zee to Indian living rooms.'[39]

FINANCIAL HIGHLIGHTS

As per annual reports, the total income of Empire Holdings Ltd in the FY 1992 was ₹33,05,429 and the total expenditure was

₹40,02,818. The loss for the year amounted to ₹6,97,389. The balance loss brought forward was ₹14,60,412. Thus, the total loss carried forward was ₹21,57,801. In FY 1993, the annual income saw an increase. It now amounted to ₹7,07,29,927 vis-à-vis the total expenses that amounted to ₹6,35,64,833. The profit then amounted to ₹71,65,094. After tax, the profit was pegged at ₹54,65,094. So the total profit of ZTL, after deducting the carried forward loss of ₹21,57,801 amounted to ₹33,07,293.

In FY 1994, the total income increased to ₹26,27,05648, whereas the total expenses amounted to be ₹16,25,87,276. The total Profit Before Taxation (PBT) amounted to be ₹10,01,18,372 and to ₹9,21,18,372. After adding the carried forward amount of ₹33,07,293, the total profit increased to ₹9,54,25,665. The proposed dividend was ₹1,64,28,000. ₹5,00,00,000 was kept as general reserve and the balance profit of ₹2,89,97,665 was carried forward to the next year.

NEW STRATAGEMS FOR A NEW DECADE

The new paradigm of entertainment business that Chandra launched, was nurtured and sustained by a slew of strategic initiatives, which included an unambiguous strategic intent enunciation, product development and diversification, strategic alliances, mergers and acquisitions, manpower and financial management practices, and supply-value chain integration.

Chandra has been of the view that in companies 'strategic intent keeps changing if the previous intent has been fulfilled. What next? Things keep evolving. You redefine your objectives, and they keep changing.'[40]

Therefore, Zee now went full throttle into developing new objectives for itself. Zee's mission statement in 1994 read:

> To be the leading TV and communications group providing the people of South Asia, wherever they live, with the finest

> entertainment, information and communications network and to provide a strong medium through which marketing organizations can enhance their business. Through these services we intend to be worthy citizens of this global village.
>
> We will be a profitable, dynamic, forward-looking and financially strong organization which cares for the welfare of its people while providing an enjoyable and rewarding work experience.

The statement of strategic intent is unequivocal about the business goals of the organization. In the modern attention economy, mass media sells the attention of the viewers to the advertisers, who help to fill the coffers of the media owners and boost the profit bottom lines. ZTL states clearly in its mission statement its intent to rope in as many viewers as possible through entertaining media products so that their viewership might find value for advertisers. It is through this route of economic well-being that ZTL hoped to become a worthy citizen of the global village. As if this were not enough, it further underlined these words by pledging to become 'a profitable, dynamic, forward-looking and financially strong organization'. There was no enunciation here of any social agenda but hard economic facts that formed the bedrock of modern business organizations. The business policy of ZTL, so enunciated, is fully reflected in the various strategic initiatives taken during this period.

In 1994, Zee Education was launched as a part of the Zee Network. The same year, the Li family sold Star TV to Rupert Murdoch's News Corporation for $2 billion. Rumours were rife about the shutting down of Zee TV in the face of a potential Hindi channel that Star would launch, and that Murdoch would cancel the Zee-Star transponder contract. In the likely event of this disaster, Chandra initiated some negotiations with the rival bosses. After some rounds of back and forth, News Corp and Zee decided to become partners with News Corp buying a stake in Asia Today (the Hong Kong-based broadcaster of Zee TV) worth 49.9 per cent. The transponder cost was also reduced from $5 million to $1.2 million. An agreement was reached. Star was to remain an English-only outlet. By 1994, Zee had claimed 65 per cent share of the Indian satellite market while STAR, which had been the catalyst for Indian television, was reduced to 15 per cent.[41]

IN A NUTSHELL

It's not everyday that a leader as visionary as Subhash Chandra takes form as the captain of a ship as humongous as the Essel Group. His journey has been nothing short of marvelous, and leads one to believe in the power of selfless aspirations. At a time when the country's agricultural output was booming with surplus, Chandra's ancestors partook in its operations by setting up an agro-based business of food production.

With the entry of Chandra into the scene, the shape and identity of the company were transformed period after period into something new, suited to cater to the imminent interests of industries and people. From his renewed efforts emerged what came to be known as the Essel Group.

It was almost as if the company had intuitive abilities strong enough to judge market and customer sensibilities, and whip into existence what the public demanded. When he took over, Chandra directed the company through various outputs, ranging from grain exports, to packaging in 1981 with Essel Packaging, and outdoor amusement in 1989 with Essel World.

But not everything can be attributed to a motive bereft of profit. One can gauge that Chandra had developed enough business acumen in all his years in his family-originated agriculture business so as to know how to read trends that swayed the market and adjust the orientation of his company accordingly.

The entrepreneurial spirit of the man who started it all invites an easy appreciation of his vision and milestones. At a time when businessmen were given to taking pragmatic steps after much deliberation, Chandra was among the few who treaded fearlessly into new avenues with only the brightness of their enthusiasm to create something novel, lighting the way.

The formative years of Zee are cast in the mould of the then available models of production and distribution of the communication and culture industry. Despite the challenges faced by Subhash Chandra in the setting up of Zee, owing to the lack of regulation of TV broadcasting in India—a space initially reserved only for the public sector, he was able to successfully channel his business expertise into the M&E industry.

The goal of kickstarting a new venture was inspired by CNN, and therefore, obviously had some high standards to match up to. Simultaneously, the necessity for private broadcasting to include a plethora of accessible news in India was understood in the course of the Gulf War.

Hurdles in the beginning were manifold, right from entering into spaces never before explored, to convincing international investors that India offered a fertile soil for profits in broadcast. During the time, India was far from being a developed country, in comparison to the metropolitan Hong Kong. Therefore, it is understandable that Chandra had trouble clinching business from there.

Aside from that, the biggest aid for Chandra and his media venture came with the relaxation of privatization laws in 1991, which allowed him to reserve a percentage of the broadcast space for himself. Moreover, since this was a newly mowed field, Zee had minimum competition from counterparts.

Zee also reaped the benefits of going public in 1993, as its stock value skyrocketed brilliantly and also got it featured on the Bombay Stock Exchange—a milestone in itself. The fact that the company overtook STAR in the satellite market in 1994 reflected that Zee had the better business model in the industry.

The most momentous development during this period, however, came with Zee Cinema and Zee TV, with their trademark Z logos that brightened up every living room in India, and are now symbols of nostalgia. The entry of these two entertainment channels completely revolutionized the TV-watching experience in the country. Media was made mainstream, and was seamlessly integrated into the daily lives of people. This venture by Chandra sought to communicate to its audiences that entertainment was no longer a luxury, and could be received on demand without leaving the house.

As rapid as Zee's popularity growth in India was, Zee TV too managed to quickly penetrate international markets. The Middle East and Asia were the main targets, owing to the large number of Indians present there, pointing to Zee's vision of assimilating and catering to the entire network of the Indian community. This experiment was a gutsy one, given that there was no way to predict its future, and that Zee was competing with international broadcast media. But more importantly, this initiative reflected an understanding that with Zee airing Hindi-language shows, no Indian was truly away from home. It was also a step in the international domain to show the world the business capacity of Indians and homegrown media business.

This phase of Zee is cast in the mould of the then available models of production and distribution of the communications and culture industry. As case histories of successful business organizations show, it is not the size and the length of corporate life that determines success but the ability to respond to changes in the environment at a rapid pace. Zee too came out of the typecast of traditional business models by seeing an opportunity in the new satellite communication technology and by capitalizing on it. Over the years, the company promoted itself as one of the most distinguished companies of the media sector. Accordingly, its mission and vision have, since the last decade, symbolized the efforts of the company to remain one of the best in the business.

2

YEARS OF CONSOLIDATION: ZEE DEVELOPS AN IDENTITY (1995-1999)

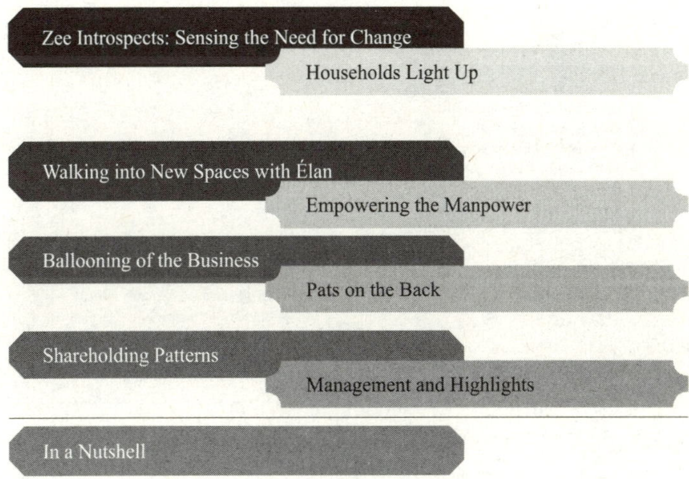

Fig. 2.1: Chapter Insights

ZEE DEVELOPS AN IDENTITY

It was after a few years of its launch that Zee began gaining an identity that made it identifiable in M&E circles. It ventured into many new segments, diversifying its product offerings and business threads. Many important milestones were achieved in consolidation of all of Zee's efforts right from the beginning.

Zee was growing at a phenomenal rate in the mid-nineties. In 1996, they realized that their stakeholders obtained value through the creation of media assets and decided there was a need to invest in more software and hardware, since there was immense pressure from the suppliers. In trademark Zee style, the company once again began climbing the charts. Redefining the strategic intent, mergers and acquisitions policy and a variety of strategic partnerships and ventures was definitive of this segment of Zee's growth chart, which led to its success.

TIMELINE 2

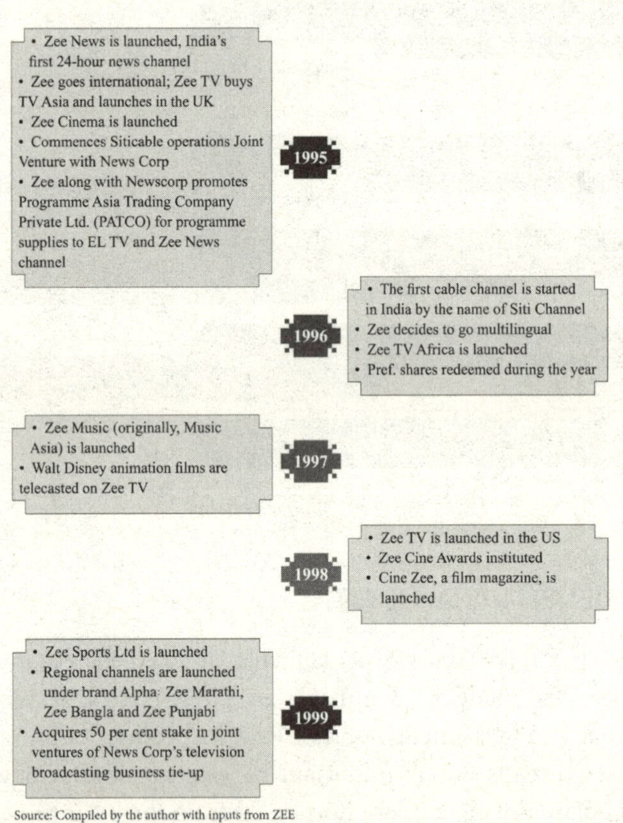

Source: Compiled by the author with inputs from ZEE

ZEE INTROSPECTS: SENSING THE NEED FOR CHANGE

1995 brought with it a slew of changes, with numerous opportunities for Zee to taste success. In this year, Zee's share of viewership peaked at 72 per cent before competition from other local providers began to eat into its dominance. Language was not the only reason for Zee's success. In Sevanti Ninan's account of growth of satellite television, *Headlines From the Heartland,* an unnamed Zee official attributed the channel's success to the fact that it was more dynamic than Doordarshan.[42] Others have noted how Zee packaged itself as an unabashed mass entertainment channel relying heavily on the popular culture of Bollywood to access the mass market. To further penetrate into this market, in 1995, the Zee Cine Awards were instituted.

During the same year, Asia Today Ltd and ZTL ventured into a sale and purchase contract for production, procurement and provision of national entertainment software from India, to be exported to Hong Kong for the transmission of the software on Zee TV. A proposal was made by the company to develop the Pay TV industry and thus they jointly promoted Zee Cinema, the first Hindi movie Pay TV Channel along with the News Corp Group. When News Corp Ltd acquired the satellite distribution business of STAR, News Corp de facto became a partner of Zee. This alliance saw the establishment of Siti Cable (Zee's cable business) and Zee Cinema (Hindi movie Pay TV channel). Also, the company promoted another company, namely Programme Asia Trading Company Private Ltd (PATCO), for the provision of programme supplies to the Zee Cinema Channel and EL TV.

STAR then purchased 50 per cent of Asia Today (the Hong Kong-based broadcaster of Zee TV). It soon became Zee's partner in India, facilitating Zee network's expansion both within India and beyond. Following their 1992 launch in the Middle East, Zee TV entered the lucrative British market in 1995, when it bought TV Asia, a company that had a 25,000-strong audience in Britain, and named it 'Zee UK'. This venture also had a local news component. While it already had access to Indian news from the parent channel, it hired British Asian journalists to produce and report on local news. The daily local news, coupled with a vast library of entertainment programming from India, was part of a strategy to position Zee UK as the voice of British Asians. Roughly 70 per cent of the content on these overseas channels consisted of Indian programming while the rest comprised local programming specific to the region.

In 1995, as per the agreement entered into between ASSPL (ATL), ASSPL was contracted as the singular canvassing agent that would book and sell advertisement slots and time slots across India, either directly or via advertising agencies, for transmitting onto Zee TV. It commenced Siti Cable operations, a joint venture with News Corp and launched Zee News and Zee Cinema.

Between 1995 and 1996, India's first privately owned 24-hour news channel was born as Zee News, this time an independent entity in its own right.

The company's flagship channel Zee TV covered almost all imaginable genres, from comedy, drama, suspense, horror to reality shows, enthralling audiences within the ambit of their homes. A part of the company's Hindi movie cluster, Zee Cinema: Home of Blockbusters, was launched in 1995. The channel showcased the best-in-class Hindi movies which cemented Zee Cinema's position as the No. 1 Hindi movie channel providing quality entertainment to over 430 million individuals in India. Zee Cinema maintained a forward outlook towards entertainment by acquiring not only recent hits, but also in-production titles with a strong industry buzz and ensemble cast. The channel's archives boasted of more than 4,200 movies from varied genres including action, comedy, romance, family entertainers, etc. Zee Cinema, India's first Hindi movie channel was launched, bringing the big screen to the comfort of the customers' homes. A prominent channel from the Zee stable, Zee Cinema has grown in audience over the years.

Zee Cinema believes in sticking to the basics: Better telecast quality, excellent packaging and presentation of material, lesser advertising clutter in the middle of telecasts, and a string of highly watched and eagerly awaited blockbuster movies and perennial favorites—all contributing to a considerably enhanced and pleasurable movie watching experience for the viewer.

'Movies. Masti. Magic.' is the channel's core proposition. It was the first channel in the history of Indian television to turn 'PAY' and was then ranked third among entertainment channels with reach of more than 75 per cent in C&S Households. Over the years, Zee Cinema made some notable developments. It had dedicated mythological movie days and dedicated black and white movie days; special screenings and retrospectives to commemorate anniversaries of past and present stars and technicians; special series *Shanivaar Ki Raat, Amitabh Ke Saath* showcasing some of the best movies of Amitabh Bachchan, *Shanivaar Ki Raat Sitaron Ke Saath*, and *Bhakti Ki Shakti*; Promax- and Abby Award-winning 2-minute films *Paap Ka Anth* and *Pyaar Ki Shuruaat*; special series *Showman Show* which showcased some of the best movies of Raj Kapoor and Subhash Ghai.

A former group editor of Zee, Zee network and Zee TV, in a conversation with the author in 2008 said that ZTL has, to some extent, defined the way people looked at Indian television and has been a trendsetter for many others. At the same time, the company promoted Siti Cable Venture with News Corp, as part of their supply-value chain integration, to establish an integrated cable network facility for all the individual cable operators on a city-by-city basis and to also act as a city TV station. News Corp held a 49 per cent stake in the cable company.

The last decade of the century saw Zee booming, with

numerous channels gracing the company's resume. Rounding up the successes during this period, Chandra in his book recounts: 'Siti Cable was moderately successful. Zee Cinema, Zee Marathi, Zee Bangla, and ETC were also making money. Even the international feeds were making money. De-risking the business—by launching more channels and earning revenues from global broadcasts—helped us survive the lower profits of the flagship channel Zee TV.'[43]

Despite the heady success, Zee in the early 1990s was still subordinate to larger global corporations that held all the financial and technological aces in the broadcasting game. Zee may have been an Indian colossus but when Rupert Murdoch's News Corporation (News Corp) bought a controlling stake in STAR TV, Zee was forced to compromise a large chunk of its ownership. It was partly Zee's success which attracted Murdoch to STAR, who described it as the most exciting challenge in broadcasting, with a reach of more than two-thirds of the entire planet. Zee was to be the passport to this market but Murdoch's overtures also exposed the cultural fault-lines that foreign broadcasting engendered.

Murdoch wanted full control over Zee as well but Chandra reportedly refused with the words, 'India is not for sale, Mr Murdoch'. It was this nationalistic streak that defined Chandra's relationship with Murdoch. But he was still forced to cede a large minority stake of 49.9 per cent in ATL, the company that broadcast Zee TV from Hong Kong, for a reported sum of $47.5 million. In a clear illustration of the uneven power dynamic, it was evident that Chandra had been reluctant to part with any control at all but had been forced to agree because News Corporation also controlled Zee's satellites. Zee did not want to be pushed off its satellites because that would affect its visibility, touching off a chain reaction that would affect ratings and advertising. Though the partnership provided Zee with funds to launch more entertainment channels and expand overseas, it also triggered a long battle of attrition between Chandra and Murdoch, which culminated only in 1999. In September 1999, Chandra bought back News Corp's 50 per cent stake in joint ventures for a consideration of $322 million (though Shine.com puts the figure at $296. 51 million.)

CABLE TV LIGHTS UP HOUSEHOLDS

According to a consulting editor, the changing environment made the management introspect its mission. They realized that they were in the media business and their stakeholders obtained value through the creation of media assets.

The year 1996 marked a turning point in the evolution of Zee. Realizing the shortcomings of reaching out to the homes of the viewing public through the then highly expensive dish antenna, Chandra hit upon the idea of cable television. This involved one cable service provider putting up a satellite dish antenna and a multitude of viewers getting access to satellite transmission through cables emanating from the cable service provider's dish antenna. This was the birth of Siti Cable in India. When News Corp Ltd acquired the satellite distribution business of STAR, News Corp de facto became a partner of Zee. This alliance saw the establishment of Siti Cable (Zee's cable business) and Zee Cinema (Hindi movie Pay TV channel) in 1996.

In 1996, Zee started the first cable channel in India, by the name of Siti Channel, and issued 3,00,000 preferential shares. It launched Zee TV Africa in 1996. As the access was now cheaply priced, Zee was able to reach out to millions of homes with the help of Siti Cable. In terms of quality of reception and the bouquet of channels it offered, the price charged by the service provider from the viewers was a pittance and gave the public broadcaster a run for their money. According to information from a Zee employee, Siti Cable entered into joint ventures with more than 6,000 cable operators across the country to distribute television channel signals received from various satellites.

To satiate the demands of music lovers, Zee Music (originally known as Music Asia) was launched in 1997.Alongside, after a deal between Buena Vista Television India and Zee, Walt Disney animation films were telecasted on Zee TV. To telecast the uniquely conceived Zee Cine Awards to millions of households across the globe, Zee tied up with PricewaterhouseCoopers, the 150-year old world audit major, and the market research firm Gallup MBA.

The author finds that the content of Zee TV covered nearly all genres—comedy, drama, suspense, horror, reality shows, etc. It had popular series like *Amanat, Hum Paanch, X-Zone, Bournvita Quiz Contest, Jeena Isi Ka Naam Hai,* etc. which ran for two to three years but went off-air in the face of increasing competition from other channels. It boasts of several successful formats like *Sa Re Ga Ma Pa, Dance India Dance, Antakshari,* etc. that have had long-running success. As is evident, Zee TV has experimented with all genres but it is 'family dramas' which is the core of its content. With more specialized channels and conceptually more successful reality shows coming up, Zee TV, in the last few years, has concentrated more on such daily soaps.

By now, Chandra had planned to get into the DTH business. He did not agree with Rupert Murdoch's monopoly over the DTH game both in the UK, as well as in India. When he approached Murdoch in relation to this prospect, the American replied, 'What do you have to do with DTH? That's my domain.'[44] But Chandra did not agree with this, and so, flew to Malaysia in 1997 to meet Ananda Krishnan, promoter of Astro Satellite, which was in the process of launching DTH operations in East Asia. Unfortunately, Krishnan too turned down Chandra's proposal and things were put on hold for the moment.

WALKING INTO NEW SPACES WITH ÉLAN

Chandra's spiritual engagement with Vipassana combined with a divergent mind that was experiencing newer heights of success, made him wonder why there were no takers for broadcasting information on ancient Indian medicine. He wrote in his autobiography, 'I commissioned some shows to promote traditional medicines. We invested about ₹30 crores on these shows... We created programming under the brand name Chakra.'[45] Unfortunately, these shows didn't strike a chord with Indian audiences anywhere. Undeterred by this small setback, Chandra prepared his company for bigger things.

In 1998, a letter of intent was signed between Zee and Echo Star Communications Corp, which detailed the launch of Zee's Hindi entertainment channel on Echo Star's DTH satellite services, which would reach a range of audiences in USA. But Zee's international flight didn't just stop there. The company also signed a deal with a business establishment called Deutsche Telecom, enabling Zee to be beamed to Germany. It also negotiated with cable companies in Sweden.

Further, in the same year, ZTL launched its cable Internet services to provide unlimited Internet access (24 hours). The year 1998 was also one of multiple mergers for Zee. First was with the Star India channels of Star Plus, Star News and Star Movies, as well as ATL, which was a 50:50 joint venture between Chandra and Murdoch, followed by Siti Cable and ZTL, which merged their operations. Zee Multimedia, which owned Zee channels in the UK, US, African and European markets, was also merged with the parent company ZTL.

ZTL was also slated to launch its first cable Internet services in approximately four to six months, through its sister outfit, Siti Cable. The company would offer unlimited Internet access 24/7 over cable, without charging its customers for browsing the net. Expanding their already vibrant reach, Zee Network forayed into the print industry, which was crowded with competitors. They launched a film magazine in August 1998, and christened it Cine Zee. All this and more were validated in a way when in 1998, Zee was voted as the Emerging Company of the Year by *The Economic Times*. Zee TV and Tata Tea Ltd together won the 1997–98 FICCI awards for the display of creativity via mediums of visual media, and for training and placing disabled and handicapped people respectively. It was as if all the grit Zee had been showing this past decade, courtesy its able management and founder, was coming to fruition in the form of reward and recognition.

EMPOWERING THE MANPOWER

The latter half of the decade ruffled up the management structure of the organization, with a renewed blueprint that included some essential new additions. The competition was only set to increase, and since this was just the beginning, the room for improvement was wide and those leading took some vital decisions during this time.

According to a senior reporter, posts of input and output heads were created between late 1997 and early 1998, owing to the telecast of back-to-back bulletins. Producers recall that subsequently in 1999, senior producers and presenters at Zee News were sent to learn the latest broadcast techniques at News Corporation's Sky TV studios in London. It was a memorable experience, one producer recounts. They had far less news than what those at Zee News had to work with, so much so that the loss of a car was being made a headline. But the way they worked was a real eye-opener. At Zee, the employees worked on shoestring budgets and a lot of the technology they used was outdated. At Sky, the trainers saw what news could become—graphics, animation, editing techniques; it was so advanced. He recalled that at Zee, they were far behind in the mechanics of the medium but this experience opened their eyes to new ideas. Of course, they worked in a different space but a lot of technical ideas were implemented when they came back from London.

In the midst of corporate aggregates, Zee never lost sight of its focus on human resource. Its people continued to remain the focus of all managerial strategies. In order to intensify the culture of excellence and inculcate a sense of ownership, Zee introduced a stock option plan in 1998–99 for employees who reach a desired level of performance.

In keeping with the tempo of a balanced emphasis on corporate growth, Zee enunciated its strategic intent of this period in its mission statement:

> To be the leading round-the-clock air-time properties provider, delighting the viewers, on the one hand, and providing value to the advertisers for their time and money, on the other. To establish the company as the creator of entertainment and infotainment products and services to feast the viewers and the advertisers. Through these services, we intend to become an integral part of the global market. As a corporation, we will be profitable, productive, creative, trendsetting and financially rugged with care and concern for all stakeholders.

Revamping the mission statement served Zee extraordinarily well. It continued with its business policy of market expansion and penetration, but not without some radical changes. Much of the time was devoted to the company's ability to sow and reap long-term growth opportunities.

BALLOONING OF THE BUSINESS

In 1999, the company took the decision to enter newer businesses like regional language programming, broadcasting, sporting events, movie production, publishing and internet services.

Zee TV was slated to launch three new channels in the English language in Europe, including a news channel by the name of Asian News Network. By taking its partner-turned-competitor STAR TV head-on, as well as starting broadcasts in eight regional languages on Indian soil during a solid action-packed expansion programme spanning six months, Zee was making a statement. Upto 1999, Zee had been running four channels, out of which three were being broadcast out of the STAR TV operations facility in Hong Kong on a lease basis. As the Zee network gradually bloomed into 11 channels, with the many launches of the DTO bouquet, Alpha channels and English channels, the management took a decision to install a facility in Singapore, fully-owned by Zee, which could play 10 channels. This facility was constructed and established in a record period of three months, and became operational in the middle of March 2000.

Zee launched broadcasts in eight regional languages in India under the brand name 'Alpha'. Zee Marathi (launched in August), Zee Bangla (launched in September) and Zee Punjabi (launched in October) were among the most popular launches. Zee Marathi was launched as a Marathi GEC covering all genres of programmes like daily soaps, game shows, talk shows, cookery, travel shows, news, films, etc. It has many significant initiatives to its credit like the Zee Gaurav Puraskar Awards and the Zee Marathi Awards. Some of its major shows were *Adhuri—Ek Kahani, Sa Re Ga Ma Pa*, *Awghachi Sansaar* and *Asambhav*. Since its inception, Zee Marathi has not only maintained its place as one of the leading Marathi GECs, but has also been the most popular and beloved channel in the hearts and minds of Marathi audience all around the world. A trendsetter in the entertainment space, this channel forms an integral part of every Maharashtrian's life; a legacy that stretches over time, emotions and relationships.

Zee Bangla was launched as a Bengali GEC, delivering programmes in almost all genres and is one of the leading Bengali channels. Some of its notable programmes are *Khela*, *Mirakkel*, *Sa Re Ga Ma Pa*, *Dance Bangla Dance* and *Erao Shatru*. Zee Bangla is the most preferred entertainment channel in Bengal. The channel offers an extremely rich and varied platter of programmes—capturing quintessential Bengali sensibilities with élan, juxtaposed with elements of aspiration and entertainment that has touched a chord with viewers across the urban and rural scapes. Zee Bangla has carved an indelible niche for itself by showcasing the culture of Bengal to the world.

Zee Punjabi is a Punjabi GEC which covers all genres of programmes. Some of its major programmes included *Excuse Me Please*, *Dial-E-Punjab*, *Jugnu Mast Mast*, *Pardesan Vich Punjabi* and *Phulkari*.

But now the buck didn't stop at entertainment for the company. In 1999, Zee Education was demerged and transferred to a separate entity called Zee Interactive Learning Systems (ZILS). ZILS, the education arm of Zee Network, was launched to overlook the education business of Zee Network, which provided technology-based education and training such as Information Technology (IT) television programmess. It consisted of distribution of software learning products, imparting education and training in IT. ZILS's purpose was to improve human capital via quality education and development and also help individuals (children and youth) realize their unique potential through a chain of pre-schools, schools, youth institutes and online ventures. ZILS planned to make substantial investments in developing new education centres for children and youth through organic and inorganic routes.

Zee also began setting up institutions in this regard across the country: Kidzee High (primary, middle, secondary and senior secondary schooling), Kidz Care (a state-of-the-art childcare centre), IECTEC (International Early Childhood Teachers'

Education Course), ZICA (Zee Institute Of Creative Arts—Classical and Digital Animation training Academy), Zed CA (Zed Career Academy) and E-learning, Kidzee (with more than 600 operational centres in India and abroad), Institute Of Media Arts And Technology (premier academy for training in aspects of TV and films) and Zee Institute of Creative Arts (premier animation training academy). There was also a collaboration with AutoDesk M&E and Design Programmes and Media Technology Centre, IIT Kanpur. British Standards Institution (BSI) accredited ZILS with ISO 9001:2000 certification for its remarkable quality practices to design and deploy educational content.

In 1999, ZTL acquired News Corp's 50 per cent stake in ATL, Siti Cable, and Programmes Asia Trading Company Ltd, later going on to own a complete 100 per cent of these businesses. The consideration paid for this deal was numbered at $296.51 million. This helped Zee to consolidate its operations and translate its strategic intent into concrete action on the ground with few organizational communication glitches and delays. The company turned in good results, surprising its most ardent critics and competitors alike. It gained positive publicity in the market for providing opportunities to budding entrepreneurs working with Zee.

ZTL also tied up with the French major Canal Plus, a forerunner of the KU-band DTH service, attracted by its proposed digital TV service. In September, 1999 Zee Multimedia Worldwide Ltd (ZMWL) was acquired by ZTL. Following this decision, all of ZMWL's international operations, including the vast broadcasting business came under ZTL's jurisdiction.

Entering the business of television entertainment had been relatively easy for Zee, but entering the business of news production and transmission was not such a cakewalk, since this sub-sector had for long remained closely guarded by the state. In 1999, the Ministry of Information and Broadcasting allowed private operators to run their own earth stations and uplink from Indian soil. Zee was the first to seize this opportunity, by initiating VSNL's (Videsh Sanchar Nigam Ltd) facilities; a direction taken by other channels too. When Zee started daily news bulletins around the same time as News Tonight on Doordarshan, other channels also followed the same model. Zee had found that surmounting the legal guidelines against broadcasting from India was easy as far as entertainment programming was concerned but news bulletins could not be recorded days in advance, as they needed immediacy. So, naturally enough, it went for direct transmission from India once the ground for that was cleared by the government.

PATS ON THE BACK

Zee's constant and consistent achievements weren't going unnoticed by the rest of the industry. Established media names were taking note of the fabulous way in which Zee was reaching its ambitious milestones, and showcasing it to the rest of the country.

In 1998–99, Zee News had a viewership percentage of over 51 per cent in its segment.[46] In 1999, it became the first 24-hour Hindi current affairs and news channel. It was, along with STAR News, the only Indian news network that ran 24/7 during the 1999 Cricket World Cup in England.

The same year, Zee was voted as the 'ninth most popular brand' in India by A&M magazine. Subhash Chandra's back-breaking efforts were also recognized, and he was accorded 'Businessman of the Year' award by *Business Standard*, and 'Entrepreneur of the Year' award by Ernst & Young in 1999.

As stated above, in September 1999, Chandra bought back News Corp's 50 per cent stake in joint ventures for a consideration of $322 million (though Shine.com puts the figure at $296.51 million) and started launching regional channels.

SHAREHOLDING PATTERNS

In 1995, 4,00,000 Redeemable Cumulative Non-Convertible Pref. shares were issued. In 1996, pref. shares were redeemed. In 1997, 3,00,000 pref. shares were issued. In 1995, ASSPL and ATL had an agreement in which the former was to be the sole canvassing agent for booking and selling advertisement slots or time slots throughout India, directly or through advertising agencies, for relaying on the Zee TV.

Table 1
Financial Highlights-ZTL (in millions)

Year Ending 31 March	*1995*	*1996*	*1997*
Income			
Sales and services	458.2	881.7	892.5
Other Income	73.6	9.3	101.98
Increase in Stocks	41.7	9.6	29.89
Total Income	573.6	900.8	1024.4
Expenditure			
Cost of Goods	335.5	605.6	563.7
Personnel Cost	4.3	7.4	26
Administrative Expenses	17	31.3	57.5
Financial Charges	4.2	9.9	36.5
Depreciation	2.2	5.9	7.7
Total Expenditure	363.4	660.3	647.4
PBT	210.2	240.4	332.6
Taxation	8.1	10.2	44.5
Profit after Tax (PAT)	202.1	230.2	288.1
Prior Period Adjustment	-	2.8	0.98
Balance Brought Forward	28.9	75	80.3

Year Ending 31 March	*1995*	*1996*	*1997*
Available for Appropriations	231.1	302.5	369.4
Appropriations			
General Reserve	100	150	100
Interim Dividend	-	6.8	0.2
Proposed Dividend	56	65.3	84
Balance Profit Carried Forward	75	80.3	136.8

Source: Compiled by the author from ZTL Annual Reports

Note: The figures of 1995 and 1996 are net consolidated results (inclusive of the erstwhile ASSL). This is to allow for meaningful comparison of figures mentioned in Annual Report 1999.

As shown in the table above, the total income of the company increased from 573 million in 1995 to 1024 million in 1997. The total expenditure amounted to 647 million in 1997. PAT was pegged at 288 million and the profit that was carried forward was 136.8 million. In the table mentioned below, all figures from 1995 to 1997 are net consolidated results (including the erstwhile ASSL. This is to allow meaningful comparison.)

Table 2
Financial Highlights-ZTL (in millions)

Year Ending 31 March	*1995*	*1996*	*1997*	*1998*	*1999*
Income From Operations	735	1230	1374	1734	2262
Other Income/ Increase in Stock	18	18	64	75	55
Total Income	753	1248	1438	1809	2317

Year Ending 31 March	*1995*	*1996*	*1997*	*1998*	*1999*
Total Expenditure	436	821	940	1144	1411
Operating Profit	299	409	434	590	851
Per Cent to Income From Operations	41 per cent	33 per cent	32 per cent	34 per cent	38 per cent
PBIDT	317	427	498	665	906
Interest	04	27	60	64	81
Depreciation	06	15	16	15	18
PBT	307	385	422	586	807
Taxation	85	84	75	149	196
PAT	222	301	347	437	611
Per Cent to Total Income	29 per cent	24 per cent	24 per cent	24 per cent	26 per cent
Dividend	56	65	84	103	103
Total Assets and Equity & Liabilities	654	1099	1425	1878	2479
Loans Funds	42	217	333	426	561
Investments	04	04	318	480	571

Source: Compiled by the author from ZTL Annual Reports

Total income of the ZTL showed an increasing trend from 1995 to 1999. It increased from 753 million to 2,317 million in this period. PBT and PAT also reflected an increasing trend. PAT shot up to 611 million in fiscal year (FY) 1999 from 222 million in FY 1995. ZTL also declared dividend in all these years. In 1998, equity shares and convertible debentures of ZTL could be purchased up to 30 per cent of its total paid-up equity capital subject to certain conditions. Enterprise value increased by more than 250 per cent during FY 1999. Zee had regained its profitability by 1999. In FY 1999, Zee procured huge advertising bookings and a jump of around 30 per cent over the previous year. The company's income from operations jumped 30 per cent to ₹2,262 million and PAT improved 40 per cent to ₹611 million. Total expenses grew at a lower pace and as a result operating profit improved 44 per cent over the previous year to ₹851 million. The company procured advertisement bookings worth ₹3,853 million, a jump of around 30 per cent over the previous year. Earnings per share jumped 40 per cent to ₹32.7 (previous year ₹23.4). Net worth of ZTL increased in this phase.

IN A NUTSHELL

This period, as we see, is marked by product diversification and market penetration. The emphasis on these two shows in the financials of the company, which note a decline from Zee's position in 1995, but the company continues to enjoy a healthy financial state. With market presence in all parts of the globe, facilitated by the Indian diaspora, and with products to suit every taste, the next phase of corporate growth laid emphasis on increasing the profitability of the company as well as that of its strategic business units. This phase of Zee's growth is marked by a new strategy to evolve and develop a new business model that takes advantage of the new communication technology.

Undoubtedly, this phase became a significant one for the media behemoth.

Also, this period of growth of Zee is marked by organizational strategic moves that focus not only on the external business environment but also on building the internal business environment capabilities. The strategic rationale for this exercise was to take advantage of joint strengths in marketing, promotions and product development globally and offer more transparency within the group, thus increasing value for investors. Eventually, the bigger balance sheet could be leveraged for further expansion. Subsequently, emerging areas of technological convergence could also be effectively tapped on a global scale.

Zee continued to spread its presence in markets across the globe, to take advantage of the Indian diaspora's need to stay connected to their roots. With the pressure such an expansion exerted on the organizational resources, Zee focused on its human resource base by co-opting them into the organization and making them a part of the organizational ownership scheme, thereby injecting the much-needed incentive to contribute to the growth of the organization.

It is worth noting that during this part of the decade, competition began increasing, especially from the already established business of news like NDTV and Doordarshan. Even so, Zee donned a fearless outlook and outpaced its competitors in making use of VSNL's facilities for uplinking, presenting a viable model that could be imitated by others in the industry.

During this period, Zee also realized the benefits of catering to a wide array of audiences. Right from launching regional channels as well as broadcasting internationally for Indian citizens, it even made a foray into the education sector. The outcomes in the latter effort weren't merely abstract, and could be seen materially through the establishment of schools and learning institutions. This was a definitive way for Zee to add to its credibility of social well-being and gain value across different demographics. And it did.

It was a period of far-reaching change, during which the company took the decision to enter newer businesses like regional language programming, broadcasting, sporting events, movie production, publishing and internet services. With the planned launch of Direct To Operator (DTO) business, the company geared itself for competing in the next millennium. During this time of change, the company continuously enhanced its market leadership. The focus was on creating value for their customers, viewers and shareowners.

It was during this period that Zee truly began asserting its identity to its counterparts, telling them that this new media company was a force to reckon with. Chandra realized his potential to stand shoulder-to-shoulder with STAR and Murdoch to let them know that Zee now possessed the capability to foray into the media business as a steady player, without depending on other big names.

Standing at the edge of a new millennium, Zee had already done great things. Despite shrinking revenues, the view from the top seemed glorious. Chandra yearned to extend his brainchild as far as the eye could see, and achieve even greater feats in the upcoming turn of the century.

3

MANTRAS OF THE MILLENNIUM: ZEE MAKES FRIENDS (2000–2002)

Fig. 3.1: Chapter Insights

THE POST-MILLENNIUM ERA

To run headlong into the new millennium, it became imperative for Zee to ride the newly rising technological wave. It posited to enlarge the scope of its business by harnessing strategies that were in line with technological paradigms on one hand, and by utilizing media properties in all forms of distribution on the other. The company aimed at spreading its network worldwide by applying all possible permutations and combinations, thereby maximizing consumer satisfaction and profits in the process.

STRATEGIC INTENT ENUNCIATION

Zee had turned in good results the past decade, surprising its most ardent critics and competitors alike. It had aimed to be a pioneer in the growth of the media industry by providing numerous opportunities to budding entrepreneurs to work with Zee and had succeeded in this endeavour. With renewed confidence and an urge to scale newer heights, Zee revamped their outlook. In 2000, ZTL emerged as a new market player on Mumbai's coveted Dalal Street.

The company's mission statement for this period was worded carefully to highlight the concern of the top management with maintaining the leadership and early gains made by their quick response to the external business environment. It read:

> To maintain the company's pioneering status as multimedia content and access provider, driven by viewer response and shareholder confidence. We will continue to aim for greater growth in creativity and productivity by adding value to our existing properties both for our viewers and advertisers. Convergence through flow of group synergies shall make innovation an inevitable part of the Zee brand.

In keeping with this statement, the company defined its value system as one with a focus on 'Customer Focus, Excellence, Creativity, Integrity and Growth.' It detailed it as follows:

> Customer Focus—Our Company's strategies are driven by the needs of the customer. Our success can be measured by the satisfaction achieved by our customers; Excellence—We accord a high premium to maintaining superlative standards throughout our Company. We encourage our employees to come up with smarter ideas within the fastest possible time; Creativity—Key to our value system is innovation and originality. We recognize and have a high regard for

> individual expression and creative freedom in our quest to provide customer satisfaction; Integrity—We observe strict ethical standards through editorial independence and creative expression, in order to earn the trust of our viewers and subscribers; Growth Driven—We are committed to delivering consistent revenue and cash flow growth in order to provide our shareholders a good return. Our objective is to grow our people, market and businesses around the world.

A senior official in Zee, in conversation with the author, informed that Chandra also gave some guiding principles for directing the company upwards. It involved building highly valuable businesses leading positions in entertainment media across the value-chain. They stayed committed to maintaining a diligent focus on the company's core business in the challenging environment surrounding them. They attempted to bring people closer to the brands through socially relevant, forward-looking programming, while also internally ensuring principles of corporate governance, vital in securing the abiding trust of investors, employees, customers and public at large.

The Annual Reports from 2000–01 and 2002–03 elaborate on Chandra's principles as follows:

> a) Our strategy is to build highly valuable businesses with leading positions in entertainment media across the value-chain. We stay committed to maintaining a diligent focus on the company's core business in the present challenging environment.
>
> b) As a television network, we owe a duty of social and ethical responsibility to the nation. We shall never cease asking ourselves how we can bring people closer to our brands.
>
> c) Sound principles of corporate governance are vital in securing the abiding trust of investors, employees,

> customers and public at large. I believe that to develop a reputation for integrity and honorable dealings, is the most important asset any company can build.

During the year, the company decided to consolidate a few operations and cut down some investments. Keeping a prudent business approach, several cost-conscious measures were implemented to streamline the overall business. Operating and expansion plans in the portal and education businesses were reduced considerably in view of the slow development of opportunity there.

In keeping with its commitment to the optimal utilization of all resources and doing away with infrastructural deadwood, in 2000, the company appointed M/s A.T. Kearney, a leading management consultancy firm, to realign the organization to best business practices. Amitabh Kumar, the former director operations of Videsh Sanchar Nigam, also came on board of ZTL as vice president of Aaccess Infrastructure and Distribution.

It appears that the strategic intent of ZTL in this phase, as manifested in their statement, reflects a primacy of business interests, brand loyalty, customer focus and product development through innovative programming.

While managerial decisions such as these were abounding, Chandra did not neglect the opportunities around him. The millennium had brought with it a flood of technological dependence, and this new wave was posited to set off something new and great. Everyone could sense it. New machines were being bought, equipment was being tested; everything was going digital.

With a similar streak of gaining operational leverages, in 2000, ZTL announced a ₹2,400 crore outlay to construct a fiber-optic and coaxial network spanning 26 cities in India. ZTL aimed at a 1:1 debt-equity ratio. Further, to ensure protection of its data flows, Zee introduced encryption with Mediaguard (a Canal Plus

Technology) Encryption System. In the same year it put up 500 Internet kiosks across the country and labeled them Zee centres, projecting its e-commerce initiatives.

TIMELINE 3

- Launches pay bouquet of channels in Asian region
- Letter of intent signed between Zee and EchoStar Communications Corp for launching DTH satellite services for USA
- Launches internet over cable services, becoming the first cable company in India to do so
- Enters in content distribution joint ventures with MGM and Viacom
- Launches 'Zed TV', an educational channel
- Zee enters a JV with Sterling Infotech for the establishment of DTH television services
- Music Asia, repositions as Zee Music
- Zee Studio, Zee Café and Zee Gujarati are launched

- Ventures into production of Hindi movies with *Gadar*, which becomes the highest-grossing box office movie
- JV of Zee and Turner International, "Zee Turner Ltd" is launched
- Zee TV partners with Cartoon Network
- Introduces Zee TV and Zee News as pay television offerings

- SitiCable became the first MSO to start HITS for implementation of CAS in India
- A separate beam of Zee TV for Middle-East and Pakistan markets are started
- Acquires controlling stakes in ETC network limited and Padmalaya Telefilms limited

Source: Compiled by the author with inputs from ZEE

GEARING UP FOR A NEW CENTURY

A share market trader, Ketan Parekh, started to accumulate the shares of Zee amounting to 8 per cent. He started buying at ₹100 and took it to almost ₹300. The end of the last decade had seen the Zee stocks shoot up to ₹1,500. Parekh then started meeting Chandra to discuss the business. But between that period and the new century, the stocks began plummeting due to the overall stock market crash. This phenomenon, begun in the USA, was termed the 'dot-com bubble,' since the stock market crash of this period was caused by an excessive 'bubble' growth in the Internet industry. The stock market continued to crash until 2001. The prices then fell sharply to ₹1,000. Parekh along with other investors bought the stock at ₹1,000, but the stock again fell to ₹800. According to Chandra, 'Many people who were our competitors/detractors became active in pushing down the stock to accelerate the decline in its price.' As a result it was reduced to ₹60. All this happened in less than 12 months. However in India, according to Chandra, things were 'blown out of proportion' and it was all deemed a 'stock market scam'.Zee's name had also come up in connection to this. SEBI sent a show-cause on the volative trade, accusing them of inside trading. Their name was cleared by the Joint Parliamentary Committee (JPC), but after many years. It did the group some damage. Chandra claims that the company lost about '$6 billion of market capitalization within months'. The business saw a setback and it affected the company's fund-raising capabilities.

Though 2000 was off to a rocky start, this event was a lesson in many ways for Chandra, which he enunciated as follows: 'Never go near the stock markets, unless you are in that business as a trader. You should leave the share price of your company to the market and the investor community. But never buy or sell your own share because you think it is overvalued or undervalued.'[47]

To capture more of the advertising rupee going to other genres, Zee started putting together 'bouquets'. It put channels like Zee TV, Zee Cinema, Zee News and regional channels together. In this way, Zee had more advertising seconds to cross-sell and ensured that all the money came into the Zee kitty.

Going by viewership numbers, Zee's entertainment channels had been receiving positive feedback from audiences. To reap more treasure, Zee brought some new channels to the fore in 2000, namely Zee Studio, Zee Café and Zee Gujarati.

Zee Studio was a 24-hour English movie channel. It projected itself as showcasing some of the best Hollywood films, other foreign cinema as well as the finest Indian cinema. It promoted itself as being passionate about showing 'good cinema' to the Indian audience. Zee Studio has had some noteworthy developments, as detailed by a Company employee in an interview with the author. It had access to over 4,000 film titles of Metro Goldwyn Mayer (MGM). Zee Studio's Hollywood fare comprised of blockbuster titles like *Batman Returns, Matrix Reloaded, Ocean's Twelve, Troy, One Fine Day, Father of the Bride, Sixth Sense, Hot Shots, Edward Scissorhands, Jumanji, 50 First Dates, Maid in Manhattan, Finally Sunday, Motorcycle Diaries, City of God* and *Schindler's list*. It also started special series like '*Thursday 9 Premiere*' (satellite and channel premieres) and '*Two Good Tuesdays*' (two movies with a common element—actor, director or genre). It also had a special '*Christmas series*' showcasing some Christmas movies.

Zee Café became the 24-hour English GEC from the ZEEL bouquet, airing international programmes that were in sync with the preferences of the national audience. It tried to cover varied genres of programmes. Their major offerings since their launch included *Friends*, *Witch Blade, Zoë, The Tonight Show with Jay Leno, The O.C., The Sopranos, The Big Bang Theory* and *Gossip Girl*. Some other programmes included *Aliens in America, Journey*

Man, Unhitched, Pushing Daisies, Back to You, Army Wives, Notes from the Underbelly, Survivor, E! News, The Wonder Years, and *The X-Files.* There have been some regular fare like *Old Skool* (the classic shows of yesteryears), *Café Xtreme, After Hrs, Top 10 Countdown* and *Showbiz India Xtreme.* Catering to English-speaking audiences, it boasts of a healthy mix of reality and scripted show offerings directly from the US. It has associations with powerful international studios such as Fremantle, Disney, WB, CBS, Sony, etc. and is currently available across all major DTH and Cable networks in India.

Zee Gujarati, on the other hand, was launched as part of Zee's regional 'Alpha' channels on 21 March 2000, positioned in similarly as its Punjabi (18 October 1999), Bengali (15 September 1999) and Marathi (15 August 1999) brethren. Zee Gujarati offered general entertainment with programming that included current affairs, news and festival-centric programmes. Some of its major programmes included *Tazza Hasgulla*, *Sangini*, *Saptadi*, *Aapni Rasoi*, *Sami Saanjna Shamana* and *Zakal Bhina Sapna*.

Other aspects of entertainment were also being taken care of. In 2000, Zee network's original music offering from 1997—*Music Asia*—was repositioned as Zee Music with a new logo and programmes. It brought daily music content for its audience, and all types and genres of music, ranging from the most retro to the most contemporary. According to an official, constant innovation and ideation were the primary drivers behind the Zee Music programming. Their main offerings were *Artist of the Fortnight, Dial M for Music, Zee Music-John Abraham Calendar, Sa Re Ga Ma Pa Challenge Hungama, Nina @ 9, Midnite Manuel, B news,* and *Cinemascope.* Members of the Bollywood music industry also came together with ZTL to present the IMI-Zee Sangeet Awards (2000). Also continuing with its bank of educational content, Zee launched 'Zed TV', an educational channel, on October 12, the same year.

An important character trait of Zee was its fearless vision of conquering even overseas markets. Neither the audience response, nor already established standards of international entertainment deterred it from its entry into foreign spaces. It stood tall, and held its own. That is how it positioned its personality, something that doesn't go unnoticed even today. By 2000, Zee was available on the Sky Network and claimed to have one million subscribers in the UK and continental Europe. It became one of the first channels to go digital in the UK, offering programming in Hindi and four other South Asian languages: Bengali, Urdu, Gujarati and Punjabi. Having acquired a base in the UK, Zee expanded into mainland Europe, after which, it also pursued a joint venture with South Africa-based platform operator, MultiChoice. A letter of intent also was signed between Zee and EchoStar Communications Corp, for the launch of DTH satellite services in USA.

THE PERKS OF PARTNERSHIP

The restructuring process was matched by a series of strategic acquisitions and tie-ups aimed to equip Zee to compete in the future. So all through 2000, Zee undertook several partnerships, which proved to be healthy for its growth.

After a very successful six-year relationship, Zee Network bought the stake of News Corp, in both the broadcasting business as well as in Siti Cable, in 2000. Following that development, it transformed itself into a major media industry player. Its operations now spanned the entire media spectrum, covering television programming, satellite broadcasting, production and distribution of films, music publishing, long distance education, creation of animation software, and news. Without prior knowledge of satellite business or technology, Chandra's success, his competitors unanimously agree, was truly inspirational.

The company entered into a joint venture with Sterling Infotech to begin DTH television services. ZTL also proposed to launch an alternative lifestyle channel positioned as a niche channel, targeting mainly the NRI population living abroad. The channel went ahead branded as Chakra. Buddha Films, the company that had been working as Zee's podium for the acquisition of sports properties was demerged from ZTL. It was spun off as a distinct, stand-alone company. In 2000, Zee and TransWorld International came together to join their bids for telecasting rights for the Cricket World Cup tournaments for the years 2003 and 2007.

ZTL also signed a Memorandum of Understanding (MoU) with Asianet Communication Ltd, a decision which consolidated Zee's admission into the genre of South Indian regional channels. It further went on to acquire a stake of 26 per cent in Aplab Ltd, which was an electronic equipment market. Chandra also made the decision to sell 50 lakh shares of ZTL to an institutional investor based in the US.

Not keeping itself tied down to one media platform, Zee launched its internet portal and mobile platform too. Zeenext, the Internet portal site of Econnect India Ltd, which was a company subsidiary, and Unimobile, which was a mobile Internet firm, came together to present zeenext.com—which presented content to audiences connected to wireless communication devices. Multichannel News International, the US-based trade publication, conferred ZTL with the prestigious Ground Breaker Award for being the top national programmer.

Further, the Zee Movies channel was repositioned as Zee MGM through a strategic partnership with Metro-Goldwyn-Mayer (MGM), with capital at a price of ₹31.52 per fully paid-up equity share. The issue opened on third MGM.The name evoked immediate awe across industries and audiences alike, given its global appeal for being one of Hollywood's leading production houses. A partnership was also commenced with Viacom for a distribution venture.

Zee Interactive Learning Systems (ZILS), which was a 100 per cent subsidiary of ZTL, came together in a venture with 'three public sector undertakings and four state governments in the country' for providing training initiatives that were web-based. The company appointed three full-time directors, namely R.K. Singh, Dev Naganad and Deepak Shourie. The subsidiary was set to expand its operations to 26 cities over a span of two years.

In May 2001, a significant turn came. ZTL decided to initiate a strategic partnership, preferably with a major international media establishment, in order to fortify its financial and technical strengths so that it could grow in the arena of convergence. The company was eyeing big names, one of them being Turner International.

However, Chandra's attempt at getting Turner International to invest as an equity partner in Zee failed. He persisted, and managed to get a joint venture agreement for distribution instead. Zee entered into a joint venture with Turner India Private Limited, a subsidiary of AOL Time Warner Inc, USA. A company by the name of Zee Turner Alliance was formed, offering a distribution of a 16-channel bouquet across the sub-continent. It included television brands such as Zee TV, Zee Cinema, Zee English, Alpha, Cartoon Network, CNN and CNBC in a single bouquet. It was decided that ZTL would hold 76 per cent stake in the distribution company, and the balance 26 per cent would be with Turner. Such distribution alliances to strengthen bouquet offerings to cable operators would prove to be the trend in future.

The year 2001 was proving to be an attractive year for Zee, with many lucrative opportunities coming their way. Zee Interactive Multimedia Ltd, set up to provide broadband and conditional access services, merged with Siti Cable Network Ltd, its holding company. Through Siti Cable, it initiated the laying of hybrid fiber optic coaxial cables as well as its project of internet over cable (IOC) in Bangalore, Delhi and Hyderabad. Around the same time, Zee Publishing, a ZTL subsidiary, was hived off as a separate company.

In keeping with the tides of the technological wave, Zee News studios introduced virtual sets in 2001. The sets, based on CyberSetNT from ORAD, provided unmatched production facilities in conjunction with online graphics provided through Frost and DVG-ORAD Systems. The studios went fully digital with matching production facilities, which were being upgraded with a Newsroom Automation System with multi-language capabilities. The same year, Zee TV and Zee News were introduced as pay television offerings. ZTL was also set to launch Basic Education Support Television in April 2001. This was to be a project aimed at educating rural regions and populations in India, through television.

Given that it wasn't alien to the world of cinema with its movie channels and partnership with MGM, Zee decided to undertake production of its own. In 2001, the Zee network took on its maiden feature film with *Gadar—Ek Prem Katha.*[48] Two of its major rivals, Sony and Star, had also already embarked upon this avenue, so it was only natural that Zee take this path. Nittin Keni, executive producer of Gadar, who had also been the first president of Zee TV and the first chief executive of Zee Cinema, said at the time, 'A film like this has not been made in India before.' Made on a ginormous budget of ₹18 crore, *Gadar* received its due and collected ₹1.33 billion, being declared as an all-time blockbuster by Box Office India. It was the highest grossing film that year.

These strategic moves were orchestrated to gain market leadership in various entertainment and communication business segments. Accordingly, the company modified its tagline to: *Sabse Pehle.* Some of Zee's shows which were prominent during this time were *Encounter, Iss Waqt, Special Correspondent, News at 9, The Inside Story, Prime Time,* and *Haqeeqat Jaisi, Khabhar Waisi.* Zee *News' Crime File,* in the 10:30–11:00 pm slot on Saturday nights, registered a 100 per cent jump in ratings over the show in the previous block. The premier programmes for Zee TV during these years were *Mehendi Tere Naam Ki, Koshish, Aashirwad, Bournvita Quiz Contest, Amanat, Hud Kar Di, Vishnu Puran, X-Zone,* and *India's Most Wanted.* From 2001, *Jeena Isi Ka Naam Hai, Simply Shekhar, Koi Apna Sa, Kitty Party* and *Lipstick* also gained prominence. Zee has always been a pioneer in everything, be it, technology or theme-based programmes.

Zee then started *Crime File* in 2002, and later *Zurm*, the patterns of which were followed by AajTak and NDTV. The employee in conversation with the author also takes the credit of making a news-based documentary on the Parliament attacks in 2001 and the attack on Akshardham.

According to market research firm Probity Research and Services Pvt. Ltd of Mumbai, ZTL was one of the 10 most valuable companies by market capitalization in India during this period, with more than 25 million viewers, the market capitalization up by 7.57 times. This carried no inkling whatsoever about the tough times that awaited the industry.

TWIRLING WITH THE TIMES

In 2002, world politics and economics went through difficult times. The year witnessed a steep fall in marketing and advertising spends and global advertising market reportedly declined by 5 per cent after a decade of solid year-on-year growth. The company experienced competitive and challenging times in the domestic markets. The company took many new initiatives to overcome economic slack and difficult competitive environment. In 2002, ZTL amalgamated four of its wholly owned subsidiaries—Kaveri Entertainment Ltd, Programme Asia Trading Company Ltd, El-Zee and Dakshin Media Ltd.

Steadfast on his path despite the obvious obstacles, Chandra was envisioning newer feats that would be in the best interests of everyone, given the external environment. His idea was to create a media-entertainment-telecoms conglomerate spanning several continents. 'I want to use all the group synergies to reach as many people as one can globally,' he claimed.[49] That year, Zee distributed two feature films, *Tere Liye* and *Bhawandar.*

In 2002, Zee TV snapped ties with Nickelodeon, courtesy its partnership with Turner. This union led to the birth of another kids' channel for the Indian market: Cartoon Network. Turner and Zee signed an agreement for an exclusive launch of Cartoon Network on Zee, a Hindi-programming block that would air twice daily—once from 8:30–9:30 am and then between 6:00–7:00 pm. The block was set to replace the slot previously accorded to Nickelodeon. Anshuman Misra, India managing director, Turner, said, 'As leaders in kids entertainment, it has been our mission to elevate animation to the level of general entertainment. The launch of Cartoon Network on Zee is a significant step in that direction. It is also a vital strategy as we continue to aggressively localize the Cartoon Network brand and product offering in India.'[50]

ZTL acquired controlling stakes in ETC Networks[51] in June 2002, following an MoU signed between the two companies. According to the MoU, Zee would acquire 57 per cent in ETC in two stages at ₹25 crore. The size of the all-cash deal for ETC Networks which owned ETC Punjabi and ETC Music was approximately ₹250 million (₹180 million for purchase of shares from promoters and ₹70 million for preferential allotment).

The same year, the company also acquired a 32.8 per cent stake in Padmalaya Telefilms Ltd, a Hyderabad-based content company and one of India's leading entertainment software houses with a significant presence in television software production and production and distribution of Hindi and regional feature films. This was done through the acquisition of a 64.3 per cent stake in PTL's holding company Padmalaya Enterprises Pvt. Ltd. Zee was to pay ₹590 million for the deal, including an open offer of 20 per cent as required by regulations.

These acquisitions brought with it much strength for Zee: a combined market share of 46 per cent in Music and 58 per cent in the Punjabi segment and opportunities to leverage Gurbani rights for driving subscriber base in international markets.

In 2002, Siti Cable became the first MSO to start digital Headend-in-the-Sky (HITS) for the implementation of a conditional access system in India. In 2002, the company started a separate beam of Zee TV for Middle-East and Pakistan markets.

Zee operated the most advanced network for networking. This network comprised of 17 VSATs with dual channel capacity on INSAT, OB Vans and DSNG terminals, which helped to link the regional news centers with the uplink facility at Noida. The transmission facilities formed an integrated part of one of the most advanced media motion architectures in the television industry. The Noida uplink facility for the Zee Network became operational in March 2002 with a dedicated 9.3 m antenna operating on the AsiaSat 3-S satellite beaming one channel, Zee News.

The transmission, which commenced with a single channel, Zee News, now covers Zee Music and the regional channels (Zee Punjabi, Zee Gujarati, Zee Bangla, Zee Marathi, etc.). Regional studios at Mumbai, Chandigarh, Ahmedabad, Chennai, Hyderabad and other locations also became fully integrated using the online network.

FINANCIAL MANAGEMENT

Table 3
Financial Highlights-ZTL (in millions)

Year Ending 31 March	*2000 Standalone*	*2001 Standalone*	*2002 Standalone*	*2002 Consolidated*
Income From Operations	2870	3847	4065	10,762
Other Income	101	511	767	792
Total Income	2971	4358	4832	11, 554
Total Expenditure	1829	2481	2835	7720
Operating Profit	1,041	1,366	1,230	3042
Per Cent to Income from Operations	36 per cent	36 per cent	30 per cent	28 per cent
PBIDT	1,142	1,877	1,997	3834
Interest	84	211	585	808
Depreciation	25	43	68	215
PBT	1033	1,623	1344	2811
Taxation	210	238	371	865
PAT	823	1,385	973	1946
Per Cent to Total Income	28 per cent	32 per cent	20 per cent	17 per cent
Dividend	161	227	227	227
Total Assets and Equity & Liabilities	37554	43333	44707	48404
Loans Funds	1,530	3,237	3,984	8491
Investments	34,328	35,139	35,369	125

Source: Compiled by the author from Annual Reports 2000–2002

Operating income of the ZTL on standalone basis increased from 2,870 million in FY 2000 to 4,065 million in FY 2002 showing an increase of 40 per cent in this period, reflecting the company's sharp capture of the market. PBT also increased from 1,033 million to 1,344 million over this period. ZTL declared dividend in all these years to maximise shareholder wealth. For consolidated figures, income from operations and operational profit increased considerably during this period. Operating profits increased to 3,042 million (consolidated) in FY 2002. During FY 2002, the company borrowed heavily and the loanable funds increased to 3,984 (standalone) and 8,491 (consolidated) from 3,237 million in the preceeding FY 2001.

During the year 2002, total revenues of the company increased by 10.9 per cent to ₹4,832 million from ₹4,358 million. The company witnessed a change in revenue profile towards the end of fiscal 2002, as it started broadcasting/uplinking the Alpha-branded channels from India. Revenues include a marginal increase in sales to ₹3,193 million and an increase of 7.5 per cent in the service revenues, including advertising commission. Total expenses increased by 14.3 per cent to ₹2,835 million from ₹2,481 million. These expenses include programming, transmission and other direct costs. Other income, including interest income on various 42 treasury operations increased by more than 50 per cent to ₹767 million. Cost of goods sold, primarily costs of programming, music publishing and acquisition/production of films, has dropped by 5.1 per cent to ₹1,70.9 million from ₹1,801 million last year. The costs of goods also include a non-recurring cost of lottery terminals worth ₹197 million purchased on behalf of Playwin Infravest. During the year, personnel expenses have increased by 29.9 per cent to ₹326 million from ₹251 million in the previous year, mainly due to the increase in compensation and benefits to employees. The PBT during fiscal 2002 was ₹1,344 million, which registered a drop of 17 per cent as compared to fiscal 2001 due to higher interest burden as mentioned above.

As far as consolidated revenues of the company are

concerned, during the year the total revenues were ₹11,554 million. Consolidated revenue streams (Sales and Services) of ZTL comprise of advertising, subscriptions and others. During FYE 31 March 2002, advertising revenues accounted for 57.2 per cent of revenues to ₹6,605 million. Subscription revenues are generated both from domestic and international operations. Zee Network channels are distributed across 80 countries through DTH and cable platforms. In domestic and other South-east Asian markets, the Pay channel bouquet is distributed and marketed by Zee Turner Ltd, which is joint venture between Zee and Turner International Ltd, an AOL Time Warner company. Siti Cable, the largest MSO in India and a subsidiary of Zee, earns subscription revenues from its franchisees and local cable operators. For FYE 31 March 2002, the company recorded subscription revenues of ₹3,169 million. The company's pay-strategy in the domestic market, over a period of last two years, has shown remarkable progress resulting in high growth in subscription revenues. Zee has been successful in deeper penetration in the US markets, which has resulted in greater capitalization of the potential. In UK, Zee has consolidated its position in the market after turning digital. Hence, subscription revenues in UK and other European markets have also shown promising trends in the current fiscal. Total expenses of the company amounted to ₹7,720 million, which includes programming, transmission, SMS and subscription and other direct and indirect costs. The company had undertaken effective cost control measures to maintain margins. Zee also witnessed savings in the transmission costs because of migration from analog to digital platform. Operating costs mainly constitutes the cost of programming and other raw materials amounting to ₹2,057 million, transmission cost of ₹686 million and subscription fees and SMS costs, mainly from international markets, amounting to ₹1,047 million. The company during the year has incurred personnel expenses amounting to ₹778 million.

During the financial year, the company incurred ₹2,507 million as other operating expenses. These expenses are 32.5 per cent of the total expenses. This also includes total non-cash write-off/amortisation amounting to ₹404 million. Consolidated, income before tax during fiscal 2002 was ₹2,811 million. The company achieved PBT margins of 24.3 per cent for the fiscal under discussion.

In 2000, ZTL's American Depository Receipts/American Depository Shares issue worth $1.5 billion. In 2002, ZTL came out with an open offer to acquire 23,39,900 fully paid-up equity shares of ₹10 each of ETC Networks. It presented 20 per cent of the voting equity share April 2002 and closed on 3 May 2002. During FY 2000, gross revenue increased to ₹2,971 million registering a growth of 28 per cent over the previous year and an increase of EBITDA to ₹1,140 million. Zee affected library sales of ₹1,890 million which has not been considered for the purpose of comparisons of results since the transaction is of a non-recurring nature. In 2002, ZTL came out with open offer to acquire 23,39,900 fully paid-up equity shares of ₹10 each of ETC Networks. It presented 20 per cent of the voting equity share capital at a price of ₹31.52 per fully paid up equity share. The issue opened on 3 April 2002 and closed on 3 May 2002.[52]

MARKETING STRATEGIES

As is clear from the financial statements for this period, advertisement revenue for 2001–02 was ₹6,577.9 million, with a contribution of 61.1 per cent to the total revenues. Similarly, in 2002–03, the advertisement revenue was ₹6,265.3 million, a decline of 4.8 per cent, mainly on account of the impact of Cricket World Cup and sluggishness in overall ad-spend. Their contribution to total revenues also decreased to 51.9 per cent. The bulk of advertising revenues were generated from the Asia-Pacific region.

Table 4
Global Reach

Regions	*2001–02*	*2002–03*
Americas (Canada, Caribbean, USA)	245,500	273,100
Europe	135,000	150,000
Africa & Middle East	37,500	166,700
Asia-Pacific	target: 50,000,000	target India: >40,000,000 rest of Asia: 218,000

Spanning five continents, Zee reached out to more than 225 million viewers in more than 80 countries. The South Asian diaspora is spread across the length and breadth of the world and financially and culturally, it is important in most countries. Even in the UK and the US, South Asians have accomplished communities. In other parts of the world like Africa and Hong Kong, they are among the wealthiest sections of society. South Asians have a strong sense of attachment with their roots, which manifests itself through culture.

IN A NUTSHELL

It could be thus seen that this phase was marked with increasing convergence of internal and external operations coupled with corporate restructuring and strategic acquisitions to work out the overall economic sluggishness that dominated all sectors of the economy, including media.

Technology was important during this period, combined with the incoming digitization. Zee was quick to undertake this approach, through means like e-commerce services, digital solutions and a digitized newsroom. Combined with the readiness to armour up and penetrate international markets, the technological embrace too was a telling feature of Zee's outlook. The company, by way of these moves, established that it was always ready to jump onto new trends, and would not shy away from surging forward, even if it was doing so alone. This manner of operation ensured that the company subsisted during the global economic turmoil, remaining unhalted in its steady endeavours.

Despite this, Zee stayed true to its refurbished mission statement. The company's decision to consolidate a few operations and cut down some investments was perhaps a wise one, given that it made up for them by engaging in significant partnerships of both national and international standard. It is worth noting that Zee was foresighted in its approach of choosing the right partners, with whom value creation would be highest. Moreover, these partnerships spanned genres, which assured the company of at least some hits among possible misses. For instance, it partnered with ETC and Padmalaya Telefilms, but also with Turner for Cartoon Network, thereby catering to a varied demographic of regional audiences and children respectively, which are also the audiences that go neglected in mainstream provisions.

This phase is obviously marked by recasting of the strategic intent and a persistent thrust on product development and diversification, business development and diversification and strategic alliances, mergers and acquisitions and promotional strategies to beat the blues of the dampened external business environment. This phase was also marked with increasing convergence of internal and external operations coupled with corporate restructuring and strategic acquisitions to work out the overall economic sluggishness which dominated all sectors of the economy including media. The company decided to consolidate a few operations and cut down some investments.

Zee has always endeavoured to establish a connect factor among Indians worldwide and its aspiration has always been to connect Indians the world over to their culture and to provide them with the best Indian entertainment.

4

THE STRATEGIC SAGA: ZEE DEMERGES (2003–2006)

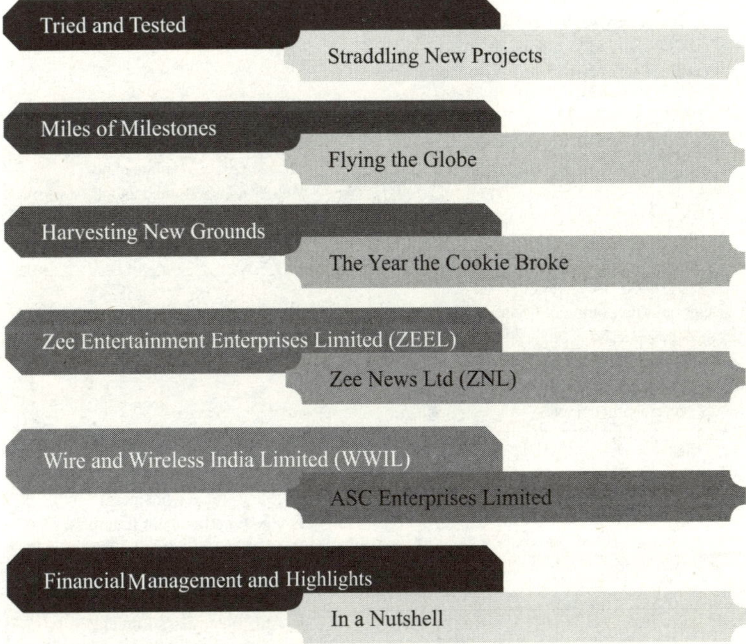

Fig. 4.1: Chapter Insights

TIMELINE 4

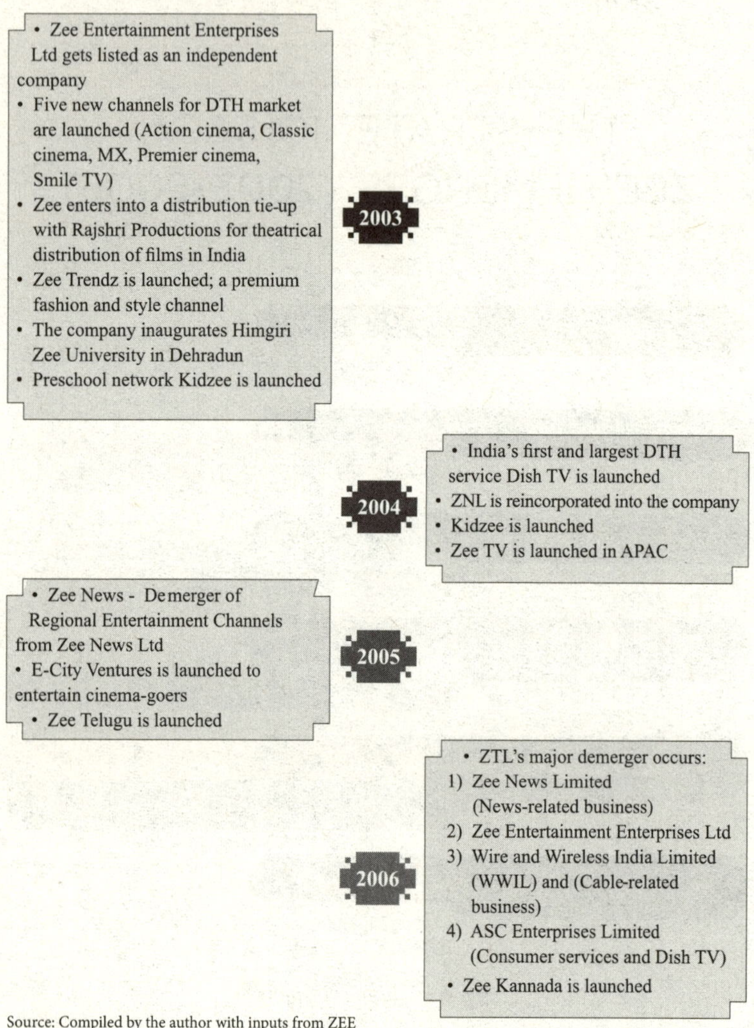

Source: Compiled by the author with inputs from ZEE

The previous chapter discussed the Zee group solidifying their presence in the Indian media market through a series of strategic partnerships and research-backed product diversification. Zee had strengthened its position as a key player in the entertainment segment, and was undoubtedly one of the key players.

Subhash Chandra proudly quoted in his book that 'there are seven categories in broadcasting: news and current affairs, general entertainment, movies, sports, children's programming, infotainment and music. We were in five of these seven categories.'[53]

The major emphasis was on growth, which yielded results for the company; there was considerable increase in the subscription revenues, launch of new programming initiatives, substantial investment in technology and upgradation of services. One major development—in the form of uplinking of some of its channels to India—meant enhancement of its operational efficiency.

A number of mergers and acquisitions, resulting in strategic alliances, were again seen during this time. Backed by multiple technology-based decisions and branding and marketing techniques, this cemented Zee's position towards financial efficiency. The group continued its foray into various allied sectors like films and music.

Alongside, the network was involved in various organizational restructuring initiatives. One of these came out as the focal point upon which the group's future was dependent. In 2006, the Zee network demerged famously into ZEEL and Zee News Ltd (ZNL). It was a momentous decision for the company, and brought with it a domino effect of changes.

TRIED AND TESTED

By 2003, the satellite cable TV entertainment industry had ceased to be the sole preserve of a handful of broadcasting companies. This phase is marked by the mushrooming of a number of TV channels and the stiffening of competition in the sub-sector of communication and entertainment.

Cognizant of the then prevailing business reality and keen to retain its early entry advantage, the *Mission Statement* of this period, as mentioned in the 2003 Annual Report, read:

> To be the leading round the clock air-time properties provider, delighting the viewers on one hand and providing value to the advertisers for their time and money on the other. To establish the company as the creator of entertainment and infotainment products and services to feast the viewers and the advertisers. Through these services, we intend to become an integral part of the global market. As a corporation, we will be profitable, productive, creative, trend-setting and financially rugged with care and concern for all stakeholders.

Chandra remarked on the goals of the year and said that with the onset of digitalization, the Indian television industry witnessed a revolution in terms of increased subscriber growth. Emerging distribution platforms like digital cable, DTH and IPTV enabled the subscriber to view superior quality customized content at a suitable cost.'

At this point, Zee's overarching objective was to create long-term, sustainable shareholder value. It remained committed to business strategies like customer focus, operational excellence, development of people and superior technology, and soon it was looking forward to a period of consolidation. It showed a strong growth overall with increased ad spending. It also built an unparalleled portfolio of programming assets strongly complemented by the distribution strengths from cable assets. There was considerable realignment of the company's organizational structure with the aim to foster a culture of disciplined management and productivity.

With the increasing competition, technological advancements and consumer expectations, the company found itself in a different position altogether. In order to assert its growing stature in the market, it had to reinvent itself. It was in, what the company calls, the 'investment' phase with several new channels added and distribution business receiving due investments for growth. There were some senior management changes also with Pradeep Guha being appointed CEO of the content business and Punit Goenka as a full-time director. However, in a later interview, Chandra recalled that he was not satisfied with Guha's managerial decisions as the CEO. In a face-off with Chandra, Guha asked him to 'increase spending without assurance of success,' leading to his expulsion from the company in 2007–08, when Goenka was ultimately made CEO.[54]

The stakes were high in 2003, and Zee's efforts, even higher. It had impressive clout in the market and among the audiences, but since technology was an easily accessible resource now, there was no telling which rival could overtake them.

The beginning of this phase saw the company register strong overall growth but witnessed a significant change in its revenue composition as its subscription revenues tended to be much more beneficial than its advertising revenues. And so, embarking upon its tried and tested methods of success, Zee continued with its golden period of partnerships. In 2003, Zee merged Asia TV (Africa), Software Supplies (International) Limited, Zee Telefilms International Limited and Zee MGM Limited with Asia Today Limited, Mauritius. Zee also hit upon a new income stream to boost revenues by permitting other international news channels to beam their exclusive footage and programmes for a fee.

An integrated subscriber management services and call centre for its worldwide operations from India were also established. It had over 8,000 km of cable plant in operation and was viewed by approximately 6.7 million cable homes, covering major areas like Delhi, Mumbai, Kolkata, Bangalore, Hyderabad, Chandigarh and Bhopal.

Zee News launched a new logo and a new advertising campaign with the tagline 'Haqeeqat Jaisi, Khabar Waisi'. In the same year, Zee News and Mid Day Multimedia inked a pact for a daily news capsule. Zee News started airing a new programme called *Zee Follow Up*. The show attempted to give a full perspective of the stories by following them to the core. The new programme would pick up the loose string of hundreds of stories that once made headlines but somewhere down the line lost their steam. Zee News was attempting to retrace history by keeping the viewers abreast of what had occurred since. Naveen Kumar, head of special investigative team of correspondents from 1996–2006, describing the procedural operations for Zee News told the author that at Zee, the management treated all the employees like family and always encouraged the reporters to file big stories. There were always various political pressures, but the management of Zee knew how to dilute those pressures. Also, the smart reporters were able to convince the management to show the stories with a different approach than to do away with the story completely.

NEW PROJECTS

During this phase of growth, the company launched a number of new products to cater to different segments of the market based on viewer preferences and language.

In 2003, the company inaugurated the Himgiri Zee University in Dehradun, Uttarakhand. The university was founded to meet the growing demand of candidates in the field of agriculture, forestry, technology, architecture, business, management, etc.

Riding high on the success of *Gadar*, in 2003 Zee began to consider its film production activities seriously. It began to commission films from filmmakers like Mahesh Bhatt and Prakash Mehra. Some titles that were produced included *Fareb*, *Phir Teri Kahani Yaad Aayee* and *Humein Jahan Pyar Mile*. It also produced a live-cum-animation film, *Bhagmati*. Zee even went international in this field, by producing a film called *One Dollar Curry* with France TV and Silhouette films. The same year, it entered into a tie-up with Rajshri Pictures for the theatrical distribution of films in India. But the modalities of this arrangement could not be worked out and it was terminated the next year.

Since Zee became the first to get a Letter of Intent for DTH operation in India, this period witnessed further increase in product diversification of their cinematic adventures with the launch of five new channels in 2003 for the DTH market viz. Action Cinema, Classic Cinema, MX, Premiere Cinema and Smile TV. Exclusively focused on the action genre, Zee Action had a collection of hundreds of movies from the last three decades. Action lovers had a blast with blockbusters such as *Ghayal, Ghatak, Tahalka, Elane Jung, Phool aur Kaante, Apradh* and *Qurbani*. Zee Action had brought the thrill home to millions of viewers. Thematics like *Teen Ka Tashan* brought the action into the living rooms of action seekers, a special experience crafted only on Zee Action. Zee Classic is India's only Hindi movie channel that showcases films from the golden era of Hindi cinema. After a short hiatus, the channel with its core slogan 'Woh Zamaana Kare Deewana', was back again on popular demand featuring an all-new look. The channel promised to recreate the magic of iconic classics and new-age cinema by showcasing not just films that shaped Indian cinema, but also acquainting viewers with the creative talent who were a part of that timeless era. Zee Premiere showcased the latest Hindi movies and never-before-seen releases. Zee Smile was a 24-hour comedy and entertainment channel with movies, cartoons, sitcoms, etc. The channel persisted with showing Thursday Bollywood blockbusters.

Zee's offering of a varied shelf in the film category however, had to be supplemented with other genres too. Hence, 2003 saw the release of one more channel, Zee Trendz. It became an international music and lifestyle channel. It also covered popular international music played every hour. Some of their product offerings were *Re-Play*, *Blingz*, *Babelicious*, *Sizzle*, *Style Q*, and *After hours*.

From 2003, Zee Cinema had the distinction of winning 'The Best Movie Channel' award for four consecutive years in a row, both at the Indian Television Academy Award and the Indian Telly Awards.

Meanwhile, Zee TV was making strides in drama shows as usual. The premier programmes for Zee TV during this time were *Khana Khazana, Lavanya, Tum Bin Jaaoon Kahan, Jeena Isi Ka Naam Hai, Sa Re Ga Ma Pa, Tumhari Disha, Sinndoor Tere Naam Ka, Kashish, Time-Bomb, Mamta, Ghar Ki Lakshmi Betiyaan, Saath Phere, Kasamh Se* and *Business Baazigar*.

This positioning of the company as a primary producer of films and general entertainment overshadowed its news production identity. For people, the mention of Zee invoked the mantra of 'Movies, Masti, Magic' since the company had been focused on entertainment broadcast from the beginning. Delving into film production and relying on pop culture trend shows (like *Khana Khazana* or *Style Q*) to expand its gallery only intensified this identity more.

Backroom upgrading of infrastructure in 2003 led to the channel fully converting to automated newsroom system. Zee had, at that time, 12 OB vans of their own, in addition to the fixed V-SAT facilities that it already had in various cities.

In 2003, there was also much back and forth between Zee, the government and the courts. During this year, the Mumbai High Court stayed Zee TV's daily and Sunday lottery draws. Once more, Zee announced its à la carte price list for bundling channels, but the government cancelled ZTL's plea for bundling its channels. Zee and Star also landed up in a fray over Siti Cable's HITS project. Some respite came when Delhi High Court permitted Zee TV to telecast *The Inside Story*.

Hindustan Lever Ltd advertisements also began to reappear on Zee TV after nearly a gap of one year. Meanwhile, the board approved a proposal to commence broadcasting of Zee TV and Zee Cinema channels from India. The company also obtained permission from the Ministry of Information & Broadcasting for the same. The board also approved the corporate restructuring of Indian and foreign subsidiaries. The High Court additionally restrained overseas firms from using Zee in domain names.

Despite hiccups, FY 2003 was a year of progress and positive change for Zee. The company was able to improve product offerings substantially. To improve the quality of earnings, time and energy were spent on improving internal processes and sharpening the focus on cash flows. There was increased communication with investors and an improved quantity and quality of disclosures. Zee-Turner International expanded their partnership with three new channels wherein Turner would be the advertising sales agent for Zee's English entertainment and lifestyle channels, Zee English, Zee MGM and the recently unveiled Trendz channel.

MILES OF MILESTONES

2004 was a year of celebration for Zee. Years of efforts had begun showing tangible results in the form of numbers. Subhash Chandra was awarded 'Global Indian Entertainment Personality of the Year' by FICCI. By the same year, Zee had reached a base of over one million subscribers overseas. It was available in more than 120 countries on all continents. The Zee brand had even entered the APAC markets with the launch of Zee TV in 2004.

Table 5
Global Reach of ZTL during 2003–2006

Regions	*2003–04*	*2004–05*	*2005–06*	*2006–07*
Americas (Canada, Caribbean, USA)	317,000	376,000	467,000	550,000
Europe	166,000	168,000	168,000	300,000
Africa and Middle East	198,000	223,000	299,000	935,000
Asia-pacific	target India: >40,000,000	target India: >610,000,000	target India: 680,000,000	3.7 million
	Rest of Asia: 230,000	Rest of Asia: 224,000	Rest of Asia: 242,000	

Source: Compiled from Annual Reports

The international audience contributed 25 per cent of its total revenues and it had nearly a million global subscribers: 33,80,000 were in the Americas, 1,71,000, in Europe, 49,000 in Africa and 40,4,000 in the Asia-Pacific region. It announced the launch of a separate encrypted beam for Singapore. It extended the South Asian beam of Zee TV to Hong Kong, Thailand, the Philippines, Indonesia and Japan. Zee was the only media company to be part of the BSE-30 Sensex. The company also looked to leverage pay revenues through distribution platforms of CAS and DTH.

Furthermore, Expand Fast Holdings, British Virgin Islands (BVI), was merged with Asia Today Limited. In the same year, Winter heath Company Limited merged with Asia Today Limited. Asia Today Limited acquired Pan Asia Infrastructure Limited. In 2004, ETC Networks Limited amalgamated with Econnect India Limited. The same year, BT Broadcast, ASCEL joined hands to offer teleport services to Zee. The company entered into an agreement with ASC enterprises limited to provide aggregate and content for DTH platform.

The major focus of the company was now the development of unique content across genres, usage of technological advancements, investments in strategic markets and aggressive marketing and branding efforts. In keeping with these efforts, the company also stressed upon developing human resources with the vision and skills to implement such a policy.

Yet another bunch of channel launches awaited the public. In 2004, Zee Jagran launched and emphasized on spirituality with themes of good living, mythology, saints, yoga and meditation. The same year, Zee Business was released to the public as a news and current affairs channel focusing on business and economy. It was proclaimed to be 'India's first Hindi business channel'. It emerged as the 'Best Business Channel' at the Consumer World Awards. Some of its major programmes were *Tax Doctor* (a programme that dispenses income tax tips), *Property Plus* (which looks at opportunities in real estate), *Bazaar, Share Bazaar Live* and *Wheelocity* (an automobile show).

Keeping in mind the emergence of the younger age group in the audiences, the company targeted this dominating sub-group in the Indian market by changing its catchphrase to 'Jiyo Zee Bhar Ke' between 2004 and 2005. This helped the company to reposition itself in keeping with the aspirations of the youth. Subhash Chandra explained the rationale behind this and said, 'Keeping in view Zee Network's growth, we decided to give Zee brand a new visual identity. The new identity retains the letter Z while its styling has been changed to represent our energy and readiness to embrace the future. The re-branding exercise weaves a thread of common identity between our many diverse brands and brings us closer to our younger audience.'

The company entered a phase wherein the focus was to consolidate as well as to ensure a steady and stable growth. With GRPs (Gross Rating Points) on the rise, the company introduced, across channels, a slew of ad sales initiatives like focus on inventory utilization, attracting higher yielding categories of business, etc. With the demerger of news, cable and direct consumer service business undertakings, the company ensured greater focus on mass entertainment.

Over at Zee News, the channel won awards at EMMVIES 2004, Indian Telly Awards and the Indian Marketing Awards. *The Inside Story*, its programme on synthetic milk, won an award at the New York festivals. India's first reality TV show was hosted by Zee News. A Zee News editor shared that the week Zee ran a 2-hour special on the *Guriya* case in late 2004 was the only week it became No. 1 in the ratings that year. He explained the rationale behind the show, 'The Guriya Show was India's first reality TV show. We set up a panchayat here, we got the Shariat experts. The issue was so big… It had a lover, a soldier, religion, a woman, religious orthodoxy, and it was from the Hindi heartland. It had all the elements. That is what made it. As far as news is concerned, it was only about politicians. We were changing that. Various human issues are now news because the canvas has widened'. Zee rounded up the entire panchayat of the village, representatives of the Muslim clergy, Guriya herself, her relatives and the first husband in the Delhi studio and asked them to decide her fate. The participants were asked not to leave the studio till they reached a decision and Zee advertised the live trial *Kis Ki Guriya*. An hour into the telecast, a Muslim cleric announced that he could resolve the dispute within five minutes, since the Shariat had clear guidelines and precedents and that television was creating an unnecessarily long debate. The panchayat ultimately decided that she should go back to her first husband. He was to bring up the unborn child for a few years before returning it to the second husband.'

PLOUGHING NEWER GROUNDS

In 2005, in a continuation of the group's sports offering, Zee Sports was officially launched as a channel to provide a multi-genre sports entertainment package to the viewers. In 2005, Zee launched Zee Arabiya (an Arabian music channel catering to the Middle Eastern audience). Zee Telugu was also launched as a Telugu GEC. It catered to the discerning Telugu viewers with a judicious programming mix. Some of its major programmes have been *Sandhyaaradhane*, *Subhashya Sheegram*, *Suddhi 180*, *Aata-The Ultimate Dance Show*, *My Name Is Mangatayaru*, and *Sa Re Ga Ma Pa Voice of Youth*. Zee Telugu was the first Southern regional channel in the Zee bouquet. The channel was launched with a vision to provide wholesome entertainment. Over the years, Zee Telugu, with its wide variety of content offerings across genres and age groups, has done just that. The channel reaches around 75 million people, week on week, across India. Meanwhile, over at Zee TV, the launch of interactive game show *Kam Ya Zyaada* was announced.

After the merger of Essel Publishers Pvt. Ltd with the company, Essel even expanded to the print sector with the DNA brand of newspapers under its belt. Diligent Media Corporation Limited (DMCL) was incorporated under the Companies Act, 1956, on 17 February 2005, as a joint venture entity of two media conglomerates viz. Essel Group and Bhaskar Group, to engage in the business of printing, publishing and distributing newspapers.

DMCL established its presence in the print media business with the launch of the Mumbai edition of *DNA* (Daily News and Analysis), an English newspaper, on 30 July 2005. The subsidiaries Diligent Media Corporation Limited (DMCL) and Pri Media Services Pvt. Ltd published *DNA* in Mumbai, Bengaluru and Pune.

Punit Goenka explained this foray into print and said, 'The fact was that the print business is largely driven through monopoly and we felt that there was a need for having a second option for the consumer. I mean, in Mumbai, *The Times of India* had the monopoly in English newspapers. And there was no second option available. That was the reason for our foray into the print business. We will keep our foot in the door but our forte will still remain electronic media as our core competence.'[55]

The year 2005 again brought with it a number of partnerships for ZTL. It teamed up with IBM Global, had an alliance with Pan Global TV, and joined hands with Malaysia's Astro to launch a Hindi channel. The same year, RPG Netcom, which later became Indian Cable Network, was sold to Siti Cable. This was a kind of reverse integration of media platforms.

THE YEAR THAT CHANGED EVERYTHING: THE DEMERGER

The year 2006 was a decisive year for Zee's future. Everything changed.

It began when Zee saw the exit of ZTL's CEO Sandeep Goyal. At this point, Chandra decided to run the company at the operational level as well and brought back his brothers Jawahar Goel and Laxmi Goel to manage Siti Cable and news businesses of Zee. These changes heralded the year of 2006, which was marked by major organizational restructuring exercises in Zee.

As the organization had grown significantly with expansion in multiple genres and territories, putting strain on the managerial span of control, Chandra thought it was time to make it leaner and more focused. The best way forward seemed to be a demerger. Big changes were in the pipeline.

Therefore, it was on 18 December 2006 that the demerger process of ZTL was initiated. The company restructured itself in a major way by demerging the main operations of the company into four separate entities: ZNL (ZNL), ZEEL, Wire and Wireless India Limited (WWIL) for cable business operations, and ASC Enterprises Limited for consumer and DTH services. In the words of one of the directors of Zee, 'With the approvals of the

Hon'ble High Courts of Bombay and Delhi, and other regulatory authorities, the company successfully concluded the process of demerger of its news, cable and direct communication business undertakings'.

Apart from providing the focus required for each of the businesses to be run effectively with varying complexities, investor expectations and a preparation required to capitalize on the technological advancement of the digital age, this restructuring was a response to the regulatory requirements. Some other discernible reasons for this decision included the formation of a clear-cut leadership and direction for all demerged businesses to be developed, incorporation of tax efficiencies, bringing all operational activities together under a suitable corporate structure with an undivided focus for unlocking shareholder value, effective optimization and exploitation of under-used cable assets, independent identification of strategic and financial partners, and exploitation of vast emerging opportunities in the cable business.

This move majorly highlighted the significance of separating news-based programmes from non-news-based programmes that had come to acquire a place in the business strategies of Zee. ZEEL and ZNL could be identified as Essel's major operations that were abuzz with the most exciting activities. They were siblings, differentiated from each other by the respective responsibilities they had to shoulder.

CORPORATE RESTRUCTURING

The company was in receipt of a high court order approving its scheme of demerger of its cable and news businesses into Wire and Wireless (India) Limited and ZNL respectively, effective from 31 March 2006. News, business and regional channels, which were hitherto a part of ZTL, were demerged into ZNL and the shareholders of ZTL would receive proportionate shares in ZNL.

After the demerger, ZNL consisted of Zee News, Zee Business, Zee Bangla, Zee Punjabi, Zee Gujarati, Zee Marathi, Zee Telugu, Zee Kannada and 24 Ghante. As per the scheme of arrangement, the cable business of Siti Cable, a 100 per cent subsidiary of ZTL and the cable-related business of ZTL were demerged into Wire and Wireless (India) Limited (WWIL). Also, it was decided that the direct consumer-related business of ZTL will be demerged into ASCEL effective 1 April 2006 subject to High Courts approval. The scheme of arrangement had already been approved by the shareholders at an EGM held on 25 July 2006.

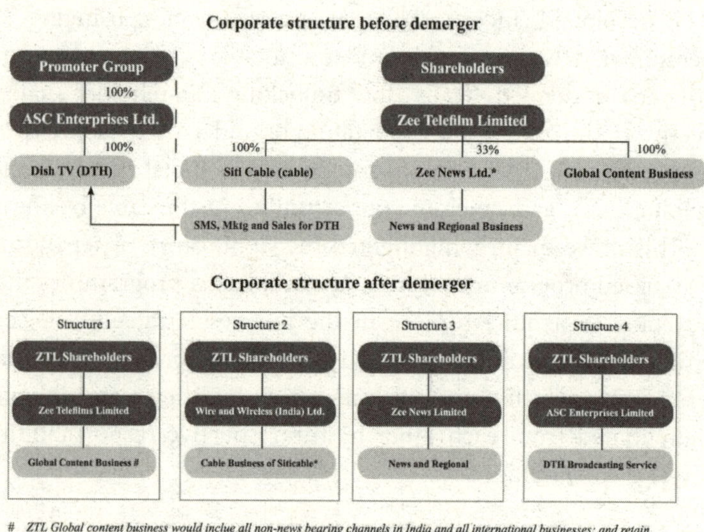

\# *ZTL Global content business would inclue all non-news bearing channels in India and all international businesses; and retain 74% investment in Zee Turner, 51% investment in ETC Networks Limited and 26% stake in Aplab Limited.*

* *Shares held by foreign promoters will be shifted to India as domestic holding to bring down the overall foreign holding to about 35% in Cable business. Foreign holding permissible is 49%.*

Source: As provided by Zee

A) Zee Entertainment Enterprises Limited (ZEEL)

Zee Entertainment Enterprises Limited was the new name given to Zee Telefilms Limited (ZTL). It owned 17 different television channels, the cable company Siti Cable, a record label Zee

Records, a production company and other businesses as well. It went on to launch several channels in the subsequent years.

B) Zee News Ltd (ZNL)

In 2006, ZNL became a separate entity after the demerger from ZTL. The channels which came under it were: Zee News, Zee Business, Zee Marathi, Zee Gujarati, Zee Telugu, Zee Kannada, Zee Punjabi, Zee Bangla, Zee 24 Taas, 24 Ghanta and Zee Talkies.

The upcoming chapters will dig deeper into the life and times of both ZEEL and ZNL (now ZMCL).

C) Wire and Wireless India Limited (WWIL)

Incepted as Wire and Wireless India Limited in 2006, the offering was later reformed to Siti Cable Network Limited as part of Essel Group. It prides itself as being India's first and one of its largest MSOs, with more than 10 million direct and indirect customers. According to a top official of Zee, the business of the company principally consisted of MSO operations, distribution of satellite channels and IOC; these were offered by WWIL. It operates across multiple services such as cable distribution of C&S channels through franchisees/local cable operators, IOC, distribution of Zee Network pay channels to the operators and providing content and infrastructure services for the DTH platform.

The WWIL product range included analogue cable, digital cable, broadband and local television channels, with all products marketed under the SITI brand. It managed to establish a national footprint in most major states and districts. Going forward, WWIL seeks to focus on market consolidation, increasing subscriber base through tapping under declaration, increasing connectivity by adding LCOs and engaging in strategic acquisitions and partnership.

D) ASC Enterprises Limited

Renamed as Dish TV India Ltd, ASC Enterprises Limited of the Essel Group held a DTH license, marking a division of duties between this arm of the group and WWIL endowed with the cable business. During the year the company was demerged, Subhash Chandra also took the decision to merge two other companies related to the consumer service business: Cornersoft Entertainment Co Pvt. Ltd and New Era Entertainment Pvt. Ltd.

Cornersoft was the force behind creating the 7,575 interactive platforms for all the Zee channels and Essel group companies to enable widespread communication between the customer and client. The positioning of Cornersoft as an entity seeking to connect audiences with stellar content and services came as a bonus to ASC Enterprises, since it would help the Dish TV market with a varied range of offerings for the subscriber base.[56] Chandra had always steered Zee with a clear-sighted vision. This decision, too, he believed would only take his company upward. When the demerger occurred, he expressed his intent behind it. He said, 'In keeping with its philosophy of building long-term shareholder value, the board of Zee had decided to restructure its various businesses. This would strengthen long-term business prospects of each individual business, by providing focused management attention.'[57]

THE RATIONALE: BEHIND THE DEMERGER

In compliance with News Uplinking Guidelines of the Govt. of India, news gathering activities were already transferred from ZTL to ZNL in respect of Zee News and all regional channels w.e.f. October 2005. With restructuring, ZTL's news business alongwith regional language channels will now vest in ZNL. Bringing all operational activities together under a suitable corporate structure with an undivided focus is the best way of unlocking shareholder value. Till date, cable assets were under-utilised and the demerger would optimize the effective use of the same.

STAKE IN TEN SPORTS AND ACQUISITION OF BCCI RIGHTS

Zee also acquired a 50 per cent stake with majority representation in the Board in M/S Taj TV Ltd, Mauritius, the company which owns 'Ten Sports' channel and a 50 per cent stake with majority representation in the Board in M/S Taj Television India Pvt. Ltd Mumbai, which is the distribution arm of Ten Sports in India. The acquisition of a stake in Ten Sports not only gave Zee a strong foothold in the arena of sports broadcasting across Asia but also strengthened its operations in the Middle East. The addition of Ten Sports gave Zee significant strength, enabling further effective exploitation of all its sports properties.

Another reason was the launch of its China operations. Zee had signed a content sharing agreement with China Central Television. Through this deal with China International—an English language news channel—it covered news, feature programmes and films.

Another important factor was implementation of CAS. TRAI issued a notification dated 31 July 2006 to the effect that Conditional Access System (CAS) be implemented w.e.f 31 December 2006 in metros. Pursuant to this, the TRAI had also set out MRPs, provisions on free-to-air (FTA) channels, quality of services, etc. With regards to this, provisions have been laid out for interconnection agreements to be entered between the broadcasters and MSOs. This ruled out any ambiguity, which can arise in future and also enabled consumers to choose the content they want to watch and to pay for the same. It also streamlined the reporting of subscriber's numbers by MSOs. TRAI also announced the pricing norms for the pay channels effective 31

December 2006 for areas in which CAS would be implemented. Among other norms, TRAI had prescribed an MRP of ₹5 per channel. Although channel bouquets could continue to be offered, pay channels would also offer on a la carte basis. Zee TV had about 10 channels, which were leaders in their respective genre. There were other channels, which commanded prominent viewership. Zee accordingly did not anticipate its subscription revenue to suffer any negative impact by the announced channel pricing or the a la carte basis of offering pay channels.

Table 6

Financial Highlights of ZTL-Standalone (in millions)

Year Ending 31 March	*2003*	*2004*	*2005*	*2006*
Income From Operations	4618	5053	6473	8314
Other Income	701	662	458	510
Total Income	5319	5715	6931	8824
Total Expenditure	3217	3371	4091	7525
Operating Profit	1401	1682	2382	789
Per cent to income from operations	30 per cent	33 per cent	37 per cent	9 per cent
PBIDT	2102	2344	2840	1299
Depreciation	90	100	139	148
PBT	1495	1874	2536	1011
Taxation	532	720	860	340
PAT	947	1154	1623	691
Per cent to total income	18 per cent	20 per cent	23 per cent	08 per cent
Dividend	227	413	413	435
Total Assets and Equity & Liabilities	43180	23160	26533	20156
Loans Funds	4044	2680	5221	4712
Investments	34356	15171	15475	13448

Source: Compiled by the author from Annual Reports 2003–2006

Note: Figures in the table are rounded off.

Total revenue increased ₹1,893.5 million, or 27 per cent from ₹6,930.7 million to ₹8,824.2 million. This increase in total revenue was majorly on account of increase in sales and services as it increased ₹1,841.5 million, or 28 per cent from ₹6,472.5 million to ₹8,314 million. The increase was mainly on account of advertisement income and sale in electronic devices. There was an increase in sale of electronic devices (set-top boxes [STBs]) from ₹325.3 million in 2005 to ₹1,773 million in 2006. Interest and other income increased by ₹52 million or 11 per cent from ₹458.2 million to ₹510.2 million. Total expenditure increased by ₹3,433.7 million or 84 per cent from ₹4,091.1 million to ₹7,524.8 million. The increase in total expenditure was due to increase in cost of goods sold, staff cost, administration and selling and distribution expenses. Also, operational cost/cost of goods increased ₹2,962.7 million, or 122 per cent from ₹2,427.7 million in 2005 to ₹5,390.4 million in 2006. Acquisition of cricket properties for Zee sports formed a major component in the increase in operational costs. Operational cost on account of STB's increased ₹1, 429.4 million from ₹310.4 million in 2005 to ₹1,739.8 million in 2006. This spurt was as a result of increase in sales of STBs. Personnel cost increased ₹55.6 million, or 14 per cent, from ₹387.7 million in 2005 to ₹443.3 million in 2006. This increase in personnel cost was due to an increase in the number of employees in both new and existing businesses, annual increments, annual incentives to employees and higher training and welfare costs.

Administrative and other expenses increased from ₹553.3 million to ₹578.6 million, an increase of ₹25.3 million or 5 per cent, selling and distribution expenses increased by ₹390.1 million or 54 per cent from ₹722.4 million to ₹1,112.5 million. This was on account of increased thrust in marketing and promotional activities and increase in channel distribution cost. Operating profit decreased ₹1,540.2 million, or 54 per cent in 2005 to ₹1,299.4 million in 2006. The main reason for this was the increase in operational costs, marketing and promotional expenses, including start up losses in new businesses/initiatives undertaken by the company. Financial expenses decreased by ₹24.8 million or 15 per cent. Depreciation increased marginally by ₹9.6 million, or 7 per cent, from ₹138.9 million to ₹148.5 million. PBT and exceptional items decreased ₹1,525.0 million or 60 per cent, from ₹2,536.0 million in 2005 to ₹1,011.0 million in 2006. Taxation decreased to ₹339.5 million (net of reversal of excess provision written back amounting ₹24.6 million) from ₹860.0 million; the decrease in provision for taxation was primarily due to offset of losses of new businesses. The effective tax rate was marginally higher. PAT for the year decreased to ₹690.8 million from ₹1,622.7 million, a decrease of almost 57 per cent.

Table 7

Financial Highlights-ZTL Consolidated (in millions)

Year Ending 31 March	*2003*	*2004*	*2005*	*2006*
Income From Operations	11,140	12,789	13,252	16,543
Other Income	785	776	521	640
Total Income	11,925	13,565	13,773	17,183
Total Expenditure	7,384	8,480	8,900	13,848
Operating Profit	3,756	4,309	4,352	2,695
Per cent to income from operations	34 per cent	34 per cent	33 per cent	16 per cent
PBIDT	4,541	5,085	4,873	3,335
Depreciation	297	319	329	360
PBT	3,477	4,183	4,338	2,787
Taxation	879	1,049	1,023	547
PAT	2,244	3,134	3,174	2,260
Per cent to total income	18 per cent	22 per cent	23 per cent	12 per cent
Dividend	227	413	413	435
Loans Funds	7,137	4,722	5,304	4,772
Investments	316	328	3,744	3,024

Source: Compiled by the author from Annual Reports 2003–2006

Operational income of ZTL consolidated touched 16,543 million in FY 2006. It showed a growth of 36 per cent in comparison to FY 2003 i.e. in a block of four years. But, the company's NPBT had declined in FY 2006 vis-à-vis FY 2005 by around 40 per cent. It came down to 2,787 million (FY 2006) from 4,338 million in FY 2005. Though there was a fall in profits, the company declared and paid dividend to its shareholders.

Total revenue increased ₹3,409.9 million or 25 per cent from ₹13,773.2 million in 2005 to ₹17,183.1 million in 2006. This increase in total revenue was principally a result of an increase in sales and services and other income that increased ₹3,291.5 million, or 25 per cent; from ₹13,252.2 million in 2005 to ₹16, 543.7 million in 2006. This increase in revenue resulted from increase in advertisement income and subscription income. Advertisement revenue has grown from ₹5,697.7 million to ₹6,566.0 million. Subscription income has increased by ₹467.8 million from ₹6,706.2 million to ₹7,174.1 million. Revenue from other sales and services increased by ₹1,955.3 million or 230 per cent: from ₹848.3 million in 2005 to ₹2,803.6 million in 2006, mainly on account of sale of electronic devices and syndication revenue.

Other income had risen by ₹118.6 million, or 23 per cent: from ₹521.0 million in 2005 to ₹639.4 million in 2006. Total expenditure increased ₹4,948.1 million, or 56 per cent: from ₹8,900.3 million in 2005 to ₹13,848.4 million in 2006. This increase in total expenditures was principally a result of increases in operational costs, selling and administration cost and personnel cost. It increased by ₹3,774.9 million, or 68 per cent: from ₹5,554.2 million in 2005 to ₹9,329.1 million in 2006. Programme/film rights cost has increased by ₹1,636.1 million from ₹2,610.9 million in 2005 to ₹4,247.1 million in 2006. This was mainly due to an increase in programme cost of the Indian channels as there was an increase in number of mega shows/

events during the year. Acquisition of cricketing rights, startup losses of new business initiatives like Zee Telugu also contributed to the rise in the programming costs.

Personnel cost increased ₹231.3 million, or 27 per cent: from ₹857.4 million in 2005 to ₹1,088.7 million in 2006. This increase in personnel cost was due to an increase in the number of employees in both new and existing businesses, annual increments and annual incentives to employees. Administrative and other expenses have increased by ₹100.1 million, or 6 per cent: from ₹1,721.8 million in 2005 to ₹1, 821.8 million in 2006. Selling and distribution expenses increased ₹841.8 million, or 110 per cent: from ₹767.0 million in 2005 to ₹1,608.8 million in 2006. Due to greater focus on marketing, there was an increase in advertisement, publicity and business promotion expenses. Operating profit fell from ₹4,352.0 million in 2005 to ₹2,695 million in 2006. This is primarily because of the increase in programming, personnel and selling and distribution expenses. Financial expenses decreased ₹19 million, or 9 per cent: from ₹206.6 million in 2005 to ₹187.7 million in 2006. Depreciation increased ₹30.9 million, or 9 per cent: from ₹328.7 million in 2005 to ₹359.7 million in 2006. This increase in depreciation is due to depreciation on assets of cable subsidiaries acquired during the year (demerged at the end of the year) and depreciation on new assets purchased during the year. PBT and exceptional items PBT and exceptional items decreased ₹1,550.3 million or 36 per cent: from ₹4,337.6 million in 2005 to ₹2,787.3 million in 2006. Provision for taxation decreased ₹476.4 million, or 47 per cent: from ₹1,023.2 million in 2005 to ₹546.8 million in 2006 to set off losses of new businesses. The effective tax rate reduced marginally from 23.6 per cent in 2005 to 19.6 per cent in 2006. PAT and before minority interest/share of profits (losses) in associate PAT and before minority interest/share of profits (losses) in associates decreased ₹914.4 million from ₹3,174.3

million in 2005 to ₹2,259.9 million in 2006.

As far as the other segments are concerned, the growth is as follows:

Access: This segment principally consists of MSO operations, distribution of satellite channels and IOC. Revenues from this segment increased by ₹1,471.5 million or 101 per cent: from ₹1,455.3 million in 2005 to ₹2,926.7 million in 2006. Operating loss before interest and tax decreased by ₹104.4 million from ₹266.8 million in 2005 to ₹162.3 million in 2006. This increase is mainly due to acquisition of Indian Cable Network Limited.

Film Production and Distribution: This segment principally consists of production, acquisition and distribution of feature films, animation films and programmes. Revenues from this segment are lower by ₹194.4 million from ₹205.9 million in 2005 to ₹11.5 million in 2006. No major activity during the year affected the results of the segment

Education: There has been an increase in the revenues from ₹112.2 million in 2005 to ₹162.4 million in 2006. Also, there has been an improvement in the operating result before interest and tax. Operating loss of ₹9.6 million in 2005 has turned in to operating profit of ₹3.8 million in 2006.

Others: This segment includes the sale of electronic devices. There has been an increase in revenues by ₹1,447.8 million over the previous year; operating profit before interest and tax in 2006 was ₹34.8 million as against ₹20.0 million in 2005.

Debt equity ratio, which was considerably higher as on 31 March 1996 at 26.50, had come down to 34.7 as on 31 March 2006, showing dependency on outside funds. Current ratio of the company had been in a comfortable position all through this period, showing that the company is never short of working capital. Fixed asset ratio which was very low at 3.50 in FY 2000–01,

Table 8

Performance Ratios of ZTL-An Analysis (Standalone) (1995 to 2006) (₹ in millions)

Year Ending 31 March	*1995*	*1996*	*1997*	*1998*	*1999*	*2000*	*2001*	*2002*	*2003*	*2004*	*2005*	*2006*
Financial Performance per cent												
Advertisement income/Income from Operations	–	–	–	–	–	–	–	1.2	25.6	37.2	50.2	45.4
Subscription Income/Income from Operations	–	–	–	–	–	–	–	0.2	7.9	17.7	32.1	21.2
Operating Profit/Income Operations	40.7	33.3	31.6	34.0	37.6	36.2	35.4	30.3	29.2	33.3	36.8	9.5
Other Income/Total Income	2.4	1.5	4.5	4.2	2.4	3.4	11.7	15.9	12.8	11.6	6.6	5.8
Programming cost/ Income from Operations	46.5	53.7	50.7	45.2	46.7	45.5	46.9	42.1	39.2	32.3	29.9	42.5
Personal cost/Income from Operations	2.3	2.8	4.0	5.3	4.7	5.4	6.5	8.0	6.2	5.5	6.0	5.3
Selling and Admin Expenses/Income from Operations	10.5	10.2	13.7	15.5	11.0	12.9	11.1	14.0	20.6	20.7	19.7	20.3
Total Operating Cost/ Income from Operations	59.3	66.7	68.4	66.0	62.4	63.8	64.6	69.7	70.8	66.7	63.2	90.5
Interest cost /Income from Operations	0.6	2.2	4.3	3.7	3.6	2.9	5.5	14.4	10.8	7.3	2.5	1.7
Tax/ Income from Operations	11.5	6.8	5.4	8.6	8.6	7.3	6.2	9.1	11.1	14.2	13.3	4.1
PAT/Total Income	29.5	24.1	24.1	24.2	26.4	27.7	31.7	20.1	17.2	20.2	23.4	7.8
Tax/PBT	27.6	21.9	17.6	25.4	24.2	20.4	14.7	27.6	35.6	38.4	33.9	33.6

Dividend Payout/PAT	25.2	21.7	24.2	23.5	16.8	19.6	16.4	23.3	24.0	35.8	25.4	59.7
Dividend Pay Out/Effective Net Worth	9.5	8	7.8	7.3	5.4	2.2	2.0	1.9	1.8	2.2	2.1	3.2
Balance Sheet												
Debt-Equity Watio (Total Loans/Eff. Net worth)	7.1	26.5	31.0	30.3	29.4	20.7	28.2	34.0	32.3	14.4	26.8	34.7
Current Ratio (Current Assets/Current Liabilities (x)	1.8	2.1	1.8	2.1	3.0	3.1	4.1	4.2	3.4	2.9	3.2	2.3
Capital Output Ratio (Inc. from Ops./ Eff. Capital Employed) (x)	1.1	1.1	1.0	0.9	0.9	0.3	0.3	0.3	0.3	0.2	0.3	0.5
Fixed Assest Turnover (Inc. from Ops/ Fixed Assets) (x)	7.2	5.8	5.7	6.5	7.3	4.9	3.5	3.2	3.7	3.4	3.6	7.2
Cash and Cash Equivalents/Total Eff. Capital Employed	–	–	–	26.3	7.2	5.9	15.3	8.0	2.5	1.3	1.6	1.3
RONW (PAT/Eff. Networth)	37.7	36.7	32.4	31.1	32.1	11.1	12.1	8.3	7.6	6.2	8.3	5.1
ROCE (PBIT/ Eff. Capital Employed) (x)	47.6	37.5	33.8	34.6	35.8	12.5	12.5	12.2	12.1	10.5	10.9	6.3
Per Share Data												
Revenue Per Share (₹)	4.0	6.7	7.7	9.7	12.4	10.2	10.6	11.7	13.3	13.9	16.8	21.4
Dividend Per Share (₹)	0.30	0.35	0.45	0.55	0.55	0.55	0.55	0.55	0.55	1.00	1.00	1.00
Indebtedness Per Share (₹)	0.22	1.17	1.79	2.3	3.0	5.2	7.9	9.7	9.8	6.5	12.7	12.7
Book value Per Share (₹)	3.17	4.41	5.77	7.5	10.2	24.0	27.8	28.4	30.4	45.0	47.3	32.9

Source: Compiled by the author from Annual Reports 1995–2006

had improved to 7.2 in FY 2005–06, showing an increase in sales level with regard to capital assets. Company declared dividend in all these years to reward its shareholders for being financial partners of the company. Book value of share of company shows an increasing trend. Revenue per share reflected positive growth trend and book value was increasing due to ploughing back of profits after payment of dividend to shareholders

Table 9

Performance Ratios—an Analysis of ZTL (Consolidated) (2002 to 2006) (₹ in millions)

Year Ending 31 March	*2002*	*2003*	*2004*	*2005*	*2006*
Financial Performance	–				
Advertisement income/ income from Operations (per cent)	61.1	51.9	42.6	43.0	39.7
Subscription Income/ income from Operations (per cent)	29.2	40.1	47.1	50.6	43.4
Operating Profit/Income Operations (per cent)	28.3	31.1	33.7	32.8	16.3
Other Income/Total Income (per cent)	6.9	6.1	5.7	3.8	3.7
Programming Cost/Income from Operations	19.21	20.2	19.7	19.7	25.7
Personal Cost Income from operations (per cent)	7.2	6.0	5.7	6.5	6.6
Selling and Admin Expenses/Income from Operations	23.3	22.6	18.5	18.8	20.7
Total Operating Cost/ Income from Operations (per cent)	71.7	68.9	66.3	67.2	83.7

Year Ending 31 March	*2002*	*2003*	*2004*	*2005*	*2006*
Interest cost/Income from Operations (per cent)	7.5	6.4	4.6	1.6	1.1
Tax/Income from Operations (per cent)	8.0	7.3	8.2	7.7	3.3
PAT/Total Income (per cent)	16.8	16.6	21.7	22.7	12.5
Tax/PBT (per cent)	30.8	25.3	25.1	23.6	19.6
Dividend Payout/PAT (per cent)	11.7	10.6	14.0	13.2	19.3
Dividend Pay Out/Effective Net worth (per cent)	1.8	1.5	1.9	1.7	2.0
Balance Sheet					
Debt-Equity ratio (Total Loans/Eff. Net worth) (per cent)	67.1	48.5	21.4	21.7	22.4
Current ratio (Current assets/Current liabilities(x)	4.5	4.3	4.1	3.4	3.4
Capital Output Ratio (Inc. from Ops./Eff Capital employed) (x)	0.5	0.5	0.5	0.4	0.6
Fixed assest Turnover (Inc. from Ops/Fixed Assets) (x)	2.9	2.9	3.1	3.1	7.5
Cash and cash equivalents/ Total Eff. Capital Employed (per cent)	8.9	5.6	4.0	5.2	4.9
RONW (PAT/Eff. Networth) (per cent)	15.4	14.5	13.3	12.8	10.1
ROCE (PBIT/Eff. Capital Employed) (x)	17.1	18.4	17.0	15.2	11.3
Per Share Data					
Revenue per share (₹)	28.00	31.2	32.9	33.4	41.7
Dividend per share (₹)	0.55	0.55	1.00	1.00	1.00
Indebtedness per share (₹)	20.6	17.3	11.4	12.9	11.6
Book value per share (₹)	30.7	35.7	53.6	59.4	51.6

Year Ending 31 March	*2002*	*2003*	*2004*	*2005*	*2006*
Earnings per share (after prior period adjustments) (₹)	4.3	5.1	7.2	7.6	5.2
Price/EPS Ratio (Share price as of 31 March)	38.9	12.2	18.6	18.3	45.9

Source: Compiled by the author from Annual Reports 2002–2006

Debt equity ratio, which was considerably higher as on 31 March 2002, at 67.10 has come down to 22.4 as on 31 March 2006 showing less dependency on outside funds. Current ratio of the company has been in a comfortable position all through this period. Fixed asset ratio, which was very low at 2.9 in the beginning, improved to 7.5 in FY 2005–06, showing increase in sales level with respect to capital assets. The return on capital employed was 17.1 in FY 2001–02, decreased to 11 in FY 2005–06. All these ratios shows good return on capital employed, which and seem to be the best and most comparable in the industry. Company declared dividend in all these years to reward its shareholders being financial partners of the company.book value of share of company shows increasing trend.

IN A NUTSHELL

This period of Zee was significant for the company, as well as for the industry as a whole. Aware of the then prevailing business conditions, the company focused on bringing about structural changes in the business by strengthening distribution and building an integrated team, improving the quality of products, offerings and earnings and improving corporate governance and financial transparency. Chandra himself was committed to bringing in the best technology for his company, with DTH and CAS services sweetening the pot.

Zee's strength always lay in the fact that it knew exactly what its customers wanted and tailor-made it for them. The need for an Indianised coterie of film channels, arranged genre-wise, would have been attractive to the public. And so, Chandra gave it to them, by finding Zee's special niche in this activity. The company came to be known for its sensitivity and inclusivity of all regional languages and areas. Also sensitive to the emerging sway of the youth on almost all market products, Zee began focusing its energies on relevant themes such as sports, even going so far as to renovate its channel tag for the modern sensibility of the young consumer. Initiatives such as Zee Trendz, with a focus on new markets like lifestyle, were also markers of the company's attempt to 'appear youthful' and in sync with the modernized Indian consumer.

A game-changer phase for Zee, 2006 was extremely important for the group in their scheme of things. Their growth across different sectors of the industry was reliant upon the decision of demerging the company into four segments. In a way, the compartmentalization of Zee in this manner created an opportunity for its leaders to manage the company better. This division ensured that each department had its job cut out for it, thereby enabling a higher potential for positive output.

Thus, in this phase of the growth of ZTL, the company focused on its strategic intent enunciation and used the modern strategic management practices of product development and diversification, organizational restructuring, mergers and acquisitions, technology-based decisions, branding and marketing techniques, manpower management and financial management.

5

NEWS BETWEEN THE NOISE: JOURNEYING FROM ZNL TO ZMCL

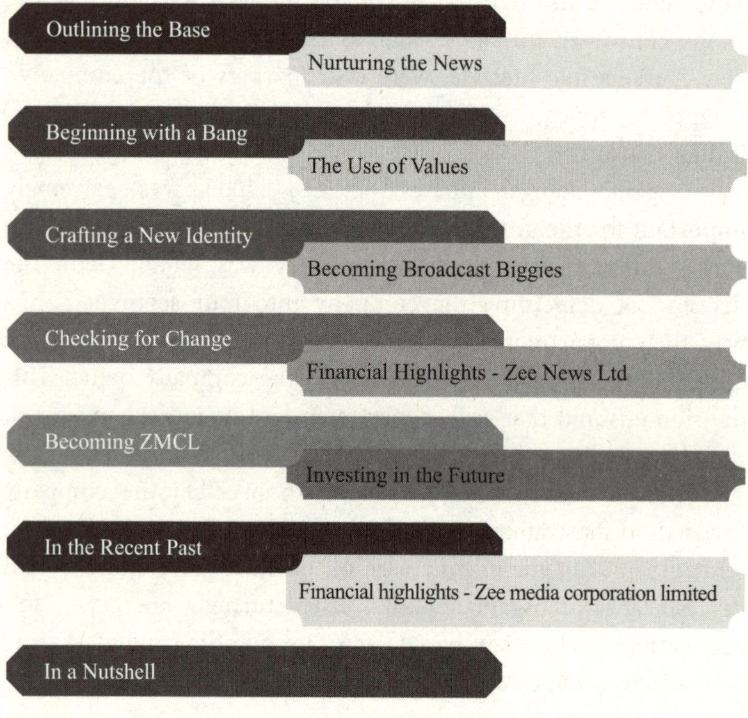

Fig 5.1: Chapter Insights

'News... a phenomenon that is continuous, global and all pervasive. What is the latest news one minute is stale the next. What is big news for one can be a trivial for the other. Local and global, scientific

and superstitious, serious and funny, path-breaking and banal... news keeps happening all the time. The challenge lies in capturing it at the right time, in the right context and with responsibility.'

—ZNL Annual Report 2006–2007

TIMELINE 5

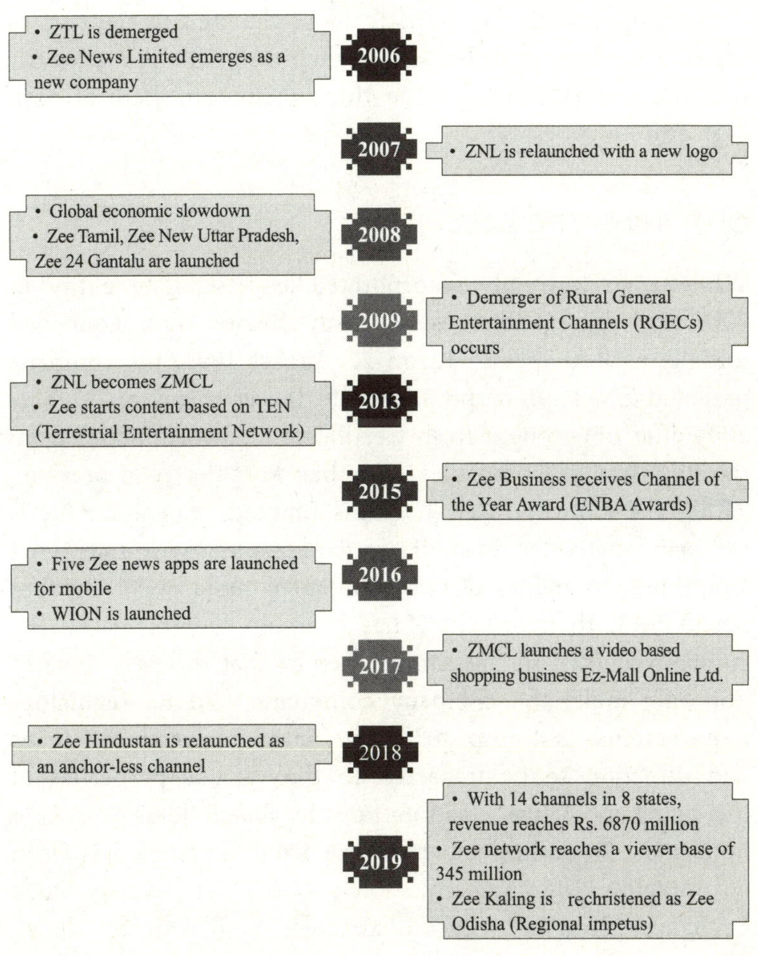

Source: Compiled by the author with inputs from ZEE

Following the demerger in 2006, a separate news segment identified as Zee News Limited (ZNL) began operating within the Essel Group. With an army of sister news channels alongside the flagship forerunner Zee News, ZNL boasted of an impressive coterie that made up its offering. Seven years hence, the company took on new dimensions as Zee Media Corporation Limited (ZMCL). With over 345 million viewers consuming multilingual news from 14 channels in eight states today, ZMCL is a resplendent branch-out. This is not to say that the company hasn't been through its fair share of both high and low tides.

OUTLINING THE BASE

While ZNL was only incorporated as a separate entity in 2006, its aggregations existed way before that. Launched initially as Zee Sports Ltd on 27 August 1999, the company predated ZNL's reincorporation into the company on 27 May 2004 after obtaining a fresh Certificate of Incorporation from the Registrar of Companies, Mumbai. Post the 2006 breakup, ZEEL, the erstwhile Zee Telefilms Limited, transferred news gathering activities to ZNL in compliance with the News Uplinking Guidelines of Government of India, w.e.f. October 2005. From then on, there has been no looking back. The company quoted in the Annual Report that this was done to not only make the company compliant with all regulatory requirements, but also to enable clear management focus and direction to be imparted to the various properties of the company. Value creation for the shareholders was kept uppermost in mind. The response from investors has been encouraging. The company soon got listed at Bombay Stock Exchange, National Stock Exchange and Calcutta Stock Exchange where the shares of the company were traded.

In its mission, Zee News claimed to strive to be the channel for the broadcasters and not for campaigners with a political philosophy, for personal likes or dislikes, for any business interests, for any compromise on the merit of news, or for anyone with scores to settle. News is one product that keeps evolving everyday and Zee News continues to change everyday, sensibly and sensitively handling this important product. 'ZNL consists of news channels and major regional channels of erstwhile Zee Telefilms limited. This bouquet covers the concerns and issues as well as the rich culture, heritage and language of various regions,' says B.V. Rao[58], the then group editor of ZNL in an interview.

Today, channels that operate under ZMCL are as follows: four national news channels (Zee News, Zee Hindustan, Zee Business, Zee Salaam); one global channel (WION); eight regional language news channels [Zee 24 Taas (Marathi), Zee Punjab Haryana Himachal (Punjabi), Zee Madhya Pradesh Chattisgarh (Hindi), Zee Rajasthan (Hindi), Zee Odisha (Odiya), Zee Bihar Jharkhand (Hindi), Zee 24 Kalak (Gujarati) and Zee Uttar Pradesh Uttarakhand (Hindi)]; and a Bangla news channel (Zee 24 Ghanta operated through Zee Akaash News Pvt. Ltd). The news channels today touch more than 119 million viewers.

ZMCL, under its digital umbrella, boasts of the following names: zeenews.com, wionews.com, and dnaindia.com.

MANAGEMENT AND EDITORIAL STRUCTURES

The management and editorial structures of ZNL in the year 2007 are reflected in the diagrams below. The management had a CEO, a group editor, director and sales department. The editorial structure also had input head, output head, bureau chief, correspondents and producers. From 1991–1996, there were no input and output heads. These posts were created in late 1997–early 1998 owing to the telecast of back-to-back bulletins, as per Mimansa Malik, senior news anchor, Zee News. As the operations of the channels increased, more posts were created. Earlier there used to be five editors and no group editor or editor-in-chief positions, which were introduced later. Besides, the emphasis was more on a flatter hierarchical structure than creating too many rungs, leading to loss of response time. According to the then editor, Satish Kumar, all the employees were so efficient that they understood the convergence in their job responsibilities. 'Here at Zee News, the employees work as a team and hierarchy is more horizontal than vertical' said most of the interviewed correspondents and deputy executive producers. 'There is a lot of freedom to work. It is not a 9-5 job but the employee is free to do any amount of work,' says an employee who works as an assignment incharge. 'At the same time, people understand their responsibilities'.

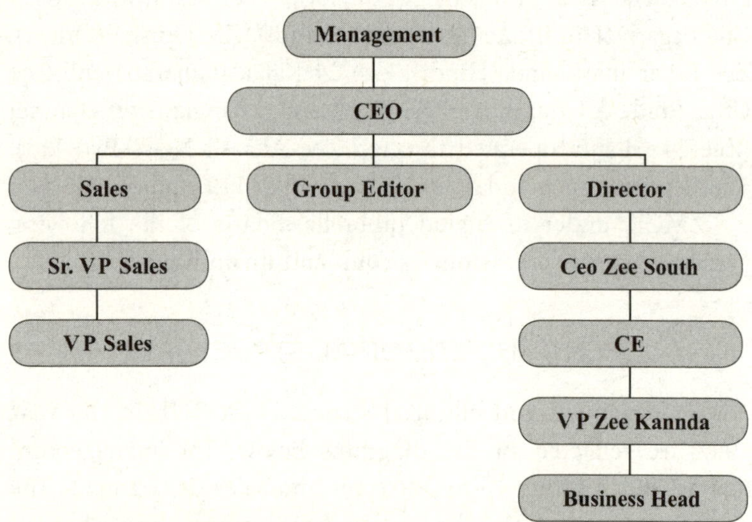

Fig. 5.2: Leadership Structure of ZNL in 2008

Source: Compiled by the author with inputs from Zee officials

According to official sources, there are 12 bureaus covering major areas like Lucknow, Mumbai, Ahmedabad, Indore, Bangalore, Noida, Bhopal, Srinagar and Jammu. These bureaus have around 225 correspondents and around 200–250 stringers. Current Board of Directors of ZMCL include Surender Singh, Amitabh Kumar, Uma Mandavgane, Raj Kumar Gupta, Rashmi Aggarwal and Dinesh Kumar Garg.

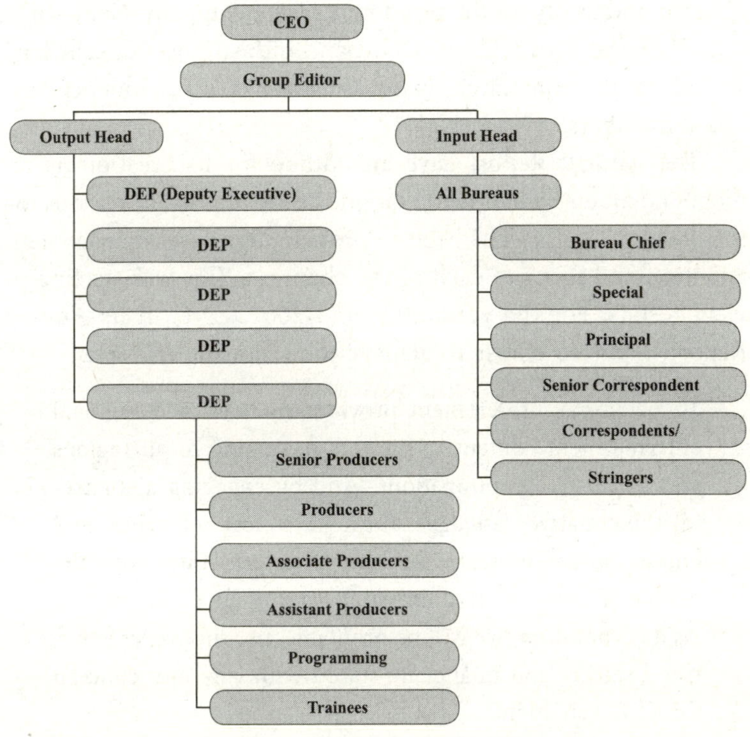

Fig. 5.3: Organizational Structiure of ZNL in 2008

Source: Compiled by the author with inputs from Zee officials.

NURTURING THE NEWS

ZNL, with its focus on reaching out to audiences across India through a complementary combination of news and regional entertainment, was uniquely positioned to ride the economic boom that India was experiencing. It had a strong leadership right at the outset. Subhash Chandra led the company as the chairman, while Laxmi Narain Goel served as the managing director and as one of the promoters of the company. Names like K.U. Rao, the then CEO of DNA, and industrialist Naresh Bajaj served on the company's board as Non-Executive Independent board members.

The Annual Report gave an outline for its creation as an independent entity and read that one of the important reasons for the creation of ZNL has been to provide high-level management attention and focus to each of the channels. This was starting to yield results. For the years 2006 and 2007, ZNL, in its Annual Report, reported efforts to achieve the following mission:

> To be India's pre-eminent provider of news and regional entertainment content to viewers belonging to all regions and linguistic denominations. And by engaging audiences in their native language through a mix of news and entertainment to truly 'Inform. Entertain. Empower' the people of India and in doing so provide value to advertisers. As a corporation, we will be profitable, productive, creative, trend setting and financially sound with care and concern for all stakeholders.

Subhash Chandra predicted that news and regional entertainment would be among the fastest growing segments in this industry. The company was in the possession of powerful, genre-leading properties and is uniquely poised to make the future count. The then managing director of ZNL, Laxmi N. Goel, also expressed belief in the 'Zee heritage', pinning future success at the 9 per cent upward growth that the Indian economy had seen that year.

BEGINNING WITH A BANG

When the company began as a demerged entity, it comprised of a total of 10 channels: Zee News, Zee Business, Zee 24 Taas, Zee Punjabi, Zee Bangla, Zee Gujarati, Zee Marathi, Zee Telugu, Zee Kannada and 24 Ghanta. Zee News was the oldest channel of the bouquet and reached millions of viewers in five continents, with a rich legacy of incisive news reporting and presentation. It was the first 24-hour Hindi current affairs and news channel in the country and broadcast tailored programming for varied viewer tastes. It had been consistently winning awards for programming and marketing activities.

India's first Hindi business channel, Zee Business redefined business news viewership in India by its aggressive programming, with a long-term mission of making business news relevant and accessible to a mass Hindi audience. Its weekend programming had been the first ever in any business channel. It was awarded the 'Best Business Channel' award at the Consumer World Awards for two years in a row.

Zee Marathi was the premium Marathi channel in Maharashtra with its different genre of programmes like daily soaps, game shows, talk shows, cookery, travel shows, films, etc. It had many significant initiatives to its credit like the Zee Gaurav Puraskar Awards and the Zee Marathi Awards. Positioned as a complete Punjabi family entertainment channel, Zee Punjabi was the only Punjabi channel available in the country. It offered entertainment across all genres including religious programmes, astrology shows, soaps, songs, comedy, etc. throughout the day.

Positioned as a wholesome entertainment channel for Gujaratis in 22 nations across the globe, Zee Gujarati provided a platform for culture preservation and promotion. Its contemporary programming included current affairs/news and festival-centric programmes. It provided a forum for local talent in literature, art, music, dance, theatre and handicrafts.

Zee Telugu catered to the discerning Telugu viewers and served a judicious programming mix along with innovative, original concepts and high-quality production. Creative ideas, constant innovation and a feel for popular taste helped the channel to usher in a radical change in viewership patterns.

Zee Bangla enjoyed maximum recall amongst the Bangla community in West Bengal and other regions. Positioned as the leading GEC, it aimed to deliver some of the finest programmes across genres: soaps, game shows, reality shows, talent hunts, stand-up comedies, musicals et al and enjoyed an unparalleled market share during prime time. Consistent offering laced with innovation was the keynote of the channel. Zee Kannada successfully completed its year of presenting unique entertaining and innovative programmes. It created a record of sorts with an overall viewership increase of 103 per cent. The channel captured the moods, sentiments and aspirations of Kannadigas with high quality programming and production.

The year 2006–2007 had seen the launch of India's first 24-hour Marathi News channel named 'Zee 24 Taas'. ZNL had acquired a 60 per cent stake in Zee Akash News Private Limited, which operated 24 Ghanta, a Bangla news channel, that recorded remarkable share gains. It covered a rich content of accurate and authentic information on politics, education, sports, business and Bengal's multifaceted cultural life. The emphasis was on accuracy, authenticity, speed, innovation, bold exposes and incisive analysis. Some of its major programmes were *Tarokar Mukhomukhi* (Celebrity Chat Show), *8ta Theke 9ta* (News Bulletin with Analysis), *Reporter Jennie* (Children's News Show), *Apnar Raay* (Celeb Talk Show of Social Nature), *Showbiz 24* (Bollywood

News Show) and *Spotlight* (Biographical Show).

Zee 24 Taas was also launched in February 2007 as a 24-hour Marathi news channel with special emphasis on local news, national outlook and international look. It covered all areas of society, offering news and insight into every aspect of life from police to politics and entertainment to economy. Some of its notable shows were *Chaska Maska* (Marathi Theatre and Bollywood News), *Adhorekhit* (News Bulletin with Analysis), *Zee 24 Taas Vishesh* (Topical Show), and *Aajcha Maharashtra* (News Bulletin). Vijay Kuvalekar, former editor in chief, elaborated on the varied intent of the channel, and the company's efforts towards regionalization. 'I can say it's a family news channel, because we don't show anything which the family cannot see. They can watch this channel sitting together, across age groups. Secondly, we cover all sections and not only politics. We focus on science and technology, for instance; we don't have cookery shows, but that is not the point. We try and are a little more serious in dealing with the topics. For instance, we run a serial on villages, which have solved their own water problems. There are many villages including Ralegan Siddhi. We focus on constructive journalism. Our editorial policy is that we support all nation-related news, we are non-aligned to any political party, we are factual, objective and pro-society, not pro-leaders.'[59]

The channel is multi-faceted. He explained, 'We started a programme called Sukhavarta—which means Positive News. Everyday, we give one positive news in the bulletins, so from Monday to Friday you get five bulletins, and these are packaged as a half-an-hour programme on Saturday and Sunday. Then we have a half-an-hour bulletin for science and technology, we have also started a programme Asha Udyachya—which means Hopes for Tomorrow. We have also started a new weekly newspaper called *Zee Marathi Disha*, that is doing very well.'[60] Punit Goenka explained the need for a print venture for the promoter group, 'We have entered the Marathi space in print because we felt that our dominance in the Marathi market needed us to come out with another media for us to cross sell.'[61]

Elaborating on the functional processes of the channel, Kuvalekar continued, 'What we have done recently, over the last 3–4 months, is that we have established an Integrated Media Newsroom and all ideas are put together. So if tomorrow I have some specific stories, they are given to IMN and then IMN circulates it to all the editions. Then each editor goes through it. It's like this—each channel has its own network. In Delhi, we have created a separate IMN cell, wherein there would be 1–2 people depending on the size of the regional channel. So that team will exchange ideas, stories with the concerned person, who will communicate and coordinate with the concerned regional channel. Suppose I want some story from Zee Punjab or Zee Hindustan, the person who is taking care of our interest and our regional channel in Delhi in IMN, he will tell them that this is the story and we want it. Then he will have a co-ordination with the output and input editors over there and get it. And vice-versa, where they want some story from us, they will get it from us.'[62]

During its first FY of operation as an independent entity, the owners of ZNL claimed that the company 'performed creditably'. The regional entertainment portfolio of the company was unmatched in terms of reach and performance. According to the Annual Report 2006-07, the highlight of the year was the sterling performance of "Zee Marathi" and "Zee Bangla", while Zee News continues to enjoy stable viewership. Zee Gujarati and Zee Punjabi have a loyal following in their respective markets. Zee Telugu is making its mark in Andhra Pradesh while Zee Kannada, launched in 2006–07, is steadily establishing itself in Karnataka in highly competitive but potentially lucrative markets.

For distribution, the company had an arrangement with Zee Turner Ltd to distribute its pay channels bouquet in India and neighbouring countries. Zee Turner was also assigned to distribute the company's bouquet of pay channels on DTH platforms. The company had an arrangement with Dish TV India Limited (one of the branchouts of the 2006 demerger, and formerly known as ASC Enterprises Limited, Asia Pacific's largest DTH company and part of Essel (Jawahar Lal Goel Group) for up-linking of its channels through their teleport.

Changes in editorial structure of ZNL also reflected the concerns mentioned in the Mission Statement. Self-admittedly, the company was well-equipped even during its first independent year. In terms of news-gathering, ZNL had the largest network of news bureaus and correspondents with a pan-India presence. The company's news-gathering capabilities were significantly enhanced by its KU Band network and strong relationships with international news agencies.

For programming, Zee used 'Velocity' software and 'Leech' as editing systems. For scripting and planning, a software called 'Octopus' was used. Zee started the concepts of phonoplate, header and split window in around 2002. The latest VT edit machine Vigartee was used. Zee had 18 OB vans and dot-com technology inter-linkages were in place. With specialized shows like *Tax Doctor, Property Plus,* and *Bazaar*, ZNL communicated to its audiences that it was a carrier of all things consequential, besides news. These shows strove to aid the public in making significant decisions for themselves. This was in keeping with the company's goal of providing a judicious blend of news, entertainment and infotainment.

However, ZNL did have some qualms about a few issues. It listed a number of risk factors, which could affect its operations negatively. Among the chief concerns was a projected lack of co-operation from local cable operators, poor implementation of measures like CAS, and hiccups caused by heavy regulations in the industry. While these were all futuristic predictions, it reflected ZNL's foresightedness and open-minded outlook towards worst-case scenarios, pointing towards a preparedness for these situations. The strategy it strived to move forward with, included the consolidation of current offerings with 360-degree monetization across platforms and markets. The channel bouquet was slated to be expanded, with a focus on building good shareholder value.

THE USE OF VALUES

The major focus of the company was now on developing unique content across genres, usage of technological advancements, investments in strategic markets and aggressive marketing and branding efforts. In keeping with these efforts, the company also laid stress upon developing human resources with the vision and skills to implement such a policy.

So, during 2006, as part of a group-wide exercise, ZNL engaged Hay Group, a reputed HR consulting firm, to undertake a Human Resource Transformation initiative in the organization. The objective of the exercise was to redesign the organization structure of the business befitting the company's vision and growth aspirations and establish robust HR processes within the structure, in order to realize the human capital. Corporate governance was one of the key strategies of the company, elaborated in Annual Report 2006–07 as follows:

> The company firmly believes that good governance is critical to sustaining corporate development, increasing productivity and competitiveness and creating shareholder wealth. The governance process should ensure that the available resources are utilized in a manner that meets the aspirations of all its stakeholders. Your company's

> essential charter is shaped by the objectives of transparency, professionalism and accountability. The company continuously endeavours to improve on these aspects on an ongoing basis.

In 2006, Chandra became a shareholder in United News of India. As reported by DNA, 'The Essel Group, promoted by Zee Telefilms chairman Subhash Chandra, is likely to join the board of news agency United News of India (UNI) as a major shareholder. The group has negotiated a deal through Mediawest, an investment vehicle, following which it will hold around 60 per cent of UNI, but group officials refused to comment on the figure.'[63] Between 2006 and 2007, the Indian M&E industry saw a healthy growth of 17 per cent. It grew from ₹190 billion to ₹226 billion in just one year. For Zee, subscription and advertising revenues were the major contributors to the upward trend the company witnessed. The year 2007 saw a relaunch and repositioning of Zee News, with a fresh logo and an even fresher vision. Going forward, ZNL was to rely on five chief values: customer focus, creativity, integrity, excellence, growth-driven. As mentioned in the ZNL Annual Report 2007-08, the Company's strategies were driven by the needs of the customer. Zee accorded a high premium to maintaining superlative standards throughout the company and encouraged the employees to come up with smarter ideas within the fastest possible time.

The company sensed that digitization was to be the new mantra of Indian TV distribution, with a widespread expansion of digital cable, DTH and IPTV. In its second year of operations after its listing as an independent entity, Zee News once again excelled in its performance. Total operating revenues increased by 52 per cent as compared to the previous year, resulting in a strong growth in PBT by a whopping 270 per cent. In 2007, the company also put out an aim to launch a global English news channel by 2010.

The flagship channel Zee News was almost unaffected by the entry of new players in the already overcrowded genre in 2007. Amongst the news channels, 24 Taas and Zee Gantalu continued to hold on to their leading position, while Zee Telugu, Zee Kannada and 24 Ghanta further consolidated their positions in their respective markets.

Table 10
Global Reach

Regions	*2003–04*	*2004–05*	*2005–06*	*2006–07*
Americas (Canada, Caribbean, USA)	317,000	376,000	467,000	550,000
Europe	166,000	168,000	168,000	300,000
Africa and Middle East	198,000	223,000	299,000	935,000
Asia-Pacific	target India: >40,000,000 rest of Asia: 230,000	target India: >610,000,000 rest of Asia: 224,000	target India: 680,000,000 rest of Asia : 242,000	3.7 million

Source: Annual Reports

CRAFTING A NEW IDENTITY

The world was hit by an economic slowdown between 2007 and 2008. Despite the shortcomings in revenue generation during this year, ZNL claimed overall positive growth. The regional growth during 2007 was, as usual, immense. The company recorded greater geographical penetration, especially in the Southern markets.

Zee News continued delivering higher revenues quarter by quarter, thus demonstrating its distinct and steady positioning as a serious and responsible news channel. Putting an end to apprehensions regarding the southern expansion, "Zee Telugu" and "Zee Kannada" registered record GRP increase. Both "Zee Marathi" and "Zee Bangla" were at their innovative best and created a class of their own by emerging as market leaders in their respective genres. The first 24-hour Marathi News channels "Zee 24 Taas" consolidated its position. The regional markets continued to grow at double-digit rates. The subsidiary operated channel "24 Ghanta" which reached close to breaking even in a record 24 months demonstrated the Company's financial prudence and determination to create value for the shareholders.'

Zee News went in for a major change in May 2008 with a new tagline—'Zara Sochiye'. The major shows that defined its new identity included *Badi Khabhar* (Sansui TV Awards 2006–07 for the Best Current Affairs programme) *Jago India, The Inside Story* and *Prime Time*. B.V. Rao, the then group editor of Zee News, in an interview with the author, revealed that news was a major casualty on news channels. In his words, 'Here at Zee News, we have changed back to NEWS'. With the new tagline, Zee News has focused on hard and relevant news. The basic idea for this, he believes, is 'you think and we also think for you'. Alka Saxena, a consulting editor and newsreader on Zee News, also supported the statement and said that in the mad race for TRPs, the channel had been more focused on infotainment. But now, she said, it has taken a U-turn towards serious news and TRPs have become second priority. She added that, with a lot of back-end support, Zee News could afford to do that and come back to hard news, which others couldn't. According to her, this helped a great deal in establishing credibility and brand value. 'Though our TRPs suffered initially, but we are not going to show any trash. Only pure news will be broadcasted'.

Satish K. Singh, the editor of Zee News, also briefed, 'We understand that the news media is very impactful and it is becoming very encompassing and has a great role to play in society. News to us is relevant and serious business; we do not believe in trivializing news. Sensible and credible news is a catalyst for positive change and we are trying hard for it.'[64] According to Sarjana[65], deputy executive producer in Zee News, 'We try to follow six minute rigid news at any cost. As far as news selection is concerned, there are a lot of meetings and discussions and the Bureau Chief suggests [an] appropriate angle to the story. He gives the practical mission statement and then the correspondents follow it.' She also informed that despite pressures, the management never interfered with their work. Talking to Mimansa Malik, another newsreader with Zee News, highlighted the criteria of news selection. She told the author, 'Two to three years back we had lots of entertainment and crime shows on the channel. But now, there are noticeable changes with regard to news selection. TRPs are not to be all in all for Zee News; there are so many perceptible changes. There was a high skew on Bollywood news, but now it is limited'.[66]

Though most interviewees accepted the fact that Zee News did produce some good content in the race for TRPs, there are some who also put emphasis on its 'changed view'. With TRPs still remaining the dominant factor at the end of the day, channels do jump the gun on many occasions. Along that line, Lynn de Souza, group director, Media Services, Lintas, remarks, 'News channels have to go beyond gossip and tackle the real issues—the country is full of issues. Niche channels are the only ones that are thinking smart to capture audiences and client spends. But, they need to do so for the sake of survival.'

BECOMING BROADCAST BIGGIES

Since ZNL had now cracked the code to expansion with a focus on regional product development, it communicated the reason behind this idea. Explaining the insistence of spreading regionally, it mentioned in its Annual Report, 'The regional entertainment genre is a nascent vertical. Given the regional diversity in language, culture and literature in India, there exists exponential growth potential of media consumption in local languages. This is reflected in the rapid proliferation and growing viewership of regional media. Increasing advertisers' preference in regional media justifies the consuming potential of regional media audience. ZNL with its current presence in most of the major language differentiated markets in the country is well-positioned to leverage the opportunity present in this diversity.'[67]

It developed its news bouquet even further, with the purpose to bring 'back the focus on hard news amidst wide-spread trivialization of news that the genre is witnessing.' Also effective 1 August 2008, Zee Talkies, a 24-hour Marathi movie channel, was transferred to the ZNL stable. There was an increase in digital subscriptions for the network, with this segment forming 34 per cent of the total subscription revenue. Moreover, all the channels witnessed a viewership share increase from 4.9 per cent of the previous year to 5.5 per cent.

ZNL also clinched a strategic partnership with Akaash Bangla channel, with a right to acquire 26 per cent equity. Subhash Chandra, explained the company intent behind this decision, 'and said that the recent strategic partnership with Akaash Bangla, a premier Bengali GEC brand, highlights their intention to grow through inorganic growth strategies as well, whenever such suitable opportunity arises.'

All this regionalization was proving to be fruitful for the company. Brajesh Kumar, Zee Business, said, 'It is very dynamic in strategy. When there was no scope for regional channels, they experimented. Some were not successful, but were stronger than their pioneer brand Zee News.'[68] However, the turnaround story of the year' was the growth of Zee Business. It rose from an average channel share of 13 per cent to a share of 25 per cent in the business channel genre. Moreover, according to official reports, Zee 24 Taas and 24 Ghanta came out with their best performance in all these years. The success of south Indian channels Zee Telugu and Zee Kannada has made ZNL a name to reckon with in the southern part of the country as well.

Laxmi N. Goel also expressed confidence in the company's re-evaluation of all its investments and expenditure plans', while saying that there would be 'greater focus on controlling costs and improving efficiencies. Sudhir Chaudhary, current editor-in-chief of Zee News, had his own views about the editorial and management policy. He said, 'Editorial and sales-marketing should never be mixed. They are two verticals and should be treated as such.'[69]

Also, there was a magnified focus on the company's CSR activities. With a view to make maximum social contribution, ZNL took various measures. It adopted schools and villages in tribal areas through Ekal Vidyalaya Foundation, an NGO that works to bring about basic literacy and health awareness amongst the tribal people. The Essel Group also supported the Global Vipassana Foundation and helped to propagate Vipassana, the non-sectarian, rational process of self-purification with the aim of bringing about peace. It also supported the Global Foundation for Civilizational Harmony, a body which aims to create a peaceful and harmonious society by resolving disputes.

ZNL, always sensitive to its customers' needs as well as its own, had set down some future perspectives, functional after the 2008 FY. L.N. Goel elaborated, 'Despite being favourably placed and having profitable operations, our company has done a critical re-evaluation of all its investments and expenditure plans. We have taken necessary steps to create a leaner and more focused organization. There is much greater focus on controlling costs and improving efficiencies across various disciplines. I am confident that ZNL will firmly establish itself as one of India's most successful and admired media companies in the years to come.'

CHECKING FOR CHANGE

As the world economy began to slowly but surely come out of the Great Recession, financial year 2009–10 proved to be one of the most eventful years for ZNL. The company continued with its strong performance in this fiscal, backed by a number of strong channels in its bouquet. To diversify and de-risk the business and lower the dependency on ads as the main revenue source, ZNL was in the process of entering the consultancy business for offering News Consultancy Services. This operation got completed in 2009, and thereby, the company announced a franchisee channel by the name of Zee 24 Ghante Chattisgarh. In April, ZNL launched Zee News Uttar Pradesh, a 24/7 Hindi news channel for the Uttar Pradesh and Uttarakhand markets, and Zee 24 Gantalu, a 24/7 Telugu news channel. 'While on one hand, the company strategically expanded its presence, on the other hand, the channels which were not likely to make profit in the near future were critically reviewed. Zee Gujarati was put off-air with effect from 31 May 2009.'

The year 2009 was a year of organizational restructuring for the company. It was to do with the demerger process of the Rural General Entertainment Channels (R-GECs), effectively concluded in March 2010. This move would considerably improve shareholders value and allow ZNL to focus on its main news area of business. Post the demerger, ZNL remained with eight 24/7 news channels, namely Zee News, Zee Business, Zee 24 Taas, Zee News UP, Zee 24 Gantalu, Zee Punjabi, Zee Tamizh, and 24 Ghanta. With the six Regional General Entertainment Channels viz., Zee Marathi, Zee Talkies, Zee Bangla, Zee Telugu,

Zee Kannada and Zee Cinemalu, getting transferred to Zee Entertainment Enterprises Limited, ZNL would now focus solely on its news-based operations.

This was the year ZNL began expressing its interest in being labeled as a 'news powerhouse', as mentioned by Subhash Chandra himself. He said, 'Having already built a nationwide news network and riding on our spectacular performance of news operations despite recession, it was a natural strategy for us to move towards creating a sensible and respectable News Powerhouse in the country. The growth potential of regional television as well as rapidly spreading digitalization would significantly fuel our endeavor.'[70] With an increase in 'literacy, consumption and disposable incomes in Tier 2 and 3 cities', this seemed like a possible dream to achieve. Their news shows and bulletins like *Nonstop@9, Badi Khabar*, *Zara Sochiye* and *Mera Ghar Meri Jeb* continued to enjoy success among its viewers, as the company leaders claimed that the time spent watching Zee had also recorded visible growth. The digital dream offered hope, after Media Partners Asia reported that India was slated to become the largest DTH market in the world, as regards subscriber numbers.

Zee News gained increased viewership share, and Zee Business continued with its supremacy during the stock market time band. During the year, Zee 24 Taas was relaunched with a completely new look and feel. It was leading the pack in Mumbai.'

Post the 2010 demerger, 2011 was the company's first year of operations as a pure news broadcaster, and the company was overjoyed to report an all-round growth across revenues, profits, reach and goodwill.

While regional channels registered stupendous returns, the company made use of brand activation to maximize its profits. At the regional level again, ZNL introduced the concept of award functions to gain visibility. The concept of 'Parishramika

Puraskaralu 2010' was initiated in Andhra Pradesh, to award deserving businessmen and industrialists. Other awards included India's Best Market Analyst Award, ASPIRE, Money Matters for Women, etc. Another innovation was Aapla Shahar Aapla Awaaz, a Marathi channel initiative which offered a platform to the common citizen for voicing their opinions and debating on issues.

Once again, ZNL initiated public service activities during the year, spearheaded by their flagship Ananya Samman—an endeavour to honour the real heroes of our country, including farmers and doctors. Another environmental campaign 'My Earth My Duty', appreciated by United Nations, was one of the largest climate awareness campaigns under which trees were planted across India. The nation's largest voter awareness initiative 'Apka Vote Apki Taqat' also created an impact in the states where elections took place. During the course of this year, ZNL however had to shut down Zee Tamil, following the dysfunction of said channel that was incurring repeated losses.

Subhash Chandra, proud of the focused hard news his channels were broadcasting, said, 'I am glad to share with you that ZNL has not only been living up to the expectation (people have) from the fourth estate but also creating industry benchmark through its prudent, responsible and sensible journalism.' During this time, ZNL emerged as India's largest news organization and the No.1 news network in terms of share in the news category. This could be credited in part to its continued regional projects. ZNL in its report mentioned, 'The biggest advantage of the television medium is that it has the power to transcend the socio-economic barriers and create an indelible impact. ZNL is the first news broadcaster to unearth the power of speaking to people in their own language. Our excellence in the regional sector comes from the fact that we lead the viewership tally in most of the markets we operate in.'[71]

FY 2010–11 was a 'news content-friendly year' for ZNL, with issues like the CWG scam, Ayodhya verdict, Delhi floods, etc. which caught the attention of viewers. This led to a 7 per cent increase in GRPs for Hindi news as compared to the previous year. To traverse the roads forward, ZNL had some good ideas, as enunciated by Punit Goenka. He mentioned a commitment to content-focused approach, better monetization of subscription revenues, and cost optimization. In an interview conducted with the author in 2018, he quoted on behalf of the promoter group, 'To keep abreast with evolving customer preferences, we need to target aggressive content delivery strategies. We will also have to align our business with technology breakthroughs and keep pace with the latest trends and technologies like HD, mobility, 3G, convergence, etc.' There was also a focus on 'building scale across the media value chain and exploring cross-media synergies', with several new partnerships. Zee Turner Ltd entered into a joint venture with Star Den Media Service Pvt. Ltd. The new company thus formed, called Media Pro Enterprise India Pvt. Ltd, would curb anomalies and piracy in the sector, and offer better digitization. Offerings like Zee Business were traversing pioneering paths with initiatives like Aspire Campaign and a Distance Learning B-School survey, which were the first of its kind undertaken by a media company.[72]

In 2011, ZNL recorded minimized business losses, which reduced from the previous year's ₹442.7 million to ₹227.4 million. Advertising revenues also grew by 2.2 per cent. All these positive returns painted a rosy picture for the company's profit chart.

Absolute digitization appeared to be on the rise. Punit Goenka commented on the impact this would have on the business of Zee News. He opined that emergence of private broadcasters in India, some three decades ago, was a breakthrough event in the history of independent India. Since then, television has made significant contribution in shaping up generations in this country. Digitization is the beginning of a new era for Indian television, wherein it will transform itself. This move will help the industry discover an organized and transparent way of working in an integrated ecosystem.

ZNL has always maintained its focus on multiple revenue sources and now it is expected that digitization shall translate into growth multiplier in subscription revenues. This, in turn, strengthens the financial position further and enable ZNL to pursue newer avenues of growth, organic as well as inorganic. With all the genres and channels being available equally, content differentiation would be the king.

Providing tangibility for ZNL's positive outlook towards digitization, their numbers also reflected well in this aspect. Zeenews.com—the mother site in English—was the fastest growing news website in India as per Comscore direct and Google Analytics. Regional websites for Zee 24 Taas and 24 Ghanta were also launched during the year in addition to the inauguration of the Hindi website. Zee 24 Gantalu and Zee Punjabi executed various events like Spoorthi (woman entrepreneur awards) and Anhad Samman (Ananya Samman) respectively, to honour the key contributors to the social and economical progress of these states. Under the Ananya Samman banner, the brand was extended to honour doctors through Swasth Bharat Samman, industrialists through Udyami Samman in Uttar Pradesh and Andhra Pradesh and farmers through Agri Awards. Over 100-odd revenue-generating events were conducted to connect with viewers and enhance brand imagery.

Subhash Chandra commented on his company's growth during the FY 2011–12 while making a new pitch for the age-old Zee value system: 'Encouraging performances like these, that too in difficult economic environment, further strengthens our belief in 'Viewer First' approach. Keeping in line with our philosophy, April 2012 onwards we have reduced our inventory significantly to live up to the consumer's interest. It is a strategic decision, which should pay rich dividend in the digitized era. Such initiatives help us foster deeper engagements with our viewers and in turn enable us to deliver quality returns to our advertisers.'[73]

In 2012, ZNL managed to reach a count of over 100 million viewers across regions and languages. Zee News, in its quest to initiate purposeful change in the country, reinvented its brand philosophy from 'Jazba Soch Ka' to 'Soch Badlo, Desh Badlo' with an objective to engage viewers in the process of positive transformation. It charted out an expansion plan in line with its vision 'To be the most respected and relevant news organization in India and the world, that connects with every conceivable community and stakeholders across platforms'.

Another Hindi news and infotainment channel for central India, by the name Zee Madhya Pradesh/Chhattisgarh, was launched, taking the ZNL bouquet of channels to eight—two national and six regional. The channel struck the right chord with its viewers within a short span of its launch. It showed tremendous scope for the thought of initiating a hybrid content of news, views analysis and features which reflect and represent the varied interests of the people of Central India.

The company sharpened its strategic edge by creating synergistic tie-ups with the group's print (DNA) and digital (india.com) businesses to provide a competitive advantage through integrated content delivery to young consumers. Considering the business synergies in print and electronic media business, the company board accorded its in-principle approval for the combination of print media business of the Group 'DNA' and the news broadcasting business of the group. An environment scan of the market during that time revealed that while traditional media like TV and print contributed the highest to media revenues, the rise of new media was creating quite a buzz. Zeenews.com continued to be the fastest growing website in the Indian news web space second year in a row. The website received 70.2 million unique visitors and 310.1 million page views.[74]

ZNL took a significant step during the year of reducing the inventory of the flagship channel, Zee News, in order to improve the viewer experience, increase the yield of the channel as well as prepare for the upcoming curbs for advertisement inventory. Events and special properties continued to be the cornerstone of the company's advertisement revenue growth strategy on the back of the Ananya Samman scheme and its likes.

All through 2012, ZNL continued to churn out a number of path-breaking editorial and marketing initiatives. These initiatives engaged with the audiences and reinforced the perception of the network being relevant and connected with the viewer on the issues affecting them. During the year, Zee News bagged the National Award from the Election Commission of India for its campaign—Aapka Vote, Aapki Taqat—that called on all voters to participate in the electoral process. Zee News also created public awareness on the importance of conservation of clean water through Saaf Paani Swasth Bharat campaign, a 2,525 km-long water rafting expedition, the longest in India, with support from Indo Tibetan Border Police. 24 Ghanta conducted the state summit to discuss the development and progress in West Bengal. For the Marathi demography, the channel rolled out a unique initiative—*Gao Tithe 24 Taas*—to connect with viewers in rural Maharashtra through on ground events and on-air programmes. It took up rural issues in the mainstream media and connected villages to their local representatives through this initiative.

Sudhir Chaudhary came on board Zee News for the second time in his timeline as a journalist in 2012. The editor-in-chief of Zee News, in an interview with the author, elucidated upon the functions and value of this news channel. In addition, he also described the conducive growth aura at Zee as 'very vibrant.'

He said, 'It helps one grow as a professional. It is very open towards the future, and has a very attractive brand value. One feels nice when they go out and tell people they are from Zee, whether nationally or internationally. These things make Zee very different. I am very happy with the kind of values and principles I have learnt here and the kind of work environment and relationship I enjoy with the promoter. What makes Zee different is the size of the portfolio and the kind of news service we are offering to people, ranging from regional to national to business news. You name it, we have it.'[75]

In answer to the changes he brought about in the strategic intent of the news group, he said he always strives to be 'pro people' and 'pro viewers'. Elaborating on his style of work, he said, 'I tried to bring in the larger picture. I always believe you are pro-system or anti-system. The system is bigger than the government; it involves the society. We are working on those goals, not on party lines.'[76] The same year, Zee group got embroiled in a controversy with Naveen Jindal, the steel magnate heading Jindal Steel and Power (JSPL). As reported by online media platform Newslaundry, 'In a complaint lodged in September 2012, the JSPL director, human resources, alleged that Zee News editor Chaudhary and Zee Business editor Ahluwalia attempted extortion to the tune of ₹100 crore from his company.'[77] The company on multiple occasions has denied this charge. Chandra and Chaudhary too have expressly claimed it to be a false case.

The footage left the audience of the Zee News segment divided. Chandra summed up the entire debacle in the penultimate chapter of his autobiography, titling it 'Stabbed in the Back'. In his justification, Chandra explains that this entire incident was part of a smear campaign initiated by Jindal over Zee News' reportage about the coal scam incident that had dragged JSPL's name out in the open.[78]

Recalling the incident, Chaudhary in an interview with the author, detailed his side of the story: 'That case was a false case. People tend to miss the legal angle of the case. In 2012, I was arrested. In 2013, a chargesheet was filed, following which the court rejected the chargesheet. They returned it, saying that the investigation was shoddy and told the police to reinvestigate the matter, and come up with a fresh chargesheet with relevant sections. From that time until now, the police have never come back with a chargesheet. It did not reach the court. Jindal later gave me in writing that no offence was committed, and whatever happened was a result of miscommunication.'[79]

In July 2018, Chandra and Jindal reached a truce which was publicly announced on social media, bringing an end to the six-year long legal battle between the two. Jindal withdrew his extortion case against Zee, a development that both parties tweeted about. Chandra wrote on Twitter, 'I am happy that JSPL and Naveen Jindal have withdrawn FIR alleging extortion with Delhi Police against Zee and its editors, similarly Zee has agreed to withdraw all complaints and cases against JSPL and Naveen Jindal. I wish Naveen very best in his life.'[80] Jindal also wrote, 'We have resolved all differences.'

A major change was stirring within the company during this time. ZNL in 2012 announced, 'As a part of future business strategy, with a view to meeting changing viewer preferences, ZNL has commenced the process of changing the content architecture of all its television channels, whereby, in addition to news, the channels of the company shall cover the entire gamut of the life of present and potential viewers. In line with this strategy, to reflect this wider gamut of media contents, in which the company proposes to transcend, a proposal for change of name of the company to Zee Media Corporation Limited has been sent to the members seeking their approval.'[81]

Table 11
Financial Highlights-ZNL (ZNL)-Standalone
(in millions)

Year Ending 31 March	*2007*	*2008*	*2009*	*2010*	*2011*	*2012*	*2013*
Total Income	2,488	3,596	5,250	5,262	2,430	2,733	2,667
Total Expenditure	2,224.36	2,903.80	4,247.42	4,213.73	2,165.79	2,330.82	2,418.10
Profit/ Loss before Tax	164.51	608.28	702.76	682.30	164.20	172.79	352.3
Profit/Loss after tax	99.42	373.03	445.60	439.65	97.79	61.99	243.0
Tax	65.09	235.25	257.16	242.65	66.40	110.79	109.3
Operating Profit	132.93	678.43	827.03	863.75	265.21	402.51	249.8
PBIDT	263.50	691.91	1,002.28	879.43	276.42	547.50	501.1
Dividend	nil	95.90	95.90	nil	nil	nil	nil
Advertising Revenue* broadcasting revenue	2,243*	3,506*	4,910*	4,966*	1,636	1,666	1,650
Total Assets and Equity and Liabilities	1,875.61	2,225.31	4,456.59	3,317.29	2,248.71	2,568.21	2,698.1
Income from Operations	2,357.30	3,582.23	5,074.46	5,077.48	2,431.01	2,733.34	-
Depreciation	47.85	78.22	88.85	104.78	92.39	101.41	106.9
Loans Funds	13.00	116.78	2,016.70	1,688.82	522.43	779.94	666.6
Financial Expenses	51.13	53.00	210.66	92.33	19.82	106.55	2,667.9
Investments	83.27	83.27	83.27	144.17	144.17	83.27	83.80

Source: Compiled by the author from ZNL Annual Reports 2007-2013

The above is the analysis of ZNL standalone data from FY 2006–07 to FY 2012–13. Income from operations increased from 2,357 million in FY 2007 to 5,077 million in FY 2010. However, it drastically come down to 2,431 million in FY 2011 and thereafter started increasing gradually. Due to drastic fall in sales in FY 2011, its net profits before tax as well as PAT came down sharply, for which reasons needs to be ascertained. The financials started improving from FY 2011–12.

Table 12
Financial Highlights-ZNL (ZNL)-Consolidated
FY 2006–07 to FY 2012–13 (in millions)

Year Ending 31 March	*2007*	*2008*	*2009*	*2010*	*2011*	*2012*	*2013*
Total Income	2,535.71	3,689.07	5,396.93	5,478.29	2,780.34	3,227.72	3,246.2
Total Expenditure	2,328.02	2,997.47	4,384.94	4,368.48	2,344.54	2,757.37	2,662.8
Profit/ Loss before Tax	104.44	601.43	706.10	736.16	319.15	303.60	422.0
Profit/Loss after tax	74.70	370.77	446.97	456.83	163.67	115.46	241.7
Tax	46.21	232.16	259.12	267.88	111.56	152.49	148.3
Operating Profit	77.09	677.64	836.36	924.38	423.95	533.54	583.4
PBIDT	207.68	691.59	1,011.98	1,109.81	435.79	689.03	583.5
Dividend	nil	96	96	nil	nil	nil	nil
Advertising Revenue	2,292	3,600	5,057	5,182	1,961	2,004	2,020
Total Assets and Equity and Liabilities	1,862.27	2,238.97	4,476.44	3,368.93	2,410.04	3,484.45	2,915.3
Income from Operations	2,405.12	3,675.12	5,221.31	5,292.86	2,768.49	3,072.22	3,038.2
Depreciation	520.96	847.55	951.92	112.27	276.79	112.09	119.5
Loans Funds	13.00	116.78	2,017.08	1,689.11	522.63	780.02	666.6
Financial Expenses	51.13	5.4	210.69	261.36	125.72	106.59	87.9
Investments	–	–	–	60.90	60.90	–	–

Source: Compiled by the author from ZNL Annual Reports 2007-2013

Income from operations increased from 2,405 million in FY 2007 to 5,293 million in FY 2010. However, it drastically came down to 2,768.49 million in FY 2011 and thereafter starting increasing gradually. Due to drastic fall in sales in FY 2011, its net profits before tax as well as PAT come down sharply, for which reasons needs to be ascertained. Financials started improving from FY 2012–13. Total assets and total liabilities also come down in FY 2010–11 to 2,410.04 million from 3,368.93 million in FY 2009–10.

BECOMING ZMCL

In 2013, Zee News received a makeover yet again, emerging with a new identity called Zee Media Corporation Limited (ZMCL). On this new identity, Subhash Chandra said, 'In line with our ambition to reach deeper into the lives of our viewers, our company changed its name to Zee Media Corporation Limited. The name along with the message of 'Vasudhaiva Kutumbakam—The World Is My Family' reflects our rich heritage as the country's pioneering media network and represents our contemporary and inclusive outlook.' The new CEO of the company, Dr Bhaskar Das, enunciated the reasons for this personality upgrade: 'It was with great conviction and a vision to grow that we looked to upgrade ourselves and change our identity to ZMCL. Our new identity forms a perfect blend of our traditional strengths with modern approach, reflecting in our wide array of media service offerings.'[82]

During the year, the company acquired 37.87 per cent equity stake in Maurya TV Private Limited, which runs Maurya TV, news and entertainment channel for the region of Bihar/Jharkhand. Additionally, consequent to amalgamation of Essel Publishers Pvt. Ltd with the company, ZNL expanded into print news media segment, through subsidiaries Diligent Media Corporation Limited (DMCL), which published DNA in Mumbai,

Bengaluru and Pune and Pri Media Services Pvt. Ltd, which is engaged in the printing inter-alia of DNA. This would enable ZNL to devise even greater synergies and offer a better quality of news to its consumers.

Rohit Gandhi, former CEO, DNA said, 'When I took over the newspaper in 2016, I wanted to give the newspaper a brand new face. Shreyasi Goenka came onboard to help build the newspaper and give it a new avatar. We realised that in the cluttered newspaper market, DNA was getting lost in the noise, as it was competing against a newspaper that had been around much longer and we were not willing to sell our soul. We wanted to remain objective news providers. The paper needed to stand out and it was only possible to do that by making it a visual interest-based newspaper. We divided up the paper in multiple sections and targeted each section with specialised news content.'

Today, ZMCL (formerly Zee News Ltd) is one of the largest news network with 14 news channels in six different languages, touching more than 220 million viewers and digital properties like zeenews.com and dnaindia.com. Zee Digital has a reach of more than a million monthly unique visitors, while the social media pages of the network have around 40 million followers.

In terms of news gathering, the company has one of the largest networks of news bureaus and correspondents with a pan India presence. The company is equipped with updated technology in content creation, packaging and broadcasting.

'The design of the paper had to be re-done along with the colour scheme and the logo. So it was a long battle to give the newspaper a brand new look within months and make all the hiring in that short span of time. Our approach was to not make hasty decisions but rather to build the right culture in the newsroom. It was not one of creating fear but one of collaboration. People were pushing the limits to deliver a different newspaper in months. It was a tall order at the time as I was also creating a brand new TV news channel from ground up.'[83]

In a short span, DNA entrenched itself into the lives of the young and dynamic readers through its news, views, analyses and interactivity with a composite unbiased picture of the city, the country and the world around them. On the other side, zeenews.com too was doing exceedingly well, generating close to 26 million users during the year, in addition to a user increase even in regional websites. In addition, through an association with India Webportal Private Limited's brand, india.com, the company also had robust digital properties. The company set up a special interest vertical team capable to generate content for all three platforms, viz., television, newspapers and digital. This Special interest Vertical team had expertise in the sectors of automobiles, luxury, women and lifestyle, and education and careers. The company was moving into newer geographies, newer content formats as well as newer content platforms. The success on all sides of the spectrum, traditional on one end and contemporary on the other, was reflective of ZMCL's all-rounded growth.

Zee also started content-based programming on TEN, a mixture of news and entertainment for some of their new channels. The company made further inroads into the Hindi heartland through the launch of Zee Marudhara, with mixture of news and entertainment-based shows for viewers in Rajasthan and Zee Kalinga, with five fiction and two non-fiction shows apart from 10 news bulletins for Odisha viewers according to the TEN format, which comprises locally produced entertainment programmes in addition to news bulletins and feature programmes. Hence, the viewers of these regions can get a variety of content on a platter. In addition to launching new channels, the company also restaged Zee News, Zee 24 Taas, 24 Ghanta, Zee Punjab Haryana Himachal (erstwhile Zee Punjabi) and Zee Sangam (erstwhile Zee Uttar Pradesh Uttarakhand) to keep up with the ever-changing viewing patterns. Zee Sangam, erstwhile Zee UP UK, was restaged by expanding its reach to key viewership cities of Delhi and Mumbai, giving its viewers news with a regional perspective. Zee Punjab Haryana Himachal, erstwhile Zee Punjabi, rebranded itself to address a much wider range of audience in the northern region of the country. There were some functional changes in the industry at this point too. There was a shift from TV Rating Point (TVRs) to TV Viewership in thousand (TVTs), which was a better representation of the increasing reach of television.

This was a year of several accolades in which the company won a number of awards, including the Best Spot News Reporting for *Maut Ke Shivir Mein Ek Raat* and Best Public Service Campaign for Aapka Vote Aap ki Taaqat, from the Exchange4Media News Broadcasting Awards in addition to Best Entertainment Show for *Double Dose*, Best Set Design for Zee News, Best Show Packaging for Daily News and Analysis and Game Changer Award for Zee News from News Television Awards.

For the upcoming future, Zee had some new things in the pipeline. They projected to provide content in highly specialized verticals like Automobiles, Luxury, Education and Career, Women and Lifestyle. Das said on future strategies, 'Advertising revenue growth, viewership consolidation and increase, faster decision-making, and getting a base for increased scope of offerings will be our priorities for the coming year. To this extent, we have gone in for a decentralized decision-making structure. We are looking to leverage our new launches to have a strong revenue growth. Looking ahead, we are going to be more focused on intensifying our efforts to dig deeper into the market with aggressive marketing and branding. With a new identity, we are looking to become a more comprehensive media corporation with one concrete focus of being relevant to our viewers. When we say the world is my family, we intend to prove it through our outreach.'[84]

The year 2014 turned out to be a great year for the news genre with the general and state elections providing a viewership boost. The business perspective shifted from expanding to monetizing the properties already owned by the company. ZMCL extended the media platform and offered 10 TV channels, one news daily, a web portal and even a mobile app, increasing the accessibility quotient and enhancing viewership simultaneously. Diversifying across media formats opened new revenue-generating options for the company. Besides, technological modernization has increased demands for satellite television and HD requirements, as well as OTT app-based media, which further strengthened revenues. BARC identified ZMCL as the No.1 in the industry in several of their surveys during this time.

All through the year, the company focused on operational excellence and strengthened its brand presence. The result was a robust financial performance. It embarked on co-creating content with the audiences; a strategy that continuously maps preferences and matches content with such preferences. It enunciated its editorial stand for the upcoming year: 'We believe in citizens before politics and countries before parties. We believe in access point aggregation. We believe in no fear and no favour. We are committed to being fair, honest and courageous in gathering, reporting and interpreting information; treating sources, subjects and colleagues with consideration; being free of obligations to any interest other than the public's right to know; and being accountable to our readers, listeners, viewers, and publishers at all times.'[85]

ZMCL showed that it believed in working holistically through its work management system. During 2014, their news-gathering network had a count of 34 news bureaus, 21 studios, 193 news reporters and 437 freelance journalists/stringers. They revealed that in addition to an expert national team of reporters and journalists to capture information from the field, there was an able back-end team to analyze and put things in perspective properly. Even internally, there was a stable system in place. ZMCL claimed: 'Internally, we operate 21 studios internationally and more than 200 high-end cameras and 52 ENG cameras. We also own 34 Live U/Dijero Units and 28 OBs, along with state-of-the-art, non-linear editing facilities. We installed [an] SMS-based app to transmit data across departments.'[86]

The company marked the year with a number of its achievements, understood majorly through its work culture. 'The company invested in quality content generation... Covering elections from the ground, engaging a star-studded expert panel for cricket and football world cup programming, and capturing international visits in a glocal perspective were some of the hallmarks of our breakthrough programming. The network's content philosophy evolved from 'update' to 'upgrade' wherein, apart from being the first one to provide reliable and accurate news, it sought to enhance its consumers' knowledge by providing a timely and detailed analysis. Moreover, through better sales management and innovations, the company increased the monetization of its channels and clocked the highest ever revenues since its existence.'[87]

The year 2015 marked another milestone for the Indian economy. India became prominent by improving its ranking in the World Bank of Business' index, as a result of which it began to attract hordes of FDIs. The new positioning of the country, which had replaced China as the top destination for foreign investments, saw global corporations wanting to invest in the Indian market. Apart from educating and creating awareness via its news channels, newspaper and news websites, the network organized user benefit programmes, such as 'Aapka Faayda' investor camps, that empowered and enabled investors to plan their investments better. 'Aapla Shahar Aapla Awaaz' provided a platform to citizens in Maharashtra to raise their civic problems with politicians and administrators. 'Emerging Business Forums' and 'SME Growth Series' provided support to the SMEs and MSMEs in their entrepreneurial journey.

The company created an integrated organization with a large network of reporters and photo-video journalists across the country. Each channel of the company could access the large national and international news network to curate the best content for its viewers. By promoting citizen journalism, the company also empowered the viewers to make a change, while simultaneously making them more accountable and responsible.

The company's flagship channel Zee News was converted to a Free to Air (FTA) channel. Moreover, a Malayalam website, zeenews.india.com/Malayalam, was launched, increasing the company's footprint in Southern India. To cater to the mobile news audience, the company also launched five new apps on Android and iOS platforms. The network further extended its offerings to the business community with the launch of web platform, zeebiz.com. Zee Purvaiya, formerly Maurya TV, the network's offering for Bihar and Jharkhand, was rebranded post acquisition of a 100 per cent stake in Maurya TV Private Limited. With a view to help improve the situation of education in Bihar, the channel provided a forum 'Education Summit 2016' for the government to interact with educators and the student community.

Rajendra Kumar Arora, the executive director at the time, said that the year had seen increased news consumption, attributable to the introduction of 4G services. As a result, there had been a growth in their online user base. He said, 'Our entire video content repository of more than 60,000 hours is being digitized and will be accessible across multiple platforms—television, print and digital media. ZMCL is investing heavily in digital platforms to suit different audiences. The company has already established a strong web presence through zeenews.com, 24ghanta.com, 24taas.com, and dnaindia.com and each one of them displayed tremendous growth in FY16. The company launched news apps for Zee News (in Hindi and in English), 24 Ghanta (in Bengali), Zee 24 Taas (in Marathi), and DNA to target the viewers who follow news on the go.' The total installs crossed 1 million marks within six months.[88]

He also pointed towards ZMCL's diversification into other varied avenues like television shopping by entering into the business through the acquisition of Today Merchandise Private Limited (TMPL) and Today Retail Network Private Limited (TRNL).[89] He quoted, 'The company is also diversifying its business by entering into television shopping business through the acquisition of Today Merchandise Private Limited (TMPL) and Today Retail Network Private Limited (TRNL). Television Shopping, with its promising potential, holds great investment value to the company.'

For ZMCL, a number of accolades were collecting on the shelf. At the 7th BCS Ratna Awards, Sudhir Chaudhary of Zee News received the Outstanding TV Journalist for the year. Zee Business received the Channel of the Year award at the ENBA Awards 2015 BARC India Business News.

INVESTING IN THE FUTURE

From 2016, ZMCL adopted a new mantra of 'Investing in Future'. To this end, it strove towards making a leap into the radio business, to add to its existing portfolio. ZMCL approved the acquisition of a 49 per cent stake in 92.7 Big FM, India's largest radio broadcast network by the Reliance group, 'and the execution of definitive agreements in relation to such acquisition.'[90] However, as per an official statement by the company, the deal valued at ₹1,592 crore was called off. Ashok Venkatramani, MD, ZMCL, was reported saying, 'For a long period it was awaiting clearance from the Ministry of Information and Broadcasting and the Home Ministry which had to be obtained… it's called off because there is no progress.'[91]

The dream that the company had seen in 2007, of launching a global English news channel by 2010, seemed now to be placed six years later than the target. In 2016, WION (World Is One News) was launched. This again reiterated their policy of 'Vasudhaiva Kutumbakam', hoping to bring the world closer through this platform. The company projected the role of WION by saying, 'The mobile/digital first platform, which will evolve into an international television channel, will report global news and issues from a South Asian lens. The channel will have its newsgathering teams across the globe equipped with mobile technology for an 'anytime-anywhere' live approach to satisfy the 'news as it happens' need of Generation Z. WION aims to be the platform which can meet the aspiration of 2 billion South Asians by delivering a global news mix that reflects a South Asian perspective. With WION and its state-of-the-art news gathering setup, the content synergy will shift gear to the next level. The strategy is in line with the company's internal orbit shifting initiative to affect a paradigm shift in the organization and to move into an exponential growth phase.'[92]

Rohit Gandhi, who also joined the WION team as the founding editor-in-chief, said, 'In 2015 when I first came on board to decide what the group wanted to build, we were still tweaking the idea. I worked directly with Dr Subhash Chandra, creating the idea from scratch, on what the network would stand for and why India had at that time reached a point where it was ready to be a global voice. I had spent years traveling through South Asia and had realised that if India and the other South Asian neighbours have to build a South Asia where its people will be fed and clothed and would have a shelter, then the most important thing was to have peace in South Asia. It is not possible to have peace without communication that is appreciative of the shared values and beliefs and clearing the air around the challenges that may exist. It was my dream to create such a template for a South Asian news exchange platform and someday be able to clear the air. The jingoism was just beginning to grow and coming from a military family I knew it is ok for people who have never sent their children to be in the army, to talk about let's have a war, but for the military personnel, the possibility of losing a loved one fighting for scraps of land, was not such a good idea. As journalists we should play the role to diffuse the tension rather than bring conflagration to the already tense situation. '

'The task involved literally building the whole platform ground up. Its financial numbers, viewer projections, viewer analysis, branding, technology, look and feel. I had a brand new staff to build all of it and it was all done in-house, including designing the set of the first studio and the bigger set for the new studio. The new building was coming up and the newsroom had to be designed and we sat down literally building the structure and workflow of the newsroom and how content flow in the new integrated setup would be and how it needed to be incorporated in the newsroom. It was a 20-hour workday with not a day off for 17 months; sometimes traveling between Mumbai and Delhi twice a week.'[93] A wionews.com digital platform was also launched later.

In an interview with the author, Punit Goenka, said, 'WION is doing extremely well in terms of the consumer feedback. I think that it's definitely something that sets us apart from the regular news channels in the country. Now, with our vision to take it global, we will only make it even bigger.'[94] Under 'Orbit Shifting', a unique ZMCL initiative to strengthen its internal programmes, the following philosophies were enunciated: 'News programming from multiple lenses; enhance and not just inform; introduction of credibility index.'[95]

The declaration of demonetization and GST by the central government was welcomed in an open-minded manner by the company leaders, who called it 'evolutionary' for the M&E industry. The user base also increased considerably with widening networks of 4G, IPL and T20 matches, and the emergence of FTA channels. The network also set itself apart from the commoditized content ecosystem through path-breaking content propositions, which are finding expression in the channels' evolved programming. Zee News experimented with several new formats, the most successful among them being *Fateh Ka Fatwa* and *Fun Ki Baat*.

Envisioning a bright future in its recently acquired teleshopping business from last year, as well as swimming with the currents of digitization, ZMCL planned on investing in the online retail and e-commerce space further down the line.

In 2017, this saw fruition. In a bid to grab a share of the rising incomes levels in rural India, ZMCL launched a video-based shopping business Ez-Mall Online Ltd. This would cater to consumers beyond Tier I cities through DTH, cable and its website Ezmall.com.

There was also the introduction of an Integrated Multimedia Newsroom (IMN), under which the 'newsrooms of all 14 television news channels and digital properties' were brought together 'to create India's largest Integrated Multimedia Newsroom.' This was done with a vision 'to strengthen the network's collaborative relationships, ensure optimum resource utilization, and build synergies among the various operations.'

The group further strengthened their television portfolio with the launch of a second national Hindi news channel, Zee Hindustan, and three new regional channels—Zee 24

Kalak (Gujarati), Zee Salaam (Urdu) and Zee Uttar Pradesh Uttarakhand (Hindi). Also, in addition to strengthening their existing English, Hindi, Bengali and Marathi sites, ZMCL increased their already strong regional presence with the addition of five more language news sites in Tamil, Telugu, Malayalam, Kannada and Gujarati, within the fold of Zeenews.com. Meanwhile, WION, which justified its position as India's first global English news channel, extended its footprint to South Asia (Sri Lanka, Bangladesh), Middle-East (Qatar, UAE), Africa and Australia. Making a creative impact during the first year of operation itself, the channel received both Gold and Silver awards in the Promax BDA Awards 2018 'Best News / Current Affairs Promo' category (Gold–Democracy and Dictatorship; Silver–WION Fishermen). The channel continued to provide exclusive on-ground coverage of significant world events including wars in Syria and Iraq, elections in Germany, BRICS summit in Xiamen, and London attacks.

In the social arena, ZMCL organized a number of notable events during the year: Fairplay Awards, GST Conclave, Education Excellence Awards, Swasthya Ratna Samman, Ek Shaam Jawano ke Naam and Zee Samman.

IN THE RECENT PAST

For FY 2018–19, Zee Media's growth measures were focused upon 'The Truth of Business' and 'The Business of Truth'. It quoted, 'In the business of truth, a lie is like a bee in a silent prayer room. Did we hear someone say truth doesn't pay? Well, for us it did pay and that too handsomely.'[96] Apparently, it did. At least in numbers. The company today continues to be one of the largest news networks in the country, touching more than 345 million viewers through its 14 News Channels in eight different languages and reaching more than 422 million users through digital channels. The latest environmental scan revealed that that 'the news genre, where the company operates, contributes only 7 per cent of the TV viewership but commands a disproportionately high share of advertising volumes. Events and activations became very important sources of revenue generation for news channels. The news genre grew at 5 per cent while the company grew at 20 per cent.'

All channels at Zee Media were attempting something new. Zee News, the flagship channel, continued to engage viewers with differentiated content and enjoyed the 'highest average time spent per viewer' in the Hindi news genre. Tapping on to the 2019 General Elections fervour, the channel kick-started its build-up early with 'India Ka DNA 2019' conclave to analyze and review the tenure of the current dispensation as well as the plan ahead, for all parties. The company relaunched Zee Hindustan as an anchor-less channel, showcasing the strength of their news content alone. The company successfully experimented with hyperlocal initiatives, with an objective to test and unleash the revenue potential in smaller towns. 24 Ghanta, the company's Bengali news offering, was rechristened Zee 24 Ghanta post the acquisition of the remaining stake in Zee Akaash News Private Limited. It showcased the contributions of Indian women, recognized their achievements and presented 'Swayam Siddha Awards' to women from different fields. The channel was reaching more than 30 million viewers across India. Zee 24 Taas continued to highlight the efforts of students who came up with innovations powerful enough to bring about a change in people's lives through the third edition of 'Young Innovator Awards'. Zeenews.com consolidated its nine languages (English, Hindi, and seven regional languages) leading to a year-on-year increase of 8 per cent in visitors.[97]

A change in the functions of the company was brought about by TRAI's new order, and was a blessing in disguise.

ZMCL announced, 'In view of TRAI's New Tariff Order, all network channels were converted to Pay channels and are being distributed as a part of the Zee Bouquet; this serves as a strong relevant offering to the customers of Zee wherein they get all the products of Zee network as a part of the bouquet(s). At the same time, it improves the proposition for Zee as a group, wherein every channel of the group adds relevance and value to the bouquet and improves the potential of Zee to enhance its reach and subscription revenue in a competitive environment.'[98]

But some of Zee's news businesses were not performing as exceedingly well as its entertainment arms. This trend was explained by Subhash Chandra to the author, 'There is not as much money in news as there is in entertainment. For instance, there are some losses in DNA.'[99] He was speaking, of course, about the company breaking up with Dainik Bhaskar on the DNA deal. On behalf of the promoter group, Punit Goenka explained further, 'I think the amount of losses that were being incurred on DNA in the early days was the reason why the shareholders at Dainik Bhaskar were not happy and that's why they chose to get out of it. It was very amicable, we are friends today so, it was a very amicable partition that happened then we took over the entire business. Today we have four editions.'[100]

The network continued to earn accolades for its exemplary news coverage and programming and has received seven awards at the 11th ENBA Awards 2018 including 'Best Hindi (Zee Business)' and 'Best Current Affairs Programme–Hindi (Zee News)'. Zee Hindustan's bold marketing campaign for its re-launch as India's first anchorless channel earned it the Afaqs! Media Innovation Award for 'The Most Innovative Marketing Campaign'. The Indian Bullion and Jewellers Association awarded Zee Business with 'Best Channel', 'Best Commodity Anchor' and 'ICON of Business Journalism'.

Through all this, news at Zee has been guided by a constant intent, of catering to its viewers firstly, and secondly, doing all that is in the best benefit of the country—an idea that has been reiterated multiple times by those at Zee News, including Sudhir Chaudhary, one of the most identifiable faces in the country and in Indian journalism today, with his 'pro-nation' stance. Summed up even in the editorial policy, as elucidated by Brajesh Kumar, 'We shouldn't be apologetic if we are talking for national interest. Major voices are critical about our editorial policy, but the public is supportive of it as it is in sync with public sentiment.'[101]

For ZMCL's future outlook, Punit Goenka outlined the following projections: 'In today's era, Digital is transforming the way content is created, accessed and consumed by the audience. Hence our Company stands committed to invest in its digital business and nurture this market of the future. We believe we have laid a strong foundation for the future wherein we will continue to take bold, meaningful strides in ensuring we stay ahead in the competitive news industry.'[102]

Table 13

Financial highlights-Zee Media Corporation limited Standalone (2014-2019) (in ₹ Million)

Year Ending 31 March	*2014*	*2015*	*2016*	*2017*	*2018*	*2019*
Total Revenue	3,301.8	3,917.11	3,945.85	4,132.07	5,240.02	6,187.40
Total Expense	2,886.1	3,812.32	3,662.34	3,533.98	4,651.58	4,791.99
Profit/ Loss before Tax	225.8	104.8	322.2	598.1	588.4	(288.5)
Profit/ Lossafter tax	188.2	61.7	221.2	383.2	406.22	(552.7)
Tax Expense	37.7	43.1	101.0	178.8	182.2	264.2
Operating Profit	162.5	406.9	581.2	857.0	1,025.4	1,279.1

Year Ending 31 March	*2014*	*2015*	*2016*	*2017*	*2018*	*2019*
PBIDT	415.7	521.8	719.1	1,008.6	1,163.6	1,395.4
Dividend	nil	nil	70.6	nil	nil	nil
Advertising Revenue	1,902	2,686	2,790	3,355	4,473	5,363
Total Assets and Equity and Liabilities	3,277.0	5,181.6	7,047.5	7,226.1	7,853.5	7,871.7
Income from Operations	3,048.6	3,802.3	3,836.1	3,980.5	5,101.8	6,071.1
Depreciation	146.4	285.7	270.4	262.6	400.9	471.6
Loans Funds	1,114.6	1,246.6	1,007.5	910.6	1,234.3	1,809.1
Financial Expenses	103.3	131.3	126.5	147.9	174.3	178.8
Investments	122.3	3,224.7	4,630.3	5,219.4	5,486.9	4,962.1

Source: Compiled by the author from ZMCL Annual Reports (2014-19)

The name of ZNL was changed to ZMCL in year 2014. From FY 2013–14 till FY 2018–19, Zee Media Corporation Ltd gave good operating results and year-on-year growth. Its operational income increased from 3,048.60 million in FY 2013–14 to 6,071.10 million in FY 2018–19; almost double in a span of five years. The above data portrays that the company is increasing its market shares considerably. PAT which was 188.20 million in FY 2013–14, dipped down to 61.70 million in FY 2014–15, but after that it continuously increased till FY 2017–18, when it touched 406.22 million. But in FY 2018–19, ZMCL booked losses of 288.50 million, for which, reasons need to be ascertained. Dividend was declared only in FY 2015–16 in the above band of years.

Table 14
Financial highlights-Zee media corporation limited Consolidated (2014–2019) (in ₹ Million)

Year Ending 31 March	*2014*	*2015*	*2016*	*2017*	*2018*	*2019*
Total Revenue	3,587.43	5,515.47	5,604.77	5,714.19	5,874	6,985.82
Total Expense	3,360.93	6,070.53	5,576.09	5,704.62	5,324.96	5,866.85
Profit/ Loss before Tax	286.39	(555.06)	(32.83)	(209.11)	503.23	492.06
Profit/ Lossafter tax	213.21	(466.51)	(69.19)	(160.59)	278.38	131.74
Tax Expense	(73.2)	(123.54)	(2.53)	(48.52)	224.85	360.32
Operating Profit	254.8	403.9	777.8	683.8	1,041.4	1,736.4
PBIDT	490.6	476.1	953.5	895.2	1,135.2	1,853.0
Dividend	nil	nil	70.6	nil	nil	nil
Advertising Revenue	2,205	3,105	3,300	3,952	5,106	6,161
Total Assets and Equity and Liabilities	4,463.63	9,942.72	11,073.05	11,875.81	10,407.46	10,424.98
Income from Operations	3,351.6	5,443.3	5,429.6	4,498.3	5,734.8	6,869.2
Depreciation	160.7	504.9	465.7	274.9	409.7	553.9
Loans Funds	1,114.6	4,386.1	3,731.9	3,959.2	1,234.3	1,809.1
Financial Expenses	103.4	526.3	486.9	149.9	175.8	180.1
Investments	39.0	22.3	–	743.6	5,247.8	4,306.2

Source: Compiled by the author from ZMCL Annual Reports (2014-19)

Total revenue as well as income from operation was on an increasing trend from FY 2013–14 to FY 2018–19. Gross revenue level increased from 3,587.43 million to 6,985.82 million, registering increase of 95 per cent in five to six years. In spite of increase in revenue in all these years, the company suffered loss in FY 2014–15, 2015–16 and 2016–17. However, it was booked profits in FY 2013–14, 2017–18 and 2018–19. Advertisement revenue of the company also showed a positive growth trend. The company's profit before interest, depreciation and taxation increased from 490.60 million in FY 2013–14 to 1,853 million in FY 2018–19 registering growth of 278 per cent in this block of six years.

CORE VALUES

Today the core values of ZMCL include: To keep the customer first and to anticipate, understand and meet needs of internal or external customers.

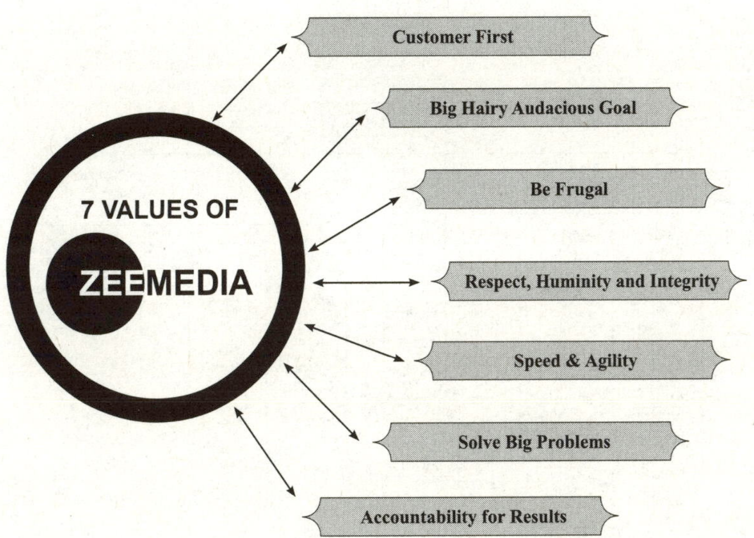

Fig. 5.4: Seven Values of Zee Media

1. Big Hairy Audacious Goal: To set clear, compelling and audacious goals.
2. Being Frugal: To focus on need based resource utilization.
3. Respect, Humility and Integrity: To respect and honour each individual's unique tale.
4. Speed and agility: To continue to deliver on responsibilities while responding to the speed and agility evolving environment.
5. Solve Big Problems: To identify and resolve problems which have a huge impact on business.
6. Accountability for Results: To take ownership of decisions or actions for self and team.

ZMCL IN CLUSTERS

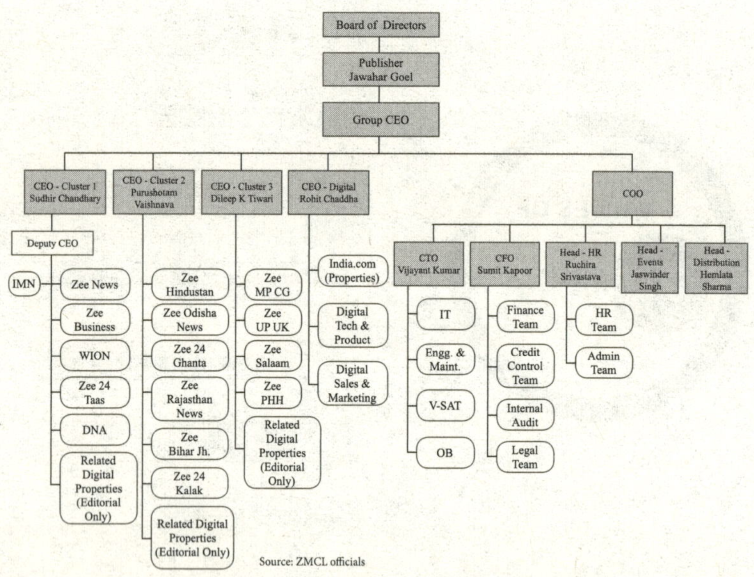

Source: ZMCL officials

Fig. 5.5: ZMCL Organizational Structure in 2019

ZMCL is categorized in various clusters at present. Sudhir Chaudhary is currently the Chief Executive Officer of Cluster 1 which includes channels like Zee News, WION, Zee Business and Zee 24 Taas. He hosts DNA, every night at Zee News. As per the website, officials at Zee News believes that, a positive change in people's thought process can bring a positive change for the whole nation. WION is India's first news channel dedicated to put forth India's perspective on emerging global issues in the world. In pursuit of this mission, WION has constituted a team of seasoned journalists coming from diverse nationalities. The channel prides itself on presenting news coverage that is distinct from the conventional media agenda existing in India. WION is also distinct in its outlook from other Indian news channels, as its vision is to create a global platform, which analyses any given issue in a geopolitical context and doesn't restrict evaluation of these issues to India alone.

Zee Business is the first Hindi Business Channel launched in India, with the aim that everybody should be made aware about the current developments in the Business World, Share Markets. Anil Singhvi is the current Managing Editor of Zee Business.

Zee Business aims to inspire and empower the entrepreneurial spirit of young India by providing the financial guidance and mentoring. It aims to bring out the entrepreneurial spirit in each one of the youth and have them chase their passion from now and not wait for the future. Zee 24 Taas is an 11-year-old Marathi TV news brand that is operating in Maharashtra with a clear objective of keeping consumer updated on the latest news offerings. Ashish Jadhao is the current Executive Editor of Zee 24 Tass.

Cluster 2 is headed by Purushottam Vaishnava as the CEO. Cluster 2 includes channels like Zee Hindustan, Zee Bihar Jharkhand, Zee Rajasthan, Zee 24 Kalak, Zee 24 Ghanta and Zee Odisha. In 2018, Zee Hindustan was relaunched as the first news channel in the country without any anchor or news reader. The idea behind the strategy of going anchor-less is aimed at giving news without any views. The basic purpose is to disseminate news in its purest form. The relaunched Zee Hindustan believes in the philosophy of 'Ab anchor nahi, khabrein khud bolengi, kyunki aap samajhdar hain'.

Zee Rajasthan sees itself as the voice of the people. By raising the concerns of the local population, the channel aims to keep the government accountable for its actions. Zee Bihar Jharkhand's content focuses on capturing the culture, language and rituals of the two states as well as showcasing their political vibrancy. The brand aims to increase regional penetration and ensure wider reach in Bihar and Jharkhand. Zee Odisha upholds the views and opinions of the common man while bringing them news from all corners of the state. Zee Odisha goes beyond the regular news bulletin and creates informative content for the viewers. Zee 24 Ghanta stands for clear, news with ample inputs from eyewitnesses on ground zero. The tagline: *Manusher jonne, manusher pashe* (For the people, By the people) epitomizes the channel vision. Keeping this unique phenomenon in mind, almost 13 years back on 31 March 2006, 24 Ghanta from Zee's stable was launched. Currently, Anirban Choudhury is the Editor of Zee 24 Ghanta.

Similar is the ethos of Zee 24 Kalak, launched on 20 August 2017. Zee 24 Kalak is a 24/7 Indian Gujarati-language news channel which believes in the saying 'Of the people, For the people, By the people'. The channel aims at dishing out authentic, accurate and factual news focused on regional issues, while keeping a watch at the larger stories in India and abroad with a Gujrat-lens. Currently Dixit Kumar is the Editor and Network Bureau Chief of Zee 24 kalak.

Cluster three is chaired by Dileep Tiwari as the CEO and includes channels like Zee MP-CG, Zee UP-UK, Zee PHH and Zee Salaam. Zee Madhya Pradesh, Chhattisgarh, acts as the voice of the people from both the states, holding true to its tagline,

'Aapki Aawaz, Aapka Bharosa'. Zee Salaam is a 24/7 Urdu News channel, which, since its inception, promotes the 'Ganga Jamuni Tehzeeb' culture of India. A channel with a flavour of 'Adab', its fundamental differentiator is that it goes beyond the traditional news domain and focusses on regional, national and international issues for our audience, standing true to its tagline 'Hindustan Ki Umeed'. Zee UP-UK, aims at providing news to 25 crore people of Uttar Pradesh and Uttarakhand, covering the length and breadth of the state with the heavy use of on-ground reporters to bring news from every nook and corner of the states and create a sense of local awareness for our audience. Zee Punjab Haryana Himachal with its diverse content portfolio of News, current affair programmes, and devotional and interactive shows, acts as a platform for people to discuss their issues.

ZMCL—A DIGITAL PUBLISHING GROUP

Zee Media Corporation Limited registers more than 500 million page views per month. ZMCL Digital Products are amongst the fastest growing websites and applications worldwide, with over 15 digital properties. Zee News App brings to you the latest news headlines, breaking news, top stories from India and around the world in five different languages— English, Hindi, Marathi (24 Taas), Bengali (24 Ghanta) and Tamil.

THE GUIDING FORCE OF ZMCL SOCIAL STRATEGY: ENGAGE, INFORM AND INNOVATE

Social media being a critical part of ZMCL's digital strategy, it delivers real-time news in various formats and languages, making them one of the most engaging social media platforms. It has more than 68,10,839 YouTube subscribers, 30,690,994 Facebook fans, 8,527,194 Twitter followers and 7,58,034 Instagram followers. At present ZMCL has 325 million users, 220 million viewers, 60 million monthly unique visitors and a fan base of 45 million fan in social media.

IN A NUTSHELL

The formation of ZNL in 2006 heralded a new dawn in the Indian news industry. With a specialized news network, the country now had a dedicated task force with a web of outgrowths, catering to different aspects of news media broadcast. Aside from mainstream news, what really sets ZNL apart was its focus on regional news channels. It was a company that believed in family-oriented growth, and always tried to walk hand in hand with each stakeholder, taking everyone forward.

Right at the beginning, without any lags, ZNL bucked up towards a strategic relaunch and redefined its intent values. The Zee News bouquet was constantly expanded to accommodate different regional news offerings, since regional media was one of ZNL's objectives even at the outset. This was even evidenced by the RGEC demerger that came in 2009. Now irrespective of whether that was a consequence of gaining more geographic ground and therefore a larger viewer base, or was simply the good-natured belief framework that functioned underneath it all, ZNL managed to conquer the hearts and minds of large masses. Though, the Hindi heartland remained its major focus.

With various shows catering to different essential genres and hence different demographics, ZNL managed to stay at the top of its game. Though the company briefly also made a turn to print, it didn't seem like a priority medium for them since efforts towards maximization remained primarily in broadcast. This was perhaps even the right decision, given the time and setting of the Indian media industry, which had been brimming with print giants since the twentieth century. In this scenario, the decision to focus on broadcast as the main channel, and then bring in print as an additional experiment had more chances to succeed, given how Zee had been among the forerunners of mainstream satellite television in India.

By the turn of the new decade in 2010, digitization as a lucrative concept had picked up pace. All media companies were trying to reap its benefits and incorporate it into their businesses in one way or another. ZNL too, by then, had joined the race and boasted of several online platforms of its broadcast news channels; an offering that was led by its primary website zeenews.com. During all its years, ZNL was sensitive to social causes. From environment to literacy, ZNL under its CSR activities pursued many such endeavours.

In 2013, ZNL changed to ZMCL. The brand name of the company had to change, to incorporate its various other media services, since previously it had only pointed towards news specialization. One of the early transformations with regard to this came with ZMCL's inclination towards acquisition of stakes in 92.7 FM, which ultimately didn't happen, and teleshopping under the India Today brand partnership.

The digital wave was still strong, with the company using latest technology for information collection, treatment and dissemination. There was even a launch of mobile apps for speedy consumption for news consumers, which could easily outpace the print segment. The company also went global with WION, a platform to connect the diaspora population with the country. ZMCL also became a pioneer in establishing an IMN in place, which brought the activities of all channels under one roof.

Over the years, the Zee media network accumulated several laurels for its efforts in the news industry—an achievement, it maintains, that has only been possible in pursuance of truth. While truth remains a subjective issue, there is one thing that cannot be denied—Zee is not a channel to be ignored.

6

AN EARNEST ENTERTAINER: THE MODERN LEGACY OF ZEEL

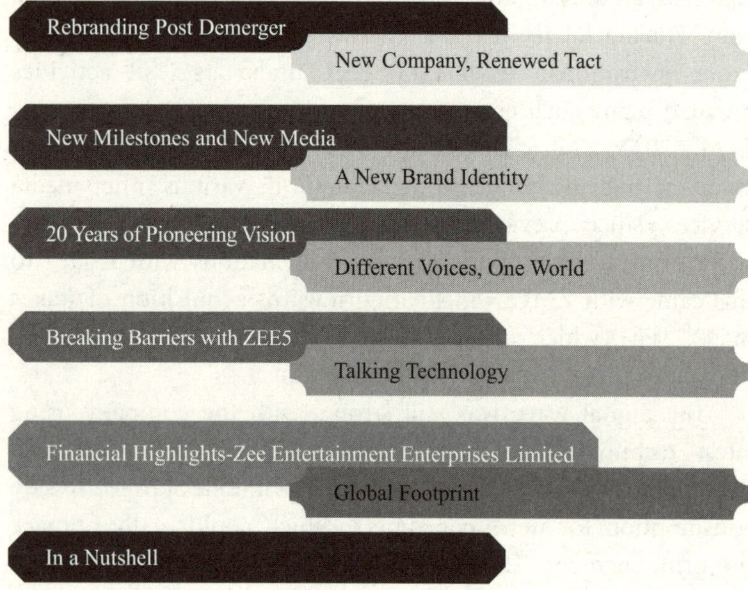

Fig. 6.1: Chapter Insights

TIMELINE 6

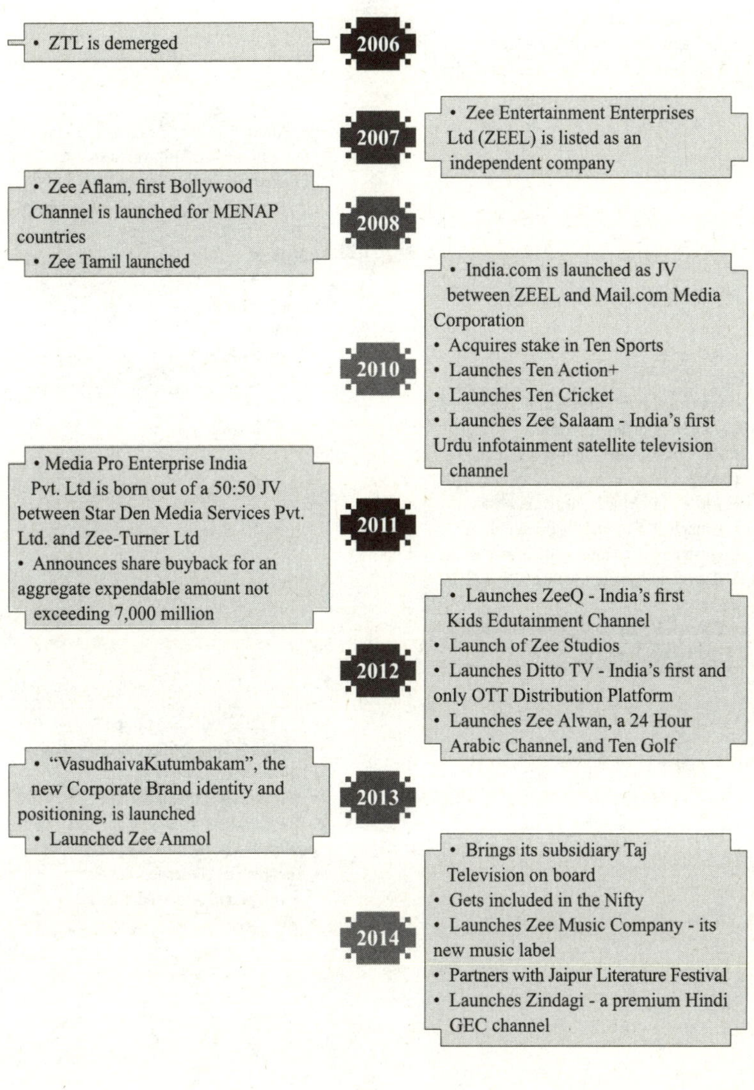
2006
• ZTL is demerged
2007
• Zee Entertainment Enterprises Ltd (ZEEL) is listed as an independent company
2008
• Zee Aflam, first Bollywood Channel is launched for MENAP countries
• Zee Tamil launched
2010
• India.com is launched as JV between ZEEL and Mail.com Media Corporation
• Acquires stake in Ten Sports
• Launches Ten Action+
• Launches Ten Cricket
• Launches Zee Salaam - India's first Urdu infotainment satellite television channel
2011
• Media Pro Enterprise India Pvt. Ltd is born out of a 50:50 JV between Star Den Media Services Pvt. Ltd. and Zee-Turner Ltd
• Announces share buyback for an aggregate expendable amount not exceeding 7,000 million
2012
• Launches ZeeQ - India's first Kids Edutainment Channel
• Launch of Zee Studios
• Launches Ditto TV - India's first and only OTT Distribution Platform
• Launches Zee Alwan, a 24 Hour Arabic Channel, and Ten Golf
2013
• "VasudhaivaKutumbakam", the new Corporate Brand identity and positioning, is launched
• Launched Zee Anmol
2014
• Brings its subsidiary Taj Television on board
• Gets included in the Nifty
• Launches Zee Music Company - its new music label
• Partners with Jaipur Literature Festival
• Launches Zindagi - a premium Hindi GEC channel

- Acquires Sarthak TV
- Launches Zee Theatre (foray into theatre production)
- Launch of ASHA 2022 project in line with the Prime Minister's Awas Yojna

- Announces the acquisition of the GECs from Anil Ambani-led Reliance Group Entities
- Launches OZEE - Its AVOD platform
- ZEAL for Unity, a peace initiative, is launched
- Sairat by Zee Studio becomes the first Marathi film to gross over ₹100 cr. worldwide
- Launch of Zee Sine, for the Philippines

- Essel Group completes 90 years
- Zee completes 25 years
- Zee Studios International is launched in Canada
- 106.2 Big FM is launched in UAE
- Launch of &Prive HD, premium English movie channel and 25 Weyyak, Video on demand service for Arabic audience
- Enters Live Business, and exits from sports broadcasting

- ZEE5 is launched online
- &flix is launched on television as a Hollywood movie channel
- Zee Bollywood is launched
- Zee Keralam, a Malayalam GEC, is launched
- Secures US patent for technology developed in Zee Media Lab

2006–ZTL IS DEMERGED

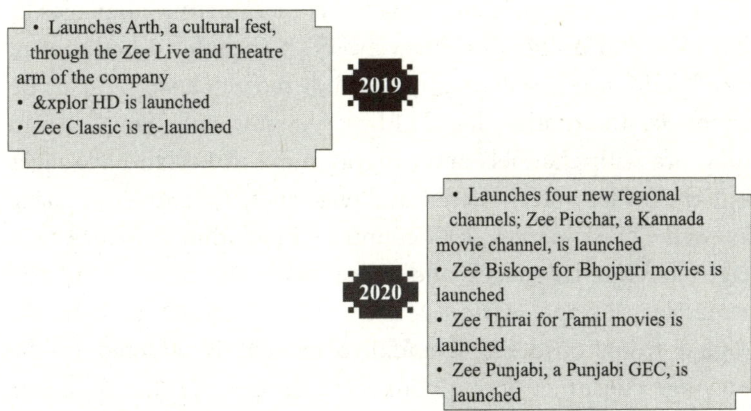

Source: Compiled by the author with inputs from ZEE

Born as a branchout of the Essel parent company in 2006, Zee Entertainment Enterprises Limited took on a life of its own from 2007. Replacing the all-subsuming umbrella of Zee, this new beast became a vessel for all things entertainment, offering all that its news-delivering sibling didn't. With a division into five verticals, ZEEL was able to create a robust legacy of business. It has strong content creation expertise, with 500+ hours of content every week across 11 languages developed through more than 28 years of institutional learnings and consumer insights. Over the years it has managed to forge strong partnerships and develop long-standing relationships across the value chain including with writers, directors and actors, and also distributors and advertisers on the other side of the spectrum. There is synergy, through the content created by one business and monetized by others, and between content creation and marketing with presence across all verticals.

Today, it has considerable clout in the market, with a presence in over 190 countries, 3,000+ brands. On the domestic front, ZEEL has 47 channels and broadcasts in 11 native languages. It has over 620 million weekly viewers. It includes a bouquet of Hindi GECs, regional channels, hindi movie cluster and niche channels. Internationally, ZEEL serves not only South Asian diaspora with channels and programming in Indian Languages but the wider International audience in their native language as well. ZEEL serves 190 countries (including broadcast in eight foreign languages and more than 120 channels in the Americas, Europe, Africa, MENA, APAC regions, etc. On the digital front, on-demand and live content is targeted to the new-age consumer across connected devices. On the domestic front Zee 5 has 150+ exclusive originals, 4,500+ movie titles, in 12 Indian languages, 125,000+ hours of on-demand content, 11.2 million+daily active users, 100 million+downloads and 100+ live channels.

Table 15
Global Reach of ZEEL

Regions	*2007–08*
Americas (Canada, Caribbean, USA)	577281
Europe	10099404
Africa and Middle East	41111670
Asia-pacific	5447523

At the International front, it is a front runner in the South Asian OTT Platform in Bangladesh and the Middle East. It has the largest presence among South Asian OTT platforms with 60+ live channels in more than 190 countries. (12 Indian and six international languages). It has 25+ global partnerships across key countries. Sugar box, a hyperlocal content distribution platform, enables users to access high-quality content even in areas with limited connectivity. This platform empowers users with seamless access to digital content and transforms existing internet connections to work twice as fast at half the cost. The daily unique reach is upwards of 24 million.

In technology and innovation, Z5X centre is an innovative technology solutions firm that addresses the trilemma of business, technology and experience. The capabilities include IoT, AI/ML, digital transformation, enterprise mobility, analytics, DevOps, automation and cloud support. It serves 160 associates that include M&E, automotive, education, publishing, automation and healthcare. And the digital publishing arm offers content across genres such as news, entertainment, technology, cricket, health and lifestyle and has 20 brands in 12 languages.

In addition to this ZEEL is into movie production and distribution, music publishing, live events and theatre. And taking the next big leap into the future of entertainment with Zee 4.0.

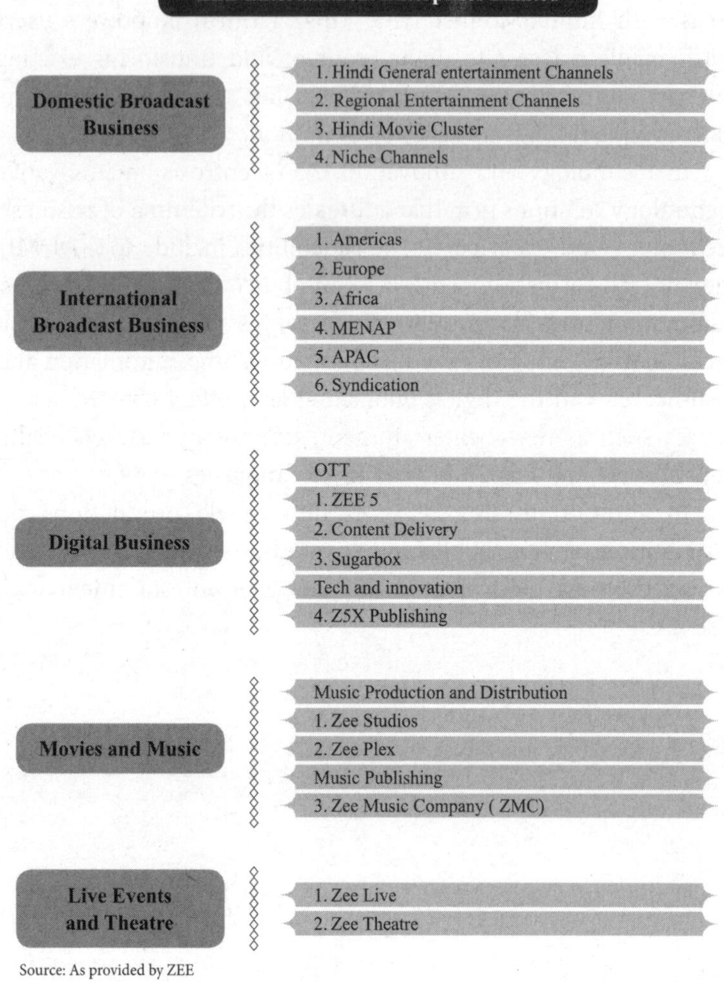

Source: As provided by ZEE

Fig. 6.2: Zee Entertainment Enterprises Limited

REBRANDING POST DEMERGER

Simply put, Zee became ZEEL. It was a matter of rebranding post the demerger in 2006. Essentially, there was a segmental division of the company according to different services. ZEEL, incorporated in 2007, became a one-stop destination for quality entertainment content. The news and current affairs business had transferred its infrastructure, editorial and production staff involved in broadcast of news and current affairs to ZNL. B.V. Rao, group editor of Zee commented, 'Zee is all set to script a new story, with the key participants taking control of their respective operations.'

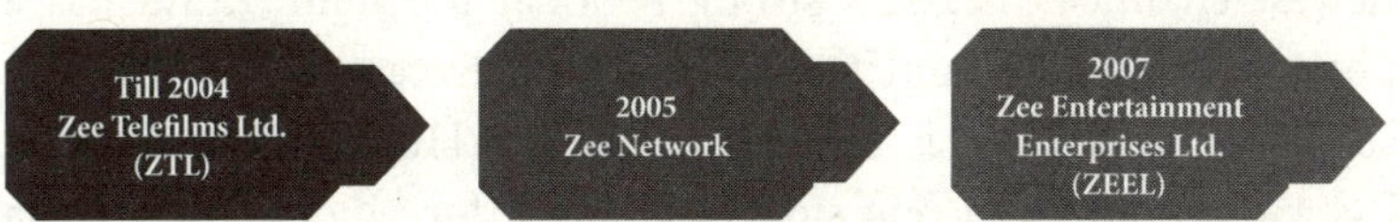

Fig. 6.3: Transition from ZTL to ZEEL

Effective 10 January 2007[103] Zee Entertainment Enterprises Limited (*ZEE*L) listed as an independent company. As the name suggests, ZEEL busied itself primarily with entertainment services, categorized under five verticals- Domestic Broadcast for Television (Hindi general entertainment, regional general entertainment, Hindi movie cluster, regional movie cluster, niche channels); Digital (ZEE5 and India Webportal Pvt. Ltd); International (with visibility in America, Europe, MENAP, Africa, APAC, and Syndication); Studios and Music (Zee Studios and Zee Music Company); and Live and Theatre (Zee Live and Zee Theatre). Today, Zee has a portfolio of four SD and two HD channels in the Hindi GEC genre.

Zee TV is the flagship channel which caters to the tastes of the entire spectrum of viewers in the Hindi speaking market. &TV, with its edgy content, is our second GEC targeted at young and urban audiences. Zee Anmol is catering to rural audiences, while Big Magic caters to the Hindi Speaking Markets through a variety of content appealing to all age groups. Zee is one of the largest providers of regional entertainment in India, with a bouquet of

GECs, movie channels and HD channels. The RGEC portfolio is spread across nine languages—Marathi, Bengali, Telugu, Kannada, Tamil, Bhojpuri, Odiya, Malayalam and Punjabi. Zee Marathi, Zee Sarthak, Zee Bangla and Zee Kannada are strong performers in the market with Zee Keralam growing steadily. ZEE's regional channels uniquely position it as a pan-India provider of high-quality entertainment content, appealing to a wide variety of audiences. Zee Punjabi, Zee Thirai, Zee Picchar and Zee Biskope are the newest channels in ZEE's strong regional portfolio. ZEEL has a portfolio of six SD and three HD channels catering to different segments of audiences and genres in the Hindi Movie Cluster. Zee Bollywood, is a one stop destination for wholesome masala Bollywood entertainers while Zee Classic showcases films from the golden era of Hindi cinema. Zee Action is exclusively focused on the action genre. &xplorHD takes viewers beyond the traditional definition of cinema. Apart from showcasing stories from different parts of India, Zee also brings international content from across the world through their niche channels. Zee Café provides the best of English entertainment to Indian audiences, while &privé HD entertains viewers with premium English movies. &flix, the latest addition to ZEE's English cluster, is the ultimate destination for hit Hollywood movies catering to avid movie fanatics with a Hollywood movie premiere every week.

Zee Global Content Sales (ZGCS), the licensing and syndication arm of ZEEL, houses one of the largest libraries of creative and broadcasting entertainment content in the world with a footprint across 190 countries including Americas, Europe, MENAP, Africa and APAC Regions. ZGCS offers 4,800+ film titles and 260,000+ hours of premium content across multiple languages including Hindi and English covering all genres: Romantic, Family, Thriller and Historic Dramas; Reality and Formats; Lifestyle and Fitness Programmes including nutrition, cooking, fitness and beauty; scripted comedy; kids; adventure and travel along with motivational real life stories.

Apart from 40 Television channels across international markets, ZGCS also offers original content across movies and television shows with a choice of dubbed or subtitled versions in many foreign languages. Extending further into international operations, Global Content Hub by Zee is the single point of access to a wide choice of content from across the world. ZEE's Global Content Hub is a major creative and broadcasting entertainment programming force, with headquarters in India and close to 40 international channels and over 1.3 billion viewers worldwide. The Global Content Hub portfolio is the go-to destination for award-winning programmes in every genre—historical, romantic, family and thriller dramas; reality and formats; adventure and travel; scripted comedy; kids; lifestyle and fitness programmes, in various languages including Hindi and English. Global Content Hub by Zee holds one of the most significant international content libraries in the world with 260,000+ hours of premium content including 4,800+ movie titles.

ALONG ROADS OF SUCCESS

Subhash Chandra defined the core values of ZEEL in the following terms: 'At ZEEL, everyone is encouraged to 'Solve Big Problems' in order to achieve their true potential. Furthermore, we have a culture that promotes 'Accountability for Results', driving the entrepreneurial spirit. 'Respect, Humility and Integrity' are fundamental to what we do. Our philosophy of 'Extraordinary Together' is not only about the way we approach our business, but also encompasses the society.'[104]

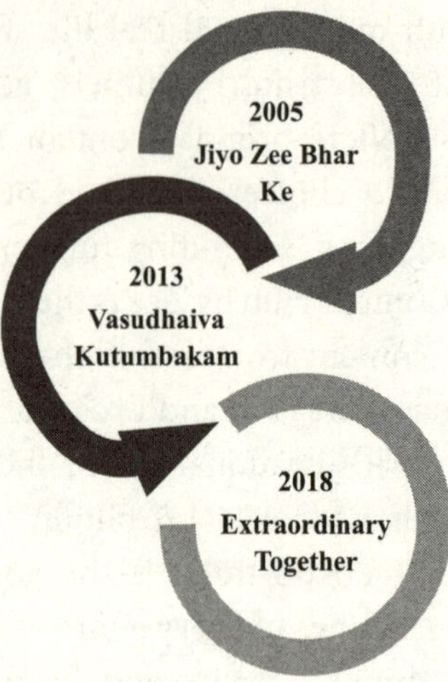

Fig. 6.4: Philosophy of ZEEL

The strategic intent for ZEEL has been quite clear with the company's forerunners. Punit Goenka elaborated on it, saying, 'In the years since we launched, our strategic intent must have changed four-five times and today what the strategic intent of the company is going forward is that we are a whole another television company. We are an entertainment powerhouse. Therefore, I need to occupy maximum mindshare of the consumers in the entertainment means. So, my competition is no longer Star or Colors or Sony. Even if you go to a restaurant to eat, that's my competition. Even if you read a newspaper, that's my competition. If you go to a theatre to watch a movie, that's my competition, because that's your entertainment. We have now evolved ourselves to be a five-vertical business.'[105]

The company was equipped with state-of-art technology in content creation, packaging and broadcasting. The transmission facility that had become operational in 2002 with a single dedicated 9.3m antenna operating on the AsiaSat 3-S satellite today, hosts over 150 broadcast channels using dedicated teleports and a complex network of optical fiber links, satellite broadcast transmissions, content contribution links and Internet streaming.

The Noida facility has been fully revamped with full HD core network, file-based media workflows, playouts with advanced media architecture and interfaces to massive archival and retrieval systems dispersed amongst ZNL's network production and transmission sites. Full file-based media workflows are achieved by an extended media network, which encompasses even the production houses on the same platform. The entire media network now operates on redundant high speed optical fiber links and connects the Playout Hub to the Mumbai Production facility, Regional Clusters as well as the company partners in media production, advertising and live events.

By 2007, ZEEL boasted of a large network of 17 channels which included the following names: Zee TV (Hindi general entertainment), Zee Next (New Hindi General Entertainment Channel with youth-centric content), Zee Cinema (Hindi movies), Zee Music (Hindi music), Zee Sports (sports content), Zee Premiere (new Hindi movies), Zee Action (Hindi action movies), Zee Classic (old Hindi movies), Zee Smile (Hindi comedy), Zee Jagran (Hindi religious content), Zee Trendz (fashion content), Zee Café (English general entertainment), Zee Studio (English movies), Zee Arabia (Arabic music), Zee Aflam (24-hour Hindi movie channel with Arabic subtitles for Middle Eastern audience), Zee MIB (general Indian entertainment channel in Malaysia, Indonesia and Brunei), and Zee Russia (general Indian entertainment and Bollywood channel with Indian films in Russian).Regional language entertainment existed through Zee Marathi, Zee Bangla, Zee Talkies, Zee Telugu, Zee Kannada, ETC Punjabi and Zee Tamizh. The company also owned cable services viz. Siti Cable and a production outfit called Zee Records.

NEW COMPANY, RENEWED TACT

An environment scan of the time, as expounded by Chandra, reveals, 'With the onset of digitalization, the Indian television industry is witnessing a revolution taking place in terms of increased subscriber growth. With emerging distribution platforms like digital cable, DTH and IPTV taking over the market, the subscriber today is at a great advantage in terms of viewing superior quality customized content at a suitable cost.'

The Mission Statement for this period as described in ZEEL's Annual Report 2006-07 read:

> To be the leading round the clock air-time proper ties provider, delighting the viewers not only through our general entertainment and infotainment channels but also through quality cinema from our new movie banners. As a corporation, we will be profitable, productive, creative, trend-setting and financially sound with care and concern for all stakeholders namely advertisers, cable operators, producers and production houses.

ZEEL continued its pre-occupation with the retention of market leadership, though the emphasis was more on new product-mix. Besides, it kept financial ruggedness as the core of its management strategy along with taking all stakeholders on board. At the same time, the Mission statement retained its interest in retaining the early entry advantage of Zee viz-a-viz other broadcasting companies. Like ZNL, ZEEL too had an arrangement with Zee Turner Ltd for distribution of pay channels bouquet on DTH platforms, and with Dish TV India Limited for up-linking of its channels through their teleport. In 2006, the Group acquired Integrated Subscriber Management Services Limited.

In November the same year, Zee Sports International Ltd Mauritius acquired a 50 per cent stake in Dubai-based Taj TV

Ltd Mauritius, which owned the Ten Sports channel. Also, the company acquired another 50 per cent stake with majority representation in the board in Taj Television India Pvt. Ltd, Mumbai, the distribution arm of Ten Sports in India.[106] ZEEL acquired a 50 per cent stake in Ten Sports in 2006, instituting an international level Indian Cricket League. This achievement came after much ado. The company had clashed with BCCI several times, due to sour relations between its leading men, and this had led to a severed relationship between the two entities.

The 20-20 idea for the league had been on Chandra's mind for a long time, something he had even pitched to the BCCI but claimed had been sidelined on account of the brewing animosity. But in Chandra's own words, 'I don't give up easily, especially when I believe in something.' He wrote, 'We went ahead and launched the league even without the BCCI's help, and created several teams… We managed the first 20-20 league event in December 2007 very well. The audience response was great.'[107] Plans were even developing to promote football in the country. The company took these initiatives with the view that it would be able to generate substantial revenues through these investments in the years to come.

Zee Kannada was launched, positioned as a Kannada general entertainment channel. The channel aimed to capture the moods, sentiments and aspirations of Kannadigas. Some of its major programmes were KuniyonuBaara (Celebrity Dance Show), Sa Re Ga Ma Pa (Musical Talent Show In Kannada), Gramophone (Musical Show), Sa Re Ga Ma Pa Little Champs and Komedy Khiladigadu (Comedy Show). Zee Kannada has already marked its position in the competitive Kannada television industry. Despite the lack of homogeneity in the viewership, this channel has carved a niche for itself by creating shows that showcases the lives of ordinary Kannadigas. The channel has been successful in introducing memorable characters the audiences could love or hate but at the end of the day identify with.

With the launch of Zee Talkies in 2007, ZEEL bridged the missing link that had existed between its kitty and Marathi cinema all these years. It was Maharashtra's first-ever 24-hour Marathi movie channel. The only Marathi movie channel which filled the gap for the amenable Marathi movie audience through a non-stop show of blockbuster movies, evergreen stars and everything about Marathi movies. Zee Talkies is a special channel that attempts to carry forward this legacy of great personalities and productions of Marathi Cinema by presenting quality movies. Zee Talkies presented the biggest library of Marathi masterpieces, right from the old classics like *Sadhi Manase, JagachyaPathiwar, Chhatrapati Shivaji, Molkarin, Gulacha Ganpati* to the most critically acclaimed *Shwaas* and all the following blockbusters from the world of Marathi Cinema. Zee Marathi has been entertaining the Marathi speaking community with content in their own language.' In 2008, however, Zee Talkies was transferred to the ZNL stable of channels.

Broadening its international base between 2006 and 2007, the company extended further into the Malaysian market with the launch of Zee Variasi, with content subtitled and dubbed in Malay, and into the Russian market with the launch of Zee Russia. Zee Russia was launched during 2007 as a 24-hour General Entertainment Channel broadcasting latest serials and movie blockbusters for its viewers in Russian and is one of the highest rated among the movie and serial genre in Russia.

With a view to comply with the regulatory requirements for Russian Broadcasting Operations, Asia TV Ltd UK an overseas subsidiary, created/acquired an indirect subsidiary called 'OOO Zee CIS Holdings Ltd' in Russia in 2008. For that purpose they acquired/created direct/indirect subsidiaries namely ZES Holdings Ltd Mauritius Zee Entertainment Studios Ltd British Virgin Islands ZES Mauritius Ltd Mauritius ZES International Ltd United

Kingdom and Zee Motion Pictures Pvt. Ltd India.[108]

A 60 per cent stake was also acquired in Venus Films. According to one of the directors of Zee, the film production and distribution division was dormant in the year 2006–07 while it observed developments in the industry and its transition to the organized sector. Zee Entertainment Enterprises Limited launched Zee Entertainment Studios in 2007 with two movie banners—Zee Motion Pictures for mainstream films and Zee Limelight for films targeted at niche audiences. Zee Studio also took the 'Subtitling Initiative'—a new category innovation of airing all English movies with English subtitles. In the same year, Zee Studios also came out with a series 'Saluting Satyajit Ray' showcasing the finest movies made by the legendary filmmaker. It also showcased some acclaimed movies of M. Night Shyamalan.

During the year 2007–08, pursuant to a scheme of amalgamation, ETC Networks Ltd a, listed subsidiary of the company merged with Zee Interactive Learning Systems Ltd, subsequently renamed as ETC Networks Ltd Asia Today Ltd For the FY 2007, Zee recorded total annual revenues of ₹15.1 billion. In 2008, Subhash Chandra's son Punit Goenka took over as CEO of Zee Entertainment.[109] That year, the company launched a new channel in the South Indian market.

On 12 October 2008, Zee launched Zee Tamil, a Tamil General Entertainment Channel (GEC) in Tamil Nadu. With the brand proposition, 'ManadhaalInaivom, MaatrathaiVaraverppom' which translates to 'let's bridge hearts and welcome change,' the channel strives to blur the divisions between age groups and generations, especially among women, urging them to come together and embrace progress in all forms. Synonymous with Tamil pride, Zee Tamil stands for progressive and onward-looking content, featuring bold and determined characters whose modern outlook is grounded by tradition and values.

For audiences in MENAP countries, Zee Aflam was launched

in 2008, a movie channel dubbed in Arabic. Zee Aflam was the first and leading free-to-air Bollywood movie channel packaged in Arabic, for the Arab Audience in the Middle East and North Africa 'connecting Arabs to Bollywood'. It is the destination for the latest and biggest Bollywood blockbuster movies with over 1000 hand-picked movies. Taking viewers to the heart of Bollywood, Zee Aflam airs the biggest movie award nights and entertaining celebrity talk shows. In the same year, ZEEL announced its plans to hive off Zee Next channel to its wholly owned Subsidiary Asia Today Limited.

The year 2009 saw a global economic slowdown. But India was able to cope well. If anything, it emerged stronger in most areas of development. Infrastructure development, increase in private equity transactions, flows from foreign institutional investors and a suitable environment for foreign direct investments, all indicated that India was capable of getting back on its feet.

During the year, India held the position of being the third largest television market in the world. This only translated into greater successes for Zee. Trying his hand once more at wellness-oriented programming, Chandra ventured into this space again with 'Veria' in 2009. This network was launched specifically for global audiences, and Indian audiences residing in America. Chandra explained the background behind this idea, 'The Americans have developed a lot of faith and interest in Ayurveda, nature cure, yoga, pilates, etc. We were keen to cash in on this need…' Since this was an ambitious undertaking that no one had attempted before, the channel didn't have adequate distribution. The select few households in America that subscribe to this channel, however, seem to enjoy it.[110]

Zee's original music offering which was launched as Music Asia in 1997, then rebranded as Zee Music in 2000, was finally relaunched yet again as Zing in April 2009. It was offered as an Indian pay television music channel owned by ZEEL, also distributed in Southeast Asia and Europe. It featured a variety of content, from humour, animation, spoofs, celebrity lifetsyle in addition to music. A non-stop musical programming block called Chill-ax Mornings was also offered on this channel. Zing was a channel for the youth and showcased youth fiction shows, music, Bollywood shows and a mix of Bollywood and Hollywood movies, thus providing an eclectic mix of content that strikes a note with the affluent youth.

In August, ZEEL launched India's first combination of talent hunt and a game show Café Mic Testing, a reality show that searched for unique talent for Zee Café. In a bid to preserve relevance, Zee Café telecast E! News and The Tonight Show with Jay Leno within a mere 12 hours of its USA telecast. Other international shows broadcast here included World Music Awards, Emmy's and leading fashion shows. Zee Café also acquired the exclusive LIVE telecast rights to the international beauty pageants Miss World 2008 and 2009. Through its Women's World Awards 2009, it recognized women's excellence and achievements. Zee Café stepped beyond the realms of a regular television channel, with the initiative of 'Green turn' (a drive for a greener earth), which found an enthusiastic response, right from viewers to advertising partners.

NEW MILESTONES AND NEW MEDIA

2010 was a landmark year for ZEEL with the release of the company's first notable Annual Report as an independent entity. It was the company's first public appearance, announcing their visions, ideas, innovations, and achievements through a compendium of data.

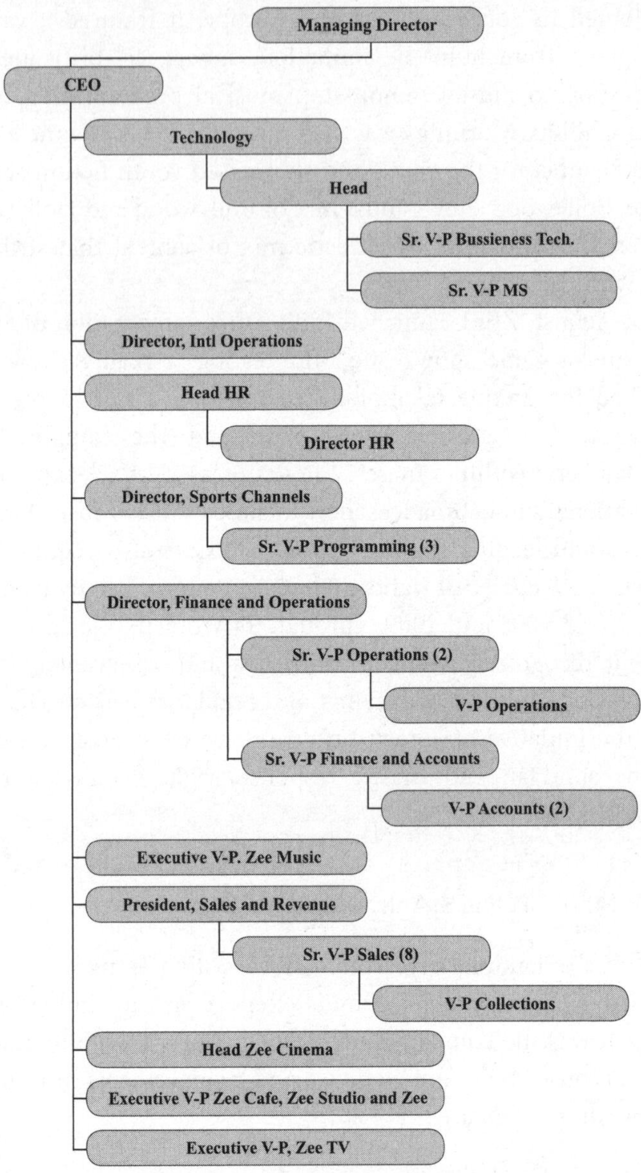

Fig. 6.5: Organizational Structure of ZEEL in 2008

Source: Compiled by the author with inputs from Zee officials

The company's mission statement going forward declared:

> To be the leading round the clock airtime properties provider and delight the viewer,s not only through our general entertainment and infotainment channels, but also through quality cinema from our movie banners. As a Corporation, we will be profitable, productive, creative, trendsetting and financially sound with care and concern for all our viewers and stakeholders namely advertisers, cable operators, producers and production houses.

It was to be based upon the foundation of the company's values of customer focus, excellence, creativity, integrity, and growth-driven development. The company's successes would be measured in the upcoming years with business restructuring, consistent network performance, digital ventures, sporting action, and international alliances.

In a recapitulation of its old and new successes, the feel of a new decade in the new century for ZEEL was declared in such way:

> It is the entertainment buffet extraordinaire of the century, and everyone is invited. We offer one of the largest spreads in the business with innumerable flavours, exciting genres, as well as a mouthwatering array of programming. The medium, the message and the media—we have a major presence in each. We bring entertainment to people in 167 countries across the globe. We are the destination for seekers of 'Indian flavoured' entertainment as well as global programming. We appeal to the intellect, as well as the emotion. We deliver fact as well as fiction. Our eclectic programming range includes prime time drama series, reality shows, television movies, theatrical films, specials and daytime dramas, sports coverage, regional and international language-based entertainment. We are

> here to provide the best in entertainment. We have made people recognise entertainment as Zee Entertainment. We are Zee Network. With innovative shows, culturally relevant content, aesthetic presentation and a truly multi genre buffet of entertainment that suits every palate… …We are here to stay![111]

The company was put across to the audiences as a fun and fresh company with big ambitions and an even bigger drive to fulfill them. Pointing towards its modernized and competent workforce, the top management mentioned, 'Almost 80 per cent of the employees at Zee Entertainment are less than 35 years of age and they thrive in a work environment that brings together bright, agile minds with varying perspectives, challenging conventional thinking and closed minds.' Alongside, it re-announced and reclaimed their position as the prime choice for entertainment and cinema. They continued, 'We are still the first choice of audiences in the Hindi GEC genre. Zee TV is the first choice Hindi entertainment channel for the South Asian diaspora worldwide. It is an ongoing festival of films everyday on Zee Entertainment Cinema channels. Zee is the one of the most favored home viewing channels for people seeking quality film entertainment. We are here to expand!'

There was a refocus on the company's regional outreach and product expansion in the multilingual sphere, within and outside India. Reflective of its personality, the Annual Report greeted its readers colourfully with 'Namaste, Sat Sri Akal, Nomoshkar, Namaskar, Namaskara, NamaskaramBaagunnara.' It continued, 'Zee's regional channels regale viewers with ethnically nuanced content, issues that are regional and entertainment that suits the specific taste of the region. Our regional channel foray is a recent one, with the merger of the regional channels into the Zee Entertainment palette.'

Recounting its international reach, the company claimed, 'Zee reaches 500 million people across 167 countries and 5 continents. Zee has nurtured this multi ethnic, multi lingual audience since its early years through a variety of platforms. Zee TV USA is the un-challenged leader in South Asian Entertainment across all Americas. Through its base in UK, Zee reaches 32 countries in Europe. Zee MENAP is the Zee arm that caters to audiences in Middle East, North Africa and Pakistan. It also caters to audiences in East and South Africa, as well as the Indian Ocean islands of Madagascar and Mauritius, as well as 43 countries in the Asia Pacific region. Zee TV and the various Zee channels deliver a taste of home culture and entertainment to the far from home...'[112]

Reminding audiences that ZEEL was the patriarch of the M&E family in India, the company recounted its firsts from the beginning, cementing its position as the pioneering force in the industry. 'Zee Entertainment is... ... the first media Company to launch a Hindi General Entertainment Channel (GEC), before it became the largest genre ... the first Indian media Company to list on a stock exchange, before the capital market became a preferred route for existing and newer entrants ... the first to launch a 24 x 7 news channel, before round-the-clock news channels became the norm ... the first to corporatise film making in India ... the first to launch and manage an MSO on a panIndia basis. Today, Zee is a name synonymous with Satellite Television in India, with a presence spanning over 167 countries. But to us, that is only the beginning.'

This was the year when the economy was almost recovered from the slopes of the global slowdown. Subhash Chandra, on this occasion, captured an environment scan of the market, with a promise to do the company's bit in placing India on the world market, 'Key indicators such as infrastructure development, surge in private equity transactions, flows from Foreign Institutional Investors (FIIs) and conducive environment for the Foreign

Direct Investments (FDI) have all augured well for the Indian economy. Today, India stands as world's second-largest wireless network with over 500 million mobile users. Digital technology is advancing at an ever-increasing pace and the boom in technology is totally redefining the meaning of entertainment. Currently, India is the third largest television market in the world and despite the size; it is one of the fastest growing markets. TV penetration in India is currently only 58 per cent and C&S TV penetration is 43 per cent. With unparalleled portfolios of programming properties, complemented by the distribution strengths from cable assets and reach of Pay TV, our Company is committed in creating operating efficiencies and developing new revenue sources for the long term.'[113] As if fulfilling the Chairman's vision, in fiscal 2010 Zee emerged with the highest viewership in the Maharashtra market, with a 35 per cent market share. Zee Cinema held the position for the No. 1 Hindi movie channel, and Zee TV made waves in USA with 53 per cent South Asian viewership. Zee TV maintained leadership in the crucial Prime Time band on weekdays and gave the viewers fiction and non-fiction shows like *Pavitra Rishta* and *Dance India Dance.* The year also marked the completion of 1000 episodes of *Saregamapa*-one of Zee TV's biggest and oldest brands.

Over at Zee Cinema, initiatives included the re-branding of the Sunday 8 PM slot as 'Lage Raho', where viewers got to see their favourite films with few breaks. Zee Telugu registered the best growth in Telugu and touched its highest ever viewership since launch. Zee Salaam, India's first Urdu infotainment satellite television channel was launched. India.com website was also launched in 2010 after a joint venture between ZEEL and Mail.com Media Corporation.It ran the fourth largest Indian Portal with 7.18 mm monthly unique visitors, owned and operated leading websites in key audience categories which include bollywoodlife.com, cricketcountry.com, health.india.com, oncars.

in, travel. india.com, and bgr.in. India.com ran the largest original production content channels on YouTube and launched 6 Original Programming Channels. It also uploaded 7,200 hours of content and 31,000 videos in 2012.

Zee International channels emerged among the top rated in markets across the US, UK, Middle East, South Africa and APAC. This placed it among the top players with regards to viewer interest in both South Asian and mainstream audiences, resulting in new advertisers and subscribers coming on board.

Over at internal quarters, Zee took full control of Taj TV by acquiring 45 per cent stake in the company and taking its holdings to 95 per cent. Ten Sports was launched, keeping sports lovers glued to their television sets. The channel broadcast 126 days of live international cricket from across the world. Alongside Ten Cricket (for cricket) and Ten Action+ (for football), Zee Sports was also making strides in the sports genre. The sports business emerged as a strong segment of the company's revenues on the back of telecast rights to 5 cricket boards, which ensured coverage of cricket of all test playing countries, and over 100 days of live cricket per year along with rights to properties like UEFA cup football, WWE wrestling, US Open Tennis, etc. Ten Cricket was also launched in the ME and USA markets.

During this time, Zee Cinema became the first-ever Hindi movie channel to launch mobile gaming. It offered its viewers an opportunity to auction celebrity costumes with 50 per cent of the proceeds to be donated to charity. Zee KhanaKhazana, the company's 24-hour food channel, was launched in December 2010. The channel brought in a rich programming mix from across India and the world that focused on culinary expertise, featuring the most popular programme led by world-renowned chef Sanjeev Kapoor.

During the year, the company undertook various initiatives to further strengthen its dominance in the geographies where it operated. In Russia, Zee signed a deal with Ukrainian DTH operator called 'MYtv'. In UK, Zee launched a new hybrid channel Zee Café, to complete the appeal of the Zee Family Pack. In Russia, Zee CIS and Sistema Mass-Media signed a Letter of Intent on cooperation in the field of TV content distribution and broadcast in India, Russia and several other countries. In Australia, four zee channels—Zee TV APAC, Zee Cinema, Zing and Zee Salaam were launched on Fetch TV further strengthening Zee's penetration across markets. Zee Entertainment Enterprises entered into a joint venture with Mail.com Media Corporation (MMC), a leading digital media Company based in Los Angeles, USA in February 2010. This joint venture marked the launch of an online and mobile entertainment portal that was purely content-centric. The portal would offer users a broad range of entertainment viewing options and other leading applications.

During fiscal 2009-2010, as per the scheme of arrangement, the company demerged the Regional General Entertainment Channel Business Undertaking (comprising of Zee Marathi, Zee Bangla, Zee Talkies, Zee Telugu, Zee Cinemalu, and Zee Kannada television channels) of Zee News Ltd (ZNL) vesting with the company on the appointed date 1 January 2010. The scheme became effective from 29 March 2010. Punit Goenka mentioned that this was the most significant development for the company during the year because it would ensure greater consolidation and synergies and result in better value creation.

ETC Networks Ltd (ETC), a listed subsidiary of the company, merged with the company with effect from appointed the date of 31 March 2010. Upon such merger the Education Business Undertaking of the company was demerged from the company and transferred to Zee Learn Ltd on the appointed date of 1 April 2010. During the year, ETC Networks Ltd (ETC), the listed subsidiary of the company, acquired the entire shareholding in Cornershop Entertainment Company Pvt. Ltd, which in turn held 100 per cent stake in Cornershop Animation Pvt. Ltd Digital Media Convergence Ltd and Re-Med Services Pvt. Ltd Subsequently these subsidiaries amalgamated with ETC from the appointed date of 1 January 2010 in pursuance of a scheme of amalgamation which became effective on 29 April 2010. Asia TV Ltd, United Kingdom, one of the overseas subsidiaries, along with its subsidiary OOO Zee CIS Holding Ltd, Russia jointly acquired 100 per cent stake in OOO Zee CIS Ltd, a broadcasting operating company in Russia.[114]

There was a multiplex-producer strike during the first quarter of the year. ETC took the initiative of getting the producers and multiplex owners together to voice their issues during the strike period. ETC also partnered in the Anti Piracy initiative drive along with several top Film Production companies. As if to mark the occasion, ZEEL was recognized as the Top Indian Company in the M&E Sector at the Dun & Bradstreet, Rolta Corporate Awards 2010. Overall, the year augured well for the channel.

A NEW BRAND IDENTITY

19 June 2011 brought a new look for the Zee logo, a flashy blue font with the company's trademark Z, with the catchphrase 'Umeed se saje Zindagi' or hope makes life blossom. The new brand identity was marked by vibrancy, effortless style, and new-age sensibilities. The brand announced the logo, and expressed the intent behind it, 'We carried out extensive research among our viewers to arrive at a new logo and programming content. It stands also for ZEE's optimism—a mirror of the aspirations of millions of Indians. To us, it is full of rigor, and life and the ultimate energy. We identify most though, with its characteristics of breaking away from clichés and norms. We are young, we are enthusiastic.' This was fitting for a company that had amassed a library of almost 1,00,000 hours of television content.

Punit Goenka, on this occasion, commented on the company's upcoming plan, 'After six years, we have introduced a new brand positioning and vision statement for Zee and are stepping into an entirely new phase. The new identity is focused particularly on showcasing relatable content, adapting to changes in society and our innovation capabilities.'

Outlining the company's other international milestones of the year, Punit Goenka said, 'Widely recognized as one of the most successful media launches of the decade, Zee Aflam has notched an all time high of 39 GRPs. Besides, Zee in Malaysia has been the consistent No.2 International channel. Zee TV in USA enjoys the highest viewership, while Zing is one of the leading Asian Channels in that market. Zee TV consistently ranks No.1 amongst Asian expatriates in UAE, and has been the leading Asian channel in South Africa.' Unlike in the previous few years, no new channel launches were seen in 2011. Meanwhile, the music channel launched in 1999 as ETC, and acquired by Zee in 2002 along with sister channel Zee ETC Punjabi (then Alpha ETC Punjabi), was renamed to Zee ETC Bollywood in 2011.[115] It complemented Zing as a music offering from the company, along with other providing information from the film industry. Zee ETC Bollywood has been catering to all the viewers, distributors, producers, exhibitors, actors and music companies. Nobody knows Bollywood as ETC does, because ETC is Bollywood's confidante.

Chandra's approach towards every undertaking has always held some amount of social objective. Between the years 2010 and 2011, Zee carried out an array of undertakings aimed at increasing their social value. Under their CSR brand, Zee Care, the key focus was on women empowerment and child education. To realise their dream of building 'one world', the company was committed to mitigating potential business risks and capitalising on emerging opportunities. The company declares, 'At ZEE, we understand the power of media to deliver messages and catalyse positive societal change. Most of our channels feature content to create awareness against social anomalies.'[116]

The social activities initiatives under the company's CSR objectives continued with its long-standing areas of development. For instance, Zee TV, in association with 'Save the Children India (STCI)', initiated support for underprivileged children and even financed the education of 100 children. Moreover, ETC Channel Punjab Initiated 'The Green Earth Campaign' involving over 50 colleges, thousands of students and many academicians, to raise environment awareness across Punjab. Zee Touch India Foundation also featured public service advertisements on breast cancer, polio, for the visually impaired, for HIV/AIDS on International Aids Day, AIDS awareness campaign by Mukti Foundation, etc. Equal in measure to the social aspect was the company's financial aspect. Clocking ₹15.8 billion through advertisement revenues and ₹13.2 billion through subscription revenues, the overall financial performance all through was stable.

The joint ventures of the company in digital distribution viz. ITM Digital Pvt. Ltd, and in India branded Entertainment Portal viz. India Webportal Pvt. Ltd commenced operations during the year. IWPL runs a suite of 24 websites focusing on entertainment, news and sports content. It was launched in partnership with Penske Media Corporation (PMC) and United Internet, and is currently the third largest content publisher in India. India.com is the flagship website and other websites including TheHealthSite.com, Bollywoodlife.com and BGR.in are leaders in their respective categories. Upon mutual agreement amongst the joint venture partners, the company acquired complete shareholding in ITM Digital Pvt. Ltd, in May 2011, thus making it a wholly owned subsidiary.

In 2011, Zee Turner Ltd entered into a 50:50 joint venture with Star Den Media Services to form MediaPro Enterprise

India Pvt. Ltd. This, Goenka said, would 'facilitate the redressal of anomalies in the distribution sector, curb piracy and enhance transparency by accelerating the digitization process. These steps would benefit stakeholders across each segment of the value chain.'[117]

Technological developments were resplendent during this FY. A series of measures were initiated in the International Delivery Network to improve functionality. Channels that were targeted for delivery across Europe and USA were being hauled via fibre systems, instead of satellite. The initiative provided a 50 per cent advantage in cost without affecting the quality. On the other hand, conversion of channels to MPEG4 would result in 40 per cent saving in bandwidth and associated costs, while improving quality.

Zee Café, Zee Trendz, Zee Studio, Zee TV Middle East and Zee KhanaKhazana were among the first channels to be converted. In broadcast operations too, the company was making strides as the trendsetter. ZEE's superior operational efficiency lay in the flexible and forward-looking traffic management and transmission play-out system it had, one of the best in the industry. Use of a superior broadcast management system (BMS) helped the company reduce its transmission log release time from the initial 72 hours to just a few hours before going on-air, maintaining the ratio of manpower to number of channels at the lowest in the industry.

During the year, both father and son laid claim to quite a few awards, some attributed to them, and others to their company. In April 2011, Punit Goenka was presented the Generation Next Business Award May, while Subhash Chandra received the 2011 International Emmy® Directorate Award. Subhash Chandra became the first ever International Emmy Directorate Award recipient from India, a proud feather in the Zee family's cap. In January the same year, Zee was presented with Certificate of

Excellence at The Second Annual Inc. India 500 Awards. Not just the company, but even channels were collecting accolades across genres. In the sphere of creative awards, Zee Cinema, Zee Studio, Ten Sports bagged three Gold Awards, while Zee Cinema and Zee KhanaKhazana bagged two Silver Awards.

20 YEARS OF PIONEERING VISION AND BEYOND

The environment in the television industry in India witnessed the introduction of the much-awaited cable digitization in 2012. Despite initial obstacles, Phase I of digitization in the four metros was rolled out smoothly resulting in much-needed transparency in the industry. Next in line was Phase II of digitization, being implemented in 38 more cities across the country. These efforts translated into enhanced subscription revenues for broadcasters and made them less dependent on advertising and enable them to drive higher value creation.

That year, Zee Entertainment completed 20 years in the business. On this occasion, Subhash Chandra is quoted to have said, 'A milestone of 20 years is a defining moment in any organization's life span. It is a reason to celebrate, when the dream we envisioned two decades ago has blossomed. We are now at an inflection point, a position from where we have to leapfrog and move to the next growth trajectory.'

Punit Goenka, who had until now headed the company with élan, envisioned bigger things and made bigger promises for the future. He said, 'With a benchmark of completing 20 years of excellence, comes a commitment to our stakeholders and partners. A promise to deliver values, fulfil dreams and realise aspirations. A promise to enrich lives and extend footprints across multiple vistas of entertainment.'[118]

The company recorded successes by marking them, 'With the completion of this milestone, we stand firm as one of India's leading M&E companies. Our pioneering steps, taken in this expedition, range from India's first satellite television channel, first 24-hour news channel, first DTH platform, to the latest Over The Top Television platform.' By this time, Zee had achieved success in 168 countries, with 30 channels and 22 international beams. Viewers were recorded at over 650 million, with 1,00,000+ hours of TV content. At the market level, 10.5 million subscribers had adopted satellite-based television services via DTH, taking the gross DTH subscriber base to 44.6 million strong in 2012.

It was an eventful year for the folks at ZEEL. According to them, 'Be it the completion of over 700 episodes of some of our leading TV shows, or the rich contribution of our Regional and Sports Channels with optimal and niche content, the successful acquisition of some of the biggest Bollywood titles, or the rapid expansion in the international markets, the year has seen it all.'[119]

Zee Alwan, the first GEC launched for Middle Eastern audiences in 2012, received commendable response from Arabic viewers within a short time span. The channel broadcast some of India's most popular television serials and shows on cookery, travel, health and fitness in Arabic, to the Middle East, considering the growing popularity of Bollywood in the Arab world. This offering was also expected to strengthen the historic and cultural bond between UAE and India. With the tagline 'Color Your Life', Zee Alwan offers exclusive Indian premieres, Turkish and East European series and lifestyle shows along with Arabic drama series and non-fiction shows over the weekend. Zee Alwan would soon also include 5 to 6 hours of local drama content per week, made specifically for Zee.

On the occasion of the launch in 2012, Punit Goenka said, 'It has taken 3 years to launch. The challenge has been in doing extensive research to find out which of our stories work in that market, then crunching 300 episodes down to 60 episodes. This is all based on research we have done in those markets. The channel launched in July, and by the end of this year we will start local production.'[120]

Strengthening the company's existence in the USA market, ZEEL launched 4 new channels, including Zee Marathi, Zee Kannada, Zing and Zee Smile, and achieved presence on newer platforms like Charter LA and Centurylink, leading to an enhanced reach. Zee Cinema International was launched with English subtitles in countries like Indonesia, Myanmar and Hong Kong with an attempt to take Bollywood across Asia. Zee also successfully conducted international events like Zee Nite in Durban, Mauritius and Reunion and Zee Bollywood Nite in Malaysia.

Zee TV also became the first Indian channel to be granted the landing rights in China. This enabled them to cater to the large audience base in China, and increase their already prevalent international base. Punit Goenka identified a three-pronged focus on these strategic priorities: creating high-quality family content, making content accessible in each of the available platforms and growing internationally.

During this time, Goenka said that there were no further plans for original production outside the Middle East, a mainly free-to-air market where advertising was making up 80 per cent of the television industry revenues. However, Zee continued to study the prospect for tailored channels elsewhere, focusing mainly on Indonesia and South Africa. At the same time, the company was also working on an English-language offering to appeal to South Asians living abroad who may still watch Bollywood, but no longer connect with homegrown soaps and dramas. Goenka said, 'A lot of research is being done on that right now. By the end of this year, we will be finalizing our plans when to launch it, and in which markets.'[121]

Back home, they moved with a mission to make 'smarter entertainment' the 'new normal', making use of new media communication channels. As outlined by Punit Goenka, they intended to scale unexplored boundaries in content distribution, following the latest launch of their OTT platform, Ditto TV, to offer content across leading genres. Ditto TV became India's first OTT service available in 176 countries across the world, offering more than 150 channels comprising premium live TV channels. It was made available on iOS, Android and Windows devices. Although it carried only linear channels, including offerings from rival broadcasters such as Sony, NDTV and Turner, Goenka was viewing this new business with a positive eye, gaining ground through on-demand content. He remarked, 'That's where the money is. You pull in the people with streaming channels, but you push them towards consuming on- demand.'

The site, which was geo-blocked for Indian audiences in the beginning, was also to go live in the US and UK by the end of the year, with a low-resolution version offering affordable daily packs for non-3G mobile devices also launching in India. It was projected that Ditto would need a critical mass of around 1 million active subscribers to start making money, a goal that was aimed to be achieved within two to three years. Goenka continued, 'It's still early days…unsure whether Ditto will develop as a mainly mobile or more multiplatform business, and how much it will appeal to existing pay-TV subs. My gut tells me the overlap with cable and satellite is not more than 5 per cent, but no-one in the world knows the answer.'[122]

Meanwhile, Zee Family.TV emerged as a dedicated OTT platform for the USA territory, offering more than 20 ZEEL channels including linear channels as well as on-demand content in Hindi and regional languages. It comprised of a rich mix of movies and GEC content. The sports offering was expanded with the launch of Ten Golf, a dedicated 24-hours golf channel with several medium- term licensing arrangements in place, and Ten HD. Ten Sports, meanwhile, completed 10 years of operation.

Zee Studios was also launched during the year as the film production and distribution arm of Zee Entertainment. It was producing differentiated and high-impact films, across several languages. Its expertise in making content for the Indian television and understanding audience preferences gave the studio an edge in successful movie making. Zee Studios established its worth in the movie business with hits like *Rustom, Sairat* and *Natsamrat.* Zee Studios has a dedicated approach method, including four areas: Focus on script and execution, because a strong script is the most important criteria for movie selection with involvement in every step of movie making with control on costs and execution; portfolio approach to produce movies across budgets and multiple languages to reduce risk; profit sharing with key talent as a way to engage with key talent, while reducing the financial risk should the movie fail; leverage presence across verticals, which provides useful consumer insights and helps promote films, wherein other business are natural buyers of movie right.

Strides were made technologically too, as per the company's broadcast operations. Between 2012–13, the Noida uplink facility was fully revamped with a full HD core network, file-based media workflows, playouts with advanced media architecture and interfaces to massive archival and retrieval systems dispersed amongst the network production and transmission sites. Full file-based media workflows are achieved by an extended media network, which encompasses even the production houses on the same platform. The entire media network operated on redundant high speed optical fiber links and connected the playout hub to the Mumbai production facility, regional clusters as well as the company partners in media production, advertising and live events.

During this financial year, Punit Goenka took the fore by receiving two accolades for his endeavours: The Businessworld Infocom ICT Award and The Generation Next Business Award.

Known as the 'content architect' of the group, Goenka attributes his success to viewer interaction. 'I just go to the viewers and asked them, 'What do you want?' What are you not getting today in entertainment?' What would you like to see? That's what we go and include.'[123]

The road ahead was visibly digital for ZEEL. The company masters quoted, 'Envisioning Zee to be a global M&E player, key strategic action points have been chalked out, in order to achieve the set goals. With the onset of digitization, arrival of 4G and elimination of anomalies, a positive industry growth is in sight, and we would implement all the planned strategies to capitalise on the opportunities. Backed with cutting edge technology support, we are surely geared up for the digital dawn.'[124] Several notable high-definition channels were launched during this year of functioning.

In 2012, ZEEL launched 'Zee BOLLYWORLD', an umbrella brand under which it consolidated its entire Indian content, including dramas, Bolly-movies, Bolly-documentaries, Bolly-travel, for syndication. Zee Bollyworld, an offering from the Zee stable, reinforces Zee's global positioning, supported by a vast content library (100,000+ hours of programming). In a first, in March 2012, Zee TV created 'Guinness World Records' for the largest Bollywood dance programme through participation of 4428 dancers as part of its *Dance India Dance* show.

Meanwhile, programmes like *Ghar ki Lakshmi Betiyaan* (protested against domestic violence), *Pavitra Rishta* (focused on injustice meted out to ageing parents), *Agle Janam Mohe Bitiya Hi Kijo* (raised awareness about girl child trafficking), *Saat phere* (battling the stigma of dark complexion) and *Aapki Antara* (which dealt with the issue of autism with sensitivity) helped in creating awareness about deep-rooted social prejudices and injustices, in accordance with Zee's early visions of trying to create an India free of such archaic social norms.

To this end, ZEEL has always played a proactive role. During this FY, the company spent approx. 0.57 per cent of its current profits towards CSR activities by way of Donations/sponsorship to various NGO's and other charitable organizations. It took initiatives to help drive social transformation during this FY too, as part of its CSR offerings. Zee Talkies and Zee Marathi had another successful campaign in 2012. Sixty hoardings were put up on the Mumbai Pune Expressways, NH4 (Mumbai-Pune), NH3 Mumbai-Nasik and other six important highways of Maharashtra, drawing attention to safe driving habits. Ekal Vidyalaya Foundation of India (EVFI) offerd free education to over 1 million rural children, as part of a drive to help eradicate illiteracy.

Zee Marathi also arranged for a symposium with the help of various social and cultural groups like Shabdagappa, Majestic group, VanitaSamaj, etc. Zee Salaam's initiative, Pehal—Ek Koshish, took up the issue of rehabilitation of sex workers and tied-up with the Jaitpur, Delhi based NGO IFRA, which addresses the issues of women forced into prostitution. An initiative by Zee Café celebrated the World Environment day by launching 'Green Turn' across four key cities: Mumbai, Delhi, Bengaluru, and Pune on the eve of World Environment day. Medium term financial support was provided by way of donation to Marrow Donor Registry (India)—MDRI, a society which facilitates Marrow and Blood Stem Cell transplants for patients with life-threatening blood diseases.

The key points of Zee's strategy during the year included taking appropriate steps to safeguard its leadership position in a high-powered competitive environment, to concentrate on additional revenues from digital pay platforms, build a foundational presence on new/alternate media platforms, rationalise on costs across different heads, fortify its expansion in the international markets, and maintain steadily high standards of corporate governance.

However, an overview of the FY revealed that margins were lower than desired, due to a spell of intense rivalry in Hindi entertainment and recent competition in regional markets, which were a key stronghold for Zee since the beginning. There were losses too, in the sports arm of the network, which dented high profitability.

According to an analytical report published in the *Asia Media Journal*, 'The ultimate goal is restoring Zee's margins to their former glory, consistently exceeding a 30 per cent cushion, an impressive performance for any broadcaster worldwide. Profits are already healthier thanks to MediaPro, a five-year distribution partnership with Star, which has helped lift growth in Zee's analog subs revenues to 16–17 per cent over the past 12 months, compared with a 6-7 per cent norm. Nonetheless, surpassing 30 per cent will be tough going until India's overloaded analog distribution networks are replaced by spacious new digital pipes.'

Punit Goenka attributed a change in the market state to digitization, 'There was a time when margins were consistently 30 per cent- plus. Today, we are in the 25-27 per cent range. We still aspire to go back to 30 per cent but it will take a few years to get there. The only way it will go back to the 30 per cent mark is if digitization happens.' This digitization dream had already been half accomplished by ZEEL in many ways. Zee's digitization of its content library was 50 per cent complete, a suite of more targeted digital channels (like the upcoming ZeeQ) was being developed, production facilities were being upgraded, etc.

In 2013, Subhash Chandra renovated the brand identity of Zee, adding an emotional flavour to it. 'Vasudhaiva Kutumbakam' (The World is My Family) now defined all that Zee stood for. This new zinger was a symbolic ode to Chandra's own early ventures into the industry with Zee and how it had developed over the years, taking along with it scores of Indians on its journey. He stressed on the fact that his organization strove to achieve this philosophy and unite the entire world with its rich and engaging content. He asserted that Zee worked for the upliftment of the society and this philosophy so far had helped it to achieve that end.

Addressing the shareholders in the company's annual report, Subhash Chandra spoke pragmatically of the business environment that enabled Zee media to flourish. After having a strong viewership of over 730 million viewers, Zee aimed to consolidate its position in the market by striving to enrich its viewer's lives by going beyond entertainment. This signifies that Zee was aspiring to become a part of people's lives and ultimately bond people and communities across countries and cultures. The opening of its markets to Indonesia and Thailand further affirmed Zee's global outlook and vision of making its brand a global entity.

Entertainment industry's favourite child, Shah Rukh Khan, expressed pride in Zee's leadership position: 'Zee is like a Family to me. My association with this Family, goes way back to the early nineties. To me, Zee resonates the word 'Entertainment'. Be it any genre, Zee has proven to be a leader. I personally like its current stance of envisioning the entire World as One Family. I think it is an extremely noble and generous approach.'[125] Employees weren't left far behind either. Zee's employee philosophy of 'Samvad' ensured top-notch human resource management. Elaborating more on his self-maintained system of management within the company, Chandra wrote in his autobiography: 'Managing so many companies is not easy. It requires a methodical approach. I meet the CEOs regularly. Then I meet all the department heads that report to the CEO. And then I meet the people who report to the department heads. All this happens at periodic intervals. I go through their HR feedback forms. This way I get to keep track of what is happening in each company, and also how each executive is performing. We call this whole process Samvad or dialogue. In the last two decades I have changed a lot and so has my management style. To me there is no difference between traditional and modern management philosophies. I can summarise it simply. Select the right person, define the right outcome and empower them.'[126]

Punit Goenka echoed his father's thoughts exactly, elaborating on how the management manner is directly proportionate to output at the company, 'Management strategy is simple—we are a people driven organization. At the end of the day, this company is because of its people; it's not because of me or any single individual. It's a collective effort of 3400 odd employees that we have in the company. More than third of that is in the content space and they are creating content on a daily basis. We produce close to 500 hours of content every week. In my view, and I could be wrong, we are the largest producer of content in the world. The amount of content we produce, I don't think any broadcaster in the world would be producing.'[127]

He said that the organization heads at Zee believe in empowering their colleagues and employees a lot. 'We are an entrepreneurial driven organization. We do not interfere in the day-to-day operations of the business heads and the teams and that empowers them to go and deliver on the goals that are set for them. That has been the key mantra for the success of Zee. If you look at our 7 values that we follow, all those have been at the core of Zee and that's what has been the success factor for us.'[128]

In 2013, a key change was also the implementation of 12-minute advertisement cap in non-news channels. This resulted in an Effective Rate (ER) increase in some genres like Hindi GECs. During the year popular movies like English Vinglish, Joker, Agneepath, and Agent Vinod premiered on Zee Cinema. Agneepath was one of the highest rated premieres of the year amongst all Hindi Movie channels, including Zee's rivals, with a rating of 4.7 TVR.

As the year progressed, Zee put up some new offerings for national and international audiences. They launched two offerings for Indian audience: Zee Q, India's first edutainment channel for kids, emphasising on learning through entertainment. The channel came into existence after thorough research by experts in order to make learning an enjoyable experience for children. The second channel was Zee Bangla Cinema, a 24/7 Bengali movie channel. Over the years, the channel has evolved into the destination for the biggest and latest Bengali films in West Bengal. Zee Bangla Cinema has always been at the forefront of innovation, with properties like Song Connection, Zee Bangla Cinema Originals and ZBC Shorts. Movie channels can assist as reliable reach and frequency builders for advertisers, and since advertiser interest in non-Hindi markets was growing during this phase, these moves stood to benefit Zee. Expansion into other genres was a good option, depending on market conditions and access to library content; however Goenka desired to secure a strong footing for the existing portfolio first.

Significantly, ZEEL strengthened their international presence with the launch of two channels in UAE (Zee TV HD and Zee Cinema HD). To further strengthen the presence in Europe, Zee channels were launched on Your TV and Yupp TV. Zee entered the Canadian market—with the launch of Zee TV HD in partnership with Ethnic Channels Group Limited (ECG), Canada's largest distributor of third language television services. Zing was launched on Rogers, while Zee Salaam and Zee Tamil were launched on Bell Fibe in Canada. The company forged a contract with Russia's third largest GSM operator Megafon, for Mobile TV and with regional analog cable operator Barshinform. Seven Zee channels were launched on the Indian Pack with TOT (IPTV) in Thailand. In UK, Zing became one of the leading Asian channel and was set to broadcast its very first daily soap-series—Cloud 9, produced in the region.

In line with its new media undertakings, Zee ventured into the production of fiction and non-fiction programming through its in-house production facility Essel Vision, earlier called ITM Digital Private Limited, which was a wholly owned Indian Subsidiary of ZEEL. Subhash Chandra explained the reason behind this: 'This is part of our backward integration strategy to be present at all the points of value creation. At the same time this will help in cost optimisation, better control on content and quick turnaround time. Further, this will enhance ZEE's capability to enter various other entertainment domains like film production in the near future. We are building a sustainable digital business model with strong cross platform presence on all devices and screens, expanding ZEE's digital business comprising the OTT platform with Ditto TV and mobile app.'[129] The company's board also approved a scheme of arrangement between the company and Diligent Media Corporation (DMCL) for the demerger of media business undertaking from DMCL and vesting into the company.[130]

Zee also designed and launched two knowledge platforms, 'Zee Leadership series' and 'Mindspace' to provide a platform for intellectuals all over the world to come together for debates, discussions and talks. ZEE's brand intellectual property, Zee Mindspace Conference aimed at bringing the marketing fraternity together to join hands and exchange discourse on new possibilities. For instance, the sessions under Zee Mindspace Conference 2016 comprised of two main themes—Previewing Tomorrow and Open Possibilities. The conference hosted names like R Ray Wang, principal analyst, founder and chairman, Constellation Research, Vanessa Clifford, deputy chief executive, News Works, Tom Goodwin, SVP of Strategy and Innovation, Havas Media, Jeff Bullas, blogger, strategist and speaker, and others.

Through its superior technology, the company covered most of Asia, through C-band on Asiasat, 3S, Insat 4A, Apstar-7 and IS-20 satellites. These covered India, Middle East, Africa,

Australia, SAARC Region and Far East.

In the financial year 2013–14, Zee spent 0.57 per cent of its profits towards various charitable organizations and NGOs. Zee focused on promoting reading and literacy in Rajasthan and Uttarakhand. Partnering with global organization, 'Room to Read', Zee enhanced literacy levels by establishing 20 primary school libraries along with providing teacher development training to 100 teachers. ZEEL was bestowed with the 'Best India Corporate Citizen Award' by the Global Association of Billionaires and Millionaires (GABM). It was to recognize ZEEL's efforts towards a commercially viable business model, which reflects its commitment towards corporate governance, fair trade and business practices.

DIFFERENT VOICES, ONE WORLD

In 2014, a 63-year-old Chandra handed over his infrastructure business through Essel Infraprojects to his younger son Amit Goenka, with a portfolio of ₹28,000 crore. Chandra's $3 billion empire now stood neatly divided between his two sons, with Punit Goenka having handled the M&E business since 2008. Chandra, with affection, explained this particular demarcation of his business, 'Amit is more of a risk-taker and has a mind of his own, while Punit is someone who creates consensus and then goes with it.'[131]

The media patriarch defined the year's vision to focus on landing amongst the top 10 global media houses by 2020, with a viewership that touched a billion, and 50 per cent revenues being drawn from overseas markets.

The ZEEL intent was renewed in 2014 with a special focus on the future outlook of the company in terms of numbers. It read:

> To become the world's leading global media company from the emerging markets. As a corporation, we are driven by

innovation and creativity that focuses on growth, while delivering exceptional value to our customers, our viewers and all our stakeholders:

- To achieve five times viewership growth by 2020
- To achieve four times growth in content consumption
- To be ranked among top media brands

The organization strove to bring in original innovations, experiment with content and design in order to grow exponentially towards the 2020 deadline. It wanted to reach out to not just its local audience but to take its world audience on board too. It wanted to project and package itself in a way that more people were attracted to it for its content and ultimately aimed to become a go-to option for the entire world. The company got included in Nifty, the National Stock Exhange's index.

In the same year, rumours began buzzing, of Zee wanting to pull out of the sports business, but not being able to since a good valuation was not available. Ten Sports, Ten Action and Ten Cricket appeared to not be doing so well. But Punit Goenka maintained that the company was committed to this enterprise. Simultaneously, except for the Zee TV flagship channel, other channels were facing tough competition from Star's general entertainment channels. Channels like KhanaKhazana and ZeeQ were also causing losses to the company. Goenka however maintained a positive outlook, and said '…they are gradually turning around.'[132]

Zee Aflam and Zee Alwan held their leadership positions in their respective genres. These channels were free-to-air and revenue was coming into the company through advertising. Punit Goenka maintained that for the time being, these channels would offer Bollywood content only, repurposed in local languages, instead of airing their usual chat shows. Pradeep Guha commended this strategy, saying, 'In TV, the more you can exploit your content across platforms and across countries, the better. All international studios do this. This will help the company turn around faster.'[133]

In Europe, the company showed marked growth through the introduction of many innovations, like the launch of the Sky Asia Pack, the addition of Zing Jukebox Live, and the introduction of an events vertical, amongst others. Meanwhile in the United States, Zee channels grew distribution by over 7.8 per cent, India.com was consolidated as the No. 2 web portal for NRIs. ZEEL also launched ZEEFamily.TV, the first South Asian anywhere, everywhere TV service.

The group's business model has always been that of market expansion and creating a global outreach. It is evident how it structurally took over the entertainment space in the Middle East, Europe and United states to achieve more dividends. It increased its viewership by diversifying content and by creating an all-inclusive platform. As such, in the Middle East, Zee TV's show 'Parwaaz' caused a surge in the channel's viewership. The channels' subscribers in the region increased by 14 per cent.

2014 brought a number of new launches within the ZEEL bouquet of channels. It launched Zee Lamhein—catring to its UK viewers. The channel took special care to customize the content and air shows which were based on the lives of migrants, thereby creating an emotional connect with the UK audience. This further ensured consolidation of Zee in a global marketplace. With a similar motive of gaining an international audience and expanding its horizons, Zee launched Zee BIOSKOP, Indonesia's first Bollywood channel, dubbed in Bahasa. Zee Bioskop featured Blockbuster Bollywood movies and premium drama series customized for the Indonesian audience. With non-stop, 24 hours entertainment, the channel brings romance, fun and drama into every living room in Indonesia, delivering exhilarating Bollywood block-busters across a range of genres from comedy to action, thriller, drama, horror and romance, premium Drama series and entertainment programmes like Talk shows and cooking shows over the weekend, all in Bahasa Indonesia! Showcasing the best of content from India, it truly is Bollywood Banget! It also launched ZeeNung, a 24/7 Bollywood movie channel in Thailand, fully dubbed and subtitled in Thai. The channel's positioning 'Bollywood Nai Thai' stays true to its personality and aims to touch the heart of all Bollywood fans in Thailand. The channel's strength lies in its library of hit movies and specially designed programme properties. Keeping up with the speed of the digital age, the company launched Zee Anmol, a Hindi GEC, which could simultaneously be streamed on mobile platform as well. With a brand positioning of 'Dil Chhoo Jaye', Zee Anmol brought back popular dramas into the viewers' lives. With television viewing universe expanding exponentially over the last few years, the channel's content was being consumed for the first-time by a vast majority of viewers across smaller towns where C&S penetration still had a lot of scope to increase. Zee Anmol's shows reaches out to innumerable new viewers across every television household in India and its consistent growth helps expand the reach of the Zee network.

The now popular &Pictures was also launched during this year, to mark its presence in the movie channel arena. An interactive Hindi movie channel, &Pictures aimed at targeting the youth, by building upon the existing film and digital resources to create a conversation with an audience that is interested in staying aware and engaged with the world around them. Being the country's first interactive movie channel, &Pictures honors India's high flying, yet rooted culture and celebrates her 'Sapnonki Udaan'. The programming of the channel is aimed to be a reflection of the subtle evolution of movies and movie viewing, which can be attributed to the evolution of the movie watching audience. Zee launched these channels to cater to a very diverse audience as the market expanded.

In 2014, ZEEL received RBI approval for FII Investment upto 100 per cent in the company. This translated into higher investment opportunity for the company, from varied quarters from around the world and therefore to expand its offering by backing itself with wealth attached to accomplished names. Zee's subsidiary Taj Television was also brought on board for increased dealings. Chandra, for the year, elaborated, 'Zee has plans to grow through inorganic growth and acquisitions, these will require funding. For example, we bid for an international company Chello, it's a Liberty Media company. We bid for $1 billion and somebody paid them 1 billion euros and we missed out. It would have fitted with our future plans on media business.'

Zee Music Company was another one of the initiatives launched by ZEEL in 2014 that sought to close the loop in terms of genre offerings from the company. The older music offering by Zee was updated and unveiled to the public as Zee Music Company. The extensive content library, network and distribution reach were synergistic, and would allow them to play a key role in this industry and benefit from its opportunities and market size. Zee Music Company's repertoire of projects comprised 36 Hindi movies, 15 Marathi movies, two Punjabi movies and 30 popular single numbers.

Launching, 'Zee Music Company', clearly points out to the expansive strategy taken by the company to make its mark in the rapidly developing Indian music industry. Digital streaming was the primary revenue source, contributing approximately 70 per cent of the revenues of music labels. ZMC is building a strong portfolio in regional markets and ZMC Youtube channel is the third most subscribed Indian channel. Aside from its Hindi music catalogue, ZMC is also present in the regional music space with a growing market share in Punjabi, Telugu, Tamil, Kannada, Gujarati and Bangla music. It boasts of a monopolistic leadership position in Marathi music.

This also affirms to the fact that the company wants to keep upgrading with the times and the technological advancements of the digital age. Further, this extends the company's boundaries to establish itself in every arena and with leading production houses to derive the maximum revenue possible. In this year, ZEEL also partnered with the Jaipur Literature Festival, the world's biggest free of cost literature fest. Drawing people from all parts of the globe, the Festival brings together some of the world's greatest minds from all walks of life from literature to history to politics, business leaders, sports and the entertainment industry. Hosting the most-renowned authors, ranging from Noble Laureates and Man Booker Prize Winners to debutants, the festival serves as a beacon of free speech around the world, and has inspired more than 200 other literature festivals of its kind across the world. With this festival, Zee aimed to revive the love and passion for the arts and inculcate an exchange of thoughts, culture and ideas. Zee JLF was awarded 'Best Festival' at the Outlook Traveller Awards in India. Dubbed 'the greatest literary show on Earth,' Zee JLF successfully expanded to London and Boulder, US too.

As far as its CSR activities for the fiscal are concerned, ZEEL partnered with 'Event and Entertainment Management Association and Film and Television Producers Guild to launch a charity concert 'Hum Hain Ummeed-E-Kashmir'... to facilitate raising funds and awareness for flood-stricken areas of Jammu and Kashmir.'

The year 2015 brought a new mantra for those at ZEEL, as they invested in tomorrow as the key strategic imperative in realising their global ambitions. This was better explained by Punit Goenka in his message to the audience in the fiscal's Annual Report, 'The key elements of our strategy going forward will be to consistently invest in growth opportunities to safeguard and grow our leadership, in a competitive environment. We will concentrate on the opportunities that digitization presents, and seek to maximise revenue from this, while operating in a prudent environment. We will consistently seek out newer markets globally, and fortify our existing ones.' His father envisioned the future with a view to achieving 'five times viewership growth' and 'four times growth in content consumption'.[134]

The key elements of ZEE's strategy during the year were to 'Invest in growth opportunities to safeguard business leadership in a competitive environment, to concentrate on additional revenues from digitization, rationalize on costs across different heads, fortify its expansion in the international markets, and to maintain consistently high standards of corporate governance.

Looking at its international achievements, the company was now identifying itself as a 'Global Content Company'. It was making supreme use of technology to the best of its abilities, sensing the changing times and changing digitized markets. It claimed: 'Zee is very much in synch with this process of change, and is geared to offer its entertainment content through 'NOW media' i.e. through digital tools and OTT platforms, among others. It is also adopting cutting-edge, advance formats like 'high definition' and '4K'. We foresee that these formats will transform the viewing experience in the near future, and content producers will have to be nimble-footed and geared up to address the technology paradigm, in addition to the content quality. The demarcation between 'on-air' and 'online' is rapidly disappearing, with almost all devices getting backward and forward integrated using the Internet.'

In 2015, INSEAD one of the world's leading and largest graduate business schools published a comprehensive case study about ZEEL. It was titled 'Act Globally, Think Globally: Zee Entertainment's Worldwide Growth' and was written by Stephen Mezias, Professor of Entrepreneurship and Family Enterprise at INSEAD and Colin J. Killick. 'It gives an account of ZEEL's international strategy with valuable insights from ZEEL MD and CEO, Punit Goenka as well as other senior management team.

The case also discusses ZEE's Global flexibility and adaptability as well as the benefits of going global.'

Mezias was quoted as saying, 'Zeel is a pioneer in private satellite TV space and has achieved noteworthy success in a short time span. The remarkable success of Zee in the global arena inspired us to research and deep dive into its entrepreneurial journey.'[135]

In 2015, ZEEL shifted base from its registered office in Worli to Lower Parel, Mumbai.[136] With the launch of Zee Unimedia the group brought the advertising sales functions within ZEEL under one roof to enable it to offer a more robust solution to the advertisers and at the same time leverage the collective strength of its businesses and channel portfolio. The company also established a new entity, Zee Digital Convergence, Limited in the financial year 2015 to consolidate its digital efforts. Other initiatives in this space included digital-first content and digital only content.

ZEEL also launched &TV, with plans to launch a bouquet of channels under this brand for the urban audience. &TV emerged as the flagship Hindi GEC amongst the '&' bouquet of channels from ZEEL. Staying true to the personification of the Ampersand, &TV stands for an aggregation of ambitions and rootedness which signifies the spirit of New Age India. Through its content offering, the channel brought together people and ideologies thus fostering unified viewing within Indian households. &TV's showcase tray included a diverse and dynamic mix of relatable fiction, high voltage non-fiction, marquee events and blockbuster movies. The channel is available in SD and HD across all Cable and DTH platforms and enjoys a leading presence in international markets including Asia Pacific, Europe, the Middle East and Americas.

The company made another foray into the entertainment channel called Zee Hiburan, which was also launched in

Indonesia for international audiences. Zee World, the first English GEC with dubbed and subtitled Indian content for mainstream African viewers, was also showcased. 'Zee World' was a step in the direction of telecasting international reality and TV shows to take the international audience on board. It was the world's first English-dubbed General Entertainment Channel showcasing Indian series, Bollywood movies, reality shows and many more action packed content. It was soon made available on DStv on channel 166 across 50 countries in Sub-Sahara Africa and the Indian Ocean Islands. Side by side, for Francophone audiences, Zee Magic was launched. Zee Magic was the world's first French-dubbed General Entertainment Channel showcasing Indian series, Bollywood movies and reality shows. The channel was available across Francophone Africa and Indian Ocean Islands. The channel is available on Canal plus channel 51 and Parabole Maurice channel 144.

This showed that the company was not stopping just at expanding their international footprint, but also introducing specialisations within it for culturally differentiated audiences. Alongside, the Zindagi channel, a premium Hindi GEC, was also launched during this year. The channel gained national prominence and positive popularity for showcasing TV serials from across the border. The Zindagi channel broadcasted productions from Pakistan, familiarizing the Indian audiences with its neighbouring culture. Positioned as 'Jodein Dilo Ko', Zindagi was a channel that believed in connecting people of different cultures while dismissing the stereotypical notions about people from other nations. Zee's launch of 'Zindagi' was a bold step taken by it at a fragile time, as Pakistan is treated as India's political adversary.

Zee Theatre was launched during this year, making ZEEL the first M&E Company to foray into theatre production. One of the reasons for this decision was the significance the art of theatre holds in Indian traditional history and ancient culture. Zee Theatre strives to bring the best of Indian theatre to the world, with an aim to revive, restore and spread this rich cultural heritage by partnering with theatre stalwarts, to bring together some of their finest works for audiences to experience. It covers theatre across genres like drama and musicals to classics, mystery, social issues and satire. Zee Theatre can be experienced live in cities across India and is available on several DTH platforms.

To add to the wagon, Zee Entertainment Enterprises acquired 100 per cent equity stake in Sarthak Entertainment, which operated 'Sarthak TV', a successful Odia channel. It was an all-cash deal at a consideration of maximum of ₹115 crore stating the lucrative abilities of the Zee group. Having an array of content which is rudimentarily Odia, Zee Sarthak makes an Odia viewer feel complete and fulfilled. Be it religious and devotional content, popular numbers, mega serials, movies or reality shows, it gives the Odia viewer a high sense of belongingness. And it is due to this connect, that the Odia viewers consider it a leading channel.

Regional television from Zee was being received well. Punit Goenka, to this effect of regionalization focus of the company, said, 'We realized early in stage that the consumption of entertainment in your mother tongue will be the way forward. India is not one country and we look at it as a conglomerate of countries. The cultures, the languages are so diverse, and that's where Dr Chandra's vision of regionalization of content will be the future and we were able to assemble a team that was capable of delivering that in an effective manner.'[137]

During this time, Zee's focus on CSR activities beamed focus on various green initiatives and literacy, with 'Room to Read' and 'Zee is Green'.

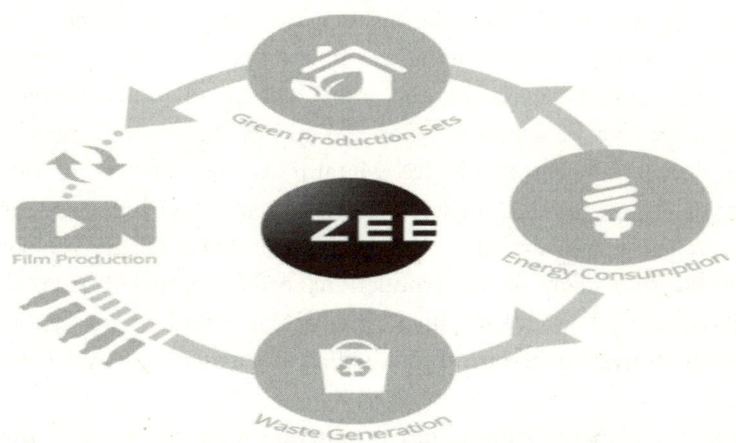

Fig. 6.6 'Zee Is Green' Initiative

Zee has done much in sustainable development and green initiatives, both internally and externally. The company proudly outlines all its initiatives in this sector. 'Sustainable living is as much a corporate responsibility as an aware individual's. We understand that our business of creation, broadcast and distribution of content needs to be in sync with today's environmental needs. To that end, we ensure that our systems and processes are constantly reviewed and best practices implemented to help us towards our goal of becoming carbon neutral. Our initiative that is focused on developing the next generation of production practices that put people and profits in sync with the planet. With our 'Zee Is Green' initiative, we aspire to translate our environmental commitment into action. The mission is to become a carbon neutral organization by 2020, raise awareness about sustainability amongst employees, build capacity to implement green initiatives, foster the widespread adoption of economically viable, environmentally restorative and socially constructive processes.'[138]

It also came up with an innovative idea of Green Studios

and Studio Tours, wherein the general public could see how the company was practicing green operations on its premises. It announced, 'After the successful implementation of green measures for key shows of Zee TV and &TV, we implemented these on key shows of Zee Marathi as well. A few of our studios have an efficient waste management system in place for segregating wet, dry and other waste. We divert 60 per cent of waste from many of our productions, originally meant to go to the landfill. We have installed a plastic shredder and an organic waste convertor at our studio which is currently shared by 8 productions. We have formulated 'Green Production Guidelines' which are shared with all our production houses. We are in the process of incorporating these guidelines as a part of legally binding contracts to ensure compliance.

To increase awareness about our green efforts, we have introduced 'Zee is Green Studio Tours', where tourists can visit our green sets and get information about the environmentally-friendly measures we have adopted. During last year, people from 18 nationalities visited our sets as a part of this initiative. The scope of green measures is not limited to our production sets, but also extends to our offices. We have installed a plastic shredder at our headquarters in Mumbai for intelligent disposal of plastic. The shredder has helped us segregate waste and divert close to 7,000 bottles a month from going to the landfill. We have also reduced the plastic bottle consumption by 40 per cent, using reusable bottles. All our conference and meeting rooms have sensors that help conserve electricity. There are messaging systems that discourage food wastage in cafeterias which has led to a 30 per cent reduction in wastage.'[139] For its legacy of success, ZEEL was the only media brand to enter into Interbrand's '30 Best Indian Brands Report 2015'.

The year also saw the launch of Essel Group's ASHA (Affordable Shelter Housing for All) 2022 project in line with the

Prime Minister's AwasYojna, aiming to construct 2 lakh homes by 2022. Chandra on this occasion elaborated, 'The Prime Minister had a vision for houses for weaker sections. This was one of his pet dreams even before he was in Delhi. When we were working on real estate projects, we wanted to contribute and hence ASHA came up.'[140]

On 14 March 2016 Zee approved in-principle an acquisition of 100 per cent equity stake in Fly By Wire (FBW) International Private Limited Bangalore. Initially Zee would acquire 49 per cent stake in FBW and the balance 51 per cent stake within five days of receipt of approval from the Ministry of Civil Aviation. FBW provided aircraft charter services under a NSOP license obtained from the Director General of Civil Aviation (DCGA) and owned one Bombardier Challenger 605 aircraft. Zee has been chartering this aircraft from FBW on an exclusive basis and the decision to acquire FBW was taken by the management with a view to save on increasing aircraft charting costs.

In 2016, ZEEL also announced acquisition of two GECs from Anil Ambani-led Reliance Group Entities. One of them was Big Magic, a channel that was originally launched in 2011. BIG Magic is a variety General Entertainment Channel which offers fresh and compelling content. With offerings across genres—comedy, mythology, action and thriller, the channel strikes a chord by showcasing content that not only entertains but also entices the viewers with strong cultural connect across key markets.

That year, another acquisition took place in Essel Group, with Dish TV announcing that it was merging with Videocon D2H. The combined Dish TV Videocon was set to have '26.4 million subscribers: 45 per cent of all active DTH subscribers in India.' Dish TV would own 36 per cent of the new entity and Videocon would own 28 per cent. Institutions and retail investors would own the rest. OZEE, an AVOD platform, was also launched. *Sairat*, a Zee Studios backed film, became the first Marathi film to ever gross over ₹100 cr. worldwide. In the social arena, a 'ZEAL for Unity' initiative was launched as part of a peace programme.

Several new channel launches graced the timeline of this FY for the company. ZEEL's international footprint expanded by entering the Philippines market with a Bollywood movie channel, called Zee Sine. Zee Sine is a first-of-its-kind dedicated offering for the Philippines. Launched in 2016 with the positioning 'Bollywood Na Tayo!', the channel is a collection of the finest flavours of Bollywood served in the local Tagalog and Taglish language round the clock. Zee Sine is available on satellite TV platform, Cignal and on cable TV, CableLink and is distributed to provincial cable operators by Cable Boss, reaching more than a million households.

In July, Zee.One was launched. Zee.One is a dedicated channel for the German-speaking audience. With the positioning of 'I Feel Bollygood', the channel is the first and only free-to-air television channel in Germany which broadcasts films, television series and other programmes from the biggest cinema industry in Asia. The channel offers a wide range of content that is tailor-made for the German-speaking audience, from movies across different genres, to series like 'Jodha Akbar' and 'Jamai Raja', non-fiction programmes like 'Namaste Yoga' and music clips with outstanding dance performances. Zee. One is available via cable (Unitymedia, Vodafone, Telecolumbus), satellite (Astra) and IPTV (Deutsche Telekom) and also via Livestream under TV Spielfilm. On this channel, Amit Goenka, CEO for the international broadcast business of ZEEL, said, 'As we did in the US Hispanic market, we conducted research and found they were craving Indian series. I am surprised to find that the series are rating higher than the movies. Germany is a market that has always been exposed to Bollywood to some extent, but never to the series. I'm really happy that our series are being well received and we're getting daily repeat viewership.'[141]

In October, Zee Mundo was launched as a 24-hour Pay-TV channel featuring never-before seen Bollywood movies and series dubbed in Spanish and in HD quality. Its programming covers five main genres: action, romance, suspense, drama and comedy. Zee Mundo's exclusive programming crosses over cultures and brings some of Bollywood's biggest stars to Spanish-language Americas. Amit Goenka said, 'We launched Zee Mundo, our Spanish channel that is targeted at the U.S Hispanic market in October 2016 on Dish LATINO and we will soon expand this channel to other markets. We have noticed that the Arabic and Hispanic cultures share a close affinity with Indian and Bollywood content. In these markets, there is very little global content coming in besides Hollywood. That is what we are trying to build and capitalize on. Zee Mundo gives us a bugger opportunity to exploit some of our existing shows for a completely new market. It's not just a movie channel. Wherever we've entered globally, we have done so with a movies offering and then quickly converted it to a more general entertainment series, telenovela kind of format.'[142]

For the national audience, it launched the likes of Zee Marathi HD, Zee Bangla HD and Zee Talkies HD, presenting a better offering to its viewers with a high-definition choice. A Telugu movie channel by the name Zee Cinemalu was also launched. With the positioning—'Dil Pai Super Hit', Zee Cinemalu, a full time Telugu movie channel, showcases movies that win the hearts of the audience. The channel library, which is a well-blended mixture of all the movie genres, has over 500 movies delivered through different packages, offering aspirational, emotional, young, light hearted and blockbuster films which appeal to the target audience.

Zee further expanded its foray into the Marathi sector in August with Zee Yuva, India's leading Marathi language television channel, which believes in providing fresh and youthful content to the audience. The tagline of the channel 'Nave Parva..YuvaSarva!'

means that the youth carries the new era and is the powerful force that would bring about change in society. Bavesh Janavlekar, business head, Zee Yuva and Zee Talkies, said about the channel launch, 'Zee Yuva has a very unique and differentiated proposition from the other offerings in the market. The content will be distinctive and based on audience insights. This is a channel for the young-at-heart. The primary motive of Zee Yuva is to deliver programmes, which are light-hearted, refreshing, youthful, and contemporary. I feel that this new and innovative step will definitely win the hearts of the audience of Maharashtra.'[143]

Under brand initiatives of intellectual property rights, the first edition of 'Zee Mindspace Awards' was launched in 2016. It aimed at recognising brands, which captured maximum 'MindSpace'. Zee partnered with Nielsen, renowned market research company, to execute a nationwide research to recognize brands which have created greatest impact on consumers. While 'Top of the Mind Recall' was the criteria given the most priority, factors like Popularity, Advocacy, Desire and Buzz were also a part of the research methodology. The winning brands were awarded at the Zee Mindspace Awards 2016 in the presence of 500+ CMOs, important public figures, and stalwarts from the marketing and advertising industry.

2017 marked ZEEL's completion of 25 years as an M&E conglomerate. The main focus for strategies for management and operation during the year were on aspects for better growth listed as: Evolve: to satisfy consumer's varied and ever changing preferences for entertainment content across different formats, language and platforms; Build: an entrenched position in content creation eco-system by partnering with the best talent; Lead: by building a strong competitive position in all their business; Sustain: through inclusive growth by managing their operations in a way that benefits all their stakeholders.

The company forayed into global production for mainstream

audiences with the launch of Zee Studios International in Canada. Also putting a foot into the radio business, following its news cousin ZMCL, ZEEL launched 106.2 Big FM in the UAE. During the year, ZEEL also entered the Live business, and bowed out of sports broadcasting. Chandra commented on the business strategy the company was pursuing internationally, 'Currently it brings about 20-25 per cent of revenue. That has to grow, because now we're going into content for the non-South Asian diaspora. We're doing this in two ways, one is repurposing our existing content to meet local needs and second, starting producing global content. In revenue terms, the US still remains our best market. Because of our expansion in Latin America we feel that we will further strengthen there as well.'[144]

On 6 October 2017 Zee announced that it had entered into a definite agreement to acquire a 100 per cent equity stake in 9X Media Private Limited and its subsidiaries from Rivendell PE LLC and other shareholders for an all-cash consideration of ₹160 crore. However, the deal did not reach fruition.

More acquisitions were in the pipeline this year. The company acquired 80 per cent stake in technology startup Margo Networks for ₹75 crore. ZEEL's longstanding partnership with Zee Turner Limited finally culminated during this year with the acquisition of the balance 26 per cent stake in the company offering. Another similar deal was finalized with the acquisition of the balance 49 per cent equity stake in ZEEL's subsidiary India Webportal Pvt. Ltd for $30.7 million.

A premium English movie channel, &Privé HD, was launched during the year. & Privé HD is a premium destination for the finest English movies in the Indian broadcast space. The channel is specifically designed for passionate cinema lovers who enjoy the details of nuanced cinema. With a brand tagline of 'Feel the Other Side', it is specifically designed for the non-conformists who go beyond the obvious and feel the soul of movies. &Privé HD has curated a list of 350 celebrated titles and 40 award winning premieres including movies like Moonlight, Jackie, Arrival, Lion and Pele.

Alongside, 25 Weyyak, a video-on-demand service for Arabic audiences graced the market. That year, two more channels for the African markets were launched, by the names Zee Bollymovies and Zee Bollynova. Zee Bollymovies was the first-of-its-kind English-dubbed Bollywood Movies Channel. Zee Bollymovies brings blockbuster movies of Bollywood to the African mainstream viewers, featuring superstars of the industry and is available in Sub Sahara Africa since January 2017. It is available on DStv channel 114 and KWESE channel 155. Zee Bollynova is the world's 2nd English-dubbed general entertainment channel launched in January 2017, showcasing the best of Bollywood and Indian content across Africa. Zee Bollynova is available on KWESE channel 150.

The company also sought to honour the 'Real Army' of women behind Indian soldiers, with a brand initiative called Army Behind the Army in 2017. It was an initiative by ZEEL to applaud the mothers, wives, daughters and sisters of soldiers and recognize that it is their support and perseverance that gives the armed forces the necessary boost to guard the nation. ZEEL aimed to honour this 'Real Army' of women behind our soldiers, by garnering respect and recognition for them at a national level.

The CSR activities for the fiscal also included initiatives like a partnership with Rashtriya Sewa Bharti (RSB), 'an NGO that implements welfare and social service programmes' for women empowerment. Meanwhile, Zee Marathi Jagruti empowered women in Maharashtra and Zee Telugu launched Lakshmi Devi ThalupuThattindi to strengthen livelihoods.

BREAKING BARRIERS WITH ZEE5

In 2018, things were getting exciting for the media industry. Everything was renovating- newer platforms, newer content, newer distribution channels. Subhash Chandra summed it up well in his Chairman's Message in the year's Annual Report, 'We are seeing discontinuous changes in all aspects of entertainment and for the consumer, freedom of choice, enhanced connectivity and multiple screens, have given new dimensions to overall entertainment consumption. The attention spans of the consumers have shortened, and the conventional boundaries of content creation have been breached. In this competitive environment, the need for innovation and creativity is certainly at its peak. In our journey of delivering extraordinary entertainment content across platforms, our Company has been at the forefront of driving change and setting trends for the industry and we are gearing-up for success in this evolving landscape. Our strong and consistent operating and financial performance give us room to invest in future growth opportunities.'

The company was pulling in revenue from several streams across the board, ranging from advertising, subscription, syndication, theatrical, music licensing, and others including movie distribution and tickets and sponsorships. This pointed to the company's extensive brand value and size.

As such, Punit Goenka quoted in Zee's Annual Report, 'Over the years, ZEEL has evolved from a single-channel network into a multi-faceted entertainment content company by consistently expanding its content offering. Till recently, television was the primary medium for taking new content to audience. However, our emerging businesses—digital, movies and music, and live events, provide us new touchpoints to reach consumers as well as to access to audience that was out of reach. This has added new dimensions to content consumption and is allowing us to experiment with new genres of content and create formats suited for smaller audience segments.'[145]

In this respect, in 2018 the company launched ZEE5, a video-on-demand platform in India on 14 February. ZEE5 offers viewers a completely integrated entertainment offering with both On-Demand and Live TV. It comes packed with 1,00,000 hours of On Demand content, including exclusive Originals, Indian and International Movies and TV Shows, Music, and Health and Lifestyle videos across languages. It also has an extensive Live TV offering with 90+ popular Live TV channels. With all this content available in one place, ZEE5 truly becomes the most comprehensive entertainment platform for language content in India and across 190+ countries around the world.

It kickstarted with Zee's already existing collection of movies, gradually adding more original shows as time passed. Content was available in 12 languages. The platform also provided the first Tamil web series in 2018 with the title America Mappillai.

ZEE5 mobile app is available on Web, Android, iOS, Smart TVs, among other devices. The platform has also partnered with global tech giants like Applicaster, Lotame, Talamoos and A.I. video enhancement startup Minute.ly to provide enhanced UI/UX and improved application performance. The company proudly announced that ZEE5 is one of the fastest growing digital entertainment platforms in India. Despite a late entry in the crowded OTT space, it has been gaining traction across all viewership parameters. ZEE5 registered 61.5 million monthly active users (MAUs) in March with an average of 31 minutes spent on the platform. It consistently ranked as one of the top five free and grossing entertainment apps in India, as per the Google Play store rankings. ZEE5 released 60+ finite-format fiction shows, reality shows, original movies and short movies, making it the biggest producer of digital content in India. It planned to release over 70 shows and movies in six languages in FY20, which will further help to consolidate its position.'

Amit Goenka, Chandra's second son, and CEO International Broadcast Business and ZEE5 Global, commented on the overwhelming success of ZEE5, explaining its intent. 'ZEE5 has rolled out several new features for its consumers and is also offering differentiated solutions to advertisers. Although the progress in year one has been satisfactory, we would have liked to have launched ZEE5 a little earlier. We always believed that the right product with a compelling content catalogue would be able to make its mark. This is just the beginning and ZEE5 will continue to scale up on the 3 pillars of content, technology and partnerships.

'With content across 12 languages, that has been the focus of ZEE5 since launch. We also understand that viewers' needs are diverse and therefore we offer a wide range of content. That is where our expansive movie library, ZEE5 Originals, TV shows, curated news, music videos, live events and cine-plays come into the picture. While ZEEL's extensive library of catch-up TV is driving organic growth on our AVOD offering, the taut storytelling of our original content has appealed to viewers and is driving SVOD adoption. ZEE5's features like navigation in 11 languages, voice search, and option to download and consume offline have been designed considering the realities of the Indian market.'

Based on the insights from their extensive research of OTT's target audience, they have devised a philosophy for original content that is based on three R's—Real, Relevant, and Resonant. It helped them to select stories from across the country's diverse cultural and linguistic backgrounds. Over the last 15 months, they created content across several genres—biopics, thrillers, horror, comedy and action. In India, young audiences (18-35 years) have been the early adopters of digital platforms and these genres have seen great success with this segment.

He continued, 'We are evaluating partnerships primarily with two objectives in mind—reaching untapped audiences and improving the viewing experience. Digital video consumption in the country is being driven by mobile, accounting for over 90 per cent of viewership. Telecom players are playing an important role in driving this growth by bundling content with their services and have become natural partners for content producers. Our partnerships with all the leading telcos boost the consumption of our AVOD content and also helps to drive our subscription service by offering SVOD content for their premium consumers. We are also partnering with device manufacturers to benefit from the rising penetration of smartphones and smart TVs. Some of our partnerships in the digital ecosystem are with businesses that already have an established user base in our target segments. In addition to providing additional touchpoints for reaching consumers, these partnerships also enable better content discovery and viewing experience.'[146]

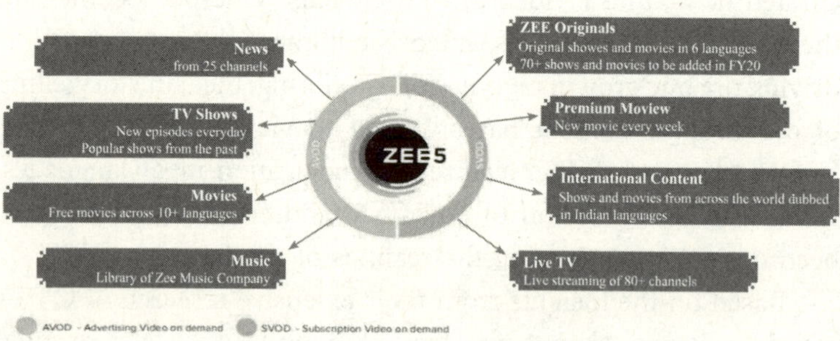

Fig. 6.7 Zee5 Content Catalogue

Zee5 had a vast library and unrivalled content catalogue. There were ZEE5 Originals, with originals in six languages, new shows every month, ranging from fiction shows, reality shows, original movies; International Content with shows from Turkey, Brazil, Pakistan, Korea etc. dubbed/sub-titled in multiple Indian languages; live, catch-up and more with over 80 live channels, catch-up content, and the best of ZEEL library shows; Movies with more than 3,500 movies in 12 languages and movie premieres every week; premium content curated from international studios, plays from Zee Theatre, health and lifestyle content and even kids entertainment.

The company was pinning several hopes upon the long-term success of ZEE5. Rohit Gupta, CFO, commented on the highs and lows and how ZEE5 was here to salvage it all, 'During FY19, domestic advertising revenues witnessed a growth of 20.9 per cent led by traction in both television and digital businesses. We became the leader in Bangla and Kannada markets and further strengthened our share in Tamil Nadu. This helped us to improve our monetization and grow ahead of the industry. Additionally, advertising revenues from ZEE5 contributed to growth. During the first three quarters, growth was relatively stronger at 22 per cent, helped by a low base and increase in ad-spends by consumer companies. However, in the fourth quarter, the growth moderated as the advertisers reduced spends due to uncertainty related to implementation of the tariff order. We believe that once the disruption is behind us, the ad growth will return to its normal growth trajectory. As ZEE5 continues to scale up, it would witness a concomitant increase in ad revenues as well. The movement of two of our FTA channels out of DD Freedish will have some impact on ad growth in the near-term but we are working with our strategy to compensate for that revenue loss through other channels. In FY19, our content cost increased by 21.7 per cent Year on Year, slightly ahead of revenue growth, resulting in our content cost-to-revenue ratio going up. Three factors contributed to this increase—ramp up of ZEE5 Originals, higher movie amortization costs, and increase in content cost of Zee Studios. Our endeavour is to continue growing ahead of the industry.'

Subhash Chandra, commenting on the vision for ZEE5, quoted: 'ZEE5 has learnt from the success of our television business, and has a really sharp focus on regional markets. ZEE5 will certainly be the vanguard of our growth in the coming years.

In the company's Annual Report, Punit Goenka quoted, 'I am pleased to see ZEE5 emerge as one of the fastest growing OTT platforms in a crowded Indian market, reaching 61 million monthly users within a year of launch. Our expanding library of commercial and niche movies in 12 languages gives consumers another reason to regularly visit ZEE5.'[147] Commenting on how Zee5 was the company's efforts at modern digitization, Goenka told the author, 'For us digital is the way forward. The ZEE5 platform is where our maximum investments are going from the company today and we will definitely emerge as a winner in that category as well. Our targets are, as I said, very audacious; we want to be the no.1 entertainment platform in the digital space in the next 18 months.'[148]

Jawahar Goel, Chairman and MD of Dish TV, talking about how the advent of OTT would affect the DTH business of the Essel Group and the industry as a whole, said 'This is a challenge to the entire broadcasting industry because we have content regulation for TV, print, and radio. However, the consumption of content online and on OTT is beyond the regulated content and that is a challenge for the broadcasters, the content creators, social scientists and even the government. It is important to avoid a scenario where there is regulation for one stakeholder and not the other; it should be uniform across the board.'[149]

During the year, ZEEL continued to increase its reach in technology spheres. It secured a US patent for a technology platform developed in Zee Media Lab, Silicon Valley. The center's innovation lab focuses on identifying media trends and provide innovative solutions for immersive experiences. Z5X Technology Center was another state-of-the-art facility by Essel group in the heart of Hitech City, Hyderabad, specializing in delivering solutions for the M&E domain. Using the portfolio of brands to differentiate their content, services and consumer services, the company seeks to develop the most creative, innovative and efficient digital hub for the world. It claims it is doing so 'To digitalize dreams by providing best digital solutions to our customer by providing them our services.'

The new distribution partnerships across USA, Europe and APAC helped it gain a wider audience. ZEE5 was made available globally in over 190 countries with a soft launch in October 2018. The platform commenced roll-out in priority markets like Bangladesh, Sri Lanka, Malaysia, Singapore and Australia. It launched #SharetheLove campaign for the neighboring countries and saw great traction from the Tamil and Bengali speaking audience in these markets.

All through the fiscal 2018–19, Zee Studios, the company's film production and distribution arm, established a robust position as India's leading content studio. In FY19, the studio released 13 movies across Hindi, Marathi and Punjabi languages—of which seven were produced or co-produced by Zee Studios. Zee Music Company acquired an expansive catalogue of music rights across 11 languages and is the only pan-India player with in-house distribution capability and key partnerships with major movie studios. To strengthen the '&' brand as a premium proposition, Zee Studios was rebranded as '&flix' in the company's English cluster. &flix, became the ultimate destination for hit Hollywood movies catering to avid movie fanatics. It even offered a movie premiere every week with a 'Leap Forth' messaging. From action and drama to comedy and animation, its library hosts a captivating mix of genres for the Indian viewers, offering an extraordinary movie-watching experienc. The channel was programmed under properties like Flix First Premiere, Best Flix Forever, Late Night Flix and FamJamFlix. Some popular movies screened were Spiderman: Homecoming, Baby Driver, Life, The Emoji Movie, Atomic Blonde, Jumanji and Blade Runner 2049 amongst others. &flix is available across DTH and digital cable platforms.

Alongside, Zee Bollywood was also launched as its counterpart, showcasing Bollywood entertainers. With a promise of '101 per cent Shuddh Bollywood', Zee Bollywood showcases passionately curated Masala Bollywood movies, firmly establishing its position as a one stop destination for wholesome masala entertainers that are not only highly entertaining but also celebrate the larger than life colorful vibrant cinema. With launch of Zee Keralam, a Malayalam GEC, in November 2018, the company now had GEC channels in all the Southern markets. Zee Keralam is a channel that reflects the radiant spirit of a true Malayali. With a brand proposition of 'NeithedukkamJeevithaVismayangal—Let's Weave Wonders in Life,' Zee Keralam aims to motivate people to rise above their conditions and carve their own roads to success.

In 2019, Zee Classic, was relaunched as India's only Hindi movie channel showcasing films from the golden era of Hindi cinema, and &xplorHD was launched for thought provoking and entertaining Hindi movies. The company positioned it as '&xplorHD will cater to every movie aficionado's entertainment cravings that are UNroutine, UNexpected and UNformula. The channel boasts of a vast repertoire of titles that explores storytelling like never before. By showcasing movies that are thought provoking yet entertaining on television, &xplorHD with its brand promise of 'Cinema Unboxed' endeavors to bring to its audience cinema that helps one explore a different world.'

Zee Live, the live events arm of ZEEL, focused on creating memorable on-ground experiences for the audiences. As the live original content and IP division of Zee Entertainment Enterprises Ltd, Zee Live aimed at creating memorable on-ground experiences for audiences across age groups in India. Zee LIVE aims to become the gateway for live entertainment experiences to the world, showcasing the best of what India has to offer, as well as to bring in wonders from the rest of the world. Currently, under its umbrella are three IPs across genres—'Arth': A Culture Fest in culture, 'Supermoon' in music and comic and 'Zee Educare' in education. The company proclaimed, 'Through our youngest business vertical, Zee LIVE, we want to push the boundaries of entertainment that we offer, creating fresh and unique concepts for different types of live events, such as music concerts, food festivals and theatre among others.'[150]

During the year, Zee Live held India's first multi-regional cultural festival, Arth, and LF91, a heritage food festival. Arth hosted 250 speakers from 11 countries, bringing a diverse cultural experience through art, literary activities and performances. More than 15,000 people attended the event over three days. Another event outside the ambit of Zee Live was the hugely successful Zee MELT—a festival of creativity and innovations in the field of marketing and communications, in partnership with Kyoorius. It is India's biggest festival for disruptive marketing and communications and caters to audiences in marketing, advertising, media and PR, emerging technology and mobility. It brings together some of the biggest names in marketing, media, digital innovation and creativity. The festival consists of a range of conferences, seminars, exhibitions, showcases, workshops and networking sessions for delegates by industry experts, catering to all experience levels. The 2018 edition was a two-day festival focused on 'Disruption in Marketing and Communications' with a sharp focus on innovation and technology. It brought together some of the biggest names in marketing, media and creativity, and was attended by over 1,400 unique visitors. It combined marketing, communication, technology, leaders and brand marketers from across the globe. With an objective to reinforce the power of television, ZEEL partnered with key industry associations like IAA and Ad Club for their flagship properties. IAA's flagship property, IAA Leadership Awards saw the CXO's of the M&E industry attend the gathering.

Punit Goenka informed, 'There were two major business developments during the year—getting into distribution contracts as per the new tariff order and conversion of our two FTA channels to pay. Both impacted our revenue growth in the short term, but we are confident that once the transitory challenges settle down, they will help us further improve our competitive position across markets.' On the subscription front, the company gained from the monetization of the recently digitized Phase-III and IV subscribers. The long-awaited TRAI tariff order was finally implemented during the last quarter of the year which led to near-term disruptions, for both subscription and advertising revenues. However, ZEEL felt that this regulation would go a long way in empowering the consumers and improving the clearness in the distribution value chain and would benefit companies with solid content creating capabilities. In the Domestic Broadcast Business, the company further strengthened its no. 1 position in the non-sports entertainment segment with an all-India viewership share of 19.7 per cent. This was led by market share gains in the regional channel portfolio and Hindi movie cluster.

Under its social initiatives, extending the brand philosophy of 'Extraordinary Together', the company launched the DibbaLautao and Revive Odisha campaigns to encourage citizens across the country to contribute to relief efforts for the natural calamity affected states of Kerala and Orissa. Their programming initiatives and on-ground activities made an attempt to alleviate the impact of drought in some parts of Maharashtra. With Project Prerna and the KisanAbhimaan initiative, the company was constantly working to bring small improvements in the lives of the farming community. Driven by a rich value system, ZEEL remains committed to bringing a positive change in the lives of its audience.

Over the last year, Zee has taken several other initiatives to strengthen its business. In an official correspondence with the author, it made public these approaches.[151] The first was the expansion of business with the release of new channels that made the company's language footprint the biggest in the country in 2020.

The company launched Zee Picchar, a Kannada movie channel with the promise of an unparalleled movie viewing experience to Kannada film lovers. The new channel went on air from 1 March, promising to leave its viewers with a 'Hit Dinada Feeling'. With 350+ films and a never-seen-before 12 premieres in 12 days, the channel aims to bring families together with unmatched entertainment and become a staple in every Kannadiga household. The specially curated library features movies across genres such as comedy, romance, action and thriller among others. In the same breath were launched Zee Thirai, a Tamil movie channel representing the passion of Tamilians for their cinema and heroic spirit through powerful movies, and Zee Biskope, the go-to destination for every Bhojpuri movie lover.

Zee Thirai is the Tamil Film Entertainment Channel of ZEE. The channel is set to emerge as the one-stop destination for fans of Tamil Cinema across the world. With a strong library of over 400+ films across genres such as horror, comedy, action-thriller, drama and so on, the channel aims to change the conversation from the 'what' to the 'why' of cinema. Zee Biskope promises to be a space where viewers can live their Bhojpuriyat to its unabashed best. With a purpose to rejoice Bhojpuriyat with every Bhojpuriya, Zee Biskope will be the go-to destination for every Bhojpuri movie lover. Stemming from the insight of 'Authenticity is more liberating than pretense', the channel aims to be as unabashed as every Bhojpuriya and rejoice true Bhojpuriyat with them. Content, channel lingo and its look and feel have been carefully curated and designed to ensure it highlights every Bhojpuriya's love for hyperbolic fun and to ensure that they never have a dull moment in life as long as they're on Zee Biskope:

Aanthon Pahariya Luta Lahariya.

Zee Punjabi also graced the product offering, emerging as the first 'Punjab ka apna GEC' which understood the pulse of the people of Punjab, bringing stories infused in the local language to them. The channel reflects the beliefs, ideas, and attitudes of a Punjabi and will narrate stories of the inherent Punjabi spark. With the brand promise 'Jazbakarvakhon da', i.e. 'Passion of making impossible possible', Zee Punjabi aims to be the fuel that will pole vault people towards their extraordinary dreams.

Next, 'digitization of distribution space led to proper accounting of subscriber base and the New Tariff Order 1.0 provided for fair distribution of revenue across the value chain. Zee was the first broadcaster to declare its new subscription packs, gaining a first mover advantage in ensuring the consumer's entertainment needs were taken care of.'[152]

Zee also made a useful investment, keeping in mind its OTT reach. It invested in the tech start-up Sugarbox—a first of its kind platform that enables internet services to work even in bad or no network areas, empowering users to access them without an active data connection. Through this investment, Zee will be able to enhance its growth in the digital ecosystem, expanding its presence beyond OTT & Adtech.

Meanwhile, the OTT presence was reaching great heights already with Zee5. ZEE5 has emerged as one of the fastest growing OTT platforms in a crowded Indian market. It is also rapidly expanding in 190+ countries across the globe. It inked several partnerships across technology players, OEMs and telcos for wider reach and easier accessibility. For technology, it partnered with global players like Applicaster, Minute.ly; for OEMs, the platform tied up with the likes of Samsung, KaiOS and with telcos like Airtel. Collaborating to co-create original content, ZEE5 inked an alliance with ALTBalaji which includes co-creation of over 60 original content series (in Hindi) which will be available exclusively to subscribers of both platforms.'

As far as other separate segments were concerned, Zee Studios, Zee Music Company and Zee Live made considerable progress. 'Zee Studios built further on the success of last year. In FY19, it not only witnessed success at box-office, but its varied portfolio of films like Article 15, Manikarnika, and Anandi Gopal amongst others, also received critical acclaim. It continued to focus on building a vigorous slate with a mix of in-house productions, co-productions and acquisitions across languages.'

'Zee Music Company firmly established itself as one of the leading music labels. Its extensive music catalogue across 11 languages is essential for the success of any Indian music streaming platform. In 2019, Zee Music released 250 film albums including 60 in Hindi and 190 in regional languages and a whopping 600+ non-film singles i.e 55 per cent market share of new Bollywood music released during the year. 'Zee Live took significant steps towards establishing its credibility in the live events space with the launch of new IPs—a first of its kind culture fest 'Arth', Supermoon—bringing the best of Indian and global artists across genres like music, comedy and more, and Educare—a first of its kind educational event for students and parents alike.' In its stride of social responsibility and cause, 'Zee proactively aligned its sustainability goals with the United Nations Sustainable Development Goals. The company took several organic steps towards greater eco-consciousness in its functioning by reducing usage of plastic, reducing energy wastage by installing occupancy sensors, recycling organic waste, implementing sustainable steps across the production ecosystem to reduce water and energy consumption, and waste generation.' Further, 'continuing to attract the best minds in the country, Zee took yet another pioneering step by announcing the M&E Industry's largest learning and development initiative 'Embark' for the capability building of frontline managers. The company has been widely recognized for fostering a culture of entrepreneurship and was adjudged the Best Place to Work in Media & Entertainment in a study conducted by the Great Place to Work Institute in 2019.'[153]

So far things were looking up for the company that had made large strides ever since its entry in the industry. It had gained considerable market clout and was at a respectable, older position than many of its youthful counterparts, which looked up to it for sustainable models and inspiration. It seemed that the company was sensing the changing pulse and size of the market well. Punit Goenka summed it up well, 'I think media has definitely become an industry in a short span of time. While newspapers and those kinds of media assets dominated the pre and post-independence period, today it is more electronic media that's dominating, and it is transforming India., whether it is YouTube or searching for news articles or whether it is entertainment content. So it's fast evolving again as an industry. While we have become a significant industry, we're still not large enough. I still think in terms of advertising, we're far behind some of the comparable economies.'[154]

Zee's success up until here was attributed to many things, but in large part, to Chandra's visionary outlook that had presented itself through the company's intent over the years. This helped Zee reach the status that it did over the years. He said, 'If I was to put a reason behind it, it has to be the entrepreneurial zeal combined with a belief that we still have to learn more. This has helped us to keep our eyes and ears open, despite the fact that we have arrived. My sons Punit and Amit also believe that they don't know enough. That helps us keep an open mind, ready to learn. The moment you say I know everything, the learning stops.'[155]

TALKING TECHNOLOGY

Per technology and broadcasting operations, ZEEL explains their Broadcast Management System and the technicalities involved, that make it a superior broadcasting vessel, 'Broadcast Management System is an internally developed media traffic & scheduling system for the fast paced, ever changing environment of television broadcast. Today it caters to more than 100 channels spread across the globe spanning Europe, the Middle East, Africa, Russia, Asia, the Far East and North & South America.'

The system carries in excess of 30,000 commercials daily to viewers, adding value to their advertisers. Electronic Data Interchange facilitates exchange of data between media houses and their local offices where the Air Time Sales teams are present. Optimization engines help maximize their revenues and air time usage by offering varied spread of commercials. BMS integrates with a host of Playout Automation systems and dynamic graphic, menu, and statutory disclaimers are generated and triggered automatically, reducing the effort required to create and schedule these events. ZEEL constantly works with their Sales teams to create and drive new revenue streams like Contextual Ad insertion, Ad Replacements for local markets, leading and lagging commercials etc.

Content management modules trigger media deliveries, optimizes usage of rights and the media repository, and compliance of viewer protection. This is achieved by integrations with DAM for media and TERMS rights related info.

Traffic Management, integrates Content management, Ad sales and Marketing while maintaining compliance with local laws (TRAI in India, BARB in UK & GFK in Germany, etc). Separation between competing product, contractual obligations, etc are enforced to protect the advertisers' interest. Accordingly, the sales returns are below 0.01 per cent of revenues. This system currently replicates over multiple server in different geographies, with trained personnel at each of these locations, to ensure business continuity.

Another technology platform that assists the company in producing content is the Digital Asset Management. Senior officials at ZEEL explain in detail how the technology functions, and why it is a leader in the media field, 'Digital Asset Management (DAM) is a modern and fully integrated platform that manages over 200K hours of content. Designed as a hub and spoke model, DAM sprawls across various locations but provides users with a single interface to browse thousands of hours of content using the regular browser. All the content and related metadata information is organized and available for advanced and intuitive search. DAM manages the entire content supply chain by automating various content workflows such as ingestion, cataloguing, post production, syndication and OTT deliveries. It supports seamless content operations across various geographies worldwide. DAM powers and automates the content syndication business. Together with a brand-new Rights Management System, DAM helps provide appropriate and automated access to the content at the click of a button.

Various value-added services are added as plug and play extensions on an ongoing basis to DAM platform for solving complex content business use cases. State-of-the-art content security solutions help us in our goal of keeping our content secure from ever-growing menace of piracy. Both offline and online Disaster Recovery (DR) solution ensures that our content is safe even in case of a massive natural calamity.'

With these developments and more, Zee has stamped its foremost position in the industry that sets it apart from the rest. It has excelled and proactively tested its limits in all aspects of media, from pioneering in satellite broadcast to technology. It would universally be agreed that Zee has been the starting point of several innovations in the country, putting India on the world map repeatedly for some development or the other. Most significantly, its mantra of taking everyone along on its extraordinary journey has made Zee stand apart. Most everything the company has initiated has been done keeping in mind even the most neglected sections of the demographic, and for that, Zee gets eternal credit.

In 2018, ZEEL took another giant step in the direction of technological development by securing the US patent for a technology platform that was developed in the Silicon Valley at Zee Media Lab. It was set up to offer an immersive experience to its audience, by using superior tools like 3D Audio, Augmented Reality (AR), Virtual Reality (VR), Digital Scent, Holograms, etc. The platform is inspired by Vedic Indian tradition that satisfies all five senses of a person. It focuses on immersive entertainment, immersive education, gaming, entertainment commerce, and home environment control. The launch of this product will allow Zee to capture the global market, including US, Europe, China, Latin America. The company announced that 'Zee Media Lab will continue to innovate in the Silicon Valley to work towards integrating technologies with a sheer focus on enhancing the overall viewer experience.'[156]

Speaking on the launch of this new initiative, Subhash Chandra said, 'At ZEE, we envisioned four or five years back, that the overall media landscape is poised to evolve at an extremely rapid pace, with content companies blending into technology companies. Hence, we started investing our time and energy in building a technology for the future, which enhances the content viewing experience by many folds. ZEE's lab in the Silicon Valley was set up in 2016 to create this robust platform, and I'm very glad that the US Patent is secured. It is a concrete step in realizing our vision of transforming ourselves from a M&E powerhouse to a technology Company, offering immersive experiences'. Adding to this Amit Goenka, CEO, Z5 Global said, 'We are extremely excited to offer this unique immersive experience to our viewers. Under the guidance of our visionary Chairman, we are building this unique platform which is futuristic in nature. The US Patent is a major milestone achieved in this process giving us the required level of confidence and reassurance. This is just the beginning of an extraordinary journey of transforming the viewers content viewing experience.'[157]

In 2020, Zee has also readily been taking steps to assist the community in the fight against the coronavirus pandemic that has been raging across India at an alarming rate. Given the uncertainty COVID–19 brought in the lives of daily wage earners, ZEEL committed itself to 'offer a financial relief to over 5000 daily wage earners, working directly or indirectly for the company in its overall production ecosystem.'[158] To keep in touch with its consumers and encourage them towards safety measures, ZEEL also undertook an initiative titled #BreakTheCoronaOutbreak, under which 'content across 40+ channels was paused for a 30 second break throughout the day, encouraging viewers to wash their hands.' Channel Zee Anmol was made free of cost for some time to allow information dissemination to all, while Standard Definition (SD) quality replaced High Definition (HD) on ZEE5 to allow easy streaming.

ZEEL also invited monetary contributions which would be directed to the PM-CARES Fund, using the 'collective strength of all consumer touchpoints of the company, including its television channels, digital platforms and social media platforms will be leveraged to urge people across the globe to join this movement.' Punit Goenka marked the event by saying, 'We firmly believe in the extraordinary power of coming together and fighting against a situation. This is a time when the entire Nation needs to come together as One Family.' Zee matched the corpus collected by the employees and the sum was donated to PM Cares Fund to help fight the pandemic.

ZEEL declared that it would donate 'over 200 Ambulances, 40,000 PPE Kits and build 100+ ICU Units across the Nation to fight against Covid–19.' In this national-level CSR drive, across 10 cities of India, the company utilised its sanctioned CSR budget to provide ambulances, humidifiers, PPE, portable ICUs, and daily meals in partnership with Akshaya Patra Foundation. Punit Goenka noted,[159] 'The effects of the Covid–19 pandemic in India have been far reaching and calamitous for vulnerable communities. It is important that we stand up during such times and step up our efforts as responsible members of the society. Zee is committed to continue its strong support towards the Government, with a key focus on strengthening the overall healthcare infrastructure, to save our Nation from this pandemic.'

Even amid the pandemic, ZEEL has continued to increase its efforts towards technological development. Despite the lockdown, it managed to provide fresh content to its audiences through technology solutions on verticals like television, digital, live entertainment, and music. On television, it announced that it would launch a set of new shows across its regional channels. Some examples of shows launched were 'Lockdown Diaries' on Zee Kannada, 'VedhBhavishyacha' on Zee Marathi, 'Mu Tame Lockdown' on Zee Sarthak, and 'AbolTabol' on Zee Bangla. Zee would also offer entertainment to its viewers through a 25-hour Live Music Marathon, 'Ek Desh Ek Raag' to raise funds for India 'COVID Response Fund' by GiveIndia.[160] The show included big industry names, music stalwarts, celebrities, and other singers.

On its digital platform, Zee5, the company launched 11 new original shows, some of which were shot entirely at the actors' homes, like 'Bhalla Calling Bhalla' and 'Kaalchakra.' Zee Music Company, alongside, released over 120 songs on its platform, the largest by any label in the music industry. ZEEL's Live Entertainment vertical, known for its outdoor experiences, also adjusted to the lockdown. It transformed its on-ground flagship

Table 16

Financial Highlights-Zee Entertainment Enterprises Limited-Standalone (in millions)

Year Ending 31 March	*2007*	*2008*	*2009*	*2010*	*2011*	*2012*	*2013*	*2014*	*2015*	*2016*	*2017*	*2018*	*2019*
Total Revenue	9291	11439	13153	13850	22,342.4	23,329	26,848	32,602	36,535	44,325	52,755	57,956	68,579
Total Expense	6,556	6,334	8,493	7,476	13,864	15,771	17,036	20,442	23,815	30,332	33,699	37,459	41,494
Profit/ Loss before Tax	2,461	4,569	3,762	6,083	8,245	7,338	9,519	11,750	12,122	11,299	15,681	27,311	26,174
Profit/Loss after tax	1,662	2,951	3,097	5,588	5,764	4,897	6,407	7,723	8,318	6,582	9,684	19,119	16,550
Tax Expense	799	1,592	690	495	2,678	2,441	3,112	4,027	3,804	4,717	6,467	8,192	9,406
Operating Profit	2,121	4,086	3,609	5,311	7,836	6,269	8,623	10,315	10,447	11,733	16,550	20,497	27,085
PBIDT	2,735	5,105	4,660	6,373	8,446	7,558	9,812	12,160	12,720	13,993	20,029	30,315	28,979
Dividend	650	868	868	1947	1,956	1,438	1,919	1,921	2,161	2,161	2,401	2,785	3,362
Advertising Revenue *broad casting Revnue	6768*	8980*	10592.60	10669.70	14,383	13,609	16,266	20,037	22,284	28,831	32,851	38,640	46,902

Total Assets and Equity & Liabilities	21,904	23,259	25,099	29,393	28,913	29,824	33,415	39,525	45,621	52,903	61,031	71,858	80,217
Income from Operations	8,677	10,420	12,102	12,787	21,700	22,040	25,659	30,757	34,262	42,065	50,249	57,956	68,579
Depreciation	85	106	119	114	167	215	280	338	580	599	860	1,398	1,589
Loans Funds	2,541	2,043	1,709	1,189	6	10	15	16	12	17,149	18,208	11,452	7,426
Financial Expenses	189	430	779	175	34	5	13	72	18	1,486	1,272	1,426	1,284
Investments	13,459	13,495	13,496	15,319	9,855	10,602	10,692	10,080	11,088	21,342	24,121	19,878	15,722

Source: Compiled by the author from Annual Reports (2007-2019)

ZEEL started its activities in FY 2006–07. Company's gross revenue on standalone basis have shown an increasing trend since inception till FY 2018–19. Company registered PAT of 1662 million in its maiden year and it went on increasing to 16550 million in FY 2018–19. Advertising and broadcasting revenue were on an increasing trend, showing increase in market share of ZEEL. Total assets of the company has increased by approximately 300 per cent from FY 2006–07 when it stood at 21904 million to 80217 million in FY 2018–19. Operating income was also in positive growth in this block of years.

Table 17

Financial Highlights-Zee Entertainment Enterprises Limited- Consolidated (in millions)

Year Ending 31 March	*2007*	*2008*	*2009*	*2010*	*2011*	*2012*	*2013*	*2014*	*2015*	*2016*	*2017*	*2018*	*2019*
Total Revenue	15906	19491	23345.30	23217.94	30986.88	31,789	38,457	46,024	51,115	60,531	66,582	71,260	81,854
Total Expense	12473	13677	16292.65	15863.20	21869.65	23,383	27,938	32,833	37,075	44,383	49,802	49,431	57,315
Profit/ Loss before Tax	3,432	5,813	5,429	6,737	8725	8,406	10,519	13,191	14,040	15,817	29,009	23,187	24,345
Profit/Loss after tax	2,375	3,832	5,123	6,344	6369	5,891	7,196	8,921	9,775	10,267	22,205	14,778	15,672
Tax Expense	999	1627	208	573	2,671	2,500	3,337	4,291	4,285	5,528	6,804	8,409	8,673
Operating Profit	3,204	5,423	5,480	6,135	8,266	7,395	9,543	12,043	12,538	15,095	19,269	20,762	25,639
PBIDT	3,951	6,561	7,053	7,355	9,117	8,779	11,004	13,850	14,816	17,111	21,509	25,165	28,154
Dividend	650	868	868	1947	1,956	1,438	1,919	1,921	2,161	2,161	2,401	2,785	3,362
Advertising Revenue	7035	9307	10592.60	10669.70	17009.80	15,841	19,369	23,801	26,603	33,652	36,735	42,048	50,367

Year Ending 31 March	*2007*	*2008*	*2009*	*2010*	*2011*	*2012*	*2013*	*2014*	*2015*	*2016*	*2017*	*2018*	*2019*
Total Assets and Equity &Liabilities	30,150	33,351	40699.55	39494.57	30,964.36	43,185	50,558	60,317	70,058	78,941	100,367	111,297	129,330
Income from Operations	15,159	18,354	21,773	21,998	30,088	30,405	36,996	44,217	48,837	58,125	64,342	66,857	79,339
Depreciation	185	232	310	285	289	323	399	501	673	777	1,152	1,821	2,347
Loans Funds	3,226	3,866	5,757	1,195	9	12	17	17	12	17149	18208	11452	7429
Financial Expenses	334	516	1,339	332	88	50	86	158	103	1598	1372	1448	1304
Investments	2,326	2,516	1,271	3,203	6964	7999	7916	8290	9755	10499	13432	15290	9765

Source: Compiled by the author from Annual Reports (2007-2019)

ZEEL started its activities in FY 2006–07. Company's gross revenue on consolidated basis are on in increasing trend since inception till FY 2018–19. Company registered PAT of 2375 million in its maiden year and it go on increasing to 15672 million in FY 2018–19. Advertising and broadcasting revenue were in increasing trend showing increase in market share of ZEEL. Total assets of the company has increased by approximately 325 per cent from FY 2006–07 when it stood at 30150 million to 129330 million in fy 2018–19. Operating income was also in positive growth in this block of years. Company declared dividend in all these years to its shareholders.

IP, Supermoon, to Supermoon Live to Home, which streamed on ZEE5 and offered consumers the best of music and comedy. Essel Vision, the company's facility in Jaipur, emerged as a hub for post-production and edit support for the employees, allowing them to use state of the art technology support. The company's Broadcast Operations & Engineering team also developed remote clients so that work-from-home became possible, a first of its kind in the industry. Functions such as editing, graphics, audio, and proxy-based workflows with edit-over-cloud solutions were available.

Punit Goenka said, 'I am very proud of our teams for making the optimal utilization of technology solutions to ensure that our consumers continued to get a fresh dosage of entertainment content, amidst the lockdown.'[161]

ZEEL further strengthened its leadership position as the top non-sports entertainment television network during the year with an all-India viewership share of 19.7 per cent. Strong performance of our regional channels and movie cluster helped viewership share improvement.

ZEE5—MONTHLY ACTIVE USERS

In its first year of operations, ZEE5 was one of the fastest growing digital entertainment platforms in India. ZEE5 witnessed a 190 per cent increase in MAUs since April 2018 driven by ZEE5 Originals, an expansive movie catalogue and the strong content library of broadcast business.

MOVIE BUSINESS REVENUE

Zee Studios' produced seven and distributed six movies across Hindi, Marathi and Punjabi languages. The significant increase in movie business revenue during the year was led by the success of three Hindi movies—*Manikarnika, Dhadak* and *Parmanu.*

Jagannath Goenka

Nandkishore Goenka with his sons—Subhash Chandra, Laxmi Goel, Jawahar Goel and Ashok Goel.

Subhash Chandra in his hometown Mandi Adampur.

Subhash Chandra

Subhash Chandra receiving the 2011 International Emmy Directorate Award.

Subhash Chandra with his sons Punit Goenka and Amit Goenka.

Amit Goenka, CEO International Business & Z5 Global, Zee.

Celebration of 25 years of Zee.

Amitabh Bachchan with Subhash Chandra at Zee's 25 year celebrations.

After the amicable resolution of the misunderstanding between Subhash Chandra and Naveen Jindal.

The Goenka family with Prime Minister Narendra Modi.

IN A NUTSHELL

Entertainment has been essential since the dawn of human civilization for rejuvenating people in the tedium of their routine. It is a sure shot way of firing peoples' imagination and helps them to turn the gaze inwards and understand the complexities of relationships. Emotion, then, is the common thread that runs across entertainment content, keeping it relevant always. By arousing emotions that people experience each day, entertainment has been able to colour lives with hues of joy and sorrow, hope and despair, pride and inferiority, awe and contempt, confidence and fear. A film, a play, a show, a symphony or a concert—it moves hearts when emotions take the foreground. ZEEL understands this and has been absorbing the intricacies of life by observing it unfold at several levels. The company has been telling stories that evoke a range of emotions and touch lives. In its storytelling journey, ZEEL has rendered tales of inspiration, picked from the lives of real people or inspired by their stories.

In tracking ZEEL's journey from being a humble man's dream to a sprawling industry denizen, one thing becomes clear—the visions this company set for itself have always been achievable and foresighted. Its identity has transformed year upon year, taking into consideration every shareholder near and far. In India, ZEEL has always stood for family-oriented entertainment, a source of living room bonding for the entire household, from the very young to the very old. Today, in retrospect too, when new media is overtaking the traditional television, one can't help but remember Zee channels playing on the idiot box without a tinge of nostalgia, reminiscent of simpler times.

The ball started rolling in 2008, when ZEEL established its position as a player in the film distribution business with a number of outlets representing it, from Zee Motion Pictures to Zee Limelight. In the beginning itself, there was a merger to form ETC Networks Asia Today and acquisition of Holdings in Russia and Mauritius. When India began gaining traction as one of the largest television markets in the world, it spelled personal victory for ZEEL. Its success was not limited to India, but was flooding overseas markets too. This was good for the company's digitization process, marked by a joint venture with a digital media company in Los Angeles which produced a new online portal.

2010 also brought a new logo for the company, displaying Zee's open-mindedness towards sailing with the tides. Amidst managerial decisions and organizational restructuring, ZEEL never lost track of its social intent which it so preached through its platforms. It partook in a number of social undertakings, like upliftment in areas such as education and mental peace to.

The company was initially investing in other regional media houses and expanding its viewership to more than 20 per cent of the population of the country in 2014. Also, the prospect of Zee Entertainment acquiring 100 per cent stake in media entities 9X Media and INX Music in an ₹160-crore cash deal in 2018 represented an upward graph.[162] But unfortunately, the deal did not get through.

The launch of ZEE5 signalled a positive use of online media in the company's digitization process. This outlet especially garnered huge responses in the market on account of a rich and compelling library, offering original content across 11 languages and attempting show themes that were 'bold' and 'daring'. It was perhaps a bit of a shocker for mainstream audiences, not just because the content was such, but because it was backed by Zee—a name that had evoked comfort in tradition for years now. Even so, ZEE5 enjoys a massive fan following today, because once the prudence was overcome, audiences discovered that the content was actually good.

Completion of 20 and then 25 years in the business were

notable milestones in the career timeline of the company. These occasions came with accolades for both the company, as well as its leaders. ZEEL, it was unanimously agreed everywhere, had done much for the music, general entertainment, and film industries. It could be envisioned as one of the foundation bricks of each of these segments, always standing behind these ventures as the old hand of experience and wise words. Punit Goenka opined, 'Till now, the growth has been primarily driven by user-generated and TV content which is monetized through advertising. I believe that the next phase of growth would be driven by content that the digital platforms are creating.'[163]

ZEEL's product offering has, all these years, been neatly categorized under 5 verticals of television for domestic broadcast, international, studios and music, digital, and live and theatre. Of these, domestic broadcast channels have been able to hit home the closest, with their varied offering of 4 broad clusters of Hindi general entertainment channels, Regional general entertainment channels, Hindi movie cluster, and Niche channels, which take care of the interests and motivations of varied spectrums of audiences across India. Even abroad, this has held true with Zee's presence in America, Europe, Africa, MENAP and APAC regions, with a footprint across 190 countries. The portfolio of channels caters to not just the Indian and South Asian diaspora but also to local audiences in international territories. Of the 40 channels in the international markets, 10 are dedicated to a non-Indian audience, offering them entertainment content in their native languages. All this has stood to reflect clearly the Zee mantra that holds each customer equally important, and in its undertaking, wishes to not leave even a single viewer out of the loop.

All through 2007 till 2020, ZEEL has made impressive growth in all its undertakings, functioning at par with its bullish counterparts. Both internally and externally, changes hung over the company.

7

ZEE ZIGZAGS: REVIEWING RICHES

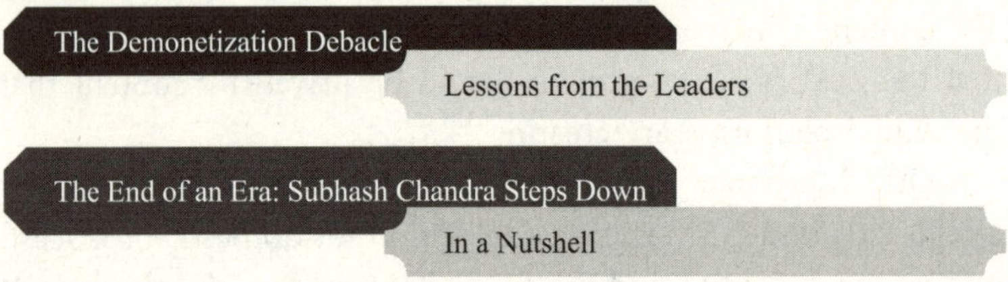

The Demonetization Debacle

Lessons from the Leaders

The End of an Era: Subhash Chandra Steps Down

In a Nutshell

Fig. 7.1: Chapter Insights

Zee, forever the pride of the Indian media industry, had become a seasoned player now. Long years of experience had taught Subhash Chandra how to steer his company around any hurdle, however impossible. A pioneer of many things novel in the country, Zee had several credits to its big name, and yet, the touchstone of its success lay in its ability to be familiar to Indians across the world as a household name.

However, inconstancy is the law of the universe. As unpredictable as Zee's initial foray into the industry, was the future that lay in wait for it. Though its foundation hadn't corroded over the years, the Zee legacy had become a skyscraping tower. Despite rock solid roots in place, the structure of Essel Group was shaking. The company had hit a few major snags along the way.

THE PERIOD POST—DEMONETIZATION

By 2018, Essel Group had announced that they were open to

selling a 50 per cent stake in ZEEL to a strategic partner. The company said in a statement, 'The proposed transaction to divest upto 50 per cent of Essel's holding to such a partner, is expected to address the Essel Group's capital allocation priorities and will allow ZEEL shareholders to capture the full value of India's largest entertainment broadcaster with an ever-strengthening bouquet.'[164]

Zee's official stance on the subject reads: 'In November 2018, the Promoters of Essel Group took a decision to find a strategic partner for Zee in order to transform the company from a Content to a Content & Technology Conglomerate. The promoters were mindful of the debt levels at the promoter level, but that was secondary at that stage. With the IL&FS collapse and the overall NBFC industry going into a difficult stage in January 2019, the scenario of the debt levels at Essel Group changed. The repayment of each and every lender emerged as the top most priority and hence the promoters of the Essel Group also initiated talks with Financial Partners for a stake in ZEE.'

'Essel Group also initiated the process of divesting its key media and non-media assets with an aim to repay all the lenders. During this divestment process, the Group received a positive response from multiple partners expressing their interest to buy a stake in ZEEL and other key non-media assets of the Group.'[165]

Annurag Batra, editor-in-chief BW BusinessWorld, asked Subhash Chandra in December 2018 who the prospective takers for the stake would be, to which Chandra had famously replied, 'This bride has many suitors.'[166]

BW quoted that 'names like Facebook, Amazon, Comcast, Apple, and Jio' were doing the rounds. Industry experts were engaged in conjecture about which giants would become attached to Zee. Karan Taurani, VP Elara Capital, said, 'The strategic partner could be either Jio, or a Video on Demand (VoD) player (Amazon or Apple) or a foreign media company that will add to

Zee's content investment initiatives for TV and digital. This is a positive move in terms of future growth prospects, as an MNC or a large-scale player will give tough competition to global VoD giants such as Netflix and others.'[167] That the partnership would be based on digital platform bases was theorized widely, seeing the potential industry trends, which were to take shape in the next 5–10 years.

Businessworld's Clifford Alvares, noted that the 'Zee group's decision of offloading its promoter's stake has gelled with analysts.'[168] Research analyst Jinesh Joshi pointed out that a strategic partnership was the done thing for anyone in media competing with bigwigs like Netflix and Amazon, since OTT platforms were to be the future.

The Essel Group appointed Goldman Sachs Securities (India) Ltd as their investment banker and named US and European based LionTree as an international strategic advisor for this exercise.[169]

2019 began with a bang for Zee Entertainment. The stocks of media giant Essel Group began spiraling downwards and had tanked 33 per cent. Subhash Chandra, in an open letter, tried to clear the air around this issue that had rocked the market. He hinted at 'negative forces' that were trying to hamper the process of stake sales he had initiated on his recent trip to London, and had thus attacked the share price. He wrote: 'From May/June 2018 onwards, a negative force which was acting against our grip as promoters, became strongly active. This was followed by some anonymous letters being sent to all Bankers, NBFCs, Mutual Funds, Shareholders, etc. Whenever we have reported some really good results from the operating Companies, the share prices were intentionally hammered by these negative forces, driving away the investors. I must also mention that there is no systematic protection against the insidious attack on us by the mentioned negative forces, but we will continue to seek the support of the system in order to thoroughly investigate the matter.'[170]

According to a report by Bloomberg Quint, 'Shares of broadcaster Zee Entertainment Enterprises Ltd fell nearly 25 per cent the most since October 2008—to ₹326.60 a piece on National Stock Exchange. The stock was on track for its worst every single-day fall since March 1999. Shares of Zee Learn Ltd fell as much 19.6 per cent its worst intraday fall. EsselPropack Ltd and Dish TV India Ltd plunged 18.6 per cent and 21.2 per cent, respectively,' the report states,[171] 'As of December 2018, Essel Group had a 41.6 per cent stake with 59.4 per cent of their holdings under pledge. On 25 January 2019, 0.6 per cent of the promoter pledged shares were offloaded in the open market by lenders thus reducing the promoter stake to 41 per cent.[172]

However, responding to the author on the fall of the company's stock price, Zee resolutely maintained its official stand by reiterating Chandra's letter and the market conditions that ordered these changes in the company dynamics. It claimed: 'Shri Subhash Chandra in an open letter on 25 January 2019, stated that certain 'negative forces' attacked the stock of Zee Entertainment to 'sabotage' the company's strategic sale process. It was not entirely based on pledged shares as a lot of companies adopt this route for business expansion. These were not real market conditions; these were created conditions.'[173]

By January 2019, the Essel group had gathered an overall debt of around ₹20,000 crore and ZEEL was the only profit-making entity of this group.[174] The promoter holding value in ZEEL during January 2019 was close to 41.62 per cent. From this 41.62 per cent, ZEEL pledged 60 per cent of the holding to take up debts. Simply put, revenue was to be loaned from the company's smooth-sailing businesses and invested in its other businesses that were flailing. Experts in the industry were making conjectures and handing out words of advice to the media establishment. For instance, Nirmal Gangwal, founder at advisory firm Brescon & Allied Partners LLP, commented, 'It is critical for Zee to find a definitive buyer for the proposed sale to arrest erosion of value of the company.'[175]

In his open letter, Chandra did not shy away from owning up to any faulty decisions he may have taken. He pinpointed some crucial business decisions that had, unfortunately, not worked in the company's favour. One of them, of course, related to the acquisition of D2H from Videocon. Chandra called it a 'key error' that cost him, and his brother Jawahar Goel, 'a fortune.'[176]

Another mistake concerned Essel Infra. He wrote: 'As most of the infra companies, even we have made some incorrect bids. In usual cases, Infra Companies have raised their hands and have left their lenders with non-performing assets, but in our case, my obsession of not walking away from the situation has made me bleed ₹4000 crore to ₹5000 crore.' He added that the situation was worsened when the IL&FS issue came to light. That 'meltdown' was cause for the roll overs to stop, which in turn put a stopper in his abilities to service his borrowings.[177]

Chandra elaborated on the steps taken from Zee's end: 'We wrote a number of complaints to the Department of Police, Home Minister of Maharashtra, SEBI and other concerned authorities, right since November 2018, but all the efforts did not result in any action. Till December, we continued to pay the due interest and principle, to all lenders. I have also given my best to expedite the stake sale of Zee Entertainment. In fact, I have just returned from London, last night itself, after a series of positive meetings with potential suitors.'[178]

He iterated and reiterated in his letter that all the troubles Zee Entertainment was facing was purely at the promoter level, and that ZEEL was performing 'exceptionally well'. He wrote, 'All Operating Companies, especially our most precious one, which is Zee Entertainment, are performing exceptionally well and are under

NO stress whatsoever. The debt burden is purely at the promoter level, which is reflecting negatively on the companies. I would like to reiterate that ALL the Companies are performing exceptionally well and there is no problem whatsoever.'[179]

Punit Goenka too echoed his father's sentiments. When asked what went south, Goenka in an interview with Business Today's Ajita Shashidhar in August 2019 said, 'We got to know of the signs last year itself. The problem was nothing but over-leveraging, which happened when we bought the asset from Videocon (the DTH business), and some of the investments in the infrastructure business didn't pan out the way they were supposed to. Therefore, we were continuously pumping in capital from family resources. It's a double-edged sword. There will come a time when you can't do it anymore, and things will go southwards. We realised that early enough and we had started the process (of debt reduction) in November itself for Zee Entertainment. We had started the process for our infrastructure assets even before that, but 25 January changed all that because it became public knowledge. We were negotiating with practically both hands tied behind our back.'[180]

Essel's infrastructure ventures, as listed in the past by Chandra, have boasted of roads, highways, power transmission and renewable energy generation, with an emphasis also on environmental infrastructure such as converting municipal solid waste into energy. But all this came to naught when the infrastructure segment suffered a setback.

Zee continues to maintain that the stock prices fell not just because of a singular reason and analysed the situation as follows, 'Several factors have impacted the stock price of the company in a largely bear market. The same is being seen with multiple scrips in the market. But ZEE's strong business fundamentals remain intact and the company has consistently delivered healthy growth quarter on quarter, beating the market estimates. Zee has been a much-loved brand for the last 27 years and is driven by a rich value system, where all its businesses are led with utmost integrity levels, keeping the customers' preferences at the epicenter. Over the years, Zee has delivered immense value to all its stakeholders and has deeply entrenched its position as the leading media & entertainment powerhouse. As a result of this, Invesco Oppenheimer Developing Markets Fund further reinforced its faith in the company by acquiring 11 per cent stake in ZEE, for ₹4224 crore at ₹400 per share. When the promoters decided to sell an additional ~16.5 per cent stake in the company in November 2019, the book was over-subscribed by approximately 3 times and some of the leading global and Indian investors picked up a stake in the company, reinforcing ZEE's strong ability to generate immense value for its stakeholders year on year.'[181]

LESSONS FROM THE LEADERS

Punit Goenka, known across the board as 'Mr Positive', was not one to capitulate to the growing tensions and a mounting loan of ₹6,776 crore payable by 30 September 2019.

Invesco Oppenheimer Developing Markets Fund had a long history of investing in India as a financial investor. The investment company registered with the US Securities and Exchange Commission, had been a financial investor in Zee Entertainment Enterprises Ltd since 2002. Therefore, Invesco Oppenheimer, which was also the largest shareholder in ZEEL, was set to buy 2.3 per cent of this 16.5 per cent stakes through the subsidiary OFI Global China Fund. Commenting upon this development, Goenka, Managing Director and CEO, ZEEL, said, 'I'm extremely glad to share that the Fund as a financial investor has further reposed its faith in ZEEL. It also gives me immense pleasure to note their strong belief and trust in the intrinsic value of our precious asset. It is the valuable belief and support of our esteemed financial investors that enables us to consistently generate great value, year after year.'[182]

The announcement of 11 per cent stake sale of ZEEL to the Fund was a bold step in the total divestment process, giving the Promoters the required financial fillip to pledge the repayment process. Zee officially told the author, 'Invesco Oppenheimer Developing Markets Fund, which has been associated with Zee for over 17 years, further reinforced its faith in ZEE's management expertise and in the company's intrinsic value. The promoters sold 11 per cent of their stake in ZEEL to Invesco Oppenheimer Developing Markets Fund at a consideration value of up to ₹4,224 Crore. For ZEE, the Values took precedence over Valuation, and hence the path of repaying every lender's money was chosen and given a priority, over everything else.'[183]

'The promoters repaid the money of some lenders by divesting their stake in ZEEL and the non-media assets of the Group. In order to meet the additional requirements, the promoters divested an additional ~16.5 per cent stake in ZEEL in November 2019 to ensure its lenders were repaid.'[184]

The stake sale was the company promoters' bid to repay their ₹11,000 crore debt. One wonders as to the changes this brought about in the different verticals of the company. Zee responded: 'The stake sale was a strategic decision taken at a Promoter level. At ZEEL, at an operational level, there was no change at all. Under the leadership of Punit Goenka and Amit Goenka, the company has been performing exceptionally well. Zee has delivered a double digit CAGR for its investors in the last two and a half decades. It has created jobs and generated immense value for its stakeholders. It has always been Business as Usual at ZEEL. Zee has beautifully transformed into a M&E powerhouse and under the leadership of the professional senior management members, it is taking all the required steps to strengthen its offerings, with an aim to entertain the world with extraordinary content.'[185]

Radiating hope for the sake of himself and the company during these uncertain times, Goenka in the interview with Shashidhar said, 'It is something that I need to learn from, that is how I am looking at it.'

Desolation was only natural, but in Goenka, the optimism seemed more overbearing. This debacle was a turning curve for the company, but a learning curve for its MD-CEO. He said: 'The two things I have learnt are that every opportunity needs to be studied thoroughly before one commits to it, and one needs to know how much to commit and how much not to. Secondly, resolution of issues needs to be handled piece by piece rather than finding an overnight solution. Overnight solutions don't work.'[186]

The company had expressed in 2018 that they would sell part off their company's stakes to a global strategic partner. However, when the time came, the stakes were sold to a financial investor. The reason behind this lay in the publicity that Essel's debt crisis received in January 2019, and the share prices of the group companies fell. Goenka explained that the decision to sell to a financial investor came during this trying period, where the focus shifted to solving the debt crisis at hand to avoid a further downward spiral for the family company. If at all a strategic investor would have come on board, it may have meant a global boom for Zee, but at the cost of the leaders' exit as promoters of the company.[187]

Among other Essel units, Zee Media Corp., SITI Networks Ltd and Shirpur Gold Refinery Ltd dipped between 18 per cent and 19 per cent. Zee Entertainment surged 17 per cent, boasting of 1.3 billion viewers across 190 countries through its 78 channels and 4,800 movie titles. Nevertheless, that recovery was less than half of the losses it saw in the previous session.[188]

There was another ₹6776 crore to be paid off, and to this

end of debt repayment meeting the deadline, diluting additional stake in Zee was also an option on the table for the decision makers in the company. There were some non-media options too. Expanding on the latter, Goenka said: 'The solar sale project deal is on the cards. We already have binding offers for three of our road projects. We are waiting for certain regulatory approvals. As soon as those are received, funding should come in. We have a non-binding deal on three other road assets, which are under due diligence. It's the same party that is buying the first three. These will give us significant liquidity.'[189]

Soon enough, it was unanimously decided among the lenders that it would be in the best interest of everyone if the deadline were extended from September 2019 to March 2020.[190]

THE END OF AN ERA: SUBHASH CHANDRA STEPS DOWN

In November 2019, Zee Entertainment released a statement: 'The founder of Zee and the pioneer of India's private satellite television industry, Shri. Subhash Chandra, during the meeting, expressed his intent to step aside as the Chairman of the company, which he founded way back in 1992. The Board accepted his resignation with regret and applauded his vision for the company and the industry at large.'[191] Chandra continued to remain on board as a representative of Essel Group, and was identified as a non-executive director of the company.

This came as a shocker for everyone. In a filing to the Bombay Stock Exchange, the media giant said: 'The Essel Group is planning to sell 16.5 per cent stake in Zee Entertainment Enterprises Limited (ZEEL) to financial investors.' [192] This move was 'in order to repay loan obligations to certain lenders of the group for whose benefit such shares are currently encumbered (and who have consented to such share sale by the group)'.[193]

The promoters even owed money to mutual funds and financial investors, including Russia's VTB Capital, which encumbered around 10.71 per cent stake in Zee Entertainment.[194]

Zee maintains that Chandra resigned because of the change in SEBI guidelines of Regulation 17 (lB) of SEBI Listing Regulations, which mandated that the chairperson of the board shall not be related to the managing director or the chief executive officer of the company.

Zee's stand on the meltdown post the collapse of Infrastructure Leasing and Financial Services (IL & FS) read, 'Amongst the external factors that led to the above changes in Zee was the IL&FS issue. Until then, the Essel Group was managing its borrowings efficiently. The IL&FS meltdown stopped the roll overs, diminishing the Group's ability to service its borrowings. The situation at hand became further unmanageable because of the overall liquidity crunch in the market after the IL&FS issue came to public light.'

'From May 2018 onwards, negative forces were acting against the promoters. This was followed by some anonymous letters being sent to all Bankers, NBFCs, Mutual Funds, Shareholders, etc. leading to an impact on the overall debt situation at the Group level. On what SEBI had directed to Zee in accordance with the external changes that were occurring, the company stated, 'SEBI has not issued any directive to Zee on the matter.'[195]

The promoters also decided to part with stakes in Zee Learn, one of their fallback options in which they held a majority stockholding. In an interview, Chandra told the author with a smile on his face, 'Media people in the country did not want to accept me as part of them. Even today a prejudice still exists. Take for instance The Kumbh Mela example. The event made front page News, but did not credit me anywhere for being the host and one of the organizers of the event. Whenever there is any news about me the media blacks it out. If they have bad news they print it. But it's okay, I have no grudges against them.'[196]

To Chandra's status as a minority in his own company, with a mere 5 per cent of ZEEL in his grip, and his future plan of action, the company responded: 'Shri Subhash Chandra continues to remain the Chairman Emeritus of Zee and is a mentor to the management. He is also the Chairman of Essel Group. Shri Subhash Chandra is an educationist, philanthropist & a parliamentarian (Member of Rajya Sabha). He invests most of his time towards working for SACH Foundation (the philanthropic arm of Essel Group), doing meaningful work for the Nation at large. He actively contributes towards the society, helping and uplifting under-privileged children, especially in the tribal areas, and is working towards rural development in many villages across the Country.'[197]

After the resignation of Subhash Chandra, another tangle awaited Zee. It was reported that two former directors, Subodh Kumar and NeharikaVohra, along with Non-Independent Director Subodh Kumar, resigned from the Zee board on 25 November.[198]

According to a regulatory filing by Zee, Kumar and Vohra had raised concerns over numerous issues, the first of which included incongruities in spending CSR funds. SEBI and the Ministry of Corporate Affairs were set to look into the matter behind the resignations, with the Ministry initiating an enquiry since it involved the spending of CSR funds. Zee, on the other hand, clarified that 'CSR funds had been allocated in compliance with the law', a claim that was certified by the chairman of the CSR committee.

After the *Moneycontrol* published its report, Bombay Stock Exchange sought clarification on the issue in hopes of getting a deeper insight.

'This is with respect to clarification sought by the exchange on 26 November 2019 and company's response dated 27 November

2019 providing details of reasons for resignation of directors. In order to ensure that adequate, accurate, explicit disclosure of information and enabling access to relevant and sufficient information for all stakeholders, you are requested to submit, as announcement to the exchange, the copies of resignation letters of all the three resigning directors mentioned in above letter,' BSE wrote to Zee.[199]

Yet another point had been raised by Kumar and Vohra, who stated that 'no action was taken on the large outstanding from Dish TV and Siti Cable for the content supplied by Zee.' Zee retorted to this claim by saying, 'The same have been secured by definitive plan and situation is being strictly monitored as instructed by the board and also discussed in various analyst calls.'[200]

Moneycontrol further wrote, 'Kumar and Vohra also raised the matter of 'a scheduled bank' appropriating '₹200 crore of the company's fixed deposits towards promoter loans and the management did not take legal action'. To this, Zee responded by saying, 'issues pertaining to the wrongful revocation of the bank guarantee stand resolved with the company being secured by the promoter companies and appropriate legal notices were sent to the bank at the relevant time'.'[201]

Kumar and Vohra also flagged the issue of 'film advances given in 2018–19 to the tune of ₹2,200 crore', to which the company responded by saying the information has already been disclosed in its annual report and clarified in various investor interactions.

As media outlets and businesses questioned Chandra's series of decisions which were apparently not boding well for the company, Punit Goenka in an open letter referenced to this in defence of his father, saying, 'I know that many of you might have questioned the steps taken by him in the recent past, but as you know, pioneers see the world through their own eyes. Had it not been for his farsightedness and vision, we would not have been able to create this great Company, or millions of jobs or for that matter, immense value for our investors. We will always be proud of his courage and determination.'[202]

Meanwhile, 'Essel Group was also said to have been in talks to unload some road projects, while its unit Dish TV India Ltd's talks to merge with Airtel Digital TV are said to have stalled.'[203]

As experts raised concerns over the company's human resources in the midst of all that was going on, Zee took a stand on the employee-employer relations that existed within this situation, with respect to job security, 'Human Capital has always been the most valuable asset at ZEE, and the company has always treated its employees as partners in its journey of growing stronger as a global media & entertainment powerhouse. All the decisions by the company and its management during this time, were taken keeping the employees' future and professional growth at the epicenter. As integral members of the Zee Family, it was important for each employee to be aware about the entire corporate development process. A consistent communication was maintained between the MD & CEO and all the employees, communicating each step of the stake sale process. All concerns and doubts raised by the employees over their job security were assuaged by Punit Goenka to ensure it was business as usual and positive energy flowed through the organization. As a result, Zee continued strengthening its businesses across all aspects including Television, Digital, Movies, Music & Live Events; delivering a good set of numbers quarter on quarter.'[204]

Chandra's personal philosophies may be instrumental in pushing the company forward, however. In an interview with Business World's Suman Jha, he expounded on these, 'I have no regrets. If you think too much about the past, there will always be regrets. Future brings anxiety. That teaching has helped me a great deal.'[205]

In the latest open letter by the company where Punit Goenka mentions the inception of the identity of Zee 4.0, going forward with the 5Gs (governance, granularity, growth, goodwill, gusto), he also makes mention of Zee's turbulent past. He wrote that 'change' was something that was necessary at Zee because the 'last 18 months have been extremely challenging, with the financial headwinds experienced by the Promoter Group. Admittedly, this event did make a dent in our goodwill, leaving us with a few things to think about.'

Along this thread, he continued, 'To all our shareholders, who have reposed their faith in us during this recent turbulent phase, I express my gratitude and assure you that we will strive to maintain and strengthen our position as one of India's premier media & entertainment powerhouse.'

'I intend to embark on this new journey of Zee 4.0, with a clean slate, immense learnings from the past and new dreams for the future.'[206]

IN A NUTSHELL

Established in 1926, Essel Group, a media conglomerate gave birth to the first Hindi language subscription channel in 1992 with Subhash Chandra being one of its founding members with the ushered privatisation of satellite rights. From then, to now, Zee Entertainment has seen several ups and downs, but the company with its strong business fundamentals has stayed resilient.

2013 also marked the origin of the growth of regional media newspapers and television channels in the southern states and north-eastern states, affecting the profit share of the larger media conglomerates. While these were general maladies plaguing all the players in the industry, the real trouble at Essel Group began in the latter half of 2018. The DTH-Videocon deal, it was unanimously agreed, had been an unfortunate decision. Zee's shares had begun their downward spiral here onwards. On the acquisition of DTH from Videocon and the trouble that ensued, Zee's official stand reads, 'The CMD of Dish TV India Ltd, Jawahar Goel has earlier stated—'I would like to reiterate that the merger of Videocon D2H with Dish TV has provided immense opportunity and is a great strategic fit. The synergies derived out of the merged business will significantly strengthen the results of our business. This is despite the fact that the merger transaction has been financially stretching for the promoters.'[207]

ZEEL had decided to sell upto 50 per cent of its stakes before this fiasco occurred. This was a natural consequence of unfortunate events, which had involved Essel Group's investments in unyielding opportunities. The Zee Media group had to face the brunt of the risk-taking attitude of its promoters risking its shares, and had to walk into debts created by investing in infrastructural projects. Now, even though this is a common market mistake that most corporations make, of aggregating their boundaries beyond control, one expects seasoned media moguls to stand their ground where specialization is concerned. Perhaps this was one of the reasons for the unexpected tumbledown.

Moreover, Chandra's resignation heralded the end of an era. The company lost its anchor, figuratively speaking. In corporate and public imagination, the name of Essel still evoked his name, even though someone else was signing the papers now. It was now his son, Punit Goenka, upon whose shoulders the company rested.

Surmounting the changes at ZEEL for the past one and a half years, in January 2020 a fresh round of fines were levied on Essel Group's other arm, ZMCL, by regulatory authorities. On the other end, it wasn't like the news businesses were going to the ruins. As claimed by its promoters, the media business was flourishing steadily. Meanwhile, Zee5 became the first Indian entertainment company to take its OTT platform to over 190 countries.[208]

However, Punit Goenka's latest acknowledgment of past mistakes could prove to be a welcome move for the company. The focus to begin again on a clean slate indicates a possible new road for Zee as a whole, but one that still won't be without its past history. It is highly unlikely that Zee would re-model their entire brand value or the 'VasudhaivaKutumbhakam' peg that has driven it forward up until now, since the foundations of the company rest on it. Zee 4.0 could probably be a refurbishing of the company's traditional stances in accordance with a modern, futuristic, more inclusive outlook.

The new directors on the Board of Directors at Zee were R Gopalan, Surender Singh and Aparajita Jain. While Surender Singh tendered his resignation due to some unavoidable personal reasons, Aparajita Jain resigned from the Board due to her professional engagements and frequent travel. In line with its commitment to strengthen the board and induct independent members with diverse experiences to build value and deliver a strong signal to the existing and new institutional investors, Zee appointed Piyush Pandey (Worldwide Chief Creative Officer, Ogilvy & Executive Chairman, Ogilvy & Mather India) and Alicia Yi (Vice Chair of Korn Ferry's Global Consumer Market) as Independent Directors on the Board of Directors at Zee with effect from March and April 2020, respectively.

As per the current shareholding pattern, the promoters own approximately 5 per cent in ZEE, while the remaining stake is held by a clutch of Global and Indian investors including Invesco Oppenheimer Developing Markets Fund, GIC, LIC and more.

8

THE BEDROCK OF BUSINESS

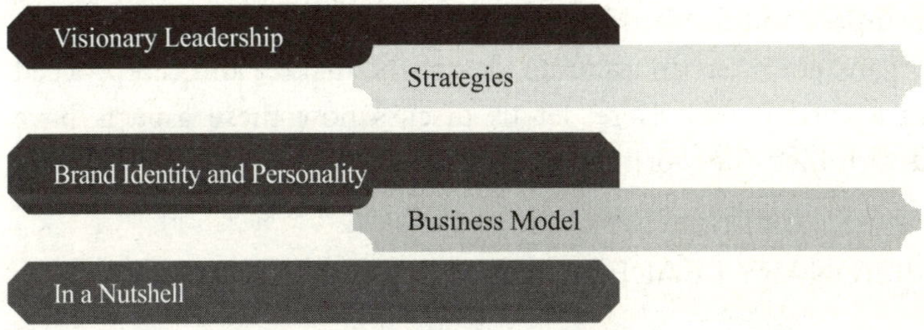

Fig. 8.1: Chapter Insights

LEADERSHIP, STRATEGIES, BRANDING, REVENUE

A lot goes into giving a company shape and form. These are usually the anchoring elements of any organization that hold it together like glue, deciding the fate of success every step of the way. It's true that audiences have the biggest effect on what a company's timeline looks like, but it is noteworthy to keep in mind that the company internally is tightening many screws in the management to strengthen the company for future growth and cater to the needs of its customers. For this, they usually rely on proper planning and a long-term outlook.

The most essential elements that guide a company on the correct path, begin from its leadership and organizational hierarchy, consisting of decision-makers and faces of the company. Next come the business strategies that the organization adopts on the way to making sound partnerships, well-timed ventures and expansion techniques to improve the international footprint. Equally important, if not more, is the brand identity that relies on the personality of the company that has to be projected to the world, ensuring that the correct message and positioning of the brand reaches the people and gains their trust. Lastly, the business model is the key function of every business, since it forms the bedrock upon which decisions are taken as to the revenue streams of the company. This function should be seamless and forward looking in its approach, to ensure that the organization has an accurate idea of the market and can proceed in a certain way. Here, let us discuss how these aspects have determined the worth of Zee for decades.

VISIONARY LEADERSHIP: PRESENT SCENARIO

Board of Directors	Chairman: R.Gopalan MD-CEO: Punit Goenka	Independent Director- Adesh Kumar Gupta, Alicia Yi, Manish Chokhani, Piyush Pandey	Non-Executive Director- Ashok Kurien
Chairman Emeritus	Subhash Chandra		
MD-CEO	Punit Goenka		
Business Leaders	President—Digital Businesses & Platforms: **Amit Goenka** Chief Business Officer—Zee Music: **Anurag Bedi** President—Content & International Markets: **Punit Misra** President—Business, South Asia-Rahul Johri Chief Business Officer—Zee Studios: **Shariq Patel**		
Chief Financial Officer	Rohit Gupta		
Chief People Officer	Animesh Kumar		
Chief Compliance Officer	Ashish Agarwal		

Source: As per data provided by ZEE

Zee has garnered respect in the industry over the years, and looms large in the country as an all-knowing, all-encompassing brand name. It goes without mentioning, but is worthy of finding mention, that this has all been possible because of the company's able and visionary leadership. While the tree stems majorly from the Goenka family, with Subhash Chandra sitting at the position of the creator and patriarch, it has branched out to include other professionals who have with their adeptness in the media field graced the company's leadership chart. The leadership begins from the Promoters of the longstanding company Essel Group. The Essel Group includes Subhash Chandra, his sons Punit Goenka and Amit Goenka, Jawahar Goel, who serves as the Chairman & Managing Director, Dish TV India Ltd, Ashok Goel, who serves as Chairman Essel World & Water Kingdom, and Atul Goel, who serves as Managing Director, E-City Ventures.

At ZEEL, the Board of Directors lists impressive titles that reflect the superiority of the brand in the industry. Subhash Chandra, who by now has managed to culminate a legendary position across spectrums, serves as the Chairman Emeritus. He also serves as an educationist, humanitarian and an elected member in the Rajya Sabha. Called the 'The Father of Indian Television', Chandra's revolutionary foresight, as regards the media industry, has presented India its first private satellite television company. He is also the Chairman of Ekal Global, an organization that works for impoverished children in tribal regions. The undertaking has instituted 86,000 schools across 22 Indian states, plus in the neighbouring country of Nepal, and has educated over 2.3 million children. It continues to work for rural development. Chandra has contributed towards society, associating his philanthropic endeavours with NGOs like TALEEM Foundation, Global Vipassana Foundation, and the Subhash Chandra Foundation.[209]

The media patriarch has been awarded several accolades over

the course of his career, for his contributions to the media scene. One of the most notable has been the 2011 International Emmy Directorate Award at the 39th International Emmy Awards, which was presented to him in New York. He also became the first Indian to receive a Directorate Award that lauded a distinction in programming for television outside USA.

Ashok Kurien, Chandra's longtime friend whose name is now familiar in the industry as the person alongside whom Chandra dared to dream big about his place in the media industry, and launched Zee, serves as a Non-Executive Director on the Board. He is a recognized personality in the advertising sphere, with experience of over 35 years. He has been part of the company since the very beginning, serving as Promoter and Director. He has been associated with brands in the fields of media, marketing, and now works for development in areas of menstrual hygiene and water filters sans electricity, for those who don't have access to these essentials. Apart from identifying as the Founder Promoter of Zee, Kurien is also the Founder and Director of Essel's offerings like Playwin Lotteries (PPIL), India.com, Dish TV, Livinguard Technologies, etc.

Adesh Gupta, serving as an Independent Director of ZEEL, is a Chartered Accountant, with a background in AMP from Harvard and a rich experience in corporate strategy of over 35 years. With a career spanning three decades with the Aditya Birla Group, Gupta has held senior positions in many sectors of the company. After he retired from his post as Whole-Time Director and CFO of Grasim Industries Ltd, he ventured into the field of Business Finance and the Corporate Service space as the Designated Partner of Progressive Consulting and Business Advisory LLP. Currently, he also serves on the Boards of two of Aditya Birla's branches. ICAI, IMA and Business Today felicitated him with the Best CFO award. He was also a member of National Accounting and Auditing Standards, a setup which was instrumental in establishing Accounting Standards in India.

Alicia Yi, who serves as an Independent Director at ZEEL, is a Harvard School alumnus with a rich background in leadership roles across top companies in consumer goods, retail, hospitality, travel, leisure, etc. Currently, she is the Vice Chair of Korn Ferry's Global Consumer Market based in Singapore. She is also a member of the Board & CEO Services Practice, Human Resources Practice, and Private Equity Practice, while also being on the Advisory Board for Women's Forum for the Economy & Society. She is an operating member of the Young President Organization (YPO): Global Learning Committee, Global Taskforce of Champion Lifecycle, Singapore Chapter Chair and Singapore Chapter Learning Officer.

Manish Chokhani, who is a Chartered Accountant with an MBA background from London Business School, ranks as one of the country's most revered investors and financial experts. With ZEEL, he serves on the Board as an Independent Director. Previously, he has been MD & CEO of Enam Securities. He has also functioned as the Chairman of TPG Growth, India and currently serves there as a Senior Advisor. He is also on the boards of establishments like Westlife Development, Shoppers Stop and Laxmi Organic. Chokhani is a member of SEBI's Alternative Investment Policy Advisory Committee, and has worked three terms as Co-Chairman of the Capital Markets Committee at IMC. He has been a visiting faculty member at IIM-Kozhikode and has worked in some roles at the London Business School as well.

Piyush Pandey, who serves as an Independent Director has an extensive experience of over 37 years in the field of advertising, primarily with Ogilvy and Mather, India. He was made the Worldwide Chief Creative Officer of Ogilvy in January 2019, and currently serves as the Executive Chairman of O&M India. Pandey is a member on the Board of Directors, of D B Corp Limited, Pidilite Industries Limited, Eighty-Two Point Five Communications Private Limited, Quintessentially Lifestyle Services (India) Private Limited and Brand David Communications Private Limited. He is the only Indian to have won three Grand Prizes at the London International Advertising Awards. He was awarded the Clio Lifetime Achievement Award in 2012 and the Lion of St. Mark at the International Festival of Creativity at Cannes 2018. In 2016, he was awarded the Padma Shri in acknowledgement of his illustrious service in the field of advertising and communication, thereby becoming the first Indian to be awarded in this field. His first book 'Pandeymonium' was published in 2015. He was also a mentor at the Berlin School of Creative Leadership. His work has won over 1,000 awards nationally and internationally.

Punit Goenka, serving as the current Managing Director and CEO of Zee, is also another name that has been around since the beginning of the brand, by virtue of being Subhash Chandra's son. He is a vibrant professional with a robust background in entrepreneurship, and originally began his professional stint with Essel Group. Much of Zee's successful identity today can be credited to Goenka who has strove to make it a brand. He has been effective in augmenting the company's functioning and has driven the company to achieve its goals. Under his management, Zee has attained hundreds of milestones and won many prestigious awards like Dun& Bradstreet Corporate Award 2015, IMC Fusion Award 2013 for Excellence in Media, Business world Infocom ICT Award 2012. He has elevated the brand to a global cadre, with his futuristic outlook and clever acumen in the domain of new media. Hehas expanded the company's international presence throughout 173 countries, and its influence to over 1.3 billion viewers.

Following his father's footsteps, Goenka has bagged many awards. He has been honored with the Business Today

'Best CEO Award' in the M&E category for 2016, MIPTV's prestigious Médailled'Honneur Award 2016, Economic Times '40 Under Forty' India's Hottest Business Leaders Award 2014, the 'Young CEO Award' by CEO India magazine in 2015 and the prestigious IAA Leadership Award 2014 under the category of 'Media Person of the Year Award'. He has also been recognized as the 'Entrepreneur of the Year' during the Asia Pacific Entrepreneurship Awards 2014. He was also felicitated as the 'IMPACT Person of the Year' in 2014, for his immense contribution to the media sphere.

R. Gopalan serves as the Chairman of the Board. He has an impressive background with Master of Public Administration & Management from Harvard University along with an MA in Economics from Boston University. He has rich background on economic dealings with many years working with the Ministry of Commerce and Industries. As an IAS officer, Gopalan has held several responsible positions including as Member of Public Enterprises Selection Board, Secretary Department of Company Affairs, and others. Through a career spanning over 25 years, Gopalan currently also serves as a member on the Boards of Directors & Audit Committee of Sundaram Clayton Ltd, Hindustan Power Projects Pvt. Ltd, and as Chairman of ANA ARC Ltd.

The specialised focus of the company is possible through its Business Leaders who serve as Vertical Heads, overlooking a certain aspect of the company.

Amit Goenka, President—Digital Businesses & Platforms, is responsible for spearheading the digital businesses of Company which include ZEE5 (Domestic AVOD—Advertising-based Video on Demand and SVOD—Subscription Video on Demand), ZEE5 Global, SugarBox and Digital Publishing. Amit has been extremely successful in pioneering ZEE5, the one-stop digital destination for Zee Entertainment and catapulting the company into its next phase of growth and aggressively expanding the company's footprint in the international arena.

Prior to this role, Amit has successfully managed the technology business of the Essel Group and has played a vital role in the setting up the state-of-the-art processes in all the group companies. Amit was also awarded the esteemed Medaille d'Honneur Award at MIPTV.

Amit's first venture was Cyquator Technologies Ltd, a company which deals with web hosting and e-solutions space. His intense knack of identifying, evaluating & pursuing new business opportunities and developing market strategies was instrumental in the phenomenal success of 'Playwin'—India's first online lottery, wherein he introduced the concept of MyPlaywin.com cards, enabling an online purchase of the lottery tickets. Furthermore, his innovative ideas gave birth to India's first pre-paid cash cards service, ITZ Cash Card, a unique payment instrument. Under his leadership, the company is taking the right steps to achieve its global ambitions, set for the year 2020. Driven by a global demand for ZEE's content, Amit is aggressively expanding the company's footprint in the international arena.

Amit has been extremely successful in pioneering ZEE5, the one-stop digital destination for Zee Entertainment and catapulting the company into its next phase of growth. Prior to this role, Amit has effectively managed the technology business of the Essel Group, and has played a fundamental role in the setting up the state-of-the-art processes in all the group companies. Amit was also awarded the revered Medaille d'Honneur Award at MIPTV.

Punit Misra serves as the CEO of President, Content & International Markets ZEEL. In his earlier phases, Misra served as Executive Director of Sales and Customer Development at Hindustan Unilever and also as a member of the Management Committee. He has a variety of experience across Sales, Marketing and General Management, with a work list that boasts of several FMCG categories.

Anurag Bedi spearheads Zee Music Company as the Chief Business Officer. Launched in 2014, Zee Music Company is one of India's leading music publishing labels. Anurag is responsible for all verticals of the music label viz. Content Acquisition, Revenue Growth, Intellectual Property, Marketing, Creative & Innovation. Today, Zee Music is the No. 2 Music Label & Publisher in India with a pan-India presence across all regional languages.

Rahul Johri is the President—Business, South Asia at Zee Entertainment Enterprises Ltd In this role, Rahul is responsible for leading the integrated revenue and monetization team to drive a more synergised monetization engine. In his previous stint, Rahul was associated with the Board of Control for Cricket in India (BCCI) as its first CEO for over four years, being the driving strength in powering the development in monetization of assets including the IPL and the BCCI Media rights. Prior to BCCI, Rahul was associated with Discovery Networks Asia Pacific for 15 years where he positively led the turnaround of the company, working across all facets of the value chain.

Shariq Patel, Chief Business Officer—Zee Studios spearheads the Movies business of Zee Entertainment Enterprises Ltd and is responsible for various aspects of the value chain viz. movie purchase/production as well as monetization, across all markets (Domestic & International). In a career of almost 25 years, Shariq has worked across industries, across diverse sectors including financial services, internet, radio, film production, and telecom.

Swaroop Banerjee serves as the COO for Zee Live, and is involved in conceptualizing and creating experiential assets for the company across genres ranging from culture, education, food to music, engaging a wide assortment of regional, national and international spectators. He has over 17 years of experience in the field that began originally with involvement in the IIFA Awards, leading to the ultimate big venture into broadcast of live entertainment. He has crafted over 15 business models with Live Original Content & IPs, which lie at the core of the businesses at MTV Asia, Star World, Star Movies, Viacom 18 INS and the Laqshya Media Group.

Rohit Gupta serves as the CFO at ZEEL, with over 25 years of experience spanning the fields of finance, accounts, investor relations, technology and telecom. Gupta has previously been associated with Chaudhary Group, Brightstar Telecommunications Ltd, NUT Ltd, Virgin Mobile India, Bharti Airtel, British Telecom Looksmart Ltd and Hutchison Max.

Animesh Kumar currently serves as the Chief People Officer at ZEEL, boasting of over 25 years of experience in the field. He has led the HR function for several reputed MNCs for over 15 years. In his professional period, he has been associated with the Future Group as the Chief People & Transformation Officer.He has also worked with the IDFC Group for 9 years and has served on Boards of various companies.[210]

Independent Directors include Alicia Yi, Piyush Pandey and Manish Chokhani.

Over at ZMCL, the leadership is equally, if not more, skilled and professional. The Board and leadership consists of Uma Mandavgane, an Associate Chartered Accountant and Certified Information Systems Auditor from ISACA, USA is a professional with experience of over 22 years in industry and consulting; Dr Rashmi Aggarwal, a PhD (Patents Law) from Law Department, Punjab University, Chandigarh; Kanta Devi Allria, an Intermediate, is a Social activist committed to prosperity and well-being of Dalits; Surjit Banga, who is a senior and experienced banker and is known for his leadership and admirable contribution to the Banking sector; Raj Kumar Gupta, a Commerce Graduate from BITS University, Pilani, Rajasthan and a Chartered Accountant, is a veteran in Finance & Accounts Profession with experience of over 5 decades, and a Senior Partner of M/s. Gupta Raj & Co., Chartered Accountants; Dinesh Kumar Garg, a Chartered Accountant with professional experience of over 25 years, associated with Essel Group for the last 14 years, including as the Chief Financial Officer of the company between 2009 to 2016. Garg was part of the core team involved in the growth of Zee Media from a 2 Channel closely held Company to a widely held, listed company currently broadcasting 14 National & Regional News Channels.

The other 2 segments that emerged after the demerger in 2016 have also been operating under renowned and capable leaders.

For Dish TV India Ltd, the Board of Directors include Dr Rashmi Aggarwal, who serves as the Non-Executive Independent Women Director on the Board of the company; Jawahar Goel, appointed as the Managing Director of Dish TV India Limited; Arun Duggal, an Independent Non-Executive member of the Board of Dish TV India Limited; Ashok Kurien, one of the Founder-Promoter and Non- Executive Director on the Board of Dish TV; B. D. Narang, an Independent Non-Executive Member of the Board of Dish TV; Eric L. Zinterhofer, an Independent Non-Executive member of the Board; Lakshmi Chand, an Independent Non-Executive Director on the Board.[211]

The SITI Cable Network Ltd has a Board of Directors which includes Brijendra K. Syngal, the father of Internet and data services in India, and who was responsible for executing a GDR issue of $527 million at VSNL, the largest GDR issue out of India to be listed on the London Stock Exchange; V.D. Wadhwa, who prior to joining SITI Cable, was with Timex Group India Limited where he was Managing Director & CEO for Business Operations in India and SAARC Countries; Sandeep Khurana, qualified in Law and a Fellow member of the Institute of Company Secretaries of India apart from being an associate member of the Institute of Cost Accountants of India; Kavita Kapahi, a Commerce Graduate from Bombay University, and an entrepreneur engaged in the Security & Surveillance Industry; Suresh Kumar Agarwal, Managing Director and major shareholder of Super Dynic Clothing Pvt. Ltd; and Vinod Kumar Bakshi, a Non-Executive Independent Board member of the company.[212]

Zee Learn has also emerged as one of the more important branches of the company, dedicated to educational services and undertakings.

BUSINESS STRATEGY

In its business overview, Zee sums up its business functions and strategies, 'Since inception, ZEEL has been entertaining its viewers by showcasing stories set in varied cultural backdrops. Over the years, it has grown from one channel to a multi-faceted entertainment content company. However, at its core, it still strives with the same enthusiasm to create content that evokes a range of emotions, provokes viewers to think beyond conventions and mirrors the cultural and societal aspects, driving a gradual change. Our five businesses—Domestic Broadcast, Digital, International, Movies & Music and Live Events—are designed to cover a vast spectrum of entertainment needs of the consumers. These businesses produce around 500 hours of original content across formats every week which is distributed through multiple platforms. Our content reaches audiences around the world in 20 languages. We continually strive to understand our viewers' evolving socio-cultural profiles to add more products and create new content to satisfy their ever-changing entertainment needs and preferences.'[213]

Zee has adopted a useful strategy since the beginning by demarcating its business into five clear verticals, namely

Domestic Broadcast, International Business, Studios and Music, Digital, and Live and Theatre, which has led to the smooth-sailing functions across all spectrums. Content is the common thread that runs across all five business verticals. All these verticals create entertainment content which is first monetized by the respective businesses. As the Intellectual Property Rights of the content produced rest with Zee, there is an opportunity to monetize the same content across other verticals as well. The company has also leveraged its presence across different verticals for effective promotion of content. Another momentous change came in 2006 with a demerger of the Zee Telefilms Ltd, and its various segments. This was helpful in compartmentalizing news, entertainment, and cable services separately.

Punit Goenka, on his company's expansion and acquisition strategies, says, 'We would not acquire something, unless we understand that market. The critical thing is for us to understand that market first, and then see whether it's an organic or inorganic entry. In this country we have evaluated practically all the deals that have happened in the last five years. We have backed out of all of them for one single reason: they want better multiples than what we trade at, so it's just not possible to do the deals.'[214]

In recent times, Zee has relied on its own blueprint for success with the creation of a highly skilled business strategy that is clear of its goals and what it wants to stir in the hearts of its customers. 'To diversify and strengthen content offering' has been one of the earliest mantras of success for Zee, and it is something that it strives to continue well into the future too. Zee notes, 'Having established leadership in television, the company is focused on scaling-up its digital, movies & music, and live events businesses. We are significantly increasing our investments in content offerings beyond television with an objective to attract new viewers and increase engagement with the existing ones.'[215] Zee's in-house know-how, along with sturdy partnerships in the content creation, aggregation and circulation eco-system, empowers it to create and deliver appealing content at a competitive cost. This has helped Zee to inflate and fortify its presence across media verticals. Presently, the company produces over 500+ hours of content every week, original content in 11 languages, and owns the IP rights of all the content they produce.

'Enhanced consumer focus' comes as the next strategic point, another longstanding tradition at Zee in sync with its diversification motives. The Zee brand has always relied on expanding itself to the effect that it subsumes every aspect of the demographic within its geographical reach. The emergence of direct-to-consumer businesses (digital, movies, live events) and the new tariff regulation for television that allows consumers to choose content, gave them greater insights into their preferences and behaviours. They started building processes which can leverage these insights to create engaging content and improve the viewing experience. Zee created synergies across businesses, and realized significant synergies, in both cost and revenue, due to a presence across markets and platforms. With superior technology today, content created for a market or a platform can travel easily to another, increasing its economic value and access. This diverse presence not only allows the company to manage the content creation and acquisition costs better but also enables cross-platform marketing. For instance, all of Zee's 40 channels in international markets run on content produced for its Indian channels, while its digital platform hosts content from TV, Movies, Music and Live Businesses.

Next, Zee seeks to 'increase its reach', by relying on factors like deeper regional penetration and expansion of its geographical impact across borders, because with Zee, viewers access content through multiple distribution channels and devices. The company assures, 'With a commitment to be available on every possible platform, ZEEL is striking partnerships with content distributors, aggregators and device manufacturers, giving more viewers an opportunity to consume its content.' This enables Zee to deliver to almost every consumer its entertainment content in India and one in ten in rest of the world. It claims that this strong reach makes it the default partner for brand building as well as the preferred partner for content creators in today's time. It has a reach of 750+ million individuals reached in India every month, a presence in 173 countries, and 3000+ brands connected with consumers through the network.

Zee seeks to 'build capabilities', since '...to succeed in an ever-evolving media landscape, the organization needs to build capabilities for the future.' To this end, ZEEL is focused on 'up-skilling its workforce, investing in data analytics, and upgrading production facilities and IT infrastructure'[216] to deliver an extraordinary entertainment experience to its users. Among its strategic assets, it counts a library with intellectual property rights of over 260,000+ hours of content, a brand value created over 28 years, and the people who believe in its saying 'Extraordinary Together.'

The World Entertained

We went International in 1995. A huge step back then. We have grown by leaps and bounds over the years, with a footprint across 173 countries around the world, covering Americas, Europe, MENAP, Africa and APAC regions.

Our portfolio of channels caters to not just the Indian and South Asian diaspora but also to local audiences in international territories.

Of the 40 channels in the international markets, 10 are dedicated to a non-Indian audience, offering them entertainment content in their native languages.

Fig. 8.2: Zee Global

Source: ZEEL, International Business Review.

Overseas, through well-planned management strategies, the company has consolidated its years of international business expansion, which have seen an exponential increase in the number of subscribers. Category 1 Channels were armed with providing Indian content to the South Asian diaspora. In this regard, Zee became the first and largest Indian broadcaster offering 28 channels to the diaspora. Category 2 Channels include dubbed and subtitled content for mainstream audiences, under which the company offers Indian content in local languages across 9 channels to local audiences around the world. Category 3 Channels offer local content to local audiences, by identifying regions having scope for production of local content in local languages. Category 4 Channels are the way forward, which will seek to provide global content to global audiences.

Amit Goenka, elaborated on the international business strategies as the CEO of Zee's International Broadcast Business and ZEE5 Global in the company's 2018–19 Annual Report, 'International opportunity for ZEE5 is sizable and we are very excited about it. Our linear network of 39 channels in over 170 countries gives us a good understanding of the relevance of our content in overseas markets. Indian and South-Asian diaspora are the primary consumers of our content and they would be the first adopters of ZEE5. It can significantly expand the addressable market amongst the diaspora as it is priced much lower than similar content available on traditional platforms. Additionally, ZEE5 Originals will help attract the younger diaspora which does not relate to Indian television content. There is an affinity for our content even beyond the Indian diaspora in several markets and ZEE5 will reach out to this audience in the next phase. We have begun the staggered roll-out of ZEE5 globally with launches in APAC countries and the response has been encouraging so far. In coming quarters, ZEE5 will be launched in markets like the MENA region, Africa, Europe and Canada.'[217]

Further in an interview, Rohit Gupta, CFO, sheds some light on ZEEL's growth and investment outlook for new businesses and initiatives on the whole, 'At ZEEL, we continue to invest and scale up new businesses to widen our content offering. Our new businesses—digital, movies and music, and live entertainment have gained traction during FY19 and are heading in the planned direction. ZEE5 completed its 1st year of operations and the platform has witnessed very encouraging response. ZEE5 released 50+ original series/movies to become the largest digital content producer in India. Investments in digital will further increase as we ramp-up production of ZEE5 Originals and movie offering across languages. These content investments will be complemented by marketing spends. Zee Studios, our movie production and distribution business, had a good run at box-office with the release of 13 movies during the year. The team has built a strong slate of movies across languages for FY20. Zee Music Company, our music publishing business, further strengthened its position by expanding its catalogue across languages. Our Movies & Music businesses are now past their investment phase. Zee Live, our live entertainment business, is at a nascent stage and is experimenting with concepts. Investments in Zee Live will be modest, relative to the size of the company. Our domestic broadcast business is preparing to launch movie channels in regional markets for which we have been building a library for some time. Incremental investments in the domestic broadcast would be limited. These content and marketing investments are expensed above EBITDA. Despite these investments, the company expects to maintain healthy margins.'[218]

BRAND IDENTITY

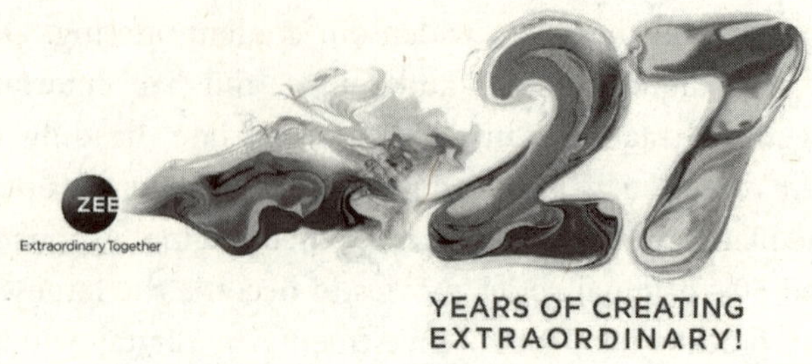

Fig. 8.3: Creative from the 27th year celebrations at ZEE

Source: As provided by ZEE

The brand identity is what makes an entity stand tall, apart from its endless sea of competitors crowding the industry markets. It is the most straightforward way, working in the most complex manner, to show customer what the company seeks to achieve and what the company seeks to provide.

For a company offering such diversified content and having wide geographic presence, it is important to pay careful attention to how it brands itself and maintains consistency. More specifically, the question steers towards what the brand architecture should be. It becomes important to note how the corporate and product brands relate to each other and derive synergy from each other while also catering to their respective markets by providing value and experiences.

Typically, firms use two types of brand architecture strategies—Branded House and House of Brands.[219] In Branded House, a single corporate brand name is used for all entities in the portfolio, something which can be seen in a brand like Philips. House of Brands involves creating distinct product brands for specific markets without linking to the corporate brand, something characteristic of HUL. Zee, by and large, is a Branded House in which everything is branded as Zee with a few exceptions like, &TV, Zing etc.

For the brand to be perceived positively and popularly, it becomes important for companies to enhance their brand identity through words and designs that succinctly portray the brand's vision to its customers. The tangible elements of a company's corporate design assets are major determiners of how the brand is perceived. Things of note include the logo, packaging, web design, social media graphics, etc.

Today, the brand Zee, is synonymous with 'entertainment for all' and is the preferred entertainment destination for audiences in India and around the world. Zee summed up its branding activities in the following words, 'The launch of Zee TV in 1992 was only the beginning. It was an era of liberalisation and the Country's economy was opening up to vibrant opportunities. Zee being a brand with young, contemporary and aspirational thoughts, capitalised these opportunities. What followed over the years was a continual string of path-breaking developments... Over the years, we have been vigilant in enhancing its brand reputation in every market in which we operate. We have developed globally competitive pricing strategies, technological advantage across the value chain and cultivated a global mindset to build on the cultural diversity. We have adopted successful practices and have given deep thought to the notions of traditional customers, values and innovation and in the process formed a beautiful family of viewers, shareholders, employees and business partners across the globe.'[220]

Over the years, Zee has been very insistent on creating a robust brand identity. Along with renovating their visions, missions and goals for each FY, due focus has also been given to the frequently evolving corporate identity of the company, which in one way or another is reflective of Zee's ideals. Not just the company, but even its separate channels have been developing their brand identity over the years with differing taglines, the most noticeable of which have come from Zee TV. The company has always believed in focusing a magnified insight into the name, logo, tone, tagline, and typeface to create an appeal for accurate audience targeting through consistent messaging.

Consistency has been one of the primary keys as to why Zee has succeeded in creating such a superior brand identity over the years. It has been an exhibition of product leadership, marketing, support, and operations, while also reflecting a good corporate culture that is working throughout to bring the perfect product to the customer. Zee has achieved this across their spectrum of products, from the website, to the announcement of their Annual Reports replete with minute details of the group, to including their consumers in every aspect of their timeline.

Ever since the company's inception in 1992 to the 2006 demerger to its current state, the company has always had clarity about its mission (the why), values (the beliefs), brand personality (defining characteristics), unique positioning (differentiation), and brand voice (communication capability). It was brought into the world keeping in mind the main shareholder- the customer. What Zee's brand personality can be defined by is what makes it better and more special than its counterparts. A lot of the brand identity portrayed by Zee comes from Subhash Chandra's ideals. The man who envisioned a revolution for the Indian media scene executed his ideas for the foremost benefit of the citizens of the country, striving to put them on a platform from where they could compete with their international counterparts. Zee has never been without the idea of connecting with people, and that is in fact, one of the mainstays of the company's visionary outlook.

Branding for any company also includes having a user-friendly and attractive website, since it is one of the most representative public indicators of a brand identity. When one hears the name Zee, a certain brand physique comes to mind, with defining words like entertainment, genres, diversified media platforms, many languages, interesting stories/content, logos, that stand out. The brand personality by extension appears creative, dynamic, exuberant, cosmopolitan and bold. It seeks to include a cultural consumer context in which the brand offers its value proposition or essence. It focuses on the cultural diversity across India and the world, elaborating upon its richness. It becomes synonymous with such values and inclusivity, humility and integrity. Zee tells the consumer that it understands their need for agility in experience and content consumption everyday. Through its expansion, the brand is understood to be comfortable with technology and embraces the virtual world as easily as it does the material one. Zee's desire to transcend the ordinary and the mundane to something bigger and uplifting is delivered in an entertaining way.

Branding well becomes doubly important for Zee since it has diversified greatly into digital and online platforms, offering a tray of varied products, the most recent one being Zee5. The platform has an easy-to-use interface and easy tools for navigation, that run on a subscription basis. The Zee5 brand offers an extremely hands-on experience for customers, with bright and bold representations of the shows it has to offer. The Zee website is one of the key places where the brand identity comes through in full force.

In order to create a differentiated visual identity, the brand has resorted and experimented with using different colours while keeping the shape and fonts consistent.

VASUDHAIVA KUTUMBAKAM
THE WORLD IS MY FAMILY

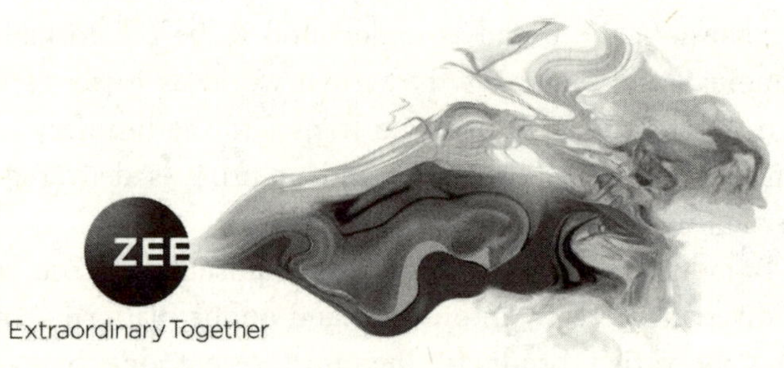

Fig. 8.4: The changing logo

Source: As provided by ZEE

In 2013, Zee Entertainment Enterprises revealed a fresh corporate brand identity and positioning termed 'Vasudhaiva Kutumbakam'. The positioning was motivated by the core message 'the world is my family', which was assimilated and crafted with the brand logo. The company on this occasion said, 'With this global cadre achieved by the brand, there was a definite need for a brand positioning statement, which differentiates Zee from the other global media brands, and establishes a strong emotional connect with the entire world. With this approach in mind, 'Vasudhaiva Kutumbakam'—The World is my Family has been launched as the positioning for Brand ZEE, which conveys the message of creating a world without borders, castes, races and strangers, hence uniting everyone as a part of one Family.'[221]

Chandra, explaining the intent behind this change, said, 'This positioning will not just be for the front-end, but going forward, would be deeply carved into the ethos of the Organization, reflecting through our communication, content and conduct.'[222]

The new branding exercise focused on the 'ancient Indian dictum of shared humanity, promoting a world where there is unity, harmony and respect for every individual irrespective of caste and creed.'[223] The positioning and identity were also extended to all communication touch points, and inculcated the group's news and digital business verticals under the Zee Media brand as well.

Punit Goenka, MD and CEO, Zee Entertainment Enterprises said in a statement, 'Zee is a cultural ambassador, uniting millions of people in India and across the world through entertainment. Zee has embraced this maxim as a belief. The identity is a balanced blend of the traditional and the modern.'[224]

M. G. Parameswaran, CEO of Draft FCB Ulka Mumbai, the creative agency behind the new positioning, said, 'Zee is rooted in true Indian values of philanthropy and spirituality. The new identity and the global positioning line tries to embody this in a succinct manner.'[225]

In 2017, to commemorate 25 years of growth of ZEEL into a M&E powerhouse, the company unveiled a new brand identity 'Extraordinary Together' which was released with a concept to offer an integrated brand experience and please consumers across the demographic spectrum by creating extraordinary experiences that transcended the ordinary. On this occasion of 25 years, the company commented, 'Our new brand ideology 'Extraordinary Together' celebrates our belief in the power of working together, that we're greater than the sum of our parts and from collaboration comes the strength to deliver the exceptional. Our mission to create extraordinary entertainment experiences for our audience could not have been achieved without the support of our employees, partners and peers, who had the faith in our vision and walked alongside us. At the cusp of our 25th anniversary, we reaffirm our commitment to work tirelessly with each of them, to create new benchmarks and deliver the extraordinary. Mosaic, an art-form made of innumerable elements, each of which is vital to the picture that emerges when they all come together, is thus a fitting motif...' The circular shape of the logo embodies the concept of permanence, connections and inclusiveness—the circle of life. The amethyst (a stone) colour in the logo is about creativity and spiritual energy. The burst of colours is the unleashing of energy that empowers all those who come into its fold. The brand purpose, clearly refers to the company's outlook of creating the extraordinary. The brand essence on the other hand is to empower the customer and company with extraordinary content and experiences.

Chandra's approach to this change was, 'We would not have been able to create the impact we did without the invaluable contributions of our employees, creative partners, distributors, peers, shareholders, and countless others who have worked behind the scenes. We firmly believe that when we collaborate with each other, our individual strengths get amplified to become greater than the sum of its parts. Our new ideology of 'Extraordinary Together' subsumes our longstanding philosophy of 'Vasudhaiva Kutumbakam—the world is one family', and celebrates this journey of collaborating with our partners, within and outside, to create and deliver extraordinary entertainment. Our philosophy of 'Extraordinary Together' is not only about the way we approach our business, but also encompasses the society. Our quest to contribute towards a better society starts with creating content that inspires, motivates and challenges the status-quo. With a renewed faith and sense of purpose, we make our way towards the future. As we write the first chapter of this new era, our dream is to be Extraordinary Together.'[226]

Explaining the new approach, Punit Goenka said, 'Our Chairman, Dr Subhash Chandra's vision and pioneering efforts caused a revolution in the country 25 years ago. Over time, Zee has evolved from a television broadcaster into a M&E conglomerate with businesses spanning across the spectrum, from broadcasting to music, movies, digital, live entertainment and theatre, providing an extraordinary range of entertainment to audiences around the world. Our new brand ideology—'Extraordinary Together' is rooted in the philosophy that from collaboration comes the strength to deliver the extraordinary. In a global company like ours, with interests across diverse verticals and businesses, we believe that our ability to win lies in us being able to effectively come together and harness this strength to be extraordinary in the market.'[227]

When asked why ZEEL thought of changing its earlier identity of 'Vasudhaiva Kutumbakam' to 'Extraordinary Together' Punit Misra maintained that the company wasn't deserting the former tag, but was instead encompassing it too within the new corporate identity. Now to reach the target of 3 billion viewers from the current 1.3 billion the MD felt the requirement for a global language that could communicate with the viewers. Misra said, 'Vasudhaiva Kutumbakam' is still part of our philosophy and our DNA group is going forward with it.'

The new brand identity, which was designed by the global visionary designer Martin Lambie-Nairn, Creative Director, ML-N, clearly represented the company's mission of celebrating the world and bringing everyone together through entertainment. The circular form of the new brand logo was symbolic of continuity, endurance and inclusiveness, representing a consistency. The amethyst colour represented a sense of creative transformation, although this colour is usually reflective of luxury and royalty in colour psychology. 'The visual property, Exuberance—a colourful explosion of creative energy makes Zee the fountainhead unleashing extraordinary potential.'

Speaking on his vision for the new identity, Martin Lambie-Nairn, Creative Director, ML-N said, '25 years is celebrating what you've achieved and far more importantly, understanding where you are going, rethinking the brand purpose and considering how to address your audiences in the future. Before conceptualising the new brand identity, our first step was to understand this rich legacy of ZEE, unravel where the viewer aspirations and expectations are headed, and then arrive at the brand purpose and ideology that is future-ready. This helped us create a truly global brand architecture that would be easy to operate across genres, businesses, and countries and more importantly, introduce magic into it. With this vastly diverse bouquet of brands and businesses that Zee owns, it was necessary to have a golden thread that runs through all the businesses—an elegant and monolithic design language that links the organization together and inspires to create the extraordinary.'[228]

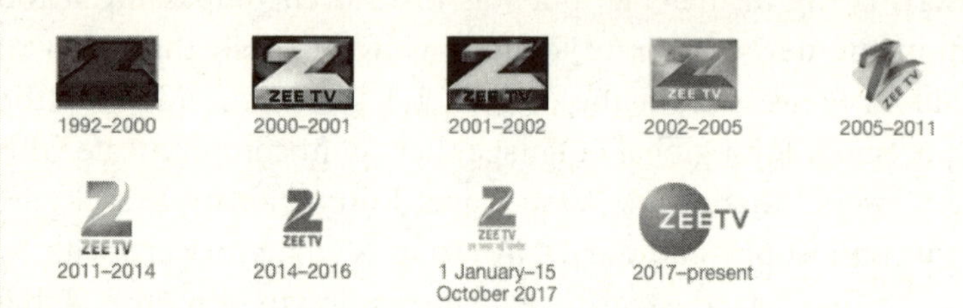

Fig. 8.5: Different logos I

Source: As provided by ZEE

Likewise, the company flagship channel, Zee TV too has undergone a change in identity over the years. In 2012, on the cusp of launching ZeeQ, the network's 32nd non-news channel, Punit Goenka brought focus to Zee's business strategy over the years. There were doubts. When Zee TV was facing stiff competition in the market for four to five years, one did feel maybe it required a different ballgame altogether. But the chairman and board knew what it takes in the long term and stood firm.

Fig. 8.6: Different logos II

Source: As provided by ZEE

The logo design of any company is the cornerstone in its brand identity. It should aim to clearly communicate what the company values and aspires towards, while giving the audience a preview into the understanding of the company's vision as a brand. The logo should without a doubt be visually appealing and uncluttered, so as not to appear too heavy on the customer's senses, and at the same time should be classic and timeless. If the company goes in for trendiness, it may have to adapt the brand identity with a higher frequency, a task that is not easy to undertake. In this arena, Zee has dabbled with many ideas over the years. While it has mostly never aimed for trendy, it has sought the quality of being open to adaptation and show to its audiences that it has the ability to change with time, according to consumer preferences.

The brand name and the logo have been adapted as per requirement across product offerings. The name Zee is consistent along with the logo shape and fonts. Where the name is concerned, the brand has by and large used 'descriptors' e.g. Zee cinema, Zee Bangla etc. However, it has also used 'modifiers' to create differentiation within the brand and its offerings e.g. Zee Café.

In the case of Zee5, the brand has clearly tried to set this apart and experimented with the shape, trying to bring out agility, dynamism, technology savviness—everything that goes with the nature of the product offering. Yet, it is very much a part of the Zee family.

The most recent and notable shifts have been detailed. In 2011, Zee TV launched a new brand identity highlighting a new logo with a slogan 'Umeed se SajeZindagi'. The channel's focus was portrayed to be once again on women and their empowerment. Developed by the in-house team, Zee TV's aqua blue logo featured a sophisticated font. It was a new age design and the upward flourish signified the skyward undertaking of desires and dreams. The abstract style of the 'Z' and vivacity of aqua blue brought in freshness and crispness to the brand: something like the unshackling of the 'Z'.[229] Some additional muscle was provided to the branding by global agency Draft FCB.

Punit Goenka, ZEEL MD and CEO said on the release of the new branding exercise, 'We believe the time is right to infuse renewed freshness into the brand and reflect an identity that truly articulates our spirit. The new positioning is about a celebration and vindication of a woman's emerging beliefs and a reflection of her changing hopes, dreams and optimism.'[230]

Then in December 2014, a new graphics package was presented. The glow and bevel effects were removed and the logo's blue shade was turned darker. The slogan was changed to 'Har Lamha Nayi Ummeed' ('A New Hope Every Moment'). Zee TV's business head, Pradeep Hejmadi, then said, 'Zee TV's core proposition of 'Ummeed Se Saje Zindagi' was about a celebration and vindication of a woman's emerging beliefs and a reflection of her changing hopes, dreams and optimism. This essence was embodied by each of our protagonists who emerged as role models and harbingers of hope for the masses. In that sense, Zee TV will always stand for Ummeed. It is the articulation that will change to reflect the changing times. Today, with India poised for growth, there is a feeling of 'a new hope, every moment'. Zee TV's new slogan 'Har Lamha Nayi Ummeed' captures this spirit and its brand philosophy as also its content will reflect the same.'

About the new packaging for the channel, he said, 'Designed and developed by the internationally acclaimed design studio Les Telecreateurs, Zee TV's aqua blue logo now makes way for a deeper shade of blue, lending it a stronger, more dynamic edge. The new motif of the packaging is a spinning top, originally derived from the left top portion of the 'Z' itself. It spins, taking the form of a beautiful flower-like element. Here, each spine is perceived as a new lamha; every show of Zee TV is a new lamha, a new emotion, a new sense of exuberance, a new moment. And from this thought stems the new brand slogan 'Har Lamha Nayi Ummeed'. The colour scheme of the new packaging is further fine-tuned to a strong blue for weekday fiction shows evoking the faith and trust of our viewers, yellow for weekend fiction signifying warmth and optimism, orange for weekend non-fiction that stands for cheer, confidence and celebration. The red packaging for movies and events represents excitement and youthful energy.'

At the same time, Zee TV rolled out a 360-degree marketing campaign across Hindi markets to unveil the new identity. The creative agency FCB Ulka conceptualised a simple yet memorable visual device of 'fingers crossed' to bring alive the new proposition. The channel also brought on board ace music industry composers Salim-Sulaiman to compose a memorable audio pneumonic to bring alive the essence of the new brand proposition.

In the wake of this brand refresh, the channel undertook an excellent brand campaign by calling out to viewers to share their 'ummeed stories'–'slices of their life that will go on to inspire content on Zee TV, as well as be showcased on digital platforms.' Some of the best crowd-sourced stories were proposed to be curated into a book by a best-selling author. Zee TV also encouraged its viewers to send in videos of their acting, dancing or singing to an online talent repository, with rewards and returns for the best entries every month.

Once again, in October 2017 during the Zee Rishtey Awards, a new orange logo was introduced for the channel. Most other Zee-branded channels, with the exception of Zing, revealed similar logos on that day. Numerous channels also launched new graphics packages, notably Zee Tamil, Zee Cinema and Zee Anmol. This was the first logo in the long history of the channel not to feature a stylised Z. *Aaj Likhenge Kal* (meaning 'we'll script tomorrow today') was introduced as a new slogan. Zee TV also introduced a new graphics package containing an orange background with orange ripples stemming from the top left corner, where the channel logo had now been relocated. Coffee & TV of London created the indents.

The primary colour of Zee has been 'Amethyst.' Amethyst is a stone of transformation. The company said they have chosen Amethyst as the core colour because of its aptitude to enlarge the higher mind. It strengthens the imagination and intuition, and refines the thinking processes, while enhancing one's creativity and passion. It helps in the assimilation of new ideas, putting thought into action, and brings projects to fruition as a talisman of focus and success.[231]

Even the sub-brands have their own unique identity and colour in line with the consumer it serves. For example, Zee Punjabi—Along with the stories and characters stimulated from the land, the philosophy of 'Jazbaa Kar Vakhon Da' is also carved out with the visual identity. The logo is a replication of inner radiance and colours from the sunrise hue palette suggesting the hope, the 'dilerJigraa' and optimism of Punjab. The colour of fuschia magenta is an ode to their welcoming and warm nature and the gold captures their chakachaund zindagi and the junoon to take on the world. The patterns of the timeless Phulkari rendered with a modern twist siginifies their strength that comes from their roots and the Bhaichaara within the community. This is juxtaposed with cascading spirals to connote their journey to their VaddeSapne.[232]

BRANDING AT ZMCL

Image plays a major role when it comes to branding. It defines the probable results of a product or company's success. Therefore, an aspect crucial to the brand identity of any company that comes hand-in-hand with the company's personality, is reputation. When a product or the company's image is damaged by untoward incidents involving either poor quality products or reckless activity, a reputation management company is the need of the hour to reconstruct and repair the damage. Oftentimes, it is re-branding that works in this case.

Zee News also took to brand rebuilding by reinforcing its role as a pillar of democracy in the industry by writing in its statement that the entire event was carried out 'to muzzle voices of dissent and interfere with the legitimate rights of the Media.' We have witnessed how both parties shook hands again and tweeted about the same eventually.[233]

REFURBISHING ANEW: PUNIT GOENKA ANNOUNCES ZEE 4.0

Recounting the entire phase of his company from 2006 to 2019, calling it Zee 3.0, Punit Goenka in a recently released open letter, said, 'It was during this phase that my journey with Zee began and I witnessed the evolution of the company, first hand. While we were busy narrating stories to the world, this phase wrote its own script about the company. A script filled with ups and downs, mergers and demergers, acquisitions and divestments, survival and growth, good decisions and the not so good ones.'

'This phase too, had one trait in common with all other phases—resilience. The lessons learnt in the previous phase brought our focus back on content, which was our key area of expertise. We also realized the need and importance of sharpening our strategic approach. This led to many important restructuring decisions, such as demerging of DTH, cable, news and education businesses from ZEE, enabling us to sharply focus on something we truly excelled at, which was 'entertainment'. We expanded our portfolio to 41 domestic and 39 international channels across genres and grew our revenue at a CAGR of 15 per cent. Even when there were headwinds such as the global recession, or influx of new competing channels backed by deep pockets, we ensured that there was no dent to our business. This was all possible because we never lost sight on what we did best—which was to judiciously create rich and engaging content. This phase saw us venture into new areas of business with the launch of our digital, movies and live entertainment businesses.'[234]

However, he specified that the final year also brought some extremely challenging 'financial headwinds experienced by the Promoter Group.' But 'Even amidst this turbulent phase it was business as usual at ZEE. I strongly believe, that what got us here will not necessarily take us further and as they say, it is not the strongest or toughest who survive, but the ones who are most responsive to change.' Harking this need for change, Goenka introduces 'a new avatar of ZEE; a version 4.0 of ZEE.' He says that Zee 4.0 would begin 'with a clean slate and focus on the following 5Gs: Governance, Granularity, Growth, Goodwill, Gusto.'

Under Governance, he says that 'Zee 4.0 has at its helm, an all-new reconstituted Board. The new esteemed members bring in the required blend of expertise, experience and wisdom. Further, we have introduced new policies which will strengthen our Governance, mitigate our Risks and safeguard our Business Interests. The focus going forward, will be to build a process-oriented structure for the future, achieving the highest levels of automation with zero manual intervention and a prudent approach towards treasury and investments.'

Granularity would bring 'a granular and transparent approach while reporting, will be an important area of focus for us. Be it segmental reporting across businesses, consistent reporting on our business KPIs, or regular communication pertaining to steps undertaken on ESG and CSR related activities; we will ensure that every single aspect is reported at the right time and on the right platforms. All of these steps will be implemented to ensure that you all get a deeper insight into our businesses.'

The focus on Growth would guide 'ZEE's constant endeavor to stay ahead of the industry performance… Apart from constantly reinventing our existing business models, the focus will be to maximize our core, expand into adjacent spaces and explore new areas of business. With an undeterred focus on growth and profitability, our aim would be to constantly enhance shareholder value.'

Under Goodwill, Goenka seeks to clear the air around the numerous controversies that have surrounded Zee these past couple of years, saying, 'Let me make one thing very clear: I am here to stay, and remain committed towards ZEE. I have taken this up as a challenge to restore the goodwill; not just for me, not just for my family, but for the entire team at ZEE.'

He further says that the 'Gusto, entrepreneurial spirit, rich expertise in content creation and the unique ability to gauge the pulse of our consumers, have been instrumental to our success.'[235]

Punit Goenka's latest acknowledgment of Zee's past mistakes and the learnings could prove to be a welcome move for the company. The focus to begin again on a clean slate, indicates a possible new road for Zee as a whole, but one that still won't be without its past history.

ORGANIZATIONAL RESTRUCTURING

On 17 October 2020, Zee announced a strategic restructuring of the organization in line with its 'Zee 4.0 Strategy'. In order to seize the opportunities developing out of the explosive evolution in content consumption across genres in India and South Asia, and to produce enhanced value in an ecosystem undergoing a paradigm shift towards content personalization, integrated advertising solutions and convergence of platforms, the company has announced the following strategic steps[236]:

- Aggregating Content Creation: The company will take a 'Content First, Cluster Centric' agenda, enabling it to take the content creation process nearer to its viewers. In order to build viewer stickiness, the company has been sharply focusing on boosting viewer intimacy, bagging and embedding sociocultural insights and the finer distinctions of the local languages & customs in its content creation process. Customer centricity has been central to the company's success in delivering rich, expressive and engaging content. This approach aims at leveraging the company's strengths in regional clusters, refining content production efficiencies, enhancing consumer insights and above all, conveying better and more cost-effective content across platforms. Hence, the company has formed an integrated content team, responsible for creating and serving content to its viewers across linear & digital platforms.
- Streamlining International Business: Under this, Zee has decided to integrate the Linear (Advt./Distribution) and Digital (AVOD/SVOD) teams in the international markets into a single team, led by the market revenue leader who will be responsible for maximizing the revenues across all formats (Linear/Digital) and revenue streams. Zee has been entertaining viewers in over 190 countries across five clusters viz. APAC; MENA; Africa; Europe and North America. The integration will also enable each international cluster leader to craft a

local-market aligned approach. With this integrated approach, the company aims to maximize revenue and drive content monetization, by optimally capitalizing the opportunities presented in the international markets.

- Integrating Digital Assets: In order to drive greater synergies across technology, data and talent, which are the three critical determinants of success in the digital ecosystem, the company will be bringing together all of its digital assets under a single umbrella, which includes ZEE5 (Domestic AVOD+SVOD), ZEE5 Global, SugarBox and Digital Publishing. While TV continues to grow in the country, digital viewership is growing at a frenetic pace, with a large number of viewers adding digital to their existing formats of content consumption. The company has been substantively investing in building its digital ecosystem, given its strategic importance for future growth.
- Movies Business: The company will be combining the different parts of its movies business, which are currently embedded in multiple domains, into a single integrated platform. This team will be responsible for both aspects of the value chain—movie purchase/production as well as monetization, across all markets (Domestic & International). Driving better line of sight through an integrated approach, this revised framework will substantially enhance the effectiveness of the company's movies business.
- Music Business: The Company's music business has gained substantial traction and it will continue to invest and grow this business to achieve market leadership.
- Integrated Revenue & Monetization team: The company will be creating an Integrated Revenue & Monetization team, combining all the existing B2B revenue

> generating teams (Linear Advt. Sales, Digital Advt. Sales, Distribution and B2B SVOD Partnerships) into a unified ecosystem. With this revised framework, the company aims to drive a more synergized monetization engine that will deliver enhanced solutions to its clients, improve wallet monetization, extend coverage to Small and Medium Enterprises (SMEs) and increase subscriber penetration across linear and digital formats.

Subsequent to this restructuring, the company has also announced the realignment of its leaders:

Punit Misra will take over as President—Content & International Markets, while Amit Goenka will take over as the President—Digital Businesses & Platforms. Tarun Katial will continue to lead the ZEE5 India business while Shariq Patel will be responsible for the integrated Movies business and Anurag Bedi will continue to drive the Music business.

Meanwhile, Rahul Johri has been appointed as President—Business, South Asia and will be responsible for leading the integrated Revenue and Monetization team. He was associated with the Board of Control for Cricket in India (BCCI) as its first CEO for over 4 years, being the driving force in powering the improvement in monetization of assets including the IPL and the BCCI Media rights.

Punit Goenka, MD & CEO, Zee Entertainment Enterprises Ltd feels Zee 4.0 will be an integrated and synergized organization, with a sharp focus on delivering world class entertainment content to their consumers across the world and enhanced value to their partners across the ecosystem. All endeavours will be to build a process-oriented structure for the future and the group's integrated approach is a strong step in this direction. 'Gusto' is an extremely important pillar of the new version of the company and as an 'Academy of Talent', Zee will continue to nurture and build leaders for the company and the Industry at large. He is certain that the collective experience and expertise of the leadership team, will help Zee immensely in achieving its set goals for the future and realize the vision chalked out for the all-new version of ZEE.

This restructuring process, implemented in line with 'Zee 4.0 Strategy', is slated to setup the company for emerging opportunities with a new version of itself. Its focus appears to be on reinventing the existing business models, maximizing its core, expanding into adjacent spaces and exploring new areas of business.

BUSINESS MODEL

Zee definitely has followed a positioning model and remained market focused ever since it began. Through the long history of its growth from a single channel to a conglomerate of more than 20 channels, to its current state, it has left many economic model doctrines of utmost value for media houses all over the world to reflect upon. If the absence of increments, reduction in pay scales and downsizing of journalists all over India have thrown some light on the aftermath of the economic slowdown in the communication sector, the sale of Star to Disney, shares of India today to the Future Group, leading 18 news channels to Reliance entertainment and the latest development of Subhash Chandra's divestment stand out as exemplary.

Self-admittedly, ZEEL draws revenue from 6 streams, namely Advertising, Subscription, Syndication, Theatrical, Music Licensing, and Other miscellaneous activities. Advertising is an important revenue stream for the domestic broadcast, international and digital businesses. Advertising revenue is primarily driven by reach and viewership of Zee content. Consumer staples, consumer durables, telecom, auto and e-commerce function as the key advertisers. Subscription revenue is generated by domestic broadcast, international and digital businesses. Content reaches through the company's distribution partners such as DTH and cable companies in case of domestic and international broadcast business. In digital, subscription revenue comes directly from consumers or through partnerships with telecom operators and other players in the digital eco-system. Syndication primarily relates to licensing of content (shows, movies etc.) in the international markets or to other broadcasters in India. Theatricals yield revenue from the theatrical release of movies produced by Zee. Music Licensing offers revenue from the licensing of the company's music catalogue to music streaming platforms and from any other events/platforms where its music titles are utilized. Other miscellaneous activities include Movie Distribution where revenues are earned through distribution of movies, and Ticketing and Sponsorships with revenues from on-ground events, live shows and theatre.

The company's summation of the Zee experience officially read, 'In its journey of crafting extraordinary entertainment experiences for audiences across the globe, Zee has been the front runner in successfully implementing several pioneering initiatives that have contributed not only to the growth of the company, but the industry at large. Emerging businesses like digital, movies and music, and live events, provide Zee new touchpoints for reaching consumers as well as greater access to audiences. This has added new dimensions to content consumption and experimentation with new genres of content and create formats which are suited for smaller audience segments. Zee has significantly ramped up content investments to capitalize on this new opportunity. The distribution landscape is also changing with audiences using multiple devices and platforms for consuming content. To enhance the reach and engagement of its products, Zee is stitching partnerships with new age content distributors, device manufacturers and other digital players. The company is also modifying its processes and developing new capabilities to sustain growth and take advantage of emerging opportunities. Investments are being made in data and analytics capabilities to use consumer insights for content creation and product design, and the workforce is being equipped for success in this new environment.'[237]

ZEEL believes in creating value for itself and its shareholders. It works 'for audiences', by providing engaging, inspirational and uplifting content to audience's satisfaction; 'for advertisers', by offering brand building solutions to reach consumers through multiple touch-points; 'for distribution partners,' by understanding that content is an integral part of offering for its distribution partners that include cable, DTH and telecom operators; 'for talent', by being instrumental in continuously bringing new talent to the industry; 'for shareholders,' through a track record of consistent financial performance and delivering significant shareholder value; and 'for people', by providing enriching experience at the work place, work life balance, adequate learning and growth opportunities.

Zee's official statement on its business model in correspondence with the author reads: 'Brand ZEE, which has been built over the last 27 years, enjoys an extremely deep consumer connect, strong 'top of mind' recall and is indeed considered a 'people's brand'. With rich and engaging content, Zee has touched over 1.3 billion people across the world. In line with its positioning and the company's rich value system, the brand has always strove to deliver extraordinary entertainment, keeping the preferences of its customers, i.e. the viewers, at the epicenter. ZEE's business model has evolved with time, it has a very nimble and agile business model. Even during tough market conditions, Zee has consistently outperformed its rivals and the industry.'[238]

It continues, 'Strong in-house capabilities, strategic content partnerships and business models designed to create an ecosystem that focuses on delivering extraordinary results, is what Zee has focused on. Zee is amongst the leading entertainment networks in India (Zee had a 18.3 per cent market share in Feb-Mar 2020). The company continues to make investments in businesses where it sees potential for growth.'

'With an aim to entrench itself deeper in the regional markets, Zee launched 4 regional channels in 2020, that made its content more accessible to audiences across the country. All 4 of these channels opened to stellar numbers and are already a strong number 1 or number 2 in their respective markets within a few months of launch. With the addition of the two new regional movie channels, Zee has the biggest movie channel portfolio in the country. On the digital front, within 2 years of its launch, ZEE5 is showing stellar growth and is well placed to become the most consumed digital entertainment platform in India. It continues to be the biggest producer of original content across Hindi and regional languages and is also inking key tech partnerships, which will enhance the content accessibility and discovery for the users at the click of a button. The platform also launched ZEE5 Kids providing access to over 4,000 hours of bespoke content for kids across nine languages. ZEE5's international expansion is seeing initial signs of success in the APAC and MENA regions, which have close affinity to Indian content.'

'Zee Studios—our movie production and distribution business, has a stellar line up of movies slated for release in 2021, our music label Zee Music Company is the No. 2 music label in the country, with a subscriber base of 52 million on YouTube. Our Live events business Zee Live continues to grow as well as it focuses on creating IPs to deliver entertainment experiences across music, arts, culture, education, kids and much more.'

'Going forward, Zee will continue on this path to affirm the strong fundamentals and intrinsic values that the company offers to its stakeholders.'[239]

Punit Goenka, commenting on the company's business model said, 'I think the business model of Zee is what you can see in the seven values that we have and that would be the crux of our business. Our first value is that we put the customer first because if we don't have a customer, we don't have a business. We look at solving big problems and not little problems. Little problems will get solved on their own. I think we focus on big-hairy audacious goals.'

'These are the kind of things that drive us significantly. Five years ago, when I sat down with my team and said that we need to take our goals from being a 12 per cent market share company to a 20 per cent market share company in the all-India viewership, the entire team felt, 'This is a task that cannot be achieved'. It's an impossible task to increase a market share by 8 per cent, but today we are at 20 per cent market share. While I would've hoped it would've taken three years, but it took us five years to get it done; so be it. But today if somebody asks me what your next goal is, I would say I don't know.'

'So that is a goal, where people say it's not doable but then we have to deliver. Being frugal is one of our key value systems. We may get the maximum bang for the buck. So, if you look today, we do almost 15-20 per cent of our production in-house, no other broadcaster in the country does that, other than news channels. That's how we keep our costs in line. We track our ratios to revenue on every per cent. I do profitability statement by shows, not by channels. We focus on being very humble, deal with people with respect and humanity; that's one of our key value systems and that's something that I personally drive. Valuing people is very critical because our biggest capital is human capital. So, our business model is ingrained in our value system. Today we pride ourselves that we are at the top end of the profitability range across the world. No media company in the world delivers the kind of profit that Zee delivers. Of course, the absolute numbers are very small.'

'It's not about billions it's about the fact that we are at 30 per cent+ margin kind of a business. The only one that comes close to us is Discovery. Everyone else, including the best in class, operates at a 20-22 per cent margin. We boast about our ability to deliver profit to our shareholders.'[240]

Continuing on this Discovery string, Goenka pointed out the differences between the two media entities, and how it is a source of motivation for his own to do better. 'I think the only company that I can say that we have not been able to figure the business out, is Discovery. That is one entity where they have built the business on factual content and they deliver very significant profits on just that one genre of content. I think that is something that has not been a big success for Zee so far. The way we run Zee is so distinctly different from any other organization that it's very difficult for me to compare myself to any other media organization. The business models are similar, but the DNA of the company is very different from any media company in the world.'

Since Essel Group was a fish that arrived late in the sea of print, it was only expected that imitating the business model of a well-established print house would be the way to go. It did not seek to pursue the trail of brand capital and private treaties that groups like Times so aggressively pushed for. Goenka, on behalf of the promoter group had said, 'We don't do that because from our perspective, our inventory is limited, unnlike in print, where you can just print more ads as and when you get them. Our inventory is capped at 12 minutes per clock hour so, we do not have too much unsold inventory that can go into private treaty kind of partnerships and now given the stringent laws, company law etc. and the SEBI laws it's even more difficult for us to get into those kinds of deals. So, we stay away from private treaty deals, we are a pure transaction-based media house.'[241]

As for the distribution between television and digital, where the traditional media forms face stiff competition from the digital revolution, Zee seems to have found a balance. The company's official statement included: 'Zee has been taking strategic steps to transform from a pure content company to a global content and technology company that can compete in a rapidly evolving digital world. With 96 per cent of TV households in India being single TV homes, the ubiquitous mobile becomes a default second screen. While digital platforms give an opportunity for personal consumption, television continues to be the single largest medium for family entertainment, delivering content to entertain an entire family as a single unit.'[242]

Amit Goenka, in his earlier role as International Broadcast Business and ZEE5 Global as CEO, commented in the company's 2018–19 Annual Report on monetizing Zee5 and how he sees the split between advertising and subscription revenues, 'India is a unique market when it comes to OTT, especially with respect to advertising and subscription. At present, television and free content dominate viewership on OTT platforms and on ZEE5 as well, catch-up TV attracts a large proportion of eyeballs. We are monetizing this viewership through advertising, and this is driving acceleration in the company's overall ad revenue growth. In the price-sensitive Indian market, digital has to compete with a very economical television offering to build a subscriber base.'

'While the digital subscription is seeing good initial traction, for sustained growth it needs to establish a strong value proposition by offering a large catalogue of differentiated content. ZEE5 is focused on creating content that caters to needs not addressed by television. ZEE5's revenues will be dominated by advertising initially but as we populate our platform with more original and premium content, we expect the subscriber base to scale up faster. In the longer term, digital subscription could be as big an opportunity as advertising in India.'[243]

The management of ZEEL under Punit Goenka and Amit Goenka has been well appreciated by all stakeholders and has reflected in the performance of the company. Speaking on where the business stands today, Jawahar Goel said, 'Punit and Amit have made the right sustainable investments for the future and the business is growing ahead on all fronts, in a focused and disciplined way.'[244]

Subhash Chandra has a simpler outlook towards the company's business model. He says, 'The Zee business model is to create the right content for its audience, and to serve them content via different kinds of distribution mechanisms, whichever way the viewer wants—mobile, computer, television. They should watch it any way they like.'

'Loss and profit is not dependent on programming, etc. Programming remains the same. In the beginning, viewership numbers are always unstable. Viewership and revenue builds gradually. We incurred losses only in our first year, but recovered everything in the second year itself. Since then Zee has only been in profit.'[245]

Part of the business model is also the sustained manner of Subhash Chandra's never-say-die attitude. In his autobiography, he writes, 'I prefer to enter segments that others ignore, especially if these seem impossible to break into. My entry into rice exports, broadcasting, packaging, amusement parks are all examples of this. I don't mind falling if I know that I tried my best. The Indian Cricket League and Agrani were my pet projects. I invested money, time, effort, resources into them. They did not work out, but I have no regrets.'

The ideals he writes about in his book, published in 2016, serve almost as justifications given in advance for the challenges he faced in 2018. The open letter reiterates what the media mogul has always maintained. He writes: 'One reason I have been able to succeed is that I have had truth by my side. But I have always said what I felt, even if it angered people. Each organization has a culture, ethos, belief. The management style may change but the ethos does not.'

Chandra is brimming with visions that seek to clear the uncertainity around the future of the group. His prospects for the future seem largely social. In his autobiography, he writes: 'One aspect of my yearning has changed though: I have decided that whatever business I do (even existing ones) will be with a social objective. An example is my ambition to develop Smart Cities. I also want to create Smart Villages that prevent needless migration and allow rural India to modernize in a sustainable manner. Life is always full of crises, hope, challenges, and enjoyment. How you look at it depends on your attitude.'[246]

9

WHICH FOOT FORWARD FOR ZEE?

'The determination to do more, to learn more, has stayed with me. Somehow, my successes have not stopped me from seeking new challenges... I remain a hungry person who 'does not want to die', who wishes to be remembered after my current journey ends someday.'

—Subhash Chandra, *The Z Factor*

With that sentence, Subhash Chandra concludes the chronicle of his life in 'The Z Factor'. It is a perfect summation of the roller coaster ride the media baron's life has been. Zee has had quite a journey since 1992, a journey worthy of finding a place in the collective memory of this country and the world, for it has, in some way or another, managed to touch many lives through screens of many shapes and sizes. The story of Zee, and of Chandra who put the founding stone in place, is a story of many wins and some losses through which it ultimately emerges a winner.

Chandra was just a young man when, freshly successful in the Essel Group business, he was overcome by a rush to venture into the media space. Though the innovation and motivation were his own, the impetus he found to start a media company was situated partly in the environment during those years, which ranged from India's newly revolutionized economic policy in 1991, to the Gulf War and the prominence it gave to relay of information across platforms. Early on in the race, Chandra realized the importance of communication. In fact, he was among the only players in the race, at a truly national level. There was Doordarshan with a monopoly over information dissemination, in the absence of other platforms allowed to privately broadcast in a varietal manner. Other competitors during the time, like STAR, were international entities, far more developed than any other media conglomerate in India. Undaunted in the face of such powerful adversaries, Chandra extended a hand of a 50:50 partnership to them, for leasing a transponder.

He was quick to encash the role of communication technology in business competitiveness, despite the roadblocks that lay on the road to launching a private satellite broadcasting channel. One of the topmost in that list was the fact that those around Chandra were not ready to take him seriously. They ridiculed him for even trying to challenge the norms of communication in the country, and for bringing up ideas that up until then had been deemed impossible. But Chandra reflected a never-say-die attitude, which even now looms over the company's values despite the troubles it is swamped in. Just as 1991 was coming to a close, he made a trip to Hong Kong to get in touch with industry bigwigs like the Li family. Even Li's opportunistic approach of making the most out of a deal with Chandra by quoting him a skyrocketing price for the transponder, could not deter the man who was known for his grit and commitment. Li's quotation exceeded Chandra's by several rungs, and even though Chandra lacked the necessary revenue, he agreed. It seemed like it had become a matter of persistent pride now that he had made up his mind to put a foot into broadcasting.

After rounds of persuasion and meetings, which in some cases even involved humiliation for Chandra, his efforts finally came home to roost in 1992, when the country beheld the launch of the first private satellite channel, Zee TV. Even at the outset, the messaging was strong—urging customers who may have been wary of the channel's intent to believe in them, and embark upon this journey with Zee. Out of this undying spirit, the company Zee Telefilms Ltd was initiated as a public offering. Zee had an enticing library of content that attracted viewers to the channel. As the love grew, so did opportunities for investment and media expansion. Even at first glance, the story of Zee seems like an extraordinary one. The visionary idea of bringing entertainment and content to people's homes was such a strong premise that it gathered immense pace even during the first year of its operation. Chandra was the first in the country to try and step into the carefully mandated broadcast bubble, thereby breaking the boundaries and making way for others whose minds were clouded with dreams and aspirations of making it big. More than a company, Zee branded itself as a people's organization, with an intent of entertaining, but also of bringing everyone up with itself, carving a road beaming with lights, upon which anyone, across different class, creed, or identity, could tread. Zee's emotional mantra was to be for the people, while its business aspirations defined a new paradigm of media, completely unseen before.

Acquisitions and subsidiaries galore, Zee was developing at breakneck speed. During one of its rounds of newfound success, Chandra picked up on a new trail of launching a news bulletin. As expected, in the exclusive presence of Doordarshan, this met with resistance from authorities. Now that Chandra was an expert in the business, he found a way around this sticky situation by masterfully uplinking programming from international locations and broadcasting it through his mediums. Thus, Zee News also came into being. During its first years, Zee broke many records with pioneering achievements, such as being the first Indian media firm to be listed on Bombay Stock Exchange.

Zee TV was a medium that gave flight to the Indian audience's imagination as the content was heavily Indianised and adjusted to their likes and dislikes.

Now that Zee was becoming well versed in the tactics of business that involved product development, diversification and alliances, it aimed to become a profitable entity backed by strong finances. Perhaps the most strategic business partnership it undertook during its nascent phase was its tie-up with Rupert Murdoch's News Corp, which had, in 1994, purchased Star TV from the Li family. Along with Zee, the company commenced Siti Cable operations, while also promoting PATCO for programme supplies. With the launch of cable service provider, Zee broke another barrier in the entertainment business. Riding high on the waves of motivated operations, Zee gathered wind under its wings and flew off to make footprints internationally. In 1995, Zee TV launched in the UK to majorly cater to the Indian diaspora audience residing there. It subsequently even made an early mark in Africa. It expanded its business operations by launching DTH services for its audience in the USA and beaming services in Germany.

By now, Zee had established itself as a buffer to the Bollywood film industry, serving as the one-stop destination for popular culture. This was catapulted further into the audience imagination with the launch of Zee Cinema, a channel reserved solely for the broadcast of popular Hindi films. The company was going full throttle to fulfill Chandra's earliest promise of bringing entertainment to the living rooms of people and making it readily available. This contributed in large part to the identity that Zee was beginning to carve out for itself in the mass market.

Specializations also began to grace the company screens, with diversified content like animated movies, award functions, and music offerings. The content tray of Zee had also expanded magnificently by now, with daily soaps and shows of all genres featuring on it. Legendary shows like Sa Re Ga Ma Pa and Jeena Isi ka Naam Hai began gaining nationwide prominence, and had such an impact that even now they evoke feelings of nostalgia whenever mentioned.

Around this time began Zee's advent into the regional sector, indicating that in its earliest form, one of Zee's primary intents were to cater to the farthest corners of the country, away from mainstream Hindi. It began broadcasting in regional languages under the brand Alpha. The first to launch were Zee Marathi, Zee Bangla and Zee Punjabi, with a plethora of shows that regional audiences could identify with. It sought to capture the essence of regional identities that were under-represented till then in media. By 1999, the company's education arm was demerged into an entity known as Zee Interactive Learning Systems for ease of specialized foray and focus on education expansion activities. It set up institutions across the country, like Kidzee, which went on to become extremely popular among parents of young children. Though education came to be a part later of Zee's CSR activities, its early entry into the education sphere indicates that, it sought to ultimately better the state of literacy and education in the country. With its diversification into this field, Zee portrayed an image of propagating all that was essential in the threads of society, and for creating India's place on the global chart.

In 1999, another decision came from the authorities that the Ministry of Information and Broadcasting had allowed private operators to run their own earth stations. Sure enough, living up to its image of being a pioneer, Zee was the first to seize this opportunity, by initiating VSNL facilities. None of Zee's achievements were going unnoticed, and in 1999, the company was recognized through many awards. Subhash Chandra's efforts as a businessman also paid off as slowly, awards at entrepreneurship and business events began to crowd his shelves.

In a display of high business acumen, the company began associations with awe-inducing names from the media industry, including giants like MGM and Viacom. Simultaneously, the pay offerings of channels on the Zee network were being updated constantly to accommodate consumer preferences. Channels were emerging more and more differentiated per their content, from Hindi General Entertainment Channels to English film channels. In doing this, Zee was fuelling the aspirations of the Indian audience further, by making them believe that the West was not a far-fetched dream. It was a highly tangible concept in which even a developing country like India could immerse itself. The international culture was not that far, and the audience here could educate themselves about it from the comfort of their homes. Even though Zee popularly stood for linking present times to the traditional past, it also served as the cross-cultural link for a variety of different societies. Previously too, and even in the future, as a mix of channels emerged to cater to many combinations of cultural societies abroad—ranging from the diaspora languages of Urdu and Gujarati to language majority of that country—Zee showed to the world that it was an institution that stood to understand the nuances of sociological impact, even if at a level of profit-making motives.

Zee's Bollywood identity came to be sharply carved out in 2001, when it stepped into first-hand production of Hindi films. Its first production was Gadar, one of the most definitive movies in Bollywood history; as regards box office collections at least. Hitting a sixer on the first go denoted that Zee was cut out for this field of operations. It pursued this line of business successfully, and Zee Studios has gone on to produce extremely profitable films like Sairat, Kesari, and Article 15, venturing into both regional as well as mainstream Hindi cinema.

Zee, in all its upcoming developments in the new decade, was openly placing emphasis on working under strong principles, with a focus on primacy of business interests, brand loyalty, customer focus and product development, all enmeshed in innovation. At the same time, covering its technological quarters too, Zee was making large strides by setting up fiber-optic and coaxial networks and boosting its e-commerce activities across the country on a large-scale basis. The news segment, Zee News, had also introduced virtual sets in its work set-up. With zeenext.com, the company could also boast of making an early entry into the digital world, though it was not a pathbreaking event, since several traditional media forms like newspapers had already made a mark online with their respective websites.

One of the most important early business developments post the new millennium however came with the Zee-Turner alliance, that immediately expanded the Zee offering in the market with a whopping 16-channel bouquet across the subcontinent. It included names like Cartoon Network, CNN, and CNBC, which sought to increase Zee's clout in the market. Around this time, the Zee tagline was modified once more, as 'Sabse Pehle', once again connotative of the primary position the customer held in the eyes of the company. Everyone was a customer, from a person in the Middle East to another person in Pakistan where Zee had begun to beam.

With the new Zee-Rajshri Productions distribution tie-up, Zee began backing large family drama movies that have now amassed legacy status in the national conscience. Films like Hum Saath Saath Hai and Maine Pyaar Kiya almost became synonymous with the Zee brand, since it was as if the public had gotten used to seeing these films with the Zee logo on the corner of the screen. Zee News was trying to invent and reinvent itself in many ways too, through new taglines, logos, and tie-ups with other media establishments for new show formats; efforts that culminated in the channel winning accolades. In 2003, Zee got listed as an independent company. That year, Zee released five new channels for the DTH market, with a broad genre offering, from lifestyle to comedy. In what may have been a risky move, Essel Group even ventured into the overcrowded print segment of the media industry with the DNA brand of newspapers. But this business decision yielded considerable success, especially since Essel pursued it in collaboration with Dainik Bhaskar Corporation, the print giant behind the Dainik Bhaskar brand of newspapers. This decision to try a hand at print seemed to come from Essel's retaliation and disagreement with the fact that the English newspaper market was dominated by the monopoly of biggies like Times of India. In a bid to offer variety to the customer to choose from, the idea for DNA was thrust forward. However, the management at Essel remained crystal about the choice of not pushing too aggressively in print, and beaming maximum attention on its electronic media core.

As Zee had by now gained veteran status, notably, there was substantial increase in subscription revenues, programming initiatives, investment in technology and service upgrades. A number of mergers and acquisitions played tunes of success for the company, that backed them by multiple technology-based decisions. As branding and marketing techniques also began gaining foreground, Zee's position as a financially efficiency profit-making institution gained prominence. During this time, India's economy and the media space was thriving, in a sense, and the broadcasting and communication sphere, which were once only open to exclusive sectors, were now free markets choked with competition. With emerging platforms like digital cable, DTH and IPTV taking over the market, subscribers and consumers were at an advantage of increased choices stemming from their purchasing capabilities and service availability. Zee was displaying strong growth backed by ad spending and sustainable shareholder value reliant on unmatched programming assets.

All these business developments consolidated in 2006, one of the most significant years on the company's timeline of events. The monumental block known with popularity as Zee Telefilms Ltd got demerged into four separate entities—ZEEL, Zee News Ltd

(ZNL), Wire and Wireless India (WWIL), and ASC Enterprises Ltd This decision was significant in the face of a company whose borders were constantly expanding without measure. The demerger, it seemed, was a necessary step in the formation of a direction for all businesses to be developed, integration of tax efficiencies, uniting operational activities under an appropriate corporate structure, unlocking shareholder value, and optimizing under-used cable assets. The independent identification of strategic and financial partners for each company henceforth would have been an easier task for the separate factions. Out of the four, ZEEL and ZNL gained the most visibility in mainstream markets, with the other two companies developing services that sought to complement its publicly present siblings.

ZNL began with a bouquet of 10 channels, led by the flagship Zee News channels and its other Hindi and regional brethren. Zee created another innovation in the field of news with a stylized and deep-focused offering of the news platter, spanning genres and languages both. This was helpful since the beginning in guiding ZNL's news coverage activities, limiting each channel's operations to specific regions, and therefore, allowing them to supply good quality and extensive journalism whose reaches expanded beyond the news that was already being covered by other media houses. But it is worth noting, and was perhaps peculiar in some sense, that ZNL did not have a news-only offering in the beginning. Though the demerged company cropped up with an intent of a sole focus on news, the ZNL offering included some General Entertainment Channels and movie channels that would have found a better place perhaps at ZEEL, which specialized in entertainment.

The concept of Integrated Media News was worked upon in news studios; a cross-channel innovation that improved the efficiency of work and invited more ideas than one, from different studios across the board. Through its KU band network and other such technologies that made for seamless transmission across platforms, ZNL made use of complex digitized outfits.

After 2006, ZNL developed regional news channels like Zee 24 Taas and 24 Ghanta over the years, which placed a special emphasis on national and international outlook, besides disseminating local news. The company admittedly relied on the highest ethical standards when it came to editorial freedom and guidelines, as it should. With newly developed taglines like 'Zara Sochiye', ZNL put forward a mantra that is very central to news—that of analysis and individual thought. This tagline was of good brand value, since it subsumed within it, the entire foundation of the field of journalism. It compelled people to wake up out of their comfort zones and think about what surrounded them or how society was structured. As it appeared, metaphorically and literally, ZNL only stood as the bridge between social events and the public audience, acting as a channel of communication. This is the ideal that journalism must always seek, instead of seeking a path where narratives are created. It should only be a good conductor of information. With this tagline, it could be inferenced, that ZNL understood the idea and tried its level-best to bring this concept to fruition.

With this supposed outlook, ZNL spread to South Indian markets as well as North Indian markets, emerging with the vision of a 'News Powerhouse'. By 2011, the company became a pure news broadcaster, after the demerger of entertainment channels between ZEEL and itself. Going forward, the management planned equal focus on commitment to content-focused approach, better monetization of subscription revenues, and cost optimization. Alongside, it emphasized its energies on building scale across the media value chain and exploring cross-media synergies. Regional news channels began additionally relying on outdoor events and marketing, by organizing live shows, which would allow audiences to directly engage with and get to know their news organization. The brand philosophy changed sometime to 'Soch Badlo, Desh Badlo', which essentially borrowed from its previous philosophy. Working on the ideology of being 'pro people', the news network fared many seas, from campaigns to awards.

However, it was not without its shortcomings. The identity and personality of news anchors began gaining prominence in the eyes of the audience, and even in the management structure. The news reader was no longer just a person relaying information to the public, but served as a symbolic representative of the news channel, personifying the news company's values. So, when prominent anchors of the network got embroiled in a controversy over the coal scam, it was detrimental to the image of the brand as a whole, not just the persons involved.

In 2013, Zee News received a brand makeover with a new identity called Zee Media Corporation Limited (ZMCL), to reach deeper into the lives of viewers, by directing its beam in a more focused manner. The company developed on a mobile app, a radio channel, an extensive and well-connected network of journalists, and a presence in large states like Rajasthan and Uttar Pradesh. A large portion of the company's approach also rested on a future based on investments. As business developed, ZMCL forayed into the English news broadcast sphere with a global news channel WION.

Shows on Zee's news channel network, since the beginning have taken it upon themselves to broadcast knowledge that wasn't common, and this it did in keeping with the company's goal of providing a sensible assortment of news, entertainment and 'infotainment'. The concept of infotainment being relayed through newsrooms may appear to be an absurd one to some, but it may well have served to capture the imagination of the Indian audience. This is a country where drama and extravagance are valued, and thoroughly enjoyed. This is more so in cases that have the scope of turning technical or jargonized, like the news. Whether infotainment as a genre is suitable for hard reporting and news or not, may be a subjective issue, since it is in essence only a way of making things more interesting, but in hindsight, this may not have served Zee News well in the long run. Today, on one side, the Zee bouquet of news channels have a large and loyal following, while on the other side, many fellow journalists in the media industry believe that Zee News today relies heavily on a sensational style of reporting, with several fake news instances pointed out by fact-checking websites.

Meanwhile, the other larger branchout called ZEEL has created a legacy of its own over the years since 2006. In 2007, it was listed as an independent company, and officially began its operations with 17 channels. It operated with five notable business verticals—domestic television, international broadcast, studios and music, digital, live and theatre. This company identified itself as an 'entertainment powerhouse' that extended its reach with impressive growth in each vertical. Sports became a fresh avenue for the company to dig through for potential. Clashing along the way with the Cricket Board, Chandra managed to stand his own and emerge victorious with the first 20-20 league cricket event in 2007.

Furthermore, expansion was pursued in previously untapped markets like Malaysia and Russia under the now iconic Zee brand. Shows from the Indian soil, beamed in foreign countries, with foreign subtitles to reach wider audiences, denoted not just an increase in Zee's brand value, but, as happens with any domestically produced content that goes global, Zee was helping India create a niche in international markets. Years ago, when it had initially begun beaming English shows from abroad, global cultures were brought to the doorsteps of Indian households. Now that the company's business operations were stable and in full order, it could manage to reverse the operations fully and make it a two-way street. Indian content was now liberally reaching foreign doorsteps, as an indication of the country's content-creating abilities, that were at par with those produced in foreign lands.

ZEEL's music offering also became very stylized, beating to the rhythms of the young and the old, with separate approaches. Since outdoor events were fast gaining traction as a fabulous way of offline marketing, ZEEL was the one to launch India's first talent hunt game show, which cemented a place for the company in the minds of the youth especially. And that was quite in sync with the company's renewed outlook. With every passing day, Zee was aiming towards a fresh outlook, signified through its often-upgraded logos and taglines, which gave a fresh spin to the Zee vision. Riding on the back of the longstanding company values of customer focus, excellence, creativity, integrity, and growth-driven development, ZEEL surged on with high fuel power. By 2010, Zee was reaching 500 million people across 167 countries and 5 continents, with a presence in the Middle East, Pakistan, Africa, USA and UK. It was a commendable feat for Zee, since it had all major regions covered; something that none of its domestic counterparts had been able to do in such a short time, that too in the wee years of digital development when the online space was not as handy as it is today. With every subsequent achievement, it could be seen that Zee was reaffirming its position as the media industry's alpha, towering higher over its counterparts. Every milestone it hit was a reminder to the other players in the entertainment space that Zee was the first born, and no conglomerate could take its place. After all, something that was synonymous with satellite television in India deserved to take that respectable position of power.

Partnerships were the fore drivers of development for ZEEL's new undertakings. Ones with Taj TV, Mail.com Media Corporation, and ETC were the most prominent and among the most profitable for the company. In a first in 2011, ZEEL launched a new flashy blue logo with the tag 'Ummeed se saje Zindagi', which was decided after extensive market research and feedback from customers. The new tagline signified something aspirational in the minds of the Indian consumer, as previously mentioned, and this idea was juiced even further this year with these branding activities. The blue logo denoted a door of capabilities and hope for the audience, which could remodel itself with new visions and new sensitivities. During the year, the company and its founders/leaders collected several awards, increasing the valuation of the Zee brand even further than it already was. Phases 1 and 2 cities were being digitized according to plan during these years, which stood to positively impact Zee's, and the entire entertainment industry's, penetration into the mainstream and remotest corners of India.

Intending to scale unexplored boundaries in content distribution, the company launched an OTT TV platform known as Ditto TV. Ditto TV became India's first OTT service available worldwide with a whopping count of over 170 countries, to offer content across leading genres. This became another genre that Zee became a pioneer in. Now that OTT platforms like Netflix and Amazon are all the rage, it becomes important in retrospect to give Zee its due for being the first in the business and envisioning a future that would become the norm in the coming years.

All this while, under its CSR plans, the company worked to add benefit in the fields of education, women empowerment and peace, by tying up with various NGOs and authorities across the country.

In 2013, the company's renowned brand philosophy and tagline of 'VasudhaivaKutumbakam' came into existence, and became a branding exercise that is celebrated like an event in the company's timeline. For all its international, domestic and regional penetrations of trying to bring the world closer, this brand tag was a fitting definition of the company's longstanding exercises, infused with a touch of the traditional, in line with Zee's original offering intent. Even within the company, this ideology was pursued with much fervor through a human resource process called 'Samvad', which invited dialogue and communication between the employees and management.

ZEEL began organizing, under its intellectual property rights banner, events like Mindspace and Arth that connected audiences from far and wide through intellectual and cultural streams of connect. Both of these, and more, have gained wide media coverage, and respect for engaging audiences and keeping the trend of debate and discussion alive. But the most notable in this genre has been the Zee Jaipur Literature Fest, which is considered to be the largest celebration of literature in the world. Annually, the Lit Fest is associated with the biggest names from across the world, from fields of journalism, media, entertainment, literature, business, etc., and is open to all walks of audiences. It has been a coveted event in the industry, grabbing eyeballs globally. It has been a success every year, and stands out as one of the largest feathers in Zee's cap. Looking at the milestones it had covered, Zee was now referring to itself as a Global Content Company, both a marker of success as well as aspiration.

In 2015, ZEEL launched the Zindagi channel, which fast gained popularity across the Indian population. The channel, which broadcast mainly Pakistani soaps, was well received in the country, despite the two countries' strained political and diplomatic relations spanning decades. But during those years, except for a few factions in the population, there was not much reason for the channel to be condemned on a national level. Come 2016, post tensions at the border after the Uri terrorist attack in India, all operations of Zindagi related to Pakistani content were stopped. All the soaps from the other side of the border were dropped from the line-up, stated by Chandra as a move to show solidarity and nationalistic sentiments with our country during this period of grief. While this, at the time, came as a welcome solution as regards economic exchanges, Pakistani soaps despite tensions between the two countries have weathered the storm, and are still popular among Indian masses due to their availability on a variety of OTT platforms.

When ZEEL became a full-blown M&E conglomerate, it soldiered forward with renewed values to evolve, build, lead and sustain. It had introduced high-definition channels with superior technology for some of its offerings, for a better viewing experience. The offerings by &TV were especially very wide, and included an array of channels even at the outset. Another feat was achieved with the launch of Zee5, an online video-on-demand website from Zee. It included exclusive content ranging from original shows, Indian and International movies, music, and health, offering new dimensions of content consumption for its audience. Much of the world was online by now, and this was now an open playing field for Zee to run enthusiastically. It was identified as the most comprehensive entertainment platform for language content in India, aside from being a massive technological leap for the company.

Beneath all the trails of success, trouble was broiling for ZEEL. The first vibrations of tremor occurred in 2018, when Zee's stocks began falling at an alarming rate. Chandra was open to divesting the powers of his company down to half and was already looking for investors and shareholders who would be interested in buying around 50 per cent of the company's shares. This was a huge chunk of the Zee property that would be lost to an investor. Talks of big names like Facebook and Apple coming on board was doing the rounds in professional circles, with no confirmed news from the media baron himself. Conglomerates like Apple are known to steer towards opportunities which have a high digital scope in them, since OTT platforms today have hogged the limelight. With the widespread use of 4G services and cheap data plans, along with the possible advent of a 5G network in the near future, more and more people are gravitating towards digital platforms for consumption of entertainment. What's more, all the television content is available online in some form or the other, making the use of broadcast, cable, and DTH services largely redundant.

The situation in 2020 is completely unprecedented. The outbreak of the novel coronavirus pandemic has put a stopper in the normalcy of businesses across the spectrum. Four rounds of a nationwide lockdown have left the economic situation battered, and the future, uncertain beyond measure. As businesses make adjustments to this new way of life, the media scape is supposed to be one of the industries that will face far-reaching consequences in their manner of functioning. Zee commented on the unpredictability of the situation and running a company amidst such severe conditions: 'The entire industry is going through unprecedented times, where no one can predict the future. At best, one can be ready with multiple plans and options with a readiness to quickly adjust to the situation. As a responsible M&E network, the health and safety of the employees and everyone working in ZEE's close ecosystem, has been paramount and all measures were taken to ensure business continuity at all levels. But at the same time, one cannot ignore the cascading impact that the pandemic will have on the entire M&E ecosystem. As a company, Zee is known for its resilience and innovation, and it will come out of this stronger. Once the situation improves, the industry and overall economy will bounce back, and the growth momentum will return. During this time, Zee is discovering newer ways of efficiency, building competencies and managing work which is stimulating for growth going forward.'[247]

'Zee embraced optimally utilizing technology solutions amidst lockdown, in order to create and offer fresh content for its consumers. The company leveraged technology and implemented various solutions across its key functions, swiftly and collaboratively, creating the bedrock for creative innovation in content offering. The teams enabled innovations through remote production of content over mobile and professional cameras by using video and audio production technologies to support broadcast, digital and social platforms. Zee launched fresh content across its TV channels shot on mobiles and edited using remote solutions. On the digital front, ZEE5 launched 11 new original shows/movies, some of which were shot entirely in the safety of the actors' homes. The live events business—Zee Live, transformed its on-ground flagship IP—Supermoon, to Supermoon Live to Home, offering a fresh dose of engaging content for its audience through digital platforms. The Company's facility in Jaipur (Essel Vision) emerged as a strong hub for post—production and edit support. Using state of the art technology support, the edit and post production of the films was completed by the editors within the safety of their homes. The Company's broadcast operating and engineering team developed remote clients through which systems could be operated remotely from home, which is a first of its kind in the industry.'[248]

Despite the uncertainty of it all today, the company's management is being handled under professionals who are working to reap the benefits of business partnerships in this day and age. The revenues cannot be made up through renovating the business model alone. So, while business is smooth, the management also seems outwardly unfazed in the face of any impending disaster.

The company is confident. It has a clear vision in sight with respect to future projections and finding a balanced co-existence between the television and digital industries together. It officially stated, 'The Media & Entertainment industry at large is certainly at an interesting juncture, with rapidly changing content consumption patterns at one end and disruptions in technology on the other. It is extremely imperative to delve deeper into the consumers' cultural nuances and deliver entertainment solutions respecting her beliefs and value system. The opportunities are immense, and they need to be seized at the right time to catapult the industry to greater heights. It is an era of co-opetition and not competition, wherein extraordinary is possible if the required synergies are drawn, keeping the consumers at the epicenter.'

'Zee believes that TV and digital will co-exist and cater to specific consumer cohorts and consumption needs through varied content offerings. It will be an AND world and not an OR world. Television growth is not going anywhere, it is still going to remain intact in terms of consumption and penetration, despite the proliferation of digital platforms.'

'In the future, digital consumption will continue to rise with faster internet and affordable devices. This increase in consumption along with a growing digital population will drive even higher investments in content and technology. Going forward, transparency and technology will be two key important aspects that will boost the M&E ecosystem. The convergence of art and technology is key to a successful approach in this highly competitive environment. The industry is blessed with rich and immense creative potential which needs to be further unleashed and capitalized in order to drive innovation and most above, generate employment.'[249]

In an interview with the author, Chandra said, 'Nothing is constant. Change is the constant. I can't say anything about the future. Lots of things are happening across the media world. Nothing can stay constant. Business will either go forth or back. It has to keep evolving.'[250] With this outlook, Zee embarks upon the 4.0 strategic future with a proud head and hopeful feet.

ACKNOWLEDGEMENTS AND SPECIAL CREDITS

At the outset, I thank Almighty God for blessing me with strength, dedication and patience to complete this work. I am extremely grateful to my husband Dr Sunil Kumar Dahiya, my parents, Sh Rajinder Bhalla and Mrs Parveen Bhalla, and my brother and sister-in-law, Sh. Aman Bhalla and Mrs Navanita, for encouraging me at every stage to complete this work and for making those heavier moments lighter. I can never forget to thank my daughter Era and my son Hritvik Neil who sacrificed their comforts to help me achieve my academic and professional goals.

It is my profound privilege to express my deep sense of gratitude to media barons, Dr Subhash Chandra and Sh Puneet Goenka for sparing time and letting me interview them for deeper insights about the evolution, functioning and business dynamics of Zee Group. Without them, the chapters would not have taken shape. I am also thankful to Sh Vijay Kuvalekar, Sh Rohit Gandhi, Sh Sudhir Chaudhary, Sh Brajesh Kumar, Ms Mimansa Malik, Sh Tarun Katial for their valuable insights and for taking time out for interviews.

I take this opportunity to thank Prof. (Dr) Alan B. Albarran, professor emeritus, The University of North Texas, USA for carefully going through the chapters and writing the foreword for this book. Words fail me in expressing my gratitude to all my mentors for suggesting to me this innovative subject to work on and for their priceless and sagacious guidance in steering me through many a difficult moment during the research and writing of this book, and for showing me the right direction. First and foremost, I would like to thank Prof. B. K. Kuthiala, chairperson, Haryana Education Board who helped me to find my way through the clutter of information that any research study throws up and to give it a focus and direction.

I would like to place on record all efforts of the Corporate Communication team of Zee to coordinate with me for the completion of this work. I would also like to thank the finance team for vetting the financial figures in the book. And last but not the least, I would like to thank the legal team for giving a go ahead for the publication of this book.

As this longitudinal case study was a tedious and time-taking work—from ideation to research about the evolution of Indian TV media, the company's growth, development, diversification, strategic intent, market expansion, technological advancements, mergers and acquisitions to writing the chapters, making timelines, cross checking text, proof reading and editing—I appreciate all the efforts of people who assisted me during different phases of making the book. The completion of this book could not have been accomplished without the support of my research and editorial assistants. I would like to sincerely thank my research assistant Ms Era Dahiya for searching data and putting it together with me, cross checking the timelines and helping me with drawing diagrams. I also thank Ms Shreyasi who accompanied me for the interview with Dr Subhash Chandra and for transcribing the interview. I would like to thank my editorial assistant, Ms Tanvi Akhauri for her help during the lockdown days in assisting me in making the book a better read.

I would also like to thank Sh Suresh Chaudhary, founder and director, Contegra Infosys LLP for graphic designing along with Sh Jyotindra Mohan Jha. I am also thankful to Sh Ramesh Tahiliani for discussing the brand identity of Zee with me and giving his valuable insights, Sh Shambhu for sparing a day for structuring the references, Ms Geeta for assisting me in completing the list of abbreviations, Ms Chetali for assisting me for few days, Sh Nikhil for cross checking the timelines and Sh Krishna for helping me cross check some financial figures.

Last but not the least, I am also thankful Ms Dipti Patel (aka Madhu Alpesh Kumar Patel) for helping me finalize the publisher. I am thankful to Sh. Dibakar Ghosh, Editorial Director for finding my work worth publishing and for giving all the motivation and support required at all stages. It will surely encourage me to write and explore more in the times to come.

ENDNOTES AND REFERENCES

1. Chandra, S. (25 September 2018). In a personal interview with Subhash Chandra (S. Dahiya, interviewer)
2. Chandra, S. (2016). *The Z Factor: My Journey as the Wrong Man at the Right Time*. Harper Collins. Pg: 238
3. 'Experience The Extraordinary, Zee Entertainment Enterprises Limited Annual Report (2017–18).' *ZEEL.*
4. Satish K. Singh, the then editor, Zee News, informed that broadcasting and content business principally consists of developing, producing and procuring television programming and film content and delivering via satellites, thereby earning revenues by way of advertisement and subscription revenues and syndication.
5. Goenka, P. (2 August 2018). In a personal interview with Punit Goenka at (S. Dahiya, interviewer)
6. Brand Zee. Retrieved 5 April 2020, from https://www.zeeentertainment.com/brand-zee/
7. 'From 'OkaraDukaan' to Zee… the complete story.' Retrieved 5 April 2020, from https://www.mxmindia.com/2012/10/from-okara-dukaan-to-zee-the-complete-story/
8. Chandra, S. (2016). *The Z Factor: My Journey as the Wrong Man at the Right Time*. Harper Collins.
9. Kohli-Khandekar, V. (5 February 2016). 'Subhash Chandra: The serial entrepreneur.' Retrieved 2 April 2020, from https://www.business-standard.com/article/companies/subhash-chandra-the-serial-entrepreneur-116020500923_1.html
10. Chandra, S. (2016). *The Z Factor: My Journey as the Wrong Man at the Right Time.* Harper Collins. Pg: 63
11. 'From "OkaraDukaan" to Zee… the complete story.' Retrieved 5 April 2020, from https://www.mxmindia.com/2012/10/from-okara-dukaanto-zee-the-complete-story/
12. Chandra, S. (2016). *The Z Factor: My Journey as the Wrong Man at the Right Time.* Harper Collins. Pg: 112
13. Chandra, S. (2016). *The Z Factor: My Journey as the Wrong Man at the Right Time.* Harper Collins. Pg: 116

14. Kapoor, C. (4 March 2016). *The Z Factory book review: Rising Against All Odds*. Retrieved 12 April 2020, from https://indianexpress.com/article/lifestyle/books/subhash-chandra-book-review-the-z-factory-book-review-rising-against-all-odds/
15. Compiled by the author with inputs from Zee Corp Comm team, in an email dated 7 September 2020
16. Adhikari A, Ajita Shashidhar, and Mahesh Nayak. (2014). 'Business Today, Passing the Baton.' Pg: 104. Retrieved from http://www.esselgroup.com/images/Business_Today_Passing_the_Baton.pdf. Accessed on 8 April 2020.
17. 'Tracing Essel Propack's Extraordinary Growth' Retreived from https://bloncampus.thehindubusinessline.com/columns/brand-basics/tracing-essel-propacks-extraordinary-growth/article29235140.ece
18. Kondratieva K, Tanya Thomas. 'Outside of Entertainment, Infrastructure biz is exciting: Subhash Chandra.' Retrieved 15 April 2020, from https://www.pressreader.com/india/the-hindu-business-line/20170513/281917363001320
19. Retrieved 2 April, 2020, from http://www.esselgroup.com/essel-group-celebrates-90-years.html, 1 June 2016, Press Release, Essel Group
20. '#youngat90: Essel Group celebrates 90 years of its existence, PM Modi says Essel's values are nation's values.' Retrieved 2 April, 2020, from https://www.dnaindia.com/india/report-essel-s-values-are-nation-svalues-pm-2438510
21. Goenka, P. (2 August 2018). In a personal interview with Punit Goenka. (S. Dahiya, interviewer)
22. Chandra, S. (2016). *The Z Factor: My Journey as the Wrong Man at the Right Time*. Harper Collins. Pg: 247
23. 'Profile: Media guru looks to the skies.' Available online at http://www.totaltele.com/view.aspx?ID=424018 (downloaded on 6 July 2016).
24. Singhal, A. and Rogers, E. M. (2001). *India's Communication Revolution*. Sage Publications.
25. Goenka, P. (2 August 2018). In a personal interview with Punit Goenka (S. Dahiya, interviewer)
26. Singh, G. *Such a Long Journey*. Business World. 2016. Pg: 38
27. 'From "OkaraDukaan" to Zee... the complete story.' Retrieved 5 April 2020, from https://www.mxmindia.com/2012/10/from-okara-dukaan-to-zee-the-complete-story/

28. Chandra, S. (25 September 2018). In a personal interview with Subhash Chandra (S. Dahiya, interviewer)
29. Kohli-Khandekar, V. (2019). *The Making of Star India: The Amazing Story of Rupert Murdoch's India Adventure*. Penguin Portfolio.
30. Chandra, S. (25 September 2018). In a personal interview with Subhash Chandra (S. Dahiya, interviewer)
31. Chandra, S. (2016). *The Z Factor: My Journey as the Wrong Man at the Right Time*. Harper Collins. Pg: 139–140
32. Chandra, S. (2016). *The Z Factor: My Journey as the Wrong Man at the Right Time*. Harper Collins. Pg: 256
33. Chandra, S. (2016). *The Z Factor: My Journey as the Wrong Man at the Right Time*. Harper Collins. Pg: 161
34. Goenka, P. (2 August 2018). In a personal interview with Punit Goenka (S. Dahiya, interviewer)
35. Chandra, S. (2016). *The Z Factor: My Journey as the Wrong Man at the Right Time*. Harper Collins. Pg: 239
36. 'Zee Chairman Subhash Chandra: "'I Always Want to Be Number One or a Strong Number Two".' Retrieved 3 July 2019, from http://knowledge.wharton.upenn.edu/article/zee-chairman-subhash-chandra-i-always-want-to-be-number-one-or-a-strong-number-two/
37. Chandra, S. (25 September 2018). In a personal interview with Subhash Chandra (S. Dahiya, interviewer)
38. Mehta, N. (2008). *India on Television*. Harper Collins.
39. Chandra, S. (2016). *The Z Factor: My Journey as the Wrong Man at the Right Time*. Harper Collins. Pg: 149–150
40. Chandra, S. (25 September 2018). In a personal interview with Subhash Chandra (S. Dahiya, interviewer)
41. Mehta, N. (2008). *India on Television*. Harper Collins.
42. Ninan, S. (2007). *Headlines From the Heartland: Reinventing the Hindi Public Sphere*. Sage Publications.
43. Chandra, S. (2016). *The Z Factor: My Journey as the Wrong Man at the Right Time*. Harper Collins. Pg: 194
44. Bamzai, K. (22 January 2016). 'Network czar—Subhash Chandra.' Retrieved 2 April 2020, from https://www.indiatoday.in/magazine/books/story/20160201-network-czar-zee-tv-promoter-subhash-chandra-esselworld-828325-2016-01-20
45. Chandra, S. (2016). *The Z Factor: My Journey as the Wrong Man at the Right Time*. Harper Collins. Pg: 231

46. *INTAM Report*. Retrieved from https://www.indiantelevision.com/keyword/intam
47. Chandra, S. (2016). *The Z Factor: My Journey as the Wrong Man at the Right Time*. Harper Collins. Pg: 209
48. Baddhan, R. (20 July 2002). Zee TV to telecast exclusive premiere of Gadar: BizAsia: Media, Entertainment, Showbiz, Brit, Events and Music. Retrieved from https://www.bizasialive.com/zee-tv-to-telecast-exclusive-premiere-of-gadar/
49. Profile: Media guru looks to the skies. Retrieved 6 August 2016, from http://www.totaltele.com/view.aspx?ID=424018
50. Cartoon Network block to replace Nickelodeon on Zee TV 1 September. (3 January 2019). Retrieved 4 April 2020, from https://www.indiantelevision.com/headlines/y2k2/aug/aug87.htm
51. Zee Punjab Haryana Himachal. (27 February 2020). Retrieved 1 April 2020, from https://www.zee.com/in-the-news/etc-board-reconstituted/
52. The Economic Times. Company History—Zee Entertainment Enterprises Ltd Available online at http://economictimes.indiatimes.com/*zee*-entertainment-enterprises-ltd/infocompanyhistory/companyid–11769.cms (downloaded on 6 July 2016).
53. Chandra, S. (2016). *The Z Factor: My Journey as the Wrong Man at the Right Time*. Harper Collins. Pg: 211
54. Singh, G. (2016). BusinessWorld. Such a Long Journey. Pg: 42
55. Goenka, P. (2 August 2018). In a personal interview with Punit Goenka (S. Dahiya, Interviewer)
56. Zee rejig: 2 companies to merge with AS C Enterprise. (4 January 2019). Retrieved 29 July 2019, from https://www.indiantelevision.com/headlines/y2k6/apr/apr350.htm
57. Retrieved from https://www.rediff.com/money/2006/dec/14zee.htm
58. Rao, B.V. In a personal interview with B.V. Rao in 2008, former Group Editor of Zee News Ltd (S. Dahiya, Interviewer)
59. Kuvalekar, V. (2 August 2018). In a personal interview with Vijay Kuvalekar, Former Editor in Chief, Zee 24 Taas (S. Dahiya, Interviewer)
60. Ibid.
61. Goenka, P. (2 August 2018). In a personal interview with Punit Goenka (S. Dahiya, Interviewer)
62. Kuvalekar, V. (2 August 2018). In a personal interview with Vijay Kuvalekar, Former Editor in Chief, Zee 24 Taas (S. Dahiya, Interviewer)

63. DNA, T. (7 September 2006). Subhash Chandra buys stake in UNI. Retrieved 17 August 2016, from https://www.dnaindia.com/business/report-subhash-chandra-buys-stake-in-uni–1051782
64. In a telephonic interview in 2008 with the author.
65. In a personal interview with the author in 2008.
66. Malik, M. (18 August 2018). In a personal interview with Mimansa Malik, Senior News Anchor, Zee News (S. Dahiya, Interviewer)
67. ZNL Annual Report 2008–09: Diversity, Growth, Sustenance. Pg: 3
68. Kumar, B. (18 August 2018). In a personal interview with Brajesh Kumar, Zee Business (S. Dahiya, Interviewer)
69. In a personal interview with Sudhir Chaudhary.
70. (2009–10). ZNL Annual Report 2009–10: Making News.Pg: 4
71. (2010–11). ZNL Annual Report 2010–11: Excellence is a Philosophy. Pg: 9
72. (2010–11). ZNL Annual Report 2010–11: Excellence is a Philosophy. Pg: 23
73. (2011–12). ZNL Annual Report 2011–12: Poised for the Next Leap. Pg: 5
74. (2012–13). ZNL Annual Report 2012–13: Reaching Out to the World. Pg: 11
75. Chaudhary, S. (17 August 2018). In a personal interview with Sudhir Chaudhary, CEO, ZMCL Cluster 1 (S. Dahiya, Interviewer)
76. Ibid.
77. Migrator. Zee-Jindal and SudhirChaudhary Tapes: The battle that never was. Retrieved 2 April 2020, from https://www.newslaundry.com/2018/07/19/zee-naveen-jindal-sudhir-chaudhary-tapes-subhash-chandra
78. Chandra, S. (2016). *The Z Factor: My Journey as the Wrong Man at the Right Time*. Harper Collins. Pg: 258
79. Chaudhary, S. (17 August 2018). In a personal interview with Sudhir Chaudhary, CEO, ZMCL Cluster 1 (S. Dahiya, Interviewer)
80. http://www.businessworld.in/article/Naveen-Jindal-and-JSPL-Withdraw-Extortion-Case-Against-Zee-Subhash-Chandra-Tweets-Truce-Message/13–07-2018–154808/
81. (2012–13). ZNL Annual Report 2012–13: Reaching Out to the World. Pg: 11
82. (2013–14). Zee Media Corporation Ltd Annual Report 2013–14: Expanding Horizons. Pg: 4–6
83. Gandhi, R. (15 August 2018). In a personal interview with Rohit

Gandhi, Ex-CEO of DNA and WION (S. Dahiya, Interviewer)

84. (2013–14). Zee Media Corporation Ltd Annual Report 2013–14: Expanding Horizons. Pg: 7
85. (2014–15). Zee Media Corporation Ltd Annual Report 2014–15: Every Story Matters. Pg: 5-23
86. (2014–15). Zee Media Corporation Ltd Annual Report 2014–15: Every Story Matters. Pg: 19–21
87. (2014–15). Zee Media Corporation Ltd Annual Report 2014–15: Every Story Matters. Pg: 90
88. (2015–16). Zee Media Corporation Ltd Annual Report 2015–16: India Positive. Pg: 7, 8, 17
89. (2015–16). Zee Media Corporation Ltd Annual Report 2015–16: India Positive.
90. https://zeenews.india.com/companies/zee-media-to-acquire-49-stake-in-reliance-broadcast-92-7-big-fm_1952634.html
91. https://www.exchange4media.com/media-radio-news/zmcls-radio-business-deal-with-rbnl-called-off-93179.html
92. (2015–16). Zee Media Corporation Ltd Annual Report 2015–16: India Positive.Pg: 6
93. Gandhi, R. (15 August 2018). In a personal interview with Rohit Gandhi, Ex-CEO of DNA and WION (S. Dahiya, Interviewer)
94. Goenka, P. (2 August 2018). In a personal interview with Punit Goenkas (S. Dahiya, Interviewer)
95. (2016–17). Zee Media Corporation Ltd Annual Report 2016–17: Investing in Future. Pg: 5
96. (2018–19). Zee Media Corporation Ltd Annual Report 2018–19: The Business of Truth, The Truth of Business. Pg: 5
97. (2018–19). Zee Media Corporation Ltd Annual Report 2018–19: The Business of Truth, The Truth of Business. Pg: 56
98. (2018–19). Zee Media Corporation Ltd Annual Report 2018–19: The Business of Truth, The Truth of Business. Pg: 58
99. Chandra, S. (25 September 2018). In a personal interview with Subhash Chandra (S. Dahiya, Interviewer)
100. Goenka, P. (2 August 2018). In a personal interview with Punit Goenka (S. Dahiya, Interviewer)
101. Kumar, B. (18 August 2018). In a personal interview with Brajesh Kumar, Zee Business (S. Dahiya, Interviewer)
102. (2018–19). Zee Media Corporation Ltd Annual Report 2018–19: The Business of Truth, The Truth of Business. Pg: 9

103. Zee Entertainment Enterprises Ltd. Retrieved 6 February 2020, from https://www.business-standard.com/company/zee-entertainmen-3126/information/company-history
104. (2018–19). Zee Entertainment Enterprises Limited Annual Report 2018–19: Evoking Emotions, Touching Lives. 2018–19. Pg: 16
105. Goenka, P. (2 August 2018). In a personal interview with Punit Goenka (S. Dahiya, Interviewer)
106. Chronology of Zee's 20-year journey. (16 April 2019). Retrieved 7 March 2020, from https://www.indiantelevision.com/headlines/y2k12/oct/oct25.php
107. Chandra, S. (2016). *The Z Factor: My Journey as the Wrong Man at the Right Time*. Harper Collins. Pg: 219
108. Zee Entertainment Enterprises Ltd Retrieved 6 February 2020, from https://www.business-standard.com/company/zee-entertainmen-3126/information/company-history
109. Zee Entertainment appoints Punit Goenka as CEO. Retrieved 18 October 2019, from https://economictimes.indiatimes.com/zee-entertainment-appoints-punit-goenka-as-ceo/articleshow/3211932.cms?from=mdr
110. Chandra, S. (2016). *The Z Factor: My Journey as the Wrong Man at the Right Time*. Harper Collins.Pg: 232
111. (2009–10). Zee Entertainment Enterprises Limited Annual Report 2009–10: Taking Entertainment Places. Pg: 3
112. (2009–10). Zee Entertainment Enterprises Limited Annual Report 2009–10: Taking Entertainment Places.Pg: 13
113. (2009–10). Zee Entertainment Enterprises Limited Annual Report 2009–10: Taking Entertainment Places.Pg: 16–17
114. Zee Entertainment Enterprises Ltd Retrieved 6 February 2020, from https://www.business-standard.com/company/zee-entertainmen-3126/information/company-history
115. Zee ETC Bollywood. Retrieved from https://logos.fandom.com/wiki/Zee_ETC_Bollywood
116. Zee Entertainment Enterprises Limited. Annual Report 2010–11, Inspired Leadership, Pg: 36-37
117. (2011–12). Zee Entertainment Enterprises Limited Annual Report 2011–12: Pioneering Vision. Pg: 24
118. (2011–12). Zee Entertainment Enterprises Limited Annual Report 2011–12: Pioneering Vision. Pg: 25
119. (2011–12). Zee Entertainment Enterprises Limited Annual Report

2011–12: Pioneering Vision. Pg: 4
120. The Asia Media Journal, Q3 2012, Zee, Pg: 18-21
121. The Asia Media Journal, Q3 2012, Zee, Pg: 21
122. The Asia Media Journal, Q3 2012, Zee, Pg: 16
123. Goenka, P. (2 August 2018). In a personal interview with Punit Goenka (S. Dahiya, Interviewer)
124. Zee Entertainment Enterprises Limited Annual Report 2011–12: Pioneering Vision. Pg: 5
125. Zee Entertainment Enterprises Limited Annual Report 2013–14: O1E World. Pg: 7
126. Chandra, S. (2016). *The Z Factor: My Journey as the Wrong Man at the Right Time.* Harper Collins. Pg: 239-241
127. Goenka, P. (2 August 2018). In a personal interview with Punit Goenka (S. Dahiya, interviewer)
128. Ibid.
129. Zee Entertainment Enterprises Limited Annual Report 2012–13: Doing >More. Pg: 29
130. History of Zee Entertainment Enterprises Ltd, Company. Retrieved 25 January 2019, from https://www.goodreturns.in/company/zee-entertainment-enterprises/history.html
131. Anand Adhikari, Ajita Shashidhar, and Mahesh Nayak. 'Passing the Baton.' Pg: 102. 2014. Available at http://www.esselgroup.com/images/ Business_Today_Passing_the_Baton.pdf. Accessed on 2 April 2020.
132. Ibid.
133. Ibid.
134. Zee Entertainment Enterprises Limited Annual Report 2015–16: Consistency and Change. Pg: 6
135. Ibid.
136. Retrieved from https://www.dynamiclevels.com/en/zee-entertainment-company-history
137. Goenka, P. (2 August 2018). In a personal interview with Punit Goenka (S. Dahiya, interviewer)
138. CSR & Sustainability at ZEEL—Zee Entertainment. Retrieved from https://www.zeeentertainment.com/about-us/csr-and-sustainability/
139. Ibid.
140. Noor Fathima Warsia. *Essellent: A Resselient Journey.* BusinessWorld. Pg: 89. 2017.
141. Worldscreen, TV Asia. Amit Goenka. 23 March 2017. Pg: 18

142. Ibid.
143. ZEEL announces the launch of Marathi youth channel Zee Yuva. Retrieved from https://www.afaqs.com/news/media/48399_zeel-announces-the-launch-of-marathi-youth-channel-zee-yuva
144. Ksenia Kondratieva and Tanya Thomas (2017) 'Outside of Entertainment, Infrastructure biz is exciting: Subhash Chandra.' *The Hindu Business* Line, 2017.
145. (2018–19). Zee Entertainment Enterprises Limited Annual Report 2018–19: Evoking Emotions, Touching Lives. Pg: 15
146. Zee Entertainment Enterprises Limited Annual Report 2018–19: Evoking Emotions, Touching Lives. Pg: 30
147. Zee Entertainment Enterprises Limited Annual Report 2018–19: Evoking Emotions, Touching Lives. Pg: 16
148. Goenka, P. (2 August 2018). In a personal interview with Punit Goenka (S. Dahiya, Interviewer)
149. Ruhail Amin. *90 years of Essel*. BusinessWorld. Pg: 100. 2017.
150. Extraordinary Together. Retrieved from https://www.zeeentertainment.com/
151. Zee's official stand in an email dated 1 June 2020.
152. Ibid.
153. Ibid.
154. Goenka, P. (2 August 2018). In a personal interview with Punit Goenka (S. Dahiya, Interviewer)
155. Chandra, S. (25 September 2018). In a personal interview with Subhash Chandra (S. Dahiya, Interviewer)
156. ZEEL, Press Release, Zee takes one more giant pioneering step—builds a technology platform to satisfy 5 senses of the viewers to offer immersive customer experience! (22 October 2018). Pg. 4
157. Ibid.
158. ZEEL Press Release dated 7 April 2020.
159. ZEEL Press Release dated 14 June 2020.
160. ZEEL, Press Release, Zee Entertainment stays ahead of the Industry in keeping Consumers Entertained & Well-Informed—Embraces Technology Solutions to create fresh content amidst lockdown. (21 May 2020). Pg. 2
161. Ibid.
162. (27 February 2018). Retrieved 12, 2019, from https://ecopack.co.in/tag/economictimes-indiatimes-com-articleshow-63085228-cmsutm_sourcecontentofinterestutm_mediumtextutm_campaigncppst/.

163. Zee Entertainment Enterprises Limited Annual Report 2018–19: Evoking Emotions, Touching Lives. Pg: 16
164. Zee Media Bureau. (14 November 2018). Essel Group plans to divest up to 50 per cent of promoter share in ZEEL. Retrieved 9 August 2019, from https://zeenews.india.com/companies/essel-group-plans-to-divest-up-to-50-of-promoter-share-in-zeel-2155302.html
165. Zee's official stand in an email dated 1 June 2020.
166. 'This bride has many suitors,' says Dr Subhash Chandra. Retrieved 2 April 2020, from https://www.exchange4media.com/media-tv-news/this-bride-has-many-suitors-says-dr-subhash-chandra-92988.html
167. BW Online Bureau. Who Will It Be For Zee? Retrieved 2 April 2020, from http://www.businessworld.in/article/Who-Will-It-Be-For-Zee-/11–12-2018–165137/
168. Alvares, C. Scripting A New Storyboard. Retrieved 2 April 2020, from http://www.businessworld.in/article/Scripting-A-New-Storyboard/11–12-2018–165138/
169. Zee Media Bureau. (14 November 2018). Essel Group plans to divest up to 50 per cent of promoter share in ZEEL. Retrieved 9 August 2019, from https://zeenews.india.com/companies/essel-group-plans-to-divest-up-to-50-of-promoter-share-in-zeel-2155302.html
170. 'Subhash Chandra apologizes to creditors, says negative forces hampering Zee stake sale.' Retrieved 28 March 2020, from https://www.moneycontrol.com/news/business/companies/full-text-subhash-chandra-apologizes-to-creditors-says-negative-forces-hampering-zee-stake-sale-3438451.html
171. Mitra, P., & Mitra, P. (29 January 2019). Zee Group linked to firm with dubious deposits post-demonetisation: The Wire reports. Retrieved 13 April 2020, from https://qrius.com/zee-group-linked-to-firm-with-dubious-deposits-post-demonetisation-the-wire-reports/
172. (14 February 2019). Zee Entertainment up 8per cen, stock rallies 52 per cent from 25 January low. Retrieved 28 March 2020, from https://www.business-standard.com/article/markets/zee-entertainment-surges-52-from-january-low–119021400512_1.html
173. Zee's official stand in an email dated 1 June 2020.
174. (27 November 2019). 'Why Subash Chandra had to Resign as Chairman of Zee.' Retrieved 13 April 2020, from https://www.newsclick.in/Subhash-Chandra-Zee-Chairman-Resings-Essel-Group
175. Essel Group, which owns Zee, rocked by allegations of ties to company under fraud probe. (28 January 2019). Retrieved 13 April

2020, from https://www.hindustantimes.com/india-news/essel-group-which-owns-zee-rocked-by-allegations-of-ties-to-company-under-fraud-probe/story-oNJB90Vz9D2vEzev0B6jKM.html

176. Subhash Chandra apologizes to creditors, says negative forces hampering Zee stake sale. Retrieved 28 March 2020, from https://www.moneycontrol.com/news/business/companies/full-text-subhash-chandra-apologizes-to-creditors-says-negative-forces-hampering-zee-stake-sale-3438451.html
177. Ibid.
178. BW Online Bureau. Chairman Of Zee And Essel Group, Subhash Chandra, Writes An Open Letter; Blames Negative Forces Hammered Share Prices. Retrieved April 13, 2020, from http://www.businessworld.in/article/Chairman-Of-ZEE-And-Essel-Group-Subhash-Chandra-Writes-An-Open-Letter-Blames-Negative-Forces-Hammered-Share-Prices/25–01-2019–166512/
179. Ibid.
180. We will find a solution to this crisis, we will rebuild the group: Zee's PunitGoenka. (14 August 2019). Retrieved 28 March 2020, from https://www.businesstoday.in/opinion/interviews/zee-puneet-goenka-we-will-rebuild-the-group-essel-group-invesco-oppenheimer/story/372550.html
181. Zee's official stand in an email dated June 1, 2020.
182. Zee Media Bureau. (1 August 2019). Essel Group announces stake sale in ZEEL. Retrieved 6 January 2020, from https://zeenews.india.com/companies/essel-group-announces-stake-sale-in-zeel-2223861.html
183. Zee's official stand in an email dated 1 June 2020.
184. Ibid.
185. Ibid.
186. We will find a solution to this crisis, we will rebuild the group: Zee's PunitGoenka. (14 August 2019). Retrieved March 28, 2020, from https://www.businesstoday.in/opinion/interviews/zee-puneet-goenkawe-will-rebuild-the-group-essel-group-invesco-oppenheimer/story/372550.html
187. https://www.businesstoday.in/magazine/the-hub/there-is-no-question-of-me-not-meeting-the-deadline/story/373483.html
188. Essel Group, which owns Zee, rocked by allegations of ties to company under fraud probe. (2019, January 28). Retrieved April 13, 2020, from https://www.hindustantimes.com/india-news/essel-

group-which-owns-zee-rocked-by-allegations-of-ties-to-company-under-fraud-probe/story-oNJB90Vz9D2vEzev0B6jKM.html

189. We will find a solution to this crisis, we will rebuild the group: Zee's PunitGoenka. (2019, August 14). Retrieved March 28, 2020, from https://www.businesstoday.in/opinion/interviews/zee-puneet-goenka-we-will-rebuild-the-group-essel-group-invesco-oppenheimer/story/372550.html
190. Aggarwal, V. (25 September 2019). Essel Group gets time till March to repay Zee debt. Retrieved 28 March 2020, from https://www.thehindubusinessline.com/companies/essel-group-gets-extension-to-repay-zees-debt/article29506364.ece
191. Zee Entertainment share price falls over 9 per cent after Subhash Chandra steps down as chairman. (26 November 2019). Retrieved March 28, 2020, from https://www.businesstoday.in/markets/company-stock/zee-entertainment-share-price-falls-subhash-chandra-resigns-chairman/story/391026.html
192. Ibid.
193. Ibid.
194. (25 November 2019). End of era for Subhash Chandra at Zee Entertainment. Retrieved 28 March 2020, from https://www.thehindubusinessline.com/companies/subhash-chandra-resigns-as-chairman-of-zee-entertainment/article30077905.ece
195. Zee's official stand in an email dated June 1, 2020.
196. In a personal interview with Subhash Chandra
197. Zee's official stand in an email dated June 1, 2020.
198. Zee Entertainment in SEBI, MCA crosshairs after exit of independent directors. Retrieved 13 April 2020, from https://www.moneycontrol.com/news/business/companies/zee-entertainment-in-sebi-mca-crosshairs-after-exit-of-independent-directors-4681541.html
199. Ibid.
200. Ibid.
201. Ibid.
202. Zee 4.0 Open Letter—From the desk of Punit Goenka, Retrieved from official Zee website.
203. 'US hedge fund asks ZEE's Subhash Chandra to exit one of his education firms.' Retrieved 13 April 2020, from https://www.livemint.com/companies/news/us-hedge-fund-asks-zee-s-subhash-chandra-to-exit-one-of-his-education-firms–11582781261439.html
204. Zee's official stand in an email dated 1 June 2020.

205. Jha, S. (2017). 90 years of Essel. In conversation. Businessworld.
206. Ibid.
207. Zee's official stand in an email dated June 1, 2020.
208. Bamzai, K., Dhingra, S., Sharma, K., &Vij, S. (2 February 2019). 'The A to Zee of media mogul Subhash Chandra's controversial and colourful life.' Retrieved 28 March 2020, from https://theprint.in/opinion/the-a-to-zee-of-media-mogul-subhash-chandras-controversial-and-colourful-life/186872/
209. Leadership at ZEEL—Zee Entertainment. Retrieved from https://www.zeeentertainment.com/about-us/about-us-leadership/
210. Ibid
211. Dish TV. Retrieved from http://www.esselgroup.com/dish-tv.html
212. Siti Networks. Retrieved from http://www.siticable.com/
213. Zee Entertainment Enterprises Limited Annual Report 2018–19: Evoking Emotions, Touching Lives. Pg : 18
214. The Asia Media Journal, Q3 2012, Zee, Pg: 18
215. Zee Entertainment Enterprises Limited Annual Report 2018–19: Evoking Emotions, Touching Lives. Pg: 16
216. Ibid.
217. Zee Entertainment Enterprises Limited Annual Report 2018–19: Evoking Emotions, Touching Lives. 31-33.
218. Ibid.
219. Strategic Brand Management: Building, Measuring, and Managing Brand Equity by Keller and Swaminathan. Fifth global edition. Pearson.
220. Zee Entertainment Enterprises Limited Annual Report 2012–13: Doing >More. Pg: 5
221. Ibid.
222. Zee Entertainment Enterprises Limited Annual Report 2012–13: Doing >More. Pg: 25
223. (27 June 2013). Zee unveils new corporate brand identity. Retrieved September 7, 2016, from https://www.thehindubusinessline.com/companies/zee-unveils-new-corporate-brand-identity/article23100438.ece
224. Ibid.
225. Ibid.
226. Zee Entertainment Enterprises Limited Annual Report 2018–19: Evoking Emotions, Touching Lives.
227. 'With its new brand ideology "Extraordinary Together"' ZEEL targets

3 billion viewers in 6 years. Retrieved 4 March 2020, from https://www.exchange4media.com/media-tv-news/with-its-new-brand-ideology-extraordinary-together-zeel-targets-3-billion-viewers-in-6-years-86964.html

228. Ibid.
229. Zee TV unveils new brand identity. (20 June 2011). Retrieved 10 October 2017, from https://www.businesstoday.in/current/corporate/zee-tv-zeel-star-plus-new-brand-identity/story/16423.html
230. Ibid.
231. As per information sent by Zee office.
232. Ibid.
233. (27 November 2012). Zee group denies extortion charges by Naveen Jindal, says arrest an attack on press freedom. Retrieved August 8, 2018, from https://www.ndtv.com/india-news/zee-group-denies-extortion-charges-by-naveen-jindal-says-arrest-an-attack-on-press-freedom-505814
234. Zee 4.0 Open Letter—From the desk of Punit Goenka, Retrieved from official Zee website.
235. Ibid.
236. Press Release issued by Zee on 17 October 2020
237. Zee's official stand in an email dated 1 June 2020.
238. Ibid.
239. Ibid.
240. Goenka, P. (2 August 2018). In a personal interview with Punit Goenka (S. Dahiya, interviewer)
241. Ibid.
242. Zee's official stand in an email dated 1 June 2020.
243. Zee Entertainment Enterprises Limited Annual Report 2018–19: Evoking Emotions, Touching Lives. Pg: 31
244. 'Essel Engages Investment Bankers to Identify Strategic Partner in ZEEL As It Transforms in a Convergent World.' Retrieved from https://www.zeebiz.com/companies/news-essel-engages-investment-bankers-to-identify-strategic-partner-in-zeel-as-it-transforms-in-a-convergent-world-71447
245. Chandra, S. (25 September 2018). In a personal interview with Subhash Chandra (S. Dahiya, Interviewer).
246. Chandra, S. (2016). *The Z Factor: My Journey as the Wrong Man at the Right Time.* Harper Collins. Pg: 271-2
247. Zee's official stand in an email dated 1 June 2020.

248. Ibid.
249. Ibid.
250. Chandra, S. (25 September 2018). In a personal interview with Subhash Chandra (S. Dahiya, Interviewer)

LIST OF ABBREVIATIONS

APAC	Asia-Pacific
AR	Augmented Reality
ASHA	Affordable Shelter Housing for All
ASSPL	Amazon Seller Services Private Limited
ATL	Asia Today Limited
AVOD	Advertising-based Video on Demand
BARB	Broadcasters Audience Research Board
BCCI	Board of Control for Cricket in India
BMS	Broadcast Management System
BSI	British Standards Institution
CAS	Conditional Access System
DAM	Digital Asset Management
DCGA	Director General of Civil Aviation
DMC	Dubai Media City
DMCL	Diligent Media Corporation Limited
DNA	Daily News and Analysis
DR	Disaster Recovery
DSC	Development Support Centre
DTH	Direct-to-Home
DTO	Direct To Operator
ECBEPL	E-City Bioscope Entertainment Pvt. Ltd
ECG	Ethnic Channels Group Limited
EGME	Essel Group Middle East
EIL	Essel Infraprojects Limited
EPL	Essel Propack Ltd
ER	Effective Rate
ESSEL	Educational Sports and Science Exhibition Land
EVFI	Ekal Vidyalaya Foundation of India
FAC	Family Activity Centers
FCI	Food Corporation of India
FDI	Foreign Direct Investments
FII	Foreign Institutional Investors
FTA	Free to Air

FZ-LLC	Free Zone Limited Liability Company
GABM	Global Association of Billionaires and Millionaires
GEC	General Entertainment Channel
GRP	Gross Rating Points
HD	High Definition
HITS	Head End in the Sky
IECTEC	International Early Childhood Teachers' Education Course
IL & FS	Infrastructure Leasing and Financial Services
IMN	Integrated Multimedia Newsroom
IOC	Internet over Cable
IPR	Intellectual Property Rights
JPC	Joint Parliamentary Committee
JSPL	Jindal Steel and Power
JV	Joint Venture
MAU	Monthly Active Users
MENA	Middle East and North Africa
MGM	Metro Goldwyn Mayer
MIPCOM	Marché International des Programmes de Communication
MMC	Mail.com Media Corporation
MoU	Memorandum of Understanding
MSO	Multi-system operators
NBFC	Non-Banking Financial Company
OTT	Over The Top
PATCO	Programme Asia Trading Company Private Ltd
PESTLE	Political, Economic, Social, Technological, Legal and Environmental
PMC	Penske Media Corporation
PPIL	Playwin Lotteries
RGEC	Rural General Entertainment Channels
RSB	Rashtriya Sewa Bharti
SD	Standard Definition
SGRL	Shirpur Gold Refinery Ltd
SME	Small and Medium Enterprises
STAR	Satellite Television for Asian Region
STB	Set Top Boxes
STCI	Save the Children India

SVOD	Subscription Video on Demand
SWOT	Strengths, Weaknesses, Opportunities and Threats
TEN	Terrestrial Entertainment Network
TMPL	Today Merchandise Private Limited
TRAI	Telecom Regulatory Authority of India
TRNL	Today Retail Network Private Limited
UNI	United News of India
VoD	Video on Demand
VR	Virtual Reality
VSNL	Videsh Sanchar Nigam Limited
WION	World is One News
WWIL	Wire and Wireless India Limited
YPO	Young President Organization
Zed CA	Zed Career Academy
ZICA	Zee Institute of Creative Arts
ZILS	Zee Interactive Learning Systems
ZMWL	Zee Multimedia Worldwide Limited
ZEEL	Zee Entertainment Enterprises Ltd
ZGCS	Zee Global Content Sales
ZMC	Zee Music Company
ZMCL	Zee Media Corporation Ltd
ZNL	Zee News Limited
ZTL	Zee Telefilms Limited

BIBLIOGRAPHY

'About DNA.' Available at https://www.dnaindia.com/investors/about.html

Adhikari. A, Shashidhar. A, and Nayak. M (2014). 'Passing the Baton.' Available at http://www.esselgroup.com/images/Business_Today_Passing_the_Baton.pdf.

Afaqs news bureau (5 July 2016). 'ZEEL announces the launch of Marathi youth channel Zee Yuva.' Available at https://www.afaqs.com/news/media/48399_zeel-announces-the-launch-of-marathi-youth-channel-zee-yuva

Aggarwal, V. (25 September 2019). 'Essel Group gets time till March to repay Zee debt.' Available at https://www.thehindubusinessline.com/companies/essel-group-gets-extension-to-repay-zees-debt/article29506364.ece

Alvares, C. (11 December 2018) 'Scripting A New Storyboard. Business World.' Available at http://www.businessworld.in/article/Scripting-A-New-Storyboard/11-12-2018-165138/

Ami, R. (2017). '90 years of Essel.' *Business World.*

Annual Report, Empire Holdings Ltd (1992): Auditor's Report to the members (as per data/ reports/ scans provided by Zee Corporate Communication Team via various emails)

Annual Reports, Zee Entertainment Enterprises Limited (ZEEL), (2006-07); (2007-08) (2008-09): Entertainment Unlimited; (2009-10): Taking Entertainment Places; (2010-11): Inspired Leadership; (2011-12): Pioneering Vision; (2012-13): Doing >More; (2013-14): O1E World; (2014-15): Investing in Tomorrow; (2015-16): Consistency and Change; (2017-18). Experience The Extraordinary; (2018-19): Evoking Emotions, Touching Lives; (2019-2020) Sharpening Consumer Focus.

Annual Reports, Zee Media Corporation Limited (ZMCL), (2013-14): Expanding Horizons; (2014-15): Every Story Matters; (2014-15): Investing in Tomorrow; (2015-16): India Positive; (2016-17): Investing in Future; (2017-18): Collaborative Strategies, Cohesive Growth; (2018-19): The Business of Truth, The Truth of Business.

Annual Reports, Zee News Limited (ZNL), (2006-07): Inform, Entertain, Empower; (2007-08): Nurturing the Minds of a Flourishing Nation; (2008-09): Diversity, Growth, Sustenance; (2009-10): Making News; (2010-11):

Excellence is a Philosophy; (2011-12): Poised for the Next Leap; (2012-13): Reaching Out to the World

Annual Reports, Zee Telefilms Limited (ZTL), (1993-1998): Auditor's Report to the members of Zee Telefilms Ltd (as per data/ reports/ scans provided by Zee Corporate Communication Team via various emails); (1998-99): Building Gateways to the Future; (1999-2000): Convergence Personified; (2000- 01); (2001-02): Big Ideas in Entertainment; (2002-03): Let us Excel; (2003-04); (2004-05): Jio Zee Bhar Ke; (2005-06): The Changing face of Entertainment.

Asia-Pacific India. (15 August 2015). Zee Chairman Subhash Chandra: 'I Always Want to Be Number One or a Strong Number Two'. Available at http://knowledge.wharton.upenn.edu/article/zee-chairman-subhash-chandra-i-always-want-to-be-number-one-or-a-strong-number-two/

B T Bureau. (20 June 2011). 'Zee TV unveils new brand identity.' *Business Today*. Available at https://www.businesstoday.in/current/corporate/zee-tv-zeel-star-plus-new-brand-identity/story/16423.html

Baddhan, R. (20 July 2020). 'ZEE TV to telecast exclusive premiere of Gadar: BizAsia: Media, Entertainment, Showbiz, Brit, Events and Music.' Available at https://www.bizasialive.com/zee-tv-to-telecast-exclusive-premiere-of-gadar/

Bamzai, K. (22 January 2016). 'Network czar- Subhash Chandra.' Available at https://www.indiatoday.in/magazine/books/story/20160201-network-czar-zee-tv-promoter-subhash-chandra-esselworld-828325-2016-01-20

Bamzai, K., Dhingra, S., Sharma, K., & Vij, S. (2 February 2019). 'The A to Zee of media mogul Subhash Chandra's controversial and colourful life.' Available at https://theprint.in/opinion/the-a-to-zee-of-media-mogul-subhash-chandras-controversial-and-colourful-life/186872/

Batra. A (16 November 2018) '"This bride has many suitors," says Dr. Subhash Chandra.' *Exchange4media*. Available at https://www.exchange4media.com/media-tv-news/this-bride-has-many-suitors-says-dr-subhash-chandra-92988.html

Bloomberg. (27 February 2020). 'US hedge fund asks ZEE's Subhash Chandra to exit one of his education firms.' Available at https://www.livemint.com/companies/news/us-hedge-fund-asks-zee-s-subhash-chandra-to-exit-one-of-his-education-firms-11582781261439.html

Brand Zee, Available at https://www.zeeentertainment.com/brand-zee/

Businesstoday.in Team. (26 November 2019) 'Zee Entertainment share price falls over 9% after Subhash Chandra steps down as chairman.' Available at https://www.businesstoday.in/markets/company-stock/zee-entertainment-share-price-falls-subhash-chandra-resigns-chairman/story/391026.html

BW Online Bureau. (11 December 2018) 'Who Will It Be for Zee?' Available at http://www.businessworld.in/article/Who-Will-It-Be-For-Zee-/11-12-2018-165137/

BW Online Bureau. (25 January 2019) 'Chairman of ZEE and Essel Group, Subhash Chandra, Writes An Open Letter; Blames Negative Forces Hammered Share Prices.' Available at http://www.businessworld.in/article/Chairman-Of-ZEE-And-Essel-Group-Subhash-Chandra-Writes-An-Open-Letter-Blames-Negative-Forces-Hammered-Share-Prices/25-01-2019-166512/

BW Online Bureau. (25 January 2019). 'Subhash Chandra apologizes to creditors, says negative forces hampering Zee stake sale.' Available at https://www.moneycontrol.com/news/business/companies/full-text-subhash-chandra-apologizes-to-creditors-says-negative-forces-hampering-zee-stake-sale-3438451.html

Chandra, S. (2016). *The Z Factor: My Journey as the Wrong Man at the Right Time.* Harper Collins.

Chandra, S. (25 September 2018). In a personal interview with Subhash Chandra at 4, Bhagwandas Road, Mahatma Jyoti Phule Marg, New Delhi (S. Dahiya, Interviewer)

Chaudhary, S. (17 August 2018). In a personal interview with Sudhir Chaudhary, CEO, ZMCL Cluster 1 (S. Dahiya, Interviewer)

Chronology of Zee's 20-year journey. (16 April 2019). Available at https://www.indiantelevision.com/headlines/y2k12/oct/oct25.php

'Company History—Zee Entertainment Enterprises Ltd.' Available at http://economictimes.indiatimes.com/zee-entertainment-enterprises-ltd/infocompanyhistory/companyid-11769.cms

'Company History of Zee Entertainment Enterprises.' Available at https://www.moneycontrol.com/company-facts/zeeentertainmententerprises/history/ZEE

'Company History.' Available at https://www.dynamiclevels.com/en/zee-entertainment-company-history

'CSR & Sustainability at ZEEL—ZEE Entertainment.' Available at https://www.zeeentertainment.com/about-us/csr-and-sustainability/

'Directors' Available at http://investors.zeenews.com/index.aspx?content=directors

'Dish TV.' Available at http://www.esselgroup.com/dish-tv.html

DNA Team. (15 May 2017). #youngat90: Essel Group celebrates 90 years of its existence, PM Modi says Essel's values are nation's values. Available at https://www.dnaindia.com/india/report-essel-s-values-are-nation-s-values-pm-2438510

DNA Team. (7 September 2006). Subhash Chandra buys stake in UNI. Available at https://www.dnaindia.com/business/report-subhash-chandra-buys-stake-in-uni-1051782

'Domestic Broadcasting Business of ZEEL—ZEE Entertainment.' Available at https://www.zeeentertainment.com/businesses/domestic-broadcasting/

'Education.' Available at http://www.esselgroup.com/education.html

'Essel engages investment bankers to identify strategic partner in ZEEL.' Available at https://www.zeebiz.com/companies/news-essel-engages-investment-bankers-to-identify-strategic-partner-in-zeel-as-it-transforms-in-a-convergent-world-71447

'Essel Finance.' Available at http://www.esselgroup.com/financial-services.html

'Essel Group Profile.' Available at http://www.esselgroup.com/group-profile.html

'Entertainment.' Available at http://www.esselgroup.com/entertainment.html

Exchange4media staff. (31 October 2017) 'With its new brand ideology 'Extraordinary Together' ZEEL targets 3 billion viewers in 6 years.' Available at https://www.exchange4media.com/media-tv-news/with-its-new-brand-ideology-extraordinary-together-zeel-targets-3-billion-viewers-in-6-years-86964.html

'Extraordinary Together.' Available at https://www.zeeentertainment.com/

Gandhi, R. (15 August 2018). In a personal interview with Rohit Gandhi, Ex-CEO of DNA and WION (S. Dahiya, Interviewer)

Goenka, P. (2 August 2018). In a personal interview with Punit Goenka at Zee Entertainment Enterprises Ltd, Marathon Futurex Building, 16th Floor, A Wing, NM Joshi Marg, Lower Parel, Mumbai on 2nd August 2018 at 3 p.m. (S. Dahiya, Interviewer)

Goenka.A. (23 March 2017) TV Asia. Worldscreen

Himgiri Zee University—[HZU], Dehradun. Available at https://collegedunia.com/university/25989-himgiri-zee-university-hzu-dehradun/admission

'History of Zee Entertainment Enterprises Ltd.' Available at https://www.goodreturns.in/company/zee-entertainment-enterprises/history.html

https://www.businesstoday.in/magazine/the-hub/there-is-no-question-of-me-not-meeting-the-deadline/story/373483.html

Indian Television Audience Measurement. (1998-99).

Indiatelevision.com. (14 August 2002).Cartoon Network block to replace

Nickelodeon on Zee TV 1 September. Available at https://www.indiantelevision.com/headlines/y2k2/aug/aug87.htm

Infrastructure. Available at http://www.esselgroup.com/infrastructure.html

INTAM Reports

Investor Info. Available at http://investors.zeenews.com/

International Business Overview. Available at https://www.zeeentertainment.com/wp-content/uploads/2017/10/zeel-internationalbusinessoverview-626102d53b2be10.pdf.

Jha, S. (2017). *90 years of Essel: In conversation*. Businessworld.

Kapoor, C. (4 March 2016). The Z Factory book review: Rising Against All Odds. Available at https://indianexpress.com/article/lifestyle/books/subhash-chandra-book-review-the-z-factory-book-review-rising-against-all-odds/

Keller and Swaminathan. *Strategic Brand Management: Building, Measuring, and Managing Brand Equity*. 5th global edition. Pearson

Kohli-Khandekar, V. (16 November 2016). The making of India's largest DTH company. Available at https://www.business-standard.com/article/specials/the-making-of-india-s-largest-dth-company-116111601911_1.html.

Kohli-Khandekar, V. (2003). *The Indian Media Business*. Sage Publications.

Kohli-Khandekar, V. (2019). *The Making of Star India: The Amazing Story of Rupert Murdoch's India Adventure*. Penguin Portfolio.

Kohli-Khandekar, V. (29 November 2016). 'Essel Group's appetite for acquisitions is growing.' Available at https://www.business-standard.com/article/companies/essel-group-s-appetite-for-acquisitions-is-growing-116112801020_1.html

Kohli-Khandekar, V. (5 February 2016). Subhash Chandra: The serial entrepreneur. Available at https://www.business-standard.com/article/companies/subhash-chandra-the-serial-entrepreneur-116020500923_1.html

Kondratieva. K., Thomas. T. (13 May 2017) 'Outside of Entertainment, Infrastructure biz is exciting: Subhash Chandra.' *The Hindu Business Line*. Available at https://www.pressreader.com/india/the-hindu-business-line/20170513/281917363001320

Kumar, B. (18 August 2018). In a personal interview with Brajesh Kumar, Zee Business (S. Dahiya, Interviewer)

Kumar, N.(2008) In a personal interview with Naveen Kumar (S. Dahiya, Interviewer)

Malik, M. (18 August 2018). In a personal interview with Mimansa Malik,

Senior News Anchor, Zee News (S. Dahiya, Interviewer).

'Management Team.' Available at http://zeelearn.com/aboutus/management-team/

Mehta, N. (2008). *India on Television.* Harper Collins.

'Middle Eaast.' Available at http://www.esselgroup.com/essel-middle-east.html

Mitra, P., &Mitra, P. (29 January 2019). 'Zee Group linked to firm with dubious deposits post-demonetisation.' Available at https://qrius.com/zee-group-linked-to-firm-with-dubious-deposits-post-demonetisation-the-wire-reports/

Mxmindia.com. (1 October 2012) 'From 'OkaraDukaan' to Zee... the complete story.' Available at https://www.mxmindia.com/2012/10/from-okara-dukaan-to-zee-the-complete-story/

N., Report, N., & 2019, 27 N. (27 November 2019). 'Why Subash Chandra had to Resign as Chairman of Zee.' Available at https://www.newsclick.in/Subhash-Chandra-Zee-Chairman-Resings-Essel-Group

Networks. Available at http://www.siticable.com/

Ninan, S. (2007). *Headlines From the Heartland: Reinventing the Hindi Public Sphere.* Sage Publications.

Partner with ZEEL—ZEE Entertainment. Available at https://www.zeeentertainment.com/about-us/key-brand-initiatives/

Precious Metals. Available at http://www.esselgroup.com/precious-metals.html

Press Release (1 June 2016) Issued by Essel Group Available at http://www.esselgroup.com/essel-group-celebrates-90-years.html

Press Release (14 June 2020). Issued by ZEE Entertainment Enterprises Ltd. (ZEEL)

Press Release (17 October 2020) Issued by Zee Entertainment Enterprises Ltd (ZEEL)

Press Release (21 May 2020). 'ZEE Entertainment stays ahead of the Industry in keeping Consumers Entertained & Well-Informed—Embraces Technology Solutions to create fresh content amidst lockdown.' Issued by Zee Entertainment Enterprises Ltd (ZEEL)

Press Release (22 October 2018). 'ZEE takes one more giant pioneering step – builds a technology platform to satisfy 5 senses of the viewers to offer immersive customer experience!' Issued by Zee Entertainment Enterprises Ltd (ZEEL).

Press Release (7 April 2020) Issued by ZEE Entertainment Enterprises Ltd. (ZEEL)

Profile: Media guru looks to the skies. Available at http://www.totaltele.com/view.aspx?ID=424018

Profile: Media guru looks to the skies. Available at http://www.totaltele.com/view.aspx?ID=424018

Promoters. Available at http://www.esselgroup.com/promoters.html

Pti. (8 July 2008). 'Zee Entertainment appoints Punit Goenka as CEO.' Available at https://economictimes.indiatimes.com/zee-entertainment-appoints-punit-goenka-as-ceo/articleshow/3211932.cms?from=mdr

Rao, B.V. (2008) In a personal interview with B.V. Rao, former Group Editor of Zee News Ltd. (S. Dahiya, Interviewer)

Reporter, S. I. (1 February 2019). Zee Entertainment up 8%, stock rallies 52% from January 25 low. Available at https://www.business-standard.com/article/markets/zee-entertainment-surges-52-from-january-low-119021400512_1.html

Sanjai. P. R, Suresh.A . (28 January 2019). 'Essel Group, which owns Zee, rocked by allegations of ties to company under fraud probe.' *Bloomberg*. Available at https://www.hindustantimes.com/india-news/essel-group-which-owns-zee-rocked-by-allegations-of-ties-to-company-under-fraud-probe/story-oNJB90Vz9D2vEzev0B6jKM.html

Service, I.-A. N. (27 November 2012). 'Zee group denies extortion charges by Naveen Jindal, says arrest an attack on press freedom.' Available at https://www.ndtv.com/india-news/zee-group-denies-extortion-charges-by-naveen-jindal-says-arrest-an-attack-on-press-freedom-505814

Sharma. T (28 November 2019). 'Zee Entertainment in SEBI, MCA crosshairs after exit of independent directors.' Available at https://www.moneycontrol.com/news/business/companies/zee-entertainment-in-sebi-mca-crosshairs-after-exit-of-independent-directors-4681541.html

Shashidhar. A (14 August 2019) 'We will find a solution to this crisis, we will rebuild the group: Zee's PunitGoenka.' Available at https://www.businesstoday.in/opinion/interviews/zee-puneet-goenka-we-will-rebuild-the-group-essel-group-invesco-oppenheimer/story/372550.html

Singh, G. (2016). *Such a Long Journey*. BusinessWorld.

Singhal, A. and Rogers, E. M. (2001). *India's Communication Revolution: From Bullock CartstoCyberMarts*. Sage Publications.

Subhash Chandra Biography. Available at https://business.mapsofindia.com/business-leaders/subhash-chandra.html

'Technology at ZEEL—ZEE Entertainment.' Available at https://www.zeeentertainment.com/about-us/technology/

'Tracing Essel Propacks.' Available at https://bloncampus.

thehindubusinessline.com/columns/brand-basics/tracing-essel-propacks-extraordinary-growth/article29235140.eceThe Hindu Business Line Team. (10 June 2019). 'Zee5 partners with Israeli firm Applicaster to improve viewer experience.' Available at https://www.thehindubusinessline.com/info-tech/zee5-partners-with-israeli-firm-applicaster-to-improve-viewer-experience/article27710084.ece

The Hindu Business Line Team. (25 November 2019). 'End of era for Subhash Chandra at Zee Entertainment.' Available at https://www.thehindubusinessline.com/companies/subhash-chandra-resigns-as-chairman-of-zee-entertainment/article30077905.ece

The Hindu Business Line Team. (27 June 2013). 'Zee unveils new corporate brand identity.' Available at https://www.thehindubusinessline.com/companies/zee-unveils-new-corporate-brand-identity/article23100438.ece

'The Zee- Volution.' Available at http://www.esselgroup.com/images/amjzee-vol-7df5f1496d1d0b4.pdf

TVP Bureau. (17 April 2018). ZEE5 launches its first Tamil original series 'America Mappillai'. Available at https://www.televisionpost.com/zee5-launches-its-first-tamil-original-series-america-mappillai/

Warsia, N. F. (2017). *Essellent. A Resselient Journey*. BusinessWorld

'Withdraw extortion case.' Available at http://www.businessworld.in/article/Naveen-Jindal-and-JSPL-Withdraw-Extortion-Case-Against-Zee-Subhash-Chandra-Tweets-Truce-Message/13-07-2018-154808/

Wire and Wireless. Available at https://www.sitinetworks.com/pdf/presentations/Wire_and_wireless.pdf.

Yo Success. (2 July 2015). 'Inspiring Success Story of Subhash Chandra—Founder of Essel Group.' Available at http://www.yosuccess.com/success-stories/subhash-chandra-essel-group/

'ZEE 2016' Available at https://www.moneycontrol.com/annualreport/zeeentertainmententerprises/ZEE/2016

'ZEE Entertainment Enterprises Ltd. (ZEEL).' Available at https://www.zeeentertainment.com/about-us/overview/#missionAndValues

'Zee media acquires 49 per cent stake in Reliance Broadcast.' Available at https://zeenews.india.com/companies/zee-media-to-acquire-49-stake-in-reliance-broadcast-92-7-big-fm_1952634.html

'Zee Media Corporation' Available at http://www.esselgroup.com/zee-media-corporation-limited.html

'Zee products platform.' Available at https://www.zee.com/products-platforms-digital-media-domestic/?pageSection=ott

'Zee Talkies: About Us.' Available at http://www.zeetalkies.com/about-us/

'Zee TV Sees Swooshes'. Available at https://www.underconsideration.com/brandnew/archives/zee_tv_sees_swooshes.php

'Zee TV: About Us.' Available at http://www.zeetelevisionafrica.com/zeetv/aboutus/

'Zee TV: History & Our Story' Available at http://www.zeetelevision.com/about-us/history-our-story.html

'Zee-Jindal and Sudhir Chaudhary Tapes: The battle that never was.' Available at https://www.newslaundry.com/2018/07/19/zee-naveen-jindal-sudhir-chaudhary-tapes-subhash-chandra

Zee 4.0 Open Letter – From the desk of Punit Goenka, Available at official Zee website.

Zee Corporate Investor Presentation (May 2019)

Zee Entertainment acquires Sarthak Entertainment. Available at https://www.exchange4media.com/media-tv-news/zee-entertainment-acquires-sarthak-entertainment-60810.html.

Zee Entertainment Company History. Available at https://stock-financials.valuestocks.in/en/zee-entertainment-company-history

Zee Entertainment Enterprises Ltd. Available at https://www.business-standard.com/company/zee-entertainmen-3126/information/company-history

Zee Media Bureau. (1 August 2019). 'Essel Group announces stake sale in ZEEL.' Available at https://zeenews.india.com/companies/essel-group-announces-stake-sale-in-zeel-2223861.html

Zee Media Bureau. (1 November 2019). 'Essel Group plans to divest up to 50% of promoter share in ZEEL.' Available at https://zeenews.india.com/companies/essel-group-plans-to-divest-up-to-50-of-promoter-share-in-zeel-2155302.html

Zee Rejig: 2 companies to merge with ASC Enterprise. (4 January 2019). Available at https://www.indiantelevision.com/headlines/y2k6/apr/apr350.htm

ZEEL International Business Overview. Available at https://www.zeeentertainment.com/wp-content/uploads/2017/10/zeel-internationalbusinessoverview-626102d53b2be10.pdf

'ZMCL radio business deal.' Available at https://www.exchange4media.com/media-radio-news/zmcls-radio-business-deal-with-rbnl-called-off-93179.html